国家出版基金项目
NATIONAL PUBLICATION FUNDING

“十二五”
国家重点图书出版规划项目

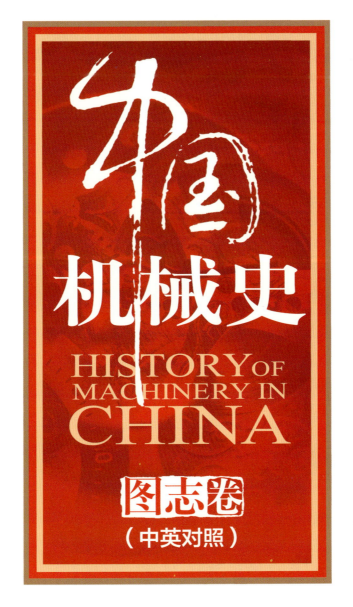

中国
机械史

HISTORY OF
MACHINERY IN
CHINA

图志卷
（中英对照）

中国机械工程学会 编
CHINESE MECHANICAL ENGINEERING SOCIETY

黄开亮 主编
HUANG KAI LIANG

中国科学技术出版社
·北 京·

图书在版编目(CIP)数据

中国机械史图志卷/黄开亮主编；中国机械工程学会编.—北京：中国科学技术出版社，2011.6（2019.1重印）

ISBN 978-7-5046-5039-9

Ⅰ.①中…　Ⅱ.①黄…　②中…　Ⅲ.①机械工业-工业史-中国-图集　Ⅳ.①F426.4-64

中国版本图书馆CIP数据核字（2010）第205942号

策划编辑	吕建华　许　英
责任编辑	吕建华　许　英　叶　翚
封面设计	中文天地
版式设计	瓦瓦酷工作室
责任校对	林　华
责任印制	李晓霖

中国科学技术出版社出版

北京市海淀区中关村南大街16号　邮政编码：100081

电话：010-62173865　传真：010-62179148

http://www.cspbooks.com.cn

中国科学技术出版社发行部发行

北京华联印刷有限公司印刷

*

开本：889毫米×1194毫米　1/16　印张：36.25　字数：820千字

2011年6月第1版　2019年1月第2次印刷

印数：2001—4000册　定价：365.00元

ISBN 978-7-5046-5039-9/F·709

中国机械史
HISTORY OF MACHINERY IN CHINA

中国机械工程学会
CHINESE MECHANICAL ENGINEERING SOCIETY

- -

顾　问　路甬祥　何光远　陆燕荪
Advisor　Lu Yongxiang　He Guangyuan　Lu Yansun

主　编　黄开亮　郭可谦
Editors-in-chief　Huang Kailiang　Guo Keqian

策　划　宋天虎　陈超志
Planners　Song Tianhu　Chen Chaozhi

编审　柳乃复
Senior editor　Liu Naifu

责任编辑　陈秀敏
Executive editor　Chen Xiumin

特约编辑　黄　慧
Special editor　Huang Hui

图志卷 编撰人员
Compilers of illustrated handbook

- -

主　编　黄开亮
Editor-in-chief Huang Kailiang

撰　文　黄开亮
Text Editor Huang Kailiang

资料图片收集整理　黄　慧　陈秀敏
Gatherers for pictures and information Huang hui Chen Xiumin

审　稿　柳乃复
Reviewer Liu Naifu

英文审订　邱廷魁
English texts finalized by Qiu Tingkui

总　序

　　中国是世界上使用与发展机械最早的国家之一。中国古代机械的发明与应用，曾长时间领先世界。在机械原理、结构设计、材料开发、动力应用和工艺技术等方面都取得了极高成就；许多古代机械制品的先进构思、精湛工艺至今尤令西方人折服；许多重要发明创造曾引领世界文明的进程。但由于种种原因，明、清两代300年以来，中国的机械制造停滞不前；在中华人民共和国成立时，已经远远落后于时代。针对中国机械工业的落后，毛泽东在1954年有过一段形象的描述："现在我们能制造什么？能造桌子、椅子，能造茶壶、茶碗，能种粮食还能磨成面粉，还能造纸，但是一辆汽车、一架飞机、一辆坦克、一辆拖拉机都不能制造。"

　　中华人民共和国成立后，特别是21世纪以来，中国机械工业的高速发展震惊世界。2009年，中国机械工业总量居世界第一位，汽车、机床、发电设备、拖拉机、船舶、轨道车辆等许多重要机械产品产量已居世界第一位。不仅研制了三峡700MW水电机组、超超临界1000MW火电机组、1000kV交流和±800kV直流等特高压输变电设备、大型液化天然气运输船、350km/h动车组等世界领先机械装备，还有卫星上天、神舟飞船等尖端技术装备系统的自主研制并发射成功。中国正由机械大国向世界机械强国奋进。

　　几千年来，中国机械工业的发展，经历了领先于世界—落后于时代—再度崛起这一兴衰过程，其中的成败教训和复兴历程，对中国机械现在与未来的发展，极富历史借鉴价值和现实意义。中国机械工业的历史还在继续，为了中国机械工业的未来，中国机械工程学会义不容辞地为几千年来中国机械工业的发展历程编撰一部较为完整的《中国机械史》。据了解，该书还可能是中国工业界的第一部行业史，不仅开工业行业史之先河，而且对促进中国机械工业新的跨越发展也极富意义。

在中国古代、近代机械的发展过程中，已产生了不少专著，该书在此基础上传承已有研究成果，重点放在对现代机械史的研究上。约请了一批知名的专家、学者撰稿，比较全面地描述了中国现代机械工业发展的全过程，记录了不同时期机械工业体制改革、技术进步、产品发展、经济社会效益、时代背景等，图文并茂。回顾历史，发人深省，催人奋进；以史为鉴，指导现实，开创未来。

　　该书的编撰构思始于21世纪初，2003年开始部署，2010年完成，历时8年。全书共分4卷：图志卷、通史卷、技术卷和行业卷。

　　我们相信，该书将对21世纪中国加快工业化进程，以信息化推动工业化，自主创新，促进以绿色、智能为特征的机械产品的研发、设计、制造和应用发挥积极的影响。

　　该书是百余位长期从事机械工业各方面工作的著名专家、学者、教授辛勤劳动的成果，谨向撰稿、编辑出版者表示衷心感谢！是为序。

2010年5月

Preface

China is one of the earliest countries that use and develop machinery in the world. The inventions and application of machinery in ancient China have been in the lead all over the world for a long time. Great achievements were made in principles of machinery, structural design, material development, power application and technology, etc. The advanced conception and exquisite workmanship of many ancient machines have convinced the occidental world. A lot of significant inventions have played leading roles in the development of world civilization. Unfortunately, China's machinery manufacture came to a standstill in 300 years from Ming Dynasty and Qing Dynasty for various reasons, and failed to keep up with the time when the People's Republic of China was founded. Mao Zedong made a vivid description of the backward machinery industry of China in 1954:"What can we produce now? We can produce tables, chairs, teapots, bowls, food, flour and paper, but we are not capable of making a car, an airplane, a tank or even a tractor. "

Swift development of China's machinery industry after the founding of PRC, especially in the 21 century, surprised the world. Gross output of China's machinery industry ranked the first and output of many significant machinery products like automobiles, machine tools, E-power equipment, tractors, ships and locomotives ranked the first in the world in 2009. Ultra-high voltage transmission and distribution equipment including 700MW hydro power generating units at Three Gorges Dam, 1000MW Ultra-supercritical thermal power generating units and 1000kV AC and ±800kV DC equipment, and advanced machines and equipment including large-sized liquefied natural gas carrier and 350km/h

Electricity Multiple Unit, were developed. Equipment systems with sophisticated technologies were successfully and independently developed for launch of satellites and the Shenzhou spaceship. China is changing from a country with great output of machinery industry to one with advanced technologies.

The history of machinery in China is the process from rise to decline and then to rise again over thousands of years, which has great historical and realistic significance for the present and future development of machinery industry in China. The machinery industry is growing in China. Chinese Mechanical Engineering Society compiled *History of Machinery in China* based on the development of that industry in China over thousands of years, for future development of that industry. As we know, this book might be the first works of industrial history in China's industrial circles, with significance to the new leap-forward development of China's machinery industry.

There are many monographs on the development of ancient and modern machinery in China. This book focuses on research of contemporary history of machinery based on existing research findings. Articles written by some well-known experts and scholars, with pictures, describe the whole contemporary history of machinery in China and record system reform, technological progress, product development, economic and social benefits and background of machinery industry in different periods. A look back into the history pushes people to think and advance,while revealing how to handle the reality and head toward the better future.

Compilation of this book took 8 years from 2003 when it was firstly planned to 2010 when it was completed. This book includes 4 volumes: Illustrated Handbook; General History; Technology; Products.

We believe this book will have positive effects on pushing China's industrialization with information-oriented construction, innovation driven, impelling the research, development, design, manufacture and application of mechanical products with green and intelligent features.

This book is based on hard work of over 100 famous experts, scholars and professors who have been engaged in machinery industry for a long time. I'd like to express my appreciating for the all writers and publishers.

Lu Yongxiang

May 2010

前　言

《中国机械史·图志卷》（简称《图志卷》），是《中国机械史》的独立分册。

《中国机械史》记载中国机械从石器时代的简单工具发展到现代化复杂机器的全过程，是记载中国古代、近代和现代机械发展的全书，是一部达800余万字的宏大巨著。该书不仅详尽地介绍了中国古代机械的发明、应用和演变，而且有大量篇幅介绍了"近代"、"现代"机械工业的诞生、发展史实；突破了行业、学科界线，首次包容了全机械工业古今发展的方方面面史实，是研究中国机械发展的重要成果。

《图志卷》既是《中国机械史》的独立分册，也是一部图文并茂的简明中国机械通史。《图志卷》由中国机械工程学会组织编纂，由中国机械工程学会与中国科学技术出版社合作出版。

按照编纂计划，《图志卷》是《中国机械史》的缩写本，也是图片直观和文字提要互补的普及本。要求以淡彩渲染出中国机械不同历史时期的发展脉络，以浓墨勾勒出中国机械不同历史时期的主要成就；要求选材精深、行文深入浅出，专业细节简约，而又能清晰、完整地陈述重要史实；要求兼有可读性和专业性，不同文化程度的中外读者都可浏览，并可供资深学者研究有关问题时参阅。为达到这样的要求，作者、编者们竭力而为，披沙拣金，确定所需内容。

《图志卷》以精练的选材、简要的文字、多彩的图片，直观地展示了中国机械工业漫长而辉煌的历史。凡属最重要的事件、成就，都尽可能包罗其中。《图志卷》包括文字10万余字、图650余幅，可以全景俯瞰机械史长河，亦可以按时代展示，而且行业与学科分陈。

为方便外国读者阅读，全书辅以英文。

《图志卷》的图片主要从国内外公开发行的书刊上收集，也有一部分系中国机械工业联合会重大装备办公室、统计与信息部、中国机械工业经济管理研究院等单位内部和个人供图。部分图片未能及时联系到原著者，希望原著者在看到本书后，能够及时联系编者，以支付图片使用费用。谢谢各方面的热情支持!

　　《图志卷》的主编是黄开亮，撰文是黄开亮，资料图片收集整理是黄慧、陈秀敏，审稿是柳乃复，英文审订是邱廷魁。虽然我们审慎其事，但由于历史跨度大，学科分布广，编译同仁水平所限，《图志卷》中的不妥之处，祈求指正。

中国机械工程学会

2010年6月

Foreword

History of Machinery in China: Illustrated Handbook (Illustrated Handbook for short), is a separate fascicule of *History of Machinery in China.*

History of Machinery in China covers the development from the simple tools in the Stone Age to the modernized complex machinery, and records the whole process of machinery development in China that spans the ancient, modern and contemporary history of machinery. The great masterpiece with more than 8 million Chinese characters not only generally introduces China's ancient machinery's invention, application and evolution, but also devotes a lot of space to presenting historical facts on the occurrence and development of "modern" and "contemporary" machinery industry. With all aspects of ancient and modern historical facts on the whole machinery industry development included for the first time, the book also makes breakthrough in terms of industry and subject and boasts a significant achievement of research on China's machinery development.

The Illustrated Handbook is not only an independent fascicule of History of Machinery in China, but also a concise comprehensive history of Chinese machinery with excellent pictures and texts. The compilation of this book is organized by Chinese Mechanical Engineering Society, and published by Chinese Mechanical Engineering Society in cooperation with China Science and Technology Press.

In accordance with the compilation plan, the Illustrated Handbook is more a popular version with vivid pictures complemented by texts than an abridged edition of History of Machinery in China. It is required to outline the major achievements and render the development of machinery in different historical periods. The materials should be selected in a careful and accurate manner and explained in simple language. With brief and concise professional details, and clear and complete statement of important facts taken into account, the book should feature readability and professionalism, which shall enable readers of different educational background at home and abroad to browse freely, but also facilitate reference for senior scholars' studies. Given our knowledge, it is difficult to meet such high standards. It could only be said that authors and editors have spared no efforts to comfirm the content.

The Illustrated Handbook visually and vividly displays the long and glorious history of China's machinery industry through refined selection, concise texts and colorful pictures. The most important events and achievements are embraced as many as possible. The book with 100 thousand Chinese characters and more than 650 pictures states in aspects of times, industries and subjects separately while delivering a panorama of the river of history.

English explanation to the whole book is presented to facilate foreign reader's understanding.

Pictures of this book are mainly collected from domestically and internationally public-released books and periodicals, but also part of the libraries of Office of Major Industrial Equipment, Statistics and Information Department of China Machinery Industry Federation, Economic & Management Institute of Machinery Industry, and some individuals. We have failed to contact the authors of certain pictures, who are expected to contact the editors for image use fees. The enthusiastic support is appreciated.

The editor-in-chief of Illustrated Handbook is Huang Kailiang. The texts are written by Huang Kailiang and the pictures are gathered and edited by Huang Hui and Chen Xiumin. The book is reviewed by Liu Naifu and the English translation is reviewed by Qiu Tingkui. While we devote deliberate efforts, it is not easy to make such a project due to great span of history, wide involvement of subjects and limited level of compilers and translators. We are open to any suggestions and criticism if any inappropriateness.

Chinese Mechanical Engineering Society
June, 2010

目　录

第一篇　中国古代机械史

第二篇 中国近代机械史

第三篇 中国现代机械史

CONTENTS

Part 2   Modern History of Machinery in China

Part 3 Contemporary History of Machinery in China

第一篇　中国古代机械史

Part 1
Ancient History of Machinery in China

■ 原始社会时期（史前时期、距今约200多万年）至晚清鸦片战争（1840年）
Primitive Society (Protohistory, about 2 million years ago) to the Opium War of the Late Qing Dynasty (1840)

引 言
Introduction

第一节 中国古代对"机械"的定义
Section 1 Definitions of Machinery in Ancient China

《庄子》（成书于战国时代）说："子贡（前520—前456年）南游于楚，反于晋。过汉阳，见一丈人方将为圃畦，凿隧而入井，抱瓮而出灌。搰搰然用力甚多而见功寡。子贡曰：'有械于此，一日浸百畦，用力甚寡而见功多，夫子不欲乎？'为圃者仰而视之，曰：'奈何？'曰：'凿木为机，后重前轻，挈水若抽，数如泆汤，其名曰槔。'"

Zhuangzi (The book of Master Chuang, written in the Warring States Period) mentioned that, "Zi Gong (520BC—456BC) had been rambling in the south in Chu and was returning to Jin. When he passed by a place on the north of the Han River, he saw an old man who was going to work on his vegetable garden. He had dug his tunnels, gone to the well and was bringing from it in his arms a jar of water for irrigation. Toiling away, he expended a great deal of strength only to get little results. Zi Gong said to him, 'There is a tool for irrigating a hundred plots in a day. It requires very little effort, but provides great results. Would you, Master, not like it?' The man looked up at Zi Gong and said, 'How does it work?' Zi Gong answered,'it is a lever made of wood, heavy behind and light in front. It raises water as quickly as you could do with your hand, or as it bubbles over from a boiler. Its name is shadoof.'"

《韩非子》（约成书于战国末年）说："舟车机械之利，用力小，致功大，则入多。"

Hanfeizi (The book of Master Hanfei, written at the end of Warring States Period or so) mentioned that, "Tools such as vessels and vehicles are favorable with the expenditure of a very little strength; the result accomplished is great with more gains."

以上记载表明，生活在公元前5世纪的子贡和公元前3世纪的韩非子，就已给"机械"下了定义，是"用力甚寡而见功多"，即能使人用力少而创造多的机械，为后人留下了关于"机械"的最早定义。表明我国早在两千多年前就对"机械"提出了定义，比西方早了4个世纪①。

The above records indicate that, Zi Gong and Master Hanfei who lived in the 5th Century BC and 3th Century BC respectively had defined "machinery" as tools "requires very little effort, but provides great results", namely tools with the expenditure of a very little strength to obtain more gains. It is the oldest definition of machinery handed down. This reflects that definitions of machinery had been given in China even more than 2000 year ago, four centuries earlier than that in the western countries[1].

第二节　古代中国机械发明
Section 2　Mechanical Inventions and Discoveries in Ancient China

中国是世界上发明与利用机械最早的国家之一。春秋时期(前770—前476年)即出现"机械"一词。

China is one of the countries in which machinery was first invented and utilized in the world. The word of "machinery" in Chinese words occurred in the Spring and Autumn Period (770BC—476BC).

古代中国机械的发明、应用，曾长时间居于世界前列。在机械原理、结构设计、材料利用、动力应用和工艺技术等方面都取得较高成就。铜、铁的应用都早于西方国家千年以上；商代(前16—前11世纪)就发明了蕴涵杠杆原理的桔槔；自东汉始，形状用途各异的齿轮广泛应用于指南车、记里鼓车、水转连磨等机械上；失蜡铸造、球墨铸铁等现代铸造技术工艺早在两千年前即在中国出现；在原动力方面，逐步从人力、畜力向利用水力、风力的方向发展；原始的机械自动化在汉代即已出现。中国古代许多机械制品的巧妙构思、精湛工艺，至今令世人折服。

Invention and application of machinery in ancient China had ever been ranking first in the world for a long time. Great achievements were made in principles of machinery, structural design, utilization of material, application of power, process engineering, etc. The application of copper and iron in China were more than one thousand years earlier than that in the western countries. Shadoof utilizing the lever principle was invented in the Shang Dynasty (16th Century BC—11th Century BC). Since the Eastern Han Dynasty, gears of different shapes and applications had been applied to machinery including compass, *li*-recording drum carriage (odometer carriage

---

① 西方第一位对机械提出定义的人，是恺撒时代（前1世纪）古罗马的一位建筑工程师维多维斯 (Vitruvius)。他的定义是"机械是由木材制造，且由具有相互联系的几部分所组成的一个系统，它具有强大的推动物体的力量。"[摘自刘仙洲编著《中国机械工程发明史》(第一编)]
① Vitruvius, a building engineer in the ancient Rome of Caesar Period (the 1st Century BC), is the first person who gave definition of machinery in the western countries. His definition is "that machinery is a system made of wood and composed of interconnected parts, and has great strength to push objects."(an excerpt of part I of *History of Mechanical Engineering Invention in China* Compiled by Liu Xianzhou)

used in ancient China) and Water powered multiple geared mills. Modern casting techniques such as dewaxing casting and spheroidal graphite iron casting occurred in China as early as 2000 years ago. Water power and wind power were gradually developed as motive power instead of manpower and animal power. Primal mechanical automation occurred in the Han Dynasty. Many mechanical products in ancient China have been amazing the world for their advanced design and superb processes until now.

中国先人对机械的大量发明、创造，推动了生产力的发展和社会进步，对人类进步产生了重大影响。大量的优秀机械发明，不但在国内产生了深远的影响，更是远播国外，改变世界，推动世界文明的进程。李约瑟在他的巨著 *Science and Civilization in China* 中，以英文字母为标号，列举了26种传到欧洲、影响巨大的中国古代杰出发明，其中机械产品19种；国内一些研究中国古代机械史的学者，曾研究确定中国古代十大机械发明，都是中国古代文明进步的里程碑、标志。研究、探讨中国古代机械的成就、规律，将可以起到借鉴历史、启发今天、激励未来的作用。

A great deal of inventions and creations on machinery by the ancient Chinese promoted development of productivity and social progress，and also had great influence on human progress. Numbers of excellent mechanical inventions not only had profound influence in China, but also were transmitted to other countries so as to change the world and initiate progression of world civilization. Joseph Needham, in his great work *Science and Civilization in China*, with alphabet labels, listed 26 outstanding inventions in ancient China which were transmitted to Europe and had great influence, among which there were 19 mechanical products.Some domestic scholars，studying ancient history of machinery in China，made researches and determined the ten major mechanical inventions in ancient China，all of which are milestones and marks of civilization progress in ancient China. Researches on and discussion of achievements and law of machinery in ancient China will have effects of drawing lessons from history, getting inspiration for the present and providing motivation for the future.

山东嘉祥汉武梁祠画石上的桔槔图

Shadoof design in Stone Relief at the Wu Liang Shrine of the Han Dynasty in Jiaxiang County, Shandong Province

李约瑟提到的26种中国古代发明、发现：

The 26 inventions and discoveries in ancient China listed by Joseph Needham are as follows:

(a) ★龙骨水车：Dragon bone waterlift;

(b) ★石碾和水力在石碾上的应用：Rollergang and application of water power to Rollergang;

(c) ★水排：Waterpower blasting combined air blowers;

(d) ★风扇车和簸扬机：Winnowing machine and fanning machine;

(e) ★活塞风箱：Piston bellow;

(f) ★平纺机和提花机：Plain loom and jacquard loom;

(g) ★缫丝、纺织和调丝机：Reeling machine, textile machine and straightening and cutting machine;

(h) ★独轮车：Wheelbarrow;

(i) ★加帆手推车：Wind powered barrow;

(j) ★磨车：Wheel driven mill;

(k) ★高效马具：Efficient harness;

(l) ★弓弩：Bow and arrow;

(m) ★风筝：Kite;

(n) ★竹蜻蜓和走马灯：Bamboo dragonfly and Craft lantern;

(o) 深钻技术：Deep drilling technology;

(p) ★铸铁：Iron casting;

(q) ★游动常平稳吊器：Traveling gimbal suspender;

(r) 拱桥：Arch bridge;

(s) 铁索吊桥：Cable suspension bridge;

(t) 河渠闸门：Canal gate;

(u) ★造船和航运：Shipbuilding and navigation;

(v) ★船尾方向舵：Stern-mounted rudder;

(w) 火药：Gunpowder;

(x) ★罗盘：Compass;

(y) 纸和印刷术：Paper making and printing;

(z) 瓷器：Porcelain.

带"★"者为机械产品

Note: Mark★ refers to mechanical products.

中国古代科技曾长期居于世界先进行列，其中机械发明占有较大比重。在众多的优秀机械发明中，许多历史学家评选出不但在国内产生了深远影响，有的还远播世界的古代十大机械发明。以出现先后为序：

Science and technology in ancient China had ever been ranking first in the world for a long time. Among others, mechanical inventions account for a large proportion. Out of many excellent mechanical inventions, numerous historians chose through public appraisal the ten major mechanical inventions in ancient China，which not only had profound influence in China but also were transmitted to countries all over the world. They are listed as follows in a order from first occurrence to late occurrence:

（1）秦陵铜车马：The Qin Shihuang Mausoleum copper combat chariots/horses;

（2）皇帝出行的仪仗车——指南车：South pointing carriage, the symbol of guard of honor used when the emperor went out in ancient times;

（3）三行条播机械——三脚耧：Animal-draw seed sow could sow three rows, a sower with three legs;

（4）水力驱动的多头碓——连机水碓：Integrated water power trip-hammer, Water-driven multiple tilt hammers;

（5）连续提水的龙骨水车：Dragon bone waterlift for continuous water lifting;

（6）水力驱动的冶金鼓风设备——水排：Waterpower blasting combined air blowers in metallurgy, combined air bellows;

（7）栈道运粮用的独轮车——木牛流马：Wooden ox and floating horse, wheelbarrow for transporting food in plank roads;

（8）风帆——船帆、可自动调节以适应风向的立轴式大风车：Wind sail, sail and vertical shaft big windmill which is self-adjustable to be adaptive to wind directions;

（9）天文仪器及机械——水运仪象台：Water-powered Armillary (sphere) and Celestial (Globe), astronomical instruments and machinery;

（10）高效的水力大纺车：Efficient water power spinning wheel.

此外还有备选的：取暖及熏香用的被中香炉；皇帝出行的另一种仪仗车——记里鼓车；舂车和磨车；可同时磨面、舂米、车水的水轮三事等。

In addition, there are also alternatives such as censer in quilt for warming and incensing; *li*-recording drum carriage, another symbol of guard of honor used when the emperor went out in ancient times; pounder and mill; and trifunctional water mill for flour grinding, rice pound and using water wheel for irrigation and drainage.

第一章　中国古代机械的发展进程与各时期发展概况

Chapter 1　Development Process of Machinery in Ancient China and Overview of Development in Various Periods

社会分期 Society division	朝　　代 Dynasty	发展概述 Overview of development
原始社会（史前时期，距今约200多万年前—前21世纪） Primitive Society (protohistory, about 2 million years ago–21st Century BC)	石器时代 Stone Age	揭开了中国机械史的序幕，这一时期主要是原始工具时期。简单机械、原始机械如腰机、陶轮已经出现 Ancient history of machinery in China began in this period, in which primitive tools predominated. Simple machines and primitive machines occurred such as waist loom and potter's wheels.
	旧石器时代 （约200多万年前—1万年前） Paleolithic Age (more than 2 million years ago–10 thousand years ago)	粗石器制作，打制石器，制成砍砸器、刮削器等原始工具，以及骨器、木棒、蚌壳等；进行原始采集和狩猎活动。这一时期已出现了较一般工具复杂的原始弓箭；出现经过磨制的骨针 Coarse stoneware manufacture began. Stoneware was forged to make primitive tools including choppers and scrapers as well as bone tools, wood bars and pearl shells for activities of primitive gathering and hunting. Bows and arrows more complicated than common tools and ground bone needles had occurred in this period.
	新石器时代 （约1万年前—前21世纪） Neolithic Age (about 10 thousand years ago–21st Century BC)	细石器制作，制作和使用磨制石器；原始农业，出现了石质犁形器等石制农具。机械开始萌芽，如狩猎用弓箭（是机械方面最早的一项发明）、缫丝纺织（踞织机），出现了独木舟和桨，已有了车等原始交通工具 Fine stoneware manufacture began, including stoneware manufacture and use of ground stoneware. In primitive agriculture, a period began with stone farm tools such as ploughs. Machines emerged, such as bows and arrows for hunting (the earliest invention in machinery), and reeling and spinning (loom with the operator in a crouching position). Pirogues and oars occurred as well as primitive vehicles such as carriages. 新石器时代的晚期，距今约5000年，相当于传说中的炎黄、尧舜时代。出现中国最早的青铜器（甘肃马家窑出土铜刀，距今已有4800年左右） The late Neolithic Age began about 5000 years ago, equivalent to the periods of Emperors Yan and Huang and Emperors Yao and Shun. The earliest bronze instrument made in China occurred (bronze knife unearthed in Majia Kiln, Gansu Province, made about 4800 years ago).

（续表）

社会分期 Society division	朝　代 Dynasty			发展概述 Overview of development
奴隶社会（前21世纪—前221年） Slave Society (21st Century BC–221BC)	夏商周三代（前21世纪—前221年） Xia, Shang and Zhou Dynasties (21st Century BC– 221 BC)			夏商周三代，是中国古代机械迅速发展阶段。冶铜技术成熟，创造了灿烂的青铜文化；开始了铁的使用，大大提高了生产工具的效率；机械技术知识的积累，为后世机械的发展提供了条件 Machinery rapidly developed in Xia, Shang and Zhou Dynasties in ancient China. With mature copper smelting technology, splendid bronze culture was created. Iron was initially used to make production tools with higher efficiency. Knowledge of machinery and technology was accumulated to prepare for development of machinery in later age.
	夏（前21—前17世纪） Xia Dynasty (21st Century BC–17th Century BC)			冶铜技术趋于成熟，开始进入青铜时代；出现了古车、加工粮食的杵臼等重要生产工具 Copper smelting technology tended to be mature and Bronze Age began. Important production tools such as ancient chariots and mortar and pestle for grain processing occurred.
	商（前17—前11世纪） Shang Dynasty (17th Century BC–11th Century BC)			青铜铸造鼎盛时期，创造了灿烂的青铜文化，著名司母戊鼎、四羊方尊都是在这一时期出现的。利用天然陨铁制造了铁刃铜钺；开始牛耕，应用桔槔汲水，出现风帆 Bronze casting reached its zenith and splendid bronze culture was created. Famous *Simuwu* quadripod and *Siyang fangzun* wine vessel were made during this period. Iron-bladed bronze tomahawk was made with natural siderite. People began to plow by cattle, lift water by shadoof and use wind sail.
	周（前11世纪—前221年） Zhou Dynasty (11th Century BC–221 BC)	西周（前11世纪—前771年） Western Zhou Dynasty (11th Century BC–771 BC)		延续和发展商代的青铜工艺；开始冶铁；应用辘轳提水；广泛使用马拉战车和车战用长柄格斗兵器，如戈、矛、戟、钺等 Bronze arts and crafts of the Shang Dynasty were extended and developed in this period. Iron smelting was started. Windlass was used to lift water. Horse-drawn chariots and combat polearms for chariot wars such as dagger-axe, lance, halberd and tomahawk were widely used.
		东周（前770—前221年） Eastern Zhou Dynasty (770 BC –221 BC)	春秋（前770—前476年） Spring and Autumn Period (770 BC –476 BC)	诸子百家争鸣，促进了古代机械技术的较快发展；铁器和生铁冶铸技术开始出现，黑心可锻铸铁、白心可锻铸铁和钢的出现，加速了铜器向铁器的过渡，铁器开始被少量应用；失蜡铸造已经成熟，叠铸工艺、错金、包金、鎏金和铸镶工艺相继出现；合金配方（六齐）定制，吴王夫差矛、越王勾践剑表明了春秋时期高超和精细的冶金工艺；出现弩，控制射击的弩机已是比较灵巧的机械装置；纺织技术得到发展，出现了斜织机等手工业机械 The hundred schools of thought in Spring and Autumn Period facilitated rapid development of ancient mechanical technology. Ironware and pig iron smelting and casting technology occurred. Emergency of blackheart malleable cast iron, whiteheart malleable cast iron and steel, hastened the transition from bronzeware to ironware. Ironware was initially used in a small quantity. Dewax casting had been mature. Overlay-casting, inlaying with gold, covering with gold leaf, gold plating and cast-inserting occurred successively. For alloy

社会分期 Society division	朝　代 Dynasty			发展概述 Overview of development
奴隶社会（前21世纪—前221年） Slave Society (21st Century BC–221BC)		东周（前770—前221年） Eastern Zhou Dynasty (770 BC–221 BC)		composition (six alloys) customization, the Spear of King Fuchai of Wu and Sword of King Goujian of Yue reflected superb and elaborate metallurgic technology in the Spring and Autumn Period. Crossbow occurred and rear works of the crossbar to control shooting were artful mechanical devices. With development of textile technology, machines of handicraft industry such as ramp loom occurred.
			战国（前475—前221年） Warring States Period (475 BC – 221 BC)	青铜器仍有发展，制造了曾侯乙编钟、曾侯乙尊盘等称为天下奇观的青铜器；铸铁柔化技术成熟，铁制农具开始普遍使用，进入铁器时代；出现最早的磁性指向器"司南"；多踪多蹑提花机开始应用；造船技术达一定水平，已经制造了大型双体船"方舟"、"舫船" Bronzeware kept developing, and the *Zeng Hou Yi* Serial Bells and *Zeng Hou Yu* Wine Vessel Plate, known as wonderous bronzeware, were made in this period. Cast iron tempering technology became mature and farm tools made of iron were universally used, which emblemized the beginning of Iron Age. The earliest south pointer called Sinan occurred. Multi-heddle and step jacquard loom was initially used. Shipbuilding technology had achieved a certain level. Large twin-hull ships called "*Fangzhou*" or "*Fangchuan*" (referring to two boats lashed side by side) were made.
封建社会（前221—1846年） Feudal society (221 BC –1846)	秦汉（前221—220年） Qin and Han Dynasties (221 BC –220)			承接春秋战国的技术积累，机械技术趋于成熟，大量创新发明，取得领先世界的辉煌成就 With accumulation of technology in the Spring and Autumn Period and the Warring States Period, machinery technology tended to be mature and took the leading position with a good deal of innovations and inventions as glorious achievement all over the world.
		秦（前221—前206年） Qin Dynasty (221 BC –206 BC)		统一全国度量衡；秦皇铜车马表明铸造技术、金属加工和组装工艺等机械制造工艺技术达到很高水平 The weights and measures system was standardized throughout the country. The *Qin Shihuang* Mausoleum copper combat chariots/horses reflect that mechanical manufacturing technology such as casting technology and metal working and assembly had achieved a very high level.
		汉（前206—220年） Han Dynasty (206 BC –220)	西汉（前206—8年） Western Han Dynasty (206BC-8)	铸铁技术继续发展，出现球墨铸铁；已有金属齿轮出现；已经广泛使用风力、水力，西汉出现了连机水碓等；开始使用绳轮传动的手摇纺车；出现了世界上最早应用常平支架的"被中香炉"、透光铜镜等先进工艺机械产品；首创领先世界的橹、舵 Iron casting technology kept developing with new progress of spheroidal graphite iron casting. Metal gears occurred. Wind power, water power had been widely used. Water-driven multiple tilt hammers were invented in the Western Han Dynasty. Hand spinning wheel driven by rope pulley was initially used. Advanced mechanical craftworks occurred such as censer in quilt, which initially utilized gimbals in the world, and Light Penetrating copper mirror. World's leading yuloh and rudder were originated.

（续表）

社会分期 Society division	朝　代 Dynasty			发展概述 Overview of development
封建社会 （前476—1846年） Feudal society (476 BC –1846)	汉 （前206—220年） Han Dynasty (206 BC –220)		新（9—25年） Xin (9–25)	制造了铜卡尺、"铜嘉量"等重要量具 During Xin (Wang Mang interregnum) (9–25) period, important measuring tools such as bronze caliper and Standard Capacity Measure of Xin were produced.
			东汉 （25—220年） Eastern Han Dynasty (25–220)	水排鼓风设备用于冶铸生铁；创制了先进的农机具，如耧车、龙骨水车、扇风车等；创制了一些先进的手工业装备，如脚踏纺车、手织机，提花机开始应用；张衡制造了地动仪（被称为世界地震仪之祖）、水运浑象仪，制造了三四层舱室的大型船舶"楼船"，装备了艉舵和高效推进工具橹 water-power blowing-engines had been applied to pig iron smelting and casting; Advanced farm machinery were created, such as animal-drawn seed sower, dragon bone waterlift and rotary winnowing fan. Some advanced equipment was created in handicraft industry, for example, treadle loom, hand loom and jacquard loom were initially used. Seismometer and water-powered armillary sphere were made by Zhang Heng, inventor of the world's earliest seismoscope. Towered ship, large vessel with three to four floors of chambers was made and provided with stern-mounted rudder and efficient pushing tool yuloh.
	三国、两晋、南北朝（220—589年） The Three Kingdoms, Jin Dynasty, and Northern and Southern Dynasty (220–589)	秦汉的统一局面结束，至此又进入割据纷争，推动古代机械的充实与提高 The unification in Qin and Han Dynasties was broken up into separation and dispute, which promoted enrichment and improvement of machinery in ancient China.		
		三国 （220—280年） The Three Kingdoms (220–280)	魏（220—265年） Wei (220–265) 蜀（221—263年） Shu Han (221–263) 吴（222—280年） Wu (222–280)	发明机械式指南车、记里鼓车，具有减速运输和自动离合装置，说明传动机构齿轮系已发展到较高水平；马钧改进了提花机；发明木牛流马（现代学者考证，多数认为是一种独轮车）；改进弩机；大型战船出现 Mechanic south pointing carriage and li-recording drum carriage were invented and provided with speed reduction and transportation device and automatic clutch device, indicating that gear train of transmission mechanism had developed to a high level. Ma Jun improved jacquard loom and crossbow and invented wooden ox and floating horse (through investigation, most modern scholars regarded it as a wheelbarrow); large warship occurred.
		两晋 （265—420年） Jin Dynasty (265–420)	西晋（265—316年） Western Jin (265–316) 东晋（317—420年） Eastern Jin (317–420)	出现低硅灰口铁 Low-silicon gray cast iron occurred. 制造水密舱船舶 Vessels with watertight bulkhead were made. 大型铜铁铸件和大型机械结构在两晋开始出现 Large copper and iron castings and large mechanical structures began to occur in the Jin Dynasty.

（续表）

社会分期 Society division	朝　代 Dynasty		发展概述 Overview of development
封建社会 （前476—1846年） Feudal society (476 BC –1846)		南北朝（420—589年） Northern and Southern Dynasty (420–589)	灌钢工艺炼制优质钢，出现舂车、磨车，发明轮船 Perfusing Steel Method was employed for smelting quality steel. Pounder and mill occurred. Motorship was invented.
	隋唐五代 （581-960年） Sui, Tang and Five Dynasties (581–960)		唐代实行对外开放政策，重视经济发展，机械技术继续发展，但与强盛的帝国声威相比仍有差距 In Tang Dynasty, opening-up policy was implemented, stress was laid on economic development and mechanical technology continued developing. However, that was not well matched with the empire which had a lot of prestige.
		隋（581—618年） Sui Dynasty (581–618)	发明雕版印刷术 Block printing was invented.
		唐（618—907年） Tang Dynasty (618–907)	发明黑色火药，制作了浑天黄道仪（浑仪） Gunpowder was invented and ecliptic armillary sphere (armillary sphere) was made.
		五代（907—960年） Five Dynasties (907–960)	沧州铁狮子重约40吨 Iron Lion of Cangzhou in Five Dynasties is about 40 tons in weight.
	宋元时期 （960—1398年） Song and Yuan Dynasties (960–1398)		此时的科学技术水平已达到中国古代的顶峰，形成古代机械科技发展高潮，众多的科学发现和技术发明为中国谱写了世界机械史的灿烂篇章 Science and technology in this period achieved the summit in ancient China, establishing a climax of scientific and technical development in ancient times. Many scientific discoveries and technical inventions in ancient China were brilliant parts of the world's history of machinery.
		两宋 （960—1279年） Song Dynasty (960–1279)	北宋 （960—1127年） Northern Song Dynasty (960–1127)	发明指南针、泥活字印刷技术；火药的制造和使用有了很大进步；苏颂制造了水运仪象台，它体现了当时中国机械工程技术水平领先于世界的卓越成就，出现"走马灯"和"喷水鱼洗"；出现活塞风箱；沈括著科学名著《梦溪笔谈》 Compass and clay movable type printing technology were invented. Great progress was made in gun powder manufacture and use. Water-powered Armillary (sphere) and Celestial (Globe) was made by Su Song, which reflected that mechanical engineering of China was far more advanced than distinguished achievements all over the world at that time. Craft lantern, fish bowl and piston-bellows occurred. Shen Kuo wrote the scientific masterpiece *Mengxi Bitan* (Which is also called *Dream Pond Essays*).
			南宋（1127—1279年） Southern Song Dynasty (1127-1279) 辽（907—1125年） Liao Dynasty (907-1125) 金（1115—1234年） Jin Dynasty (1115-1234)	发明木活字印刷；水罗盘用于航海；纺织技术进一步发展，出现了花本提花机，水转大纺车的出现大大提高了纺纱效率 Wooden movable type printing was invented. Water compass was used for navigation. For textile technology, jacquard loom with endless paper card occurred, and water power spinning wheel greatly improved spinning efficiency.

社会分期 Society division	朝　　代 Dynasty	发展概述 Overview of development
封建社会（前476—1846年） Feudal society (476 BC –1846)	元（1206—1368年） Yuan Dynasty (1206-1368)	机械技术继续发展，研制和装备了许多先进装备和仪器，总体处于当时世界先进水平。出现多色多版木印，发明转轮活字盘，活字印刷趋于完备；出现效率极高的32个纺锭的水轮大纺车；火药技术成熟，制造了火铳、炮，标志着冷兵器向火器过渡的完成；制成支撑式指南仪器，指南针广泛用于航海；制造1200吨的运粮船；制造了简仪，首次应用了滚柱轴承 Since the Song Dynasty, mechanical technology had kept developing, in which many advanced equipment and apparatus were developed and provided. It generally took the world's leading position at that time. Multi-color and multi-screen wooden printing occurred. Rotary typetray was invented. Movable-type printing tended to be complete. Extremely efficient water power spinning wheel with 32 hasps occurred. Powder technology tended to be mature. Gun barrel and gun were manufacture, which emblemized completion of transition from cold weapons to firearms. Supported south pointing apparatus were made and compass was widely applied to navigation. Grain carrier with capacity of 1200 tons was made. Abridged armilla was made, and roller bearing was initially employed.
	明（1368—1644） Ming Dynasty (1368-1644)	西方先进机械制造开始传入中国，但受限制，朝廷采取思想禁锢政策，机械技术发展缓慢；万户进行喷气飞行试验；郑和下西洋，造船和航海技术达到当时世界最高水平。沿海地区广泛使用八面立帆的立轴式风车；火器制作有较高水平，制造了世界最早的二级火箭；铸造了永乐大钟，重46吨；宋应星著《天工开物》 Western advanced machinery manufacturing technology was initially introduced to China. However, it was restrained by mental slavery policy of government, which resulted in slow development of mechanical technology. Wan Hu carried out jet fuel flight test. During Zheng He's maritime expedtions, shipbuilding and navigation technology once achieved top position all over the world. Vertical shaft windmills with 8 vertical sails were widely used in coastal areas. Firearms manufacture was advanced and the world's earliest two-stage rocket was made. The Yongle Bell was cast with weight of 46 tons. Song Yingxing wrote *Tiangong Kaiwu* (Which is also called *The Exploitation of the Works of Nature*).
	清（1644—1911年） （古代机械史截至1840年） Qing Dynasty (1644-1911) (Ancient history of machinery in China ended in 1840)	制造了不少新奇钟表；西学东渐，西方机械技术开始传入中国 Quite a few fancy clocks and watches were made. In that period, western learning was progressively extending to the East, and western mechanical technology was initially introduced into China.

第一节 原始工具
Section 1 Primitive Tools

　　史前时期，人类所制造的工具是经打击而制成的粗糙石器，只是改变原材料的形状，这是最简单的加工方法。人类使用打制石器的时代称为旧石器时代。

In prehistoric era, ancient people used knapped stone tools. It is the simplest machining method which only change the shape of raw materials. Human beings used knapped stone tools during the Paleolithic Age.

　　中国旧石器时代早期的人类，如距今200万—240万年前繁昌人字洞（1998年发现）人，170万—180万年前的元谋人，50万—60万年前的北京人，已会对石块进行敲击和初步修整，制成各种形状粗糙的刮削器、砍砸器和三棱形尖状器等原始工具。

Human beings living in China in lower Paleolithic Age, such as *Renzidong* site (discovered in 1998) man living in Fanchang 2—2.4 million years ago, Yuanmou Man living 1.7—1.8 million years ago and Peking Man

石钺 （新石器时代） 长13.8cm，宽8.2cm。扁平、弧刃、穿孔，材质颇佳，制作精细，不但有磨制精良的刃部，而且钻出非常规矩的圆孔，反映了石兵器的发展与进步。江苏淮安出土。

Stone battle-axe (in the Neolithic Age): 13.8 cm in length and 8.2 cm in width. It is flat with an arc cutting edge and a through hole. It was made with quality materials by elaborate processes. Not only its well ground cutting edge but also the regular round hole drilled reflects development and advancement of stone weapons. It was unearthed in Huaian, Jiangsu Province.

living 500—600 thousand years ago, were capable of knapping and preliminarily shaving stone blocks to various primitive tools with crude shape such as scrapers, choppers and triquetrous points.

约在距今4万—5万年前的旧石器时代晚期，资阳人、山顶洞人等已掌握了初步的磨削技术，许多石器都已比较光滑，刃部也较锋利。山顶洞人不仅使用了磨制过的骨针、石珠，稍晚还使用了带孔石珠、兽骨、鹿角等。大约2万—3万年前，人们已会利用材料的弹性，制造比一般工具更为复杂的弓箭。早期的石镞（箭头）与木杆是用绳索捆绑在一起的。

In the upper Paleolithic Age about 40—50 thousand years ago, Ziyang Man and Upper Cave Man had mastered primary grinding technology. Most stoneware was relatively smooth with sharp cutting part. Upper Cave Man not only used ground bone needles and stone beads, but also used perforated stone beads, animal bones, deer horns, etc. later. About 20—30 thousand years ago, people could utilize elasticity of materials for creating bows and arrows more complicated than common tools. Early stone arrowhead (arrow head) was tied up with wooden poles by ropes.

石镞　中石器时代的石箭头。中国使用石镞大约起源于2.8万年以前。内蒙古赤峰市林西县出土。

Stone arrowhead: Arrow head in the Mesolithic Age. Stone arrowhead was initially used in China about 28 thousand years ago. It was unearthed in Linxi County, Chifeng, Inner Mongolia Autonomous Region.

大约1万多年前，人类开始进入了一个新的历史时期——新石器时代。进入精制工具阶段，虽然生产工具主要仍是石器，但采取了磨制的加工技术，有较为精细的打磨工艺，能对石器进行雕刻、穿孔、开槽，从而进入新石器时代。甘肃省出土了一种精致的约5000年前的石刃骨刀，它以开有细长柄的兽骨为刀体，内装磨制的石刃。这种刀反映了新石器时代综合运用不同材料制造工具的能力，可视为后世组合刀具的先驱。公元前8000—前2800年期间出现了陶轮（制陶用转台）、陶纺轮、踞织机、独木舟等简单的机械，农具大约出现在公元前6000—前5000年，已有石斧、石刀、石锄、石镰和骨耜等。

About 10 thousand years ago, ancient people entered the Neolithic Age, a new historic period. Fine tool period began. Although stoneware was still main production tool, working technology of grinding was added and fine grinding processes were employed to help graving, perforation and grooving on stoneware. Hence, the Neolithic Age began. An exquisite stone-edged bone blade made about 5 thousand years ago was unearthed in Gansu Province. It has a body which was made of animal bones with long and thin shank and internally provided with ground stone edge. The blade reflects the capability of comprehensively applying various materials to tool manufacture in the Neolithic Age. It can be regarded as the precursor of combined tools in later ages. Between 8000 BC and 2800 BC, simple machines occurred such as potter's wheels (revolving tables for potting), ceramic spinning wheels, loom with the operator in a crouching position and canoes.

Farm tools occurred about between 6000BC and 5000BC. Stone axes, stone knives, stone hoes, stone sickles, spade-shaped bone instruments, etc. had occurred.

骨耜、木耜　当时重要的农业工具。6000—7000年前，中国人的祖先已进入农业社会。

Spade-shaped bone instruments and spade-shaped wooden instruments: They were important farm tools at that time. 6000—7000 years ago, ancestor of the Chinese had entered agricultural society.

石凿、石锛　出土于广西桂林甑皮岩洞穴（新石器时代早期）。

Stone chisels and stone adzes: In the lower Neolithic Age, unearthed from Zengpiyan Cave site in Guilin, Guangxi Zhuang Autonomous Region.

石磨盘与石磨棒　河南新郑裴李岗出土，约为7000年前文物。石磨盘状如鞋底，下面有4个柱状足。操作者手持石磨棒，在磨盘上来回碾磨谷物。

Stone roller and quern: Unearthed from Peiligang site in Xinzheng County, Henan Province, as relics from about 7000 years ago. The stone quern is like a sole of shoe in shape with four cylindrical legs. It can be imagined that an operator is reciprocatingly grinding grains on the quern with stone roller in hand.

骨针、骨针筒　约为新石器时代文物，包头市东郊阿善遗址出土。

Bone needles and needle cylinder: In the Neolithic Age，unearthed from Ashan site in east suburbs of Baotou.

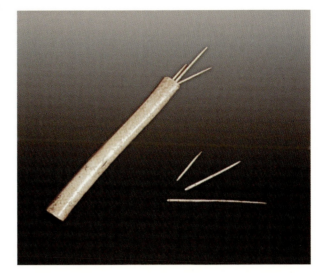

骨梭　新石器时代的骨梭，是原始的引纬工具。山东泰安大汶口出土。

Bone shuttle: Bone shuttle of the Neolithic Age is a primitive wefting tool. It was unearthed from Dawenkou site, Taian, Shandong Province.

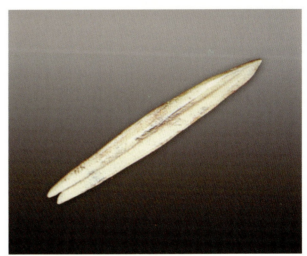

石纺轮　石纺轮是7000多年前的河姆渡人给纤维加捻的工具。浙江余姚河姆渡出土。

Stone spinning wheel: Hemudu Man living more than 7000 years ago used stone spinning wheel for twisting of fibre. It was unearthed from Hemudu site in Yuyao, Zhejiang Province.

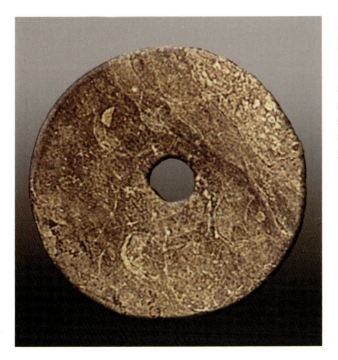

第二节 简单机械
Section 2 Simple Machines

杠杆、滑轮在物理学上被称作简单机械。

Levers and pulleys are called simple machines physically.

杠杆，是中国古代应用最普遍的简单机械。杠杆在中国的典型发展是秤的发明和广泛应用。在一根杠杆上安装吊绳作为支点，一端挂上重物，另一端挂上砝码或秤锤，就可以称量物体的重量。实物发现最多的是在湖南长沙、常德、衡山等古楚墓出土的衡器。它们是公元前4—前3世纪的制品，是等臂称，不等臂称可能早在春秋时期就已经使用了。

Levers are the most commonly used simple machines in ancient China. Representative development of levers in China is reflected by invention and extensive application of steelyards. Objects can be weighed by a lever provided with lifting ropes as the fulcrum and load hung at one end and balance weights or the sliding weight at the other end. Most physical levers discovered are

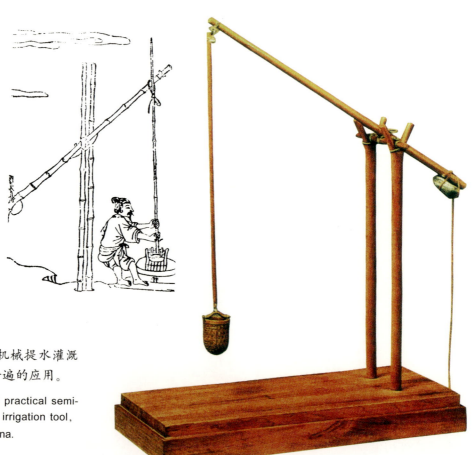

桔槔 简单而实用的半机械提水灌溉工具，在中国古代得到普遍的应用。

Shadoof: It is a simple and practical semi-mechanical water lifting and irrigation tool, universally used in ancient China.

weighing apparatus unearthed from the tombs of Chu State in Changsha, Changde and Hengshan Mountain of Hunan Province. Levers were produced between the 4th Century BC and the 3rd Century BC as equal-arm scales. Unequal-arm scales might have been used in the Spring and Autumn Period.

桔槔，亦称吊杆，提升机械。王祯著《农书》记载商初成汤时遇大旱，伊尹发明桔槔，"教民田头凿井灌田"。桔槔的结构简单，利用杠杆原理，在水边竖一立木或就地利用树杈，架上一根横木，一端绑上配重(石块)，另一端系上水桶，当把水桶入水中打满以后，由于杠杆末端的重力作用，便能轻易提上来。桔槔早在春秋时期便被普遍使用，而且沿用几千年，是农村历代通用的旧式提水器具。

Shadoof, also called hanger rod, is a lifting machine. Wang Zhen recorded in the *Nongshu* (Book of Agriculture) that absolute drought occurred during Emperor Cheng Tang's reign in the early Shang Dynasty, and Yi Yin invented shadoof and "taught farmers to dig wells for irrigation at the edge of fields". The machine is easily made by, based on the lever principle, erecting a vertical timber at waterside or using tree branches locally and building a cross bar spanning the timber with balance mass (stone blocks) tied at one end and a water bucket at the other end. When the water bucket is immersed and filled with water, due to gravity action at the other end of the lever, the bucket can be easily lifted. Shadoof was universally used as early as in the Spring and Autumn Period and the following thousands of years. It was a general water lifting instrument for generations in rural areas.

辘轳，是轮轴与杠杆原理相结合的简单提水工具。据宋朝高承著《事物纪原》记载："史佚始作辘轳"，史佚是西周史官，实际的运用可能更早。至春秋战国，广泛应用于农田灌溉，也用于矿业开采、工程建筑、军事等方面。辘轳的应用在我国时间较长，新中国成立前在我国北方缺水地区，仍在使用辘轳提水灌溉。至今，一些地下水很深的山区，也还在使用辘轳从深井中提水。

双辘轳结构示意图

Two-way windlass structural representation

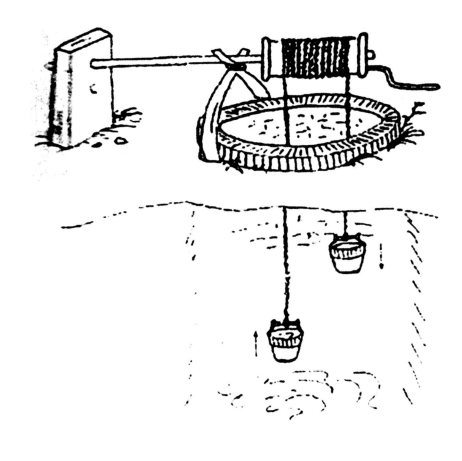

Windlass is a simple water lifting tool combining axle with lever principle.

It was recorded in *Shiwu Jiyuan* (On the Origins of Things and Affairs) by Gao Cheng of the Song Dynasty that "Shi Yi initiated windlass." Shi Yi is the name of a historiographer of the Western Zhou Dynasty. In fact, windlass may be used earlier. Up to the Spring and Autumn Period and the Warring States Period, it was widely applied to farmland irrigation as well as mining, engineering construction, military affairs, etc. Windlass has been used in China for a long time. Before foundation of the People's Republic of China, windlass had been used for water lifting and irrigation in areas of water shortage in North China. Even now windlass is still used in some mountainous areas with deeply buried groundwater for lifting water from deep wells.

单辘轳　采自《天工开物》

One-way windlass：from *Tiangong Kaiwu*

第三章 青铜器与高超的铸造工艺
Chapter 3 Bronzeware and Superb Casting Techniques

第一节 古代铸造技术的发展进步
Section 1 Development and Improvement of Casting Technology in Ancient China

铸造在我国古代的金属加工工艺中占有突出地位。最初的铸造技术是使用石范，由于石料不易加工，又不耐高温，其后创造了泥范铸造和失蜡铸造两大传统铸造工艺。

Casting predominated in metal working techniques in ancient China. Stone molds were used in casting technology initially. Considering that stone molds were not easily worked or high temperature resistant, two major traditional casting techniques of clay mold casting and dewax casting were created afterwards.

泥范铸造
Clay Mold Casting

在近代砂型铸造之前的三千多年时间里，泥范铸造一直是最主要的铸造方法之一。泥范铸造的工艺一是制模；二是翻外范；三是制内范；四是合范；五是浇铸。古人在制作复杂造型的青铜器时，还采用了分铸法，即将复杂的器物分为若干简单的部件，大型部件化为小型部件分别铸造，最后压铸成一体。我国在商代早期就有了泥范铸造，商代中期已达到极高的范铸工艺技巧。司母戊方鼎、四羊方尊、虢伯簋、方卣等旷世奇珍都是用这种方法铸造成功的。如西周的虢伯簋的铸造共用了36块泥范（包括8块活块范）和5块泥芯，经6次浇铸（包括铸接）而成。

Clay mold casting remained one of the most important casting processes throughout more than three thousand years till sand mold casting occurred in recent times. Clay mold casting consisted of five processes: molding, external mold reproduction, internal mold forming, mold folding and pouring. The ancients also employed separate casting technique in making bronzeware in complicated shape, namely, a complicated ware was divided into some simple parts, separate casting was performed to form small parts as integral parts of large parts and finally die casting was performed for integration. Clay mold casting can be traced back to the early Shang Dynasty in China. In the middle Shang Dynasty, mold casting craft became superb level. Rare treasures such as Simuwu Quadripod, Siyang Fangzun Wine Vessel, *Yu Bo Gui* and Square You-vessel were molded by this process. For example, *Yu Bo Gui* was made with totally 36 clay molds (including 8 movable piece molds) and 5 clay cores by pouring (including cast bonding) six times in the Western Zhou Dynasty.

失蜡铸造（又称熔模铸造）
Dewax Casting (also Called Investment Casting)

失蜡铸造是以蜡型制模型，然后在模上面多次涂挂泥浆，待泥干后加热铸型，蜡便熔化并流出而成型。失蜡法不存在块范法的分型问题，可以一次铸成形状相当复杂、纹饰特别细致的器物。我国失蜡法至迟起源于春秋时期，河南淅川下寺出土的春秋时代铜禁是迄今得到的最早的失蜡法铸件；战国时期的曾侯乙尊盘，其沿口透空附饰由细小的铜梗组成，重重叠叠，玲珑剔透，如丝瓜络子，即使用现代工艺铸造，也极为困难，可见当时失蜡铸造技术的出神入化，巧夺天工。

In dewax casting, the mold is made in wax patterns, the mold is then dipped into slurry many times, the slurry is left to dry and heated for pouring mold, and the wax is melt and flows out to form a cavity. Dewax casting does not require splitting in piece-mold casting, so can be used to form wares in complicated shape with delicate decorative patterns in one piece. Dewax casting technique at the latest started from the Spring and Autumn Period in ancient China. The copper Jin of the Spring and Autumn Period unearthed in Xiasi, Xichuan，Henan is the oldest casting made by dewax casting process among the castings discovered till now. As for Zeng Hou Yi Wine Vessel Plate made in the Warring States Period, its pierced decorations at the rim consisting of fine bronze stems, overlapped and exquisite, like the loofah, can even hardly be cast with modern techniques. Obviously, dewax casting technique at that time attained to perfection with wonderful workmanship excelling nature.

中国传统的失蜡铸造技术，对世界的冶金发展有很大影响。现代的熔模精密铸造就是从传统的失蜡法发展而来，虽然其所用蜡料、制膜、造型材料、工艺方法等方面，随着时代的进步，都有很大不同，但工艺原理是一致的。20世纪40年代美国工程师奥斯汀创立以他名字命名的现代熔模铸造技术时，曾从中国云南、贵州等地得到启示。1955年奥斯汀提出首创失蜡法发明专利的申请，日本学者鹿取一男以中国和日本历史早已有使用失蜡法的事实表示异议，最后鹿取一男胜诉。

Traditional dewax casting technique in China has great influences on development of metallurgy industry in the world. Modern investment casting develops from the traditional dewax casting technique. Though they are quite different from each other in terms of wax stock used, mold making, forming materials, technological processes, etc. with development of the times, they have the same process principles. In the 1940s, when Austin, an American engineer, created the modern investment casting technology named after him, he got inspiration from Yunnan Province and Guizhou Province of China. In 1955, Austin submitted a patent application for invention of creation of dewax casting. Kazuo Katori, a Japanese scholar raised an objection to the application by bringing out the fact that dewax casting was used in the history of China and Japan and finally won.

第二节　青铜器
Section 2　Bronzeware

　　我国在新石器时代晚期，就进入了铜、石并用的时代。大约在距今4000年前，即公元前21世纪的夏代进入青铜时代，历夏、商、西周至春秋早期迎来鼎盛期，冶铜技术、铸造工艺趋于成熟，创造了灿烂的青铜文化。气势雄伟的司母戊鼎、精美绝伦的四羊方尊、大气磅礴的战国编钟、设计巧妙的长信宫灯、姿态优美的铜奔马、巧夺天工的曾侯乙尊盘……这些荟萃了工艺技巧与文化艺术，令人叹为观止的杰作，将中国青铜冶铸技术推向高峰，站在了世界的先进行列。世界冶金学权威克里尔说："即使把美国和欧洲一流的技师集合起来，并使用近代科学技术，也不能做出比殷商时代更好的青铜器。"中国古代所创造的灿烂辉煌的青铜文明，对于推动整个世界金属材料的进步和铸造技术的发展起到了巨大的作用。

　　In the upper Neolithic Age China had entered the age which copper and stone were all used. The China's Bronze Age began in the Xia Dynasty about 4000 years ago, namely in the 21st century BC and reached a period of great prosperity in the early Spring and Autumn Period after Xia Dynasty, Shang Dynasty and Western Zhou Dynasty successively. At that time, bronze smelting and casting tended to be mature, establishing the splendid bronze culture. Magnificent Simuwu Quadripod, artistic Siyang Fangzun Wine Vessel, momentous chimes of the Warring States Period, aesthetic Changxin Palace Lantern, magnificent Bronze Horse in Gallop and superb Zeng Hou Yi Wine Vessel Plate are marvelous craftworks which integrated craftsmanship and culture and arts and propelled bronze smelting and casting in China to reach the Summit, edging into the advanced ranks in the world. Creel, an authoritative person in the world, said that, "even if all the best masters were collected in USA and Europe while modern science and technology were used, bronzeware of the Shang Dynasty could not be expelled." The splendid bronze civilization in ancient China greatly facilitated improvement of metallic materials and development of casting technology throughout the world.

司母戊大方鼎　已更名为后母戊鼎，为国家博物馆的镇馆之宝。高133cm，长111cm，宽79cm，重875kg，腹的四面腹部都环以饕餮纹、夔龙纹，是中国发现的青铜礼器中最大的一件。司母戊鼎用块范法分铸铸接成形，应是用多个竖炉同时熔炼、浇注而成的。其材质为含铜84.77%、锡11.64%、铅2.79%的青铜。出土于河南安阳。

Simuwu Quadripod: It has been renamed Houmuwu quadripod now and is one of the most valuable treasure of the National Museum. 133 cm in height, 111 cm in length, 79 cm in width, 875 kg in weight; four faces of the center encircled with Taotie patterns and Genglong patterns; and the largest one among the bronze ritual vessels discovered in China. Simuwu Quadripod was formed by separate piece-mold casting and bonding. It shall be smelted and poured with multiple shaft furnaces at The same time. It was made of bronze containing 84.77% of copper, 11.64% of tin and 2.79% of lead. It was unearthed in Anyang, Henan Province.

中国出土和传世的青铜器很多，以用途而言，大致有农具与工具、礼器、兵器、食器、酒器、水器、乐器、杂器（包括生活用具、车马器、货币、度量衡、符印）等；按器形分，有鼎、鬲、瓦、簋、簠、盨、豆、卣、尊、觥、盉、罍、壶、彝、斝、盘、匜、洗、钟、镈、鼓、戈、剑、镜等。

Numerous bronze wares were unearthed and handed down in China. They were mainly classified as farm implements and tools, ritual vessels, weapons, food vessels, wine vessels, water vessels, musical instruments and miscellaneous (including utensils, chariot, horse and implements, ancient money, weights and measures and talisman-bearing seals) according to application, and as *Ding, Li, Wa, Gui, Fu, Xu, Dou, You, Zun, Gong, He, Lei, Hu, Yi, Jia, Pan, Yi, Xi, Zhong, Bo, Gu, Ge, Jian, Ting* etc. according to shape of vessels.

司母戊大方鼎
Simuwu Quadripod

公元前12世纪，商代后期王文丁为祭祀其母戊而铸造，因鼎内壁有铭文"司母戊"而得名（已更名为"后母戊鼎"）。鼎重875千克，结构复杂，身、耳、足分别铸成后，再合铸成一个整体，像这种古而重的青铜器在世界上是绝无仅有的。它造型凝重而优美，纹饰华丽而神秘，显示出商代青铜冶炼工艺的精湛和巧妙，体现了商代辉煌的文化艺术和技术成就，是商代青铜文化顶峰时期的代表作。

It was cast by the King Wending of the late Shang Dynasty for offering sacrifice to his mother in the 12th century BC. The vessel was named for the inscription "Simuwu" on the inner wall of the vessel(renamed Houmuwu later). The vessel's weight is 875 kg with a complicated structure. Its body, sides and legs were separately cast and then assembled into a whole part. Such a heavy ancient bronze vessel is unique in the world. It has dignified and magnificent shape and sumptuous and mystical decorative patterns. It indicated superb and elaborate bronze smelting technique and brilliant culture, arts and technology achievements and was the representative works in the peak period of bronze culture in the Shang Dynasty of China.

四羊方尊、方卣、纵目人面具
Siyang Fangzun Wine Vessel, Square You-Vessel and Bronze Mask in a Shape of Figure with Protruding Eyes

青铜器四羊方尊，它器型独特，精细复杂，铸造难度很大，制作精美绝伦，是商代铜器艺术创作具有代表性的精品，被誉为臻于极致的青铜典范；青铜方卣，器形复杂，纹饰细腻；青铜纵目人面具，冶铸工艺很高。三者都是商代铸造的，都有极高的工艺水平。分别在湖南宁乡、江西新干和四川广汉三星堆出土，显示高度发达的商代文化，已从中原地区远播至南方地区，其青铜器冶铸工艺水平，与中原地区已难分高下。

Bronze Siyang Fangzun Wine Vessel has unique shape, delicate and complicated. In spite

四羊方尊　为国家博物馆镇馆之宝。肩之四隅各饰一立雕羊首，通体饰以细密纹饰，做工极为精良。抗战时期曾被炸为碎片，建国后修复完整。羊首用分铸法铸造，再与尊体铸接，表现出极高的范铸工艺技巧。商代铸造，湖南宁乡月山铺出土。

Siyang Fangzun Wine Vessel: It is one of the most valuable treasre of the National Museum. Four corners on the shoulder are decorated by a vertical ram sculpture respectively. The whole body is decorated by close patterns with superb workmanship. It had been blown apart in the Anti-Japanese War and was repaired after the founding of the P.R.C. Ram heads were made by separate casting and then cast bonded with the vessel body, reflecting superb mold casting craftsmanship. It was cast in the Shang Dynasty and unearthed in Yueshanpu, Ningxiang County, Hunan Province.

of great difficulty in casting, the vessel is produced artistic; it is typical elaborate works of artistic creation on copper ware and is praised as the bronze model that reached its acme in the Shang Dynasty. Bronze square You-vessel has complicated shape and subtle decorative patterns. Bronze Mask in a Shape of Figure with Protruding Eyes was made by superb smelting and casting processes. All the three were cast by superb processes in the Shang Dynasty. They were separately unearthed in Ningxiang County, Hunan Province, Xin'gan County, Jiangxi Province and Sanxingdui site, Guanghan, Sichuan Province. It reflects that highly developed Shang Dynasty Culture had been transmitted from the Central Plains to as far as the South. Bronze smelting and casting of the South had become almost as good as that of the Central Plains.

方卣　卣腹为正方形，中央有十字形通孔，镂空圈足有假底。以蛇形片饰连接盖和提梁，提梁与卣肩环耳套接。整个方卣纹饰规整、细腻，也是以块范法铸造成形的。器形的复杂对范与芯的组合要求严格，铜芯撑的使用解决了这一困难，这是此卣铸造工艺的关键。出土于江西新干大洋洲。

Square You-vessel: The center of the You-vessel is square with central cross through holes. The pierced circular leg has a false bottom. Snake decorations are used to connect the lid and the hoop handle which is sheathed with circular sides on the shoulder of the You-vessel. The whole Square You-vessel is decorated by neat and subtle patterns and was also formed by piece-mold casting. Complexity of the vessel shape requires strict combination of molds and the core. This problem is solved by use of copper core support, which is critical to casting process of this You-vessel. It was unearthed in Dayangzhou Village, Xin'gan County, Jiangxi Province.

青铜纵目人面具 此面具双目突出，内部中空，壁厚均匀。具有强烈的非中原文化特色。出土于四川广汉三星堆商代祭祀坑。

Bronze Mask in a Shape of Figure with Protruding Eyes：The mask has jutting eyes, hollow inside and even wall thickness. It has outstanding features of culture of non-central plains. It was unearthed from the sacrifice pit of Shang Dynasty in Sanxingdui site, Guanghan, Sichuan Province.

弭伯簋、毛公鼎
Yu Bo Gui and Maogong Tripod

弭伯簋和毛公鼎都是西周铸造的青铜器。宝鸡弭国墓地出土，弭伯簋代表了西周早期的风格和工艺水平，这件铜器的铸造，共用了36块泥范（包括8块活块范）和5块泥芯，经6次浇注（包括铸接）而成。

弭伯簋 双耳，圈足，立于方座上，底有铜铃，饰细密花纹，系块范法分铸铸接成形。出土于陕西省宝鸡弭国墓地。

Yu Bo Gui：It has two ears, a circular leg standing on a square base, and copper bells at the bottom decorated with subtle patterns. It was formed by separate piece-mold casting and cast bonding.It was unearthed in Baoji, Shaanxi Province.

Yu Bo Gui and Maogong Tripod are bronze vessels cast in the Western Zhou Dynasty. Unearthed from the tomb of Yu State, Yu Bo Gui of Yu represents the style and level of technology in the early Western Zhou Dynasty. The bronze vessel was made with totally 36 clay cores (including 8 movable piece molds) and 5 clay molds by pouring 6 times (including cast bonding).

毛公鼎是西周晚期的青铜铸件，青铜礼器上多有铭文，商代器物铭文多为族徽和制器者名号，比较简短；西周器物铭文往往较长，或记事功，或书赏赐，以为鉴证并告诸后世，毛公鼎铭文最长，有495字，这些铭文是随器物用块范法一次铸成。

Maogong Tripod is a bronze casting in the late Western Zhou Dynasty. Most bronze ritual vessels are provided with inscription. Most vessels of the Shang Dynasty have brief inscription of clan emblems and name of the maker. Inscription on vessels of the Western Zhou Dynasty is usually long, either recording achievements and successes or carved with awards as certification for the later generation. Inscription on Maogong Tripod is the longest with 495 characters. The inscriptions were made by piece-mold casting along with the vessels at one time.

毛公鼎

Maogong Tripod

龙凤方案、十五连盏灯
Dragon and Phoenix Table, 15-Branch Lamp

春秋战国时期，块范法仍然是青铜器制作的主导工艺。河北中山王墓出土的龙凤方案共有40个铸接点、60个焊接点，先后用186块泥范经过多次铸接和焊接成形。同墓出土的十五连盏灯则分8段以块范法铸造，或以块范法分铸后焊接于一体，各段之间则以不同形状的榫卯连接，表现出了高超的执简就繁的范铸工艺技巧。

龙凤方案　高36.2cm，长47.5cm。案顶为方形铜框，原镶有木板，并为铜斗拱承托，立于四条龙额顶。中间四龙与四凤相间交错纠结，四凤悬空，四龙立于圆盘上，而圆盘为四鹿支持，四鹿二牝二牡。整个方案错以金银，与精巧的造型相映生辉。河北平山中山王墓出土。

Dragon and Phoenix Table：It is 36.2 cm high and 47.5 cm long. The top is of square copper frame originally inlaid with wood board, and is supported by copper bracket set, standing on the forehead of four dragons. In the middle, the four dragons overlap and interlace with four phoenixes. The four phoenixes are hung up and the four dragons are standing on a circular tray which is supported by four deer, two females and two males. The whole table inlaid with gold and silver decorations is brilliant with its elaborate shape. It was unearthed from the tomb of King of Zhongshan, Pingshan County, Hebei Province.

During the Spring and Autumn Period and the Warring States Period, the piece-mold casting remained predominant in bronzeware making. Dragon and Phoenix Table unearthed from the tomb of King of Zhongshan in Hebei Province has 40 cast bonding points and 60 welding points. It was formed with 186 clay molds by cast bonding and welding many times successively. 15-branch Lamp unearthed from the same tomb was made by piece-mold casting in 8 sections or by separate piece-mold casting and welded to form a whole part. The sections are connected in tenons and mortises of different shapes. This emblemizes superb mold casting craftsmanship to control the complexity by controlling the simplicity.

十五连盏灯 高82.9cm。灯作树形，15盏灯错落有致地分布于灯树上。干枝间饰有蟠龙和顽猴。底座作轮形，以两具双身兽承负全器。底座采用分铸接成形。而灯树分17节铸作，再以榫卯结合。河北平山中山王墓出土。

15-Branch Lamp: It is 82.9 cm high. The lamp takes the shape of tree. Fifteen lamps are scattered on the lamp tree. Decorations of coiled dragon and naughty monkeys are arranged between the trunk and branches. The base is like a wheel, with two two-body beasts to support the whole lamp. The base was formed by separate cast bonding. The lamp tree was cast in 17 sections and connected by tenons and mortises. It was unearthed from the tomb of King of Zhongshan, Pingshan County, Hebei Province.

曾侯乙编钟
Zeng Hou Yi Serial Bells

曾侯乙编钟是战国时期楚国的乐器，其中中层甬钟是用了12种模具，制作出136块泥范组成铸型一次铸造而成。它融音乐、艺术和青铜工艺于一体，被称为天下奇观。

Zeng Hou Yi Serial Bells are musical instruments of Chu in the Warring States Period, among which handled bells were formed by making 136 clay molds with 12 types of molds to constitute the cast form for casting in one piece. It integrates music, arts and bronze casting processes and is reputed Marvelous Spectacle of the World.

钟是古代祭祀或宴飨时用的乐器。钟体上部称为"钲"，下部为"鼓"，即发声的部位。钟口呈弧形弯曲，称为"于"。由于钟口弯曲，钟体表面铸有钟乳。形成声音衰减较快，并有双音的特点。用多件频率不同的钟按大小不同依次排列，编成一组，构成合律合奏的音阶，称为编钟。曾侯乙编钟规模恢宏，音律完备，纹饰纤若毫发，音质很好，音阶准确，至今仍可演奏乐曲。

Bells were musical instruments used in sacrifice or feasts in ancient times. The upper part of body is called "*Zheng*" (mandarin pronunciation of Chinese character "钲") and the lower part is called "*Gu*" (mandarin pronunciation of Chinese character "鼓"), namely where sound is produced. The bell mouth is bent like arc and so called "*Yu*" (mandarin pronunciation of Chinese character "于"). Due to the bent mouth, the body is cast with swell on the surface. Therefore, the

sound attenuates quickly and is characterized by double tone. Chimes are formed by arranging multiple bells in different frequencies in proper order according to size to form a set to constitute tempered musical scale for ensemble. Zeng Hou Yi Serial Bells have magnificent scale, complete temperament and decorative patterns as fine as hair. It has excellent tone quality and accurate musical scale, and can still be used to play music up to now.

在曾侯乙编钟的钟架和挂钩上有三千多字的乐学律学铭文，内容分为：铭记、标音、乐律关系以及音名、阶名、八度组、各国律名对应关系等乐律知识。可以说是一部先秦时代的乐律全书和珍贵文献。它证明春秋战国时代，中国已经制定并建立了完整的乐律学体系，而且能够在实际操作中实现旋宫转调，融金属工艺与声学技艺于一体，是中国文化史上的经典之作。

Music and temperament inscription with more than three thousand characters is on bell rack and hooks of the Zeng Hou Yi Serial Bells, indicating music and temperament knowledge on enshrinement, transcription, relationship between music and temperament as well as pitch name, scale name, octaves and coincidence relation of pitch names of various countries. The inscription can be said a complete book on tone-system and precious literature in Pre-Qin times. It demonstrates that during the Spring and Autumn Period and the Warring States Period, complete tone-system had been prepared and established in China, and change of keys and inflexion could be performed in practice. It integrates metal working processes and acoustic arts，being a classical craftwork in the history of China's culture.

曾侯乙编钟　湖北随州擂鼓墩出土，系曾侯乙的随葬品。由1件镈钟、45件甬钟和19件钮钟组成，分三层悬挂于曲尺形钟架上，上边长7.48m，高2.65m，短边长3.35m，高2.73m。每件钟都标有音铭，并且都能发两个音，音高准确，12个半音齐备。整套钟音频在64.8—2329.4赫兹之间，共有5个八度音程。可以旋宫转调。

Zeng Hou Yi Serial Bells: The chimes were unearthed in Leigudun site, Suizhou County, Hubei Province. It is one of funerary objects of Marquis Yi of Zeng. The chimes consist of one Bo bell, 45 Yong Bells （handled bells） and 19 Niu bells （knobbed bells） which are hung on the bell rack in the shape of try square in three layers. The upper edge is 7.48 m long and 2.65 m high and the short edge is 3.35 m long and 2.73 m high. Each bell is marked with tone inscription and can produce two tones at accurate pitch, with all 12 semitones. The complete set of bells is within frequency range of 64.8—2329.4 Hz, with totally 5 octaves. Change of keys and pitch are possible.

曾侯乙尊盘
Zeng Hou Yi Wine Vessel Plate

湖北随州曾侯乙墓出土。战国时期制作的曾侯乙尊盘是采用失蜡铸造的精品。

Zeng Hou Yi Wine Vessel Plate was unearthed from the tomb of Marquis Yi of Zeng in Suizhou County, Hubei Province. It was an elaborate craftwork made by dewax casting in the Warring States Period.

该件以其工艺之复杂，工艺之精美，冠古来青铜器之首。不但运用了前代已有泥范浑铸、分铸、接铸和焊接等技术。而且娴熟地运用了失蜡铸造工艺。其沿口的透空附饰由细小的铜梗组成，重重叠叠，如丝瓜络子。即使用现代铸造工艺来铸造也极为困难。经鉴定铜尊和铜盘颈部透空附饰都是用失蜡法铸成的。如铜尊颈部图案系由19种变体蟠虺文构成12种花纹单元，再按一定的排列方式与层次汇合成极华丽多姿的整体花环。高低参差与对称排比相结合，制造出玲珑剔透、节奏分明的艺术效果。如此精细优美的铸件铸造成功，充分反映了失蜡铸造技术已发展到了十分成熟的阶段，已达到出神入化、巧夺天工的境界。

It is second to none among bronze vessels in the ancient times with its complicated and exquisite craftsmanship. Not only technologies such as whole casting, separate casting, cast bonding and welding with clay molds which occurred in the former dynasties were applied, but also dewax casting process was freely applied. Its pierced decorations at the rim consisting of fine copper stems, overlapped and exquisite, like the loofah, can hardly be cast even by modern casting processes. Pierced decorations in the neck of bronze Zun and bronze Pan were made by dewax casting through identification. For example, patterns in the neck of bronze Zun were delicate one-piece garland formed by gathering 12 patterns cells consisting of 19 variant Panhui patterns according to certain arrangement method and hierarchy. Combination of irregular height and symmetric arrangement in order results in artistic effect of brightness and sharp pattern. Successful casting of such an exquisite casting fully reflects that dewax casting technique had entered into a very mature development stage, attaining to perfection with wonderful workmanship excelling nature.

曾侯乙尊盘　由尊、盘两件组合成套。尊和盘都是在块范法铸造的主体外，附有众多的附饰和多层透空装饰，造型复杂、华美。透空附饰也是分段分块以失蜡法铸造，再铸接或镴焊于主体之上。湖北随州擂鼓墩曾侯乙墓出土。

Zeng Hou Yi Wine Vessel Plate: It is a set combining *Zun* and *Pan*. Both *Zun* and *Pan* are provided with many decorations and multi-layer pierced decorations in addition to the body made by piece-mold casting, forming complicated and magnificent shape. The pierced decorations are also made by dewax casting in sections and pieces, and cast bonded or soldered onto the body. It was unearthed from the tomb of Marquis Yi of Zeng in Leigudun site, Suizhou County, Hubei Province.

夫差矛和勾践剑、铜奔马

the Spear of King Fuchai and the Sword of King Goujian，Bronze Horse in Gallop

吴王夫差矛

The Spear of King Fuchai

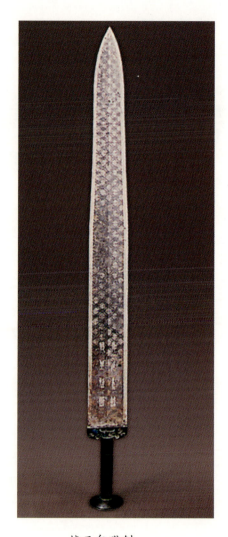

越王勾践剑

The Sword of King Goujian

吴王夫差矛 春秋晚期兵器，长29.5cm，宽3cm，矛狭，起牛脊，下端作鱼尾形，通体有朱字格暗纹。

The Spear of King Fuchai: It is a weapon made in the late Spring and Autumn Period. It is 29.5 cm long and 3 cm wide. The spear is narrow with protruding ridge of cattle and fishtail shape at the lower end. The whole body is provided with subtle patterns of radial cells.

越王勾践剑 春秋晚期兵器，长55.6cm，宽4.6cm，剑身有菱形暗纹，格上花纹嵌蓝琉璃及绿松石。出土时插在素漆木鞘中，茎上缠有丝绳。

The Sword of King Goujian: It is a weapon made in the late Spring and Autumn Period. It is 55.6 cm long and 4.6 cm wide. The body is provided with diamond subtle patterns, with cell patterns inlaid with blue obsidian and turquoise. When unearthed, it was inside the unpainted wood sheath with the handle wound by silk tassels.

夫差矛、勾践剑 春秋战国时期的青铜兵器制作十分发达，自古以来被人们赞不绝口的名剑——"干将"、"莫邪"、"巨阙"、"纯钩"等，都是这个时期制作的，在中国广大地区都有出土。1965年在湖北江陵望山一号墓出土的越王勾践剑，制成距今已有2400多年，出土时仍宝光四射，锋利无比，可断发丝，表明了春秋时期制剑工艺的高超和精细。1983年，在湖北江陵又出土了吴王夫差矛，形制精美。它们都是古代兵器中的瑰宝。

The Spear of King Fuchai and the Sword of King Goujian: Manufacture of bronze weapons was developed in the Spring and Autumn Period and the Warring States Period. Praiseful famous swords such as "Ganjiang Sword", "Moye Sword", "Juque Sword" and "Chunjun Sword" since ancient times were made during this period and unearthed in vast regions of China. In 1965, the Sword of King Goujian unearthed from Tomb No.1 of Wangshan in Jiangling, Hubei Province was made 2400 ago. It was still pearlescent and sharp enough to cut down hair when unearthed. This indicates superb and subtle sword making technology in the Spring and Autumn Period and the Warring States Period. In 1983, the Spear of King Fuchai was also unearthed in Jiangling, Hubei Province, with delicate shape and structure. They are both treasures in ancient weapons.

铜奔马 1969年甘肃武威雷台出土。东汉晚期制作，通称"马踏飞燕"。马造型雄俊非凡，昂首嘶鸣，如风驰电掣状，三足腾空，一足蹄下踏燕，其姿态之优美，在遗存的同时期作品中无与伦比，反映了东汉时期杰出的制作工艺和铸造水平。现在作为我国旅游的标志物。

Bronze Horse in Gallop: It was unearthed in Leitai, Wuwei, Gansu Province in 1969. It was made in the late Eastern Han Dynasty, and is generally called "Galloping Horse Treading on a Flying Swallow". The horse with a smart figure looks as if it were neighing, holding its head high, and treading a swallow under a hoof with the other three prancing hoofs, as swift as wind and thunder. Its exquisite posture is unique among the works of the same period remained. This reflects outstanding workmanship and casting technology in the Eastern Han Dynasty. Now it is regarded as a mark of Chinese tourism.

东汉铜奔马

Bronze Horse in Gallop of the Eastern Han Dynasty

汉代错金博山炉、"诅盟"贮贝器和北魏释迦立佛像
Gold Inlaid Boshan Burner of the Han Dynasty, Oath Shell-container and Standing Sakyamuni Buddha Statue of North Wei Dynasty

　　秦汉时期冶铸技术和工艺继续进步。河北满城刘胜墓出土的错金博山炉是这一时期失蜡铸造的代表作；同期云南晋宁石寨山出土的大批贮贝器或铸有祭祀场面，或铸有战争格斗场面，场景、人物与建筑物皆栩栩如生，表示了在云南发达的失蜡法工艺水平，"诅盟"贮贝器为其代表作。南北朝时期的佛像铸造也多用失蜡法，且多鎏金，北魏正光五年（524年）的释迦立佛像是这一时期的代表作。

Smelting and casting technology and processes kept advancing in the Qin and the Han dynasties. Gold Inlaid Boshan Burner unearthed from the tomb of Liu Sheng in Mancheng County, Hebei Province is a representative craftwork made by dewax casting in that period. Numbers of shell-containers unearthed in Shizhai Mountain, Jinning County, Yunnan Province were either cast with the scene of sacrifice or with the scene of combat in battles. The scene, characters and buildings are vivid, reflecting developed dewax casting technology in Yunnan Province. Oath Shell-container is a representative craftwork thereof. Buddha statues were mostly made by dewax casting in Northern and Southern Dynasties. Most of them were plated with gold. Standing Sakyamuni Buddha Statue made in the 5th year of Zhengguang region in the Northern Wei (524 AD) is a representative craftwork in this period.

错金博山炉　炉盖形如多层峰峦，有人物、走兽隐现其间，通体错金，精致华美。河北满城汉中山墓出土。

Gold Inlaid Boshan Burner: The burner cover is like overlapping ridges and peaks in shape, with indistinct characters and beasts therein. The whole body is inlaid with gold decorations, exquisite and luxuriant. It was unearthed from the tomb of King of Zhongshan in Mancheng County, Hebei Province.

"诅盟"贮贝器 盖面铸杀人祭祀场面；干栏式房屋中央坐一妇女，是主祭者，边缘有拴虎、豹的圆柱，有被捆绑、被枷、被大蛇吞吃的人，当是供牺牲的奴隶。参加祭祀的有击鼓者、杀牛羊者、骑马者、捧食者等，云南晋宁石寨山西汉墓出土。

Oath Shell-container: The cover face is cast with the scene of human sacrifice. A woman sitting in the center of a stilt house is the officiant, and on the periphery are columns for tying tigers and leopards and persons being tied up, wearing cangues or being devoured by serpents as slaves for sacrifice. Participants include drummers, cattle-sheep killers, riders and food holders. It was unearthed from the tomb of the Western Han Dynasty in Shizhai Mountain, Jinning County, Yunnan Province.

释迦立佛像 北魏正光五年（524年）造。释迦立于四足方形莲座上，神情温和，背负透雕火焰纹舟形背光，上绕飞天11尊，主尊两侧置菩萨8尊，方座两侧为力士像，内有神兽一对。河北正定县出土。

Standing Sakyamuni Buddha Statue: It was made in the 5th year of Zhengguang region in the Northern Wei (524 AD). Sakyamuni is standing on a square seat in the form of a lotus flower with four legs, gentle and kindly. On his back is boat-shaped mandorla of openwork flaming patterns.11 Flying Apsaras statues are around at the top. The major statue is provided by 8 Buddha statues on both sides. Images of warriors are on both sides of the square seat with a pair of legendary beasts inside. It was unearthed in Zhengding County, Hebei Province.

第四章 铁器时代与冶铁鼓风设备
Chapter 4 Iron Age and Blowers for Iron Smelting

蕴含着巨大力量的铁器，在春秋战国时期已初露锋芒，在秦汉时期迎来了铁器时代。

Powerful ironware began to show its function in the Spring and Autumn Period and the Warring States Period. Iron age began in the Qin and Han Dynasties.

铁器时代的奠定，主要有赖于冶炼设备与工艺的进步。战国时期出现的竖式炼铁炉，秦汉时期向大型化发展，郑州古荥镇冶铁遗址，炼铁高炉炉底面积约8.4m²，高5—6m，有效容积约为50m³，日产铁1吨。按其耐火材料等内部结构分析，炉温可达1460℃，据其炉渣结痂情况分析，炉温已达1250—1280℃，已达相当高的水平，保证了古代中国铁冶炼技术领先于世界。随着炉体的增大，为保证中心温度，必须改革炉内结构，提高送风量。鼓风技术的改进与提高是钢铁冶炼向大型化发展的基础。山东滕县宏道院出土的东汉冶铁鼓铸石刻图反映了汉代的鼓风皮囊应用情况。此画左边画有一鼓风大皮囊，皮囊上方排列有4根吊杆，右方则是接炼炉的风管，左方还有许多人在运作。

Progress of smelting equipment and processes is important for establishment of Iron Age. Vertical blooming furnace occurred in the Warring States Period and was enlarged in the Qin and Han Dynasties. In the iron smelting site in Guxing Town, Zhengzhou, blast furnace hearth has the area of about 8.4m², height of 5—6m and active volume of about 50 m³, with daily iron output of 1t. Based on analysis of internal structures such as refractory materials, furnace temperature can reach 1460℃ and based on analysis of cinder caking, furnace temperature had reached 1250—1280℃, reflecting technology at high level and ensuring that iron smelting technology in ancient China was superior to that of the world. As furnace body was increased, internal structure of the furnace must be reformed to increase air delivery in order to ensure central temperature. Improvement and promotion of blast technology provided foundation for expansion of steel and iron smelting. Stone carving of iron smelting by blast furnace of the Eastern Han Dynasty unearthed in Hongdao Temple, Tengxian County, Shandong Province reflects application of airblower in the Han Dynasty. On the left of the carving is a big airblower with four hanger rods arranged above; on the right is a blast pipe of the smelting furnace with many operators on the left.

汉画像石冶铁图

Picture of Iron Smelting of Stone Sculptures of the Han Dynasty

人类早期的鼓风器大都是皮囊，古代又叫橐。一个炉子用好几个橐，放在一起，排成一排，就叫"排囊"或排橐。其动力从人力鼓风发展到应用畜力鼓风，有"牛排"、"马排"；随后应用水力鼓风，叫"水排"。东汉初年，南阳太守杜诗(?—38年)发明水排，因为它"用力少，见功多，百姓便之"。

Most of early air blowers used by people are leather bags, also called *tuo* (pronunciation of the Chinese character "橐" referring to airblower) in ancient times. For one furnace, quite a few airblowers were arranged in one row, called "blowing leather bags" or airblowers. Blowers were powered by manpower and later by animal power such as "cattle-power blower" and "horse-power blower". Afterwards blowers were powered by water and called "water-power blower". In the early Eastern Han Dynasty, Du Shi (?—38), prefect of Nanyang Prefecture, invented water-power blower for it "required little efforts but provided great results, which provided an easy way for common people".

三国时期的韩暨把它推广到魏国官营冶炼作坊，用水排代替人排、马排。水力鼓风有十分重要的意义，它加大了风量，提高了风压，增加了风力在炉里的穿透能力，从而能扩大炉缸，加高炉身，增大有效容积。足够大的鼓风能力，才能有足够大的高炉，才可以炼出更多生铁，促进了冶铁业的发展，直到20世纪70年代，中国一些地方还在使用。欧洲人能在14世纪炼出生铁来，和水力鼓风的应用有一定关系。水排的发明是人类利用自然力的一次伟大胜利。

Han Ji of the Three Kingdoms period promoted it into official smelting workshops of the Wei State to replace manpower blowers and horse-power blowers with water-power blowers. Water-power blowing had great significance in increasing air volume and air pressure，and improving penetrating power of air force in furnaces so as to enlarge crucible hearth, heighten furnace body and increase useful volume. Only when blowing capacity is sufficient, can blast furnaces be large enough to smelt more pig iron. It facilitated development of iron smelting industry. Till 1970s, it had been used in some areas of China. The European could smelt pig iron in the 14th Century due to application of water-power blowing in a degree. Invention of water-power blowing-engine is a great victory of mankind to utilize natural forces.

汉代水排的具体构造现在已经很难了解，由同一时期的水碓结构推测，大约也是一种轮轴拉杆传动装置。中国古代水排构造的详细记述最早见于元代王祯的《农书》，依水轮放置方式的不同，分成立轮式和卧轮式两种。它们都是通过轮轴，拉杆以及绳索把圆周运动变成直线往复运动，以此达到关闭风扇和鼓风的目的。

It is very difficult to understand specific construction of water-power blower of the Han Dynasty. It is supposed from structure of water-driven tilt hammer that water-power blower is also similar to a wheel shaft and tie rod gearing. The earliest detailed description of construction of water-power blower in ancient China was recorded in *Nongshu* written by Wang Zhen, stating that there were vertical wheel type and horizontal wheel type according to different placement ways of water wheel. For both types, circular motion was changed to straight reciprocating motion by wheel shafts, tie rods and ropes in order to close fan and blow in and out.

鼓风器最早是皮囊，后来是风扇，再后是风箱。风扇大约发明于公元10世纪以前。北宋《武经总要》前集的行炉图、元代王祯《农书》的水排图中都有风扇的图像，活塞或风箱最早见于明代著作《天工开物》中。

Leather bags were the earliest air blowers and then fans and bellows. Fans were invented before the 10th Century AD approximately. Fans occurred in the picture of transportable kiln in the former collection of *Wujing Zongyao* (Collection of the Most Important Millitary Technique) of the Northern Song Dynasty and in the picture of water-power blower in the *Nongshu* written by Wang Zhen of the Yuan Dynasty. Pistons or bellows first occurred in *Tiangong Kaiwu* of the Ming Dynasty.

冶铁水排模型　冶铁水排是利用水力进行鼓风的装置，由水轮、凸轮、皮橐、输风管等部件组成。汉代利用水轮和凸轮等机械系统在世界上处于领先地位。

Model of Water-power Blower for Iron Smelting: Water-power blower is a device utilizing water power for blowing and consisting of parts such as water wheel, cam wheel, leather blower and air supply pipe. Utilization of mechanical systems such as water wheels and cam wheels of the Han Dynasty took leading position in the world.

活塞式木风箱　用于冶炼金属的鼓风装置。它的两端各设一个进风口，口上设有活门。箱侧有风道。侧端各有一个带活门的出风口，通过伸出箱外的拉杆，推拉活塞作往复运动，使活门一启一闭，连续鼓风。

Wooden Piston Bellows：It is a blowing device for metal smelting. One air inlet is provided at both ends of it respectively. Valves are provided at air inlets. Air duct is provided on the lateral side of the bellow. Lateral ends are provided with one air outlet respectively. The piston is pushed and pulled by tie bar protruding the bellow to do reciprocating motion to allow the valves to open and close alternately for continuous blowing.

第五章 古代农业机械
Chapter 5 Agricultural Machinery in Ancient China

在中国几千年的文明史上，以农立国，劳动人民发明创造了多种多样的农业生产工具，而且许多是世界上出现最早的农业生产工具。

In the history of Chinese civilization over thousands of years, agriculture was the basis for establishment of the state. The laboring people invented and created diverse agricultural production tools, most of which occurred earlier than in other countries in the world.

西汉初年，铁农具已经在很大程度上取代了铜、骨、木、石器具，由于冶铁业的重大发展，铁制农具得到了广泛应用，水平很高的发明创造很多，影响较大的有犁、三脚耧、龙骨水车、水碓和风扇车等，由于实用、方便，多数设备沿用至今，已有2000多年历史。

In the early Western Han Dynasty, iron farm tools had been substituted for bronze, bone, wood and stone instruments to a great extent. Due to significant development of iron smelting industry, iron farm tools were widely used. There were numerous superb inventions and creations. Among others, plough, animal-drawn seed sower with three legs, dragon bone waterlift, water-driven tilt hammer and winnower were greatly influential. Most of the instruments have been used so far for more than 2000 years due to utility and convenience.

耕地机械——犁
Plough—a Tool Used in Farming for Initial Cultivation of Soil

中国很早就发明了耒耜用来翻整土地，随着农业生产的发展，古人又将耒耜发展成犁。由于冶铁业的兴起，战国时期已出现了铁制的耕犁。河北易县和河南辉县都出土过战国时期的铁犁铧。铁犁铧是项了不起的成就，它标志着人类社会发展的新时期。汉代耕犁已有铁犁壁，能起翻土碎土作用。根据中外史料记载，在整个古代社会，我国耕犁的发展水平，一直处于世界农业技术发展的前列，欧洲的耕犁直到公元

11世纪才有犁壁的记载。中国至迟到汉代就有了犁壁的装置，比欧洲要早约1000年。中国第一部农具专著，陆龟蒙（?—881年）的《耒耜经》，虽然篇幅很短，但却详记江东犁(曲辕犁)的部件、尺寸和作用，其构造已和现代耕犁基本相同。

Leisi (Chinese mandarin pronounciation of "耒耜" referring to a kind of plough-like farm tool) was invented early in ancient China for soil preparation. With development of agricultural production, ancient people developed Leisi into ploughs. Due to emergence of iron smelting industry, iron plough occurred in the Warring States Period. Iron ploughshare of the Warring States Period was unearthed in Yixian County, Hebei Province and Huixian County, Henan Province. Iron ploughshare is a marvelous achievement which marks the new development period of human society. In the Han Dynasty, plough had been provided with iron plough wall to turn and crush soil. According to records of historical materials of China and overseas, in the entire ancient society, development level of ploughs in China were ranking first in development of agricultural technology all over the world. For ploughs in Europe, recorded plough wall did not occur until the 11th Century AD. The device of plough wall occurred at latest in the Han Dynasty in China, which was about 1000 years earlier than in Europe. Lu Guimeng (?—881) recorded detailed parts, size and function of Jiangdong Plough (curve-beam plough) in his book *Lei Si Jing* (Book on Fieldwork), the first special work on farm tools in China, with very short pieces. Its construction was almost the same as modern ploughs.

战国铁镢 铸造生产铁质工具始于战国时期。河南辉县出土。

Iron Hoe of the Warring States Period: Iron tools were initially cast and produced in the Warring States Period. It was unearthed in Huixian County, Henan Province.

汉代套有双侧犁壁的铁犁铧 双侧犁壁可将翻耕的土壤翻到犁的两侧，它还可以开沟漕，是较进步的组合耕具。陕西礼泉出土。

Iron Ploughshare Provided with Double-sided Plough Wall of the Han Dynasty: Double-side plough wall can turn soil to both sides of the plough and be used to open grooves. It is advanced tiller combine. It was unearthed in Liquan, Shaanxi Province.

战国铁犁头 可以翻耕土地的铁犁头的使用，对农业生产的发展具有重要意义。河南辉县出土。

Iron Ploughshare of the Warring States Period: Use of iron ploughshare for plowing is of great significance for development of agricultural production. It was unearthed in Huixian County, Henan Province.

汉代铁铧 铁铧是翻土的农具。陕西斗鸡台出土。

Iron Spade of the Han Dynasty: Iron spade is a farm tool to turn the soil. It was unearthed in Doujitai, Shanxi Province.

播种机械——耧车
Sowing Machine—Animal-Drawn Seed Sower

战国时期就有了播种机械，汉武帝时（前140—前87年）赵过在一脚耧、二脚耧的基础上发明了三脚耧，这是现代播种机的始祖。现在最新式的播种机是把开沟、下种、覆盖和压实四道工序接连完成。而中国2000多年的三脚耧已把前三道工序连在一起，由同一机械来完成，是中国古代在农业机械方面的重大发明之一。三脚耧的出现，大大提高了当时播种（撒播、点播等）工作的效率和质量，汉武帝曾经下令在全国推广这种先进播种机，还改进了其他耕耘工具，这对当时农业生产发展起到了推动作用。耧车通体用木，只有耧脚（开沟器）为铁制。有一脚、二脚、三脚、四脚之分，因耕地土质及牛力等条件而异，三脚耧（即三行播种器）使用最广泛。

Sowing machines occurred in the Warring States Period. Zhao Guo in the period of Emperior Wu of Han Dynasty（140BC—87BC）invented animal-drawn seed sower with three legs based on that with one leg and two legs respectively. It is origination of modern sowing machines. The latest modern sowing machine is used to conduct four procedures such as trenching, seeding, covering and compaction successively. However, for animal-drawn seed sower with three legs used more than 2000 years ago in China, the first three procedures had been conducted in succession by the same machine. It was one of significant inventions in agricultural machinery in ancient China. Upon occurrence of animal-drawn seed sower with three legs, efficiency and quality of seed sowing (such as broadcast sowing and spot sowing) were greatly improved. Emperior Wu of Han Dynasty once gave orders for nationwide promotion of this advanced sowing machine as well as improvement of other tilling machines, which facilitated development of agricultural production at that time. The whole body of animal-drawn seed sower with three legs was made of wood except that the legs (opening share) were made of iron. There wcre animal-drawn seed sowers with one leg, two legs, three legs and four legs respectively according to different conditions such as quality of soil of cultivated land and cattle power. Animal-drawn seed sowers with three legs (namely three-row seeders) were most widely used.

耧车（模型）

Animal-Drawn Seed Sower

(Model)

《天工开物》中的龙骨水车图

Picture of Dragon Bone Waterlift in
Tiangong Kaiwu

灌溉机械——龙骨水车、立轴式大风车
Irrigation Machine—Dragon Bone Waterlift and Vertical-Shaft Big Windmill

龙骨水车是一种刮板式连续提水工具，又名翻车。《后汉书》记有汉灵帝时（186年）毕岚发明，三国时马钧加以完善。它是最早出现的采用链传动的机械，实现了由间歇式提水变为连续提水。比原有的辘轳、滑轮、绞车等提水机械，效率大大提高，操作搬运方便，是农业灌溉机械的一项重大进步。它是中国应用最广泛、效果最好、影响最大的灌溉机械，沿用至今已有两千年。龙骨水车的动力可由人力(手动、脚踩)、畜力、风力或水力等驱动。畜力龙骨水车，大约出现在南宋，距今已近900年。水转龙骨水车在元代王祯《农书》有记载，这一发明大约在元初，有约700年的历史，这是元代机械制造方面的一项巨大进步。

汉代龙骨水车（模型）

Dragon Bone Watertift of the
Han Dynasty (model)

Dragon bone waterlift is a scraper tool for continuous water lifting. It is also called square pallet chain-pump. It was recorded in *The History of the Later Han* that Bi Lan of the period of Emperor Ling of Han Dynasty（186）invented and Ma Jun of the Three Kingdoms period improved the tool. It is the earliest machine that is driven by chains. Compared with previous waterlift machines such as windlass, pulley and winch, it achieved continuous water lifting from intermittent water lifting. As a result, efficiency was greatly improved and operation and transportation are convenient. It is a significant progress in agricultural irrigation machinery. It is the irrigation machine which was most widely used with best effect and greatest influence in China. It has been used so far for 2000 years. Dragon bone waterlift can be driven by manpower (hand motion or treading), animal power, wind power or water power, etc. Animal-power dragon bone waterlift occurred in the Southern Song Dynasty, nearly 900 years ago. Water-power dragon bone waterlift was recorded by Wang Zhen of the Yuan Dynasty in the *Nongshu*. It was invented in early Yuan Dynasty with history of about 700 years. It is a great progress in mechanical manufacture in the Yuan Dynasty.

立轴式大风车是中国古代利用风力驱动的机械，按轴的位置有卧轴式风车和立轴式风车。卧轴式风车起源于汉代，立轴式风车起源于南宋。南北朝时已有人试用风力推动载人车辆，南宋时已有风力驱动的翻车，所用风车可能是立式的。明代沿海地区广泛使用风车驱动翻车提水。这种风车采用八角形木架，上面有八面立帆，驱动立轴转动。

Wind powered machines in ancient China were divided into horizontal-axle windmill and vertical-shaft windmill according to different axle positions. Horizontal-axle windmill originated from the Han Dynasty and vertical-shaft windmill from the Southern Song Dynasty. People tried to use wind power to drive passenger carrying vehicles in the Southern and Northern Dynasty. Wind powered square pallet chain-pump was used in the Southern Song Dynasty, windmill for which might be vertical type. Windmill was widely used to drive square pallet chain-pump for water lifting in coastal areas of the Ming Dynasty. This windmill was made of octagonal wooden stand with eight vertical sails to drive the vertical axle to rotate.

国内学者对中国立轴式风车十分重视，有较多记载。立轴式风车的优点：一是有风向调节系统，能自动适应各方向来风，使风车工作不受风向不同的影响。二是当风速有变时，可控制风帆的升降，改变风帆受风面积，保证风车的转速稳定。三是风车可架设得很高。人在风车架下进行各种操作，防止立轴风车占地面积过多。

Scholars in China paid special attention to vertical-shaft windmill in ancient China, which is demonstrated by many records. vertical-shaft windmill has the following advantages: first, it has wind direction control system, which can automatically adapt to wind from various directions to allow windmill to work without being affected by difference of wind direction; second, in case of change of wind speed, wind sails can be ascended or descended to change the area of wind sails exposed to wind in order to ensure steady rotary speed of windmill; and third, windmill can be erected very high; people conducted operations below windmill stand, allowing vertical-shaft windmill to occupy less area.

立轴风车　由八面立帆及木架组成的立轴式动力装置，俗称"走马灯"，明朝时沿海很多地方都使用这种大风车。立轴下端的水平大齿轮可驱动一至两部翻车。这种大风车的优点是能够适应来自任何方向的风。

Vertical-Shaft Windmill: it is a vertical-shaft power device made up of eight vertical sails and a wooden carcases. It is commonly called "Revolving scenic lantern". Such as big windmill was used in many coastal areas in the Ming Dynasty. Horizontal bull wheels at the lower end of the vertical axle can drive one or two square pallet chain-pumps. Its advantage is capable of adapting to wind from all directions.

粮食加工机械——风扇车、水碓、水磨
Grain Processing Machine—Winnower, Hydraulic Pestle Set and Watermill

风扇车　公元前1世纪，西汉时出现，欧洲约1400年后才有类似的风车。解决谷物清选的风车，效果很好，沿用至今。风扇车的发明，可能是离心式风机的最早应用。

Winnower: It occurred in the Western Han Dynasty in the 1st Century BC and similar winnowers only occurred in Europe about 1400 years later. Winnowers for cereal cleaning have good effect and have been used so far. Invention of winnowers may be the earliest application of centrifugal fans.

水碓　它是利用水力舂米的机械，出现于西汉，比杵臼、踏碓的效率提高很多，而且利用水碓可以夜以继日加工粮食。根据水的流量，碓头数多少不一，叫连机水碓，有的多达8个碓头。

Hydraulic Pestle Set: It is a machine which pounds rice by water power. It occurred in the Western Han Dynasty. It worked much more efficiently than mortar and pestle and treadle pestle. In addition, Hydraulic Pestle Set can be used to process grains day and night. Hydraulic Pestle Set had uncertain number of pestle heads according to different water flow. Some had eight pestle heads.

风扇车（模型）

Winnower (model)

磨　最初叫硙，汉代才叫磨，是粮食加工机械。磨有用人力的、畜力的和水力的，用水力作为动力的磨，大约在晋代就发明了，随着机械制造技术的进步，后来人们发明一种一个水轮能带动几个磨，在王祯《农书》上有记载。

Mill was initially called "Kai" (Chinese mandarin pronunciation of "硙") and then "Mo" (Chinese mandarin pronunciation of "磨") in the Han Dynasty. It is a grain processing machine. There were manpower, animal-power and water power mills. Water powered mill was invented around the Jin Dynasty. With progress of mechanical manufacturing technology, people invented multi-mill driven by one water wheel, which was recorded by Wang Zhen in the *Nongshu*.

唐代的水力利用机械有了较大发展，将水轮巧妙地用于提水灌溉，即在轻便的立式水轮上装上竹筒，制成筒车。除了翻车和筒车之外，还有一种能垂直提水的井车。

Machines utilizing water power were greatly developed in the Tang Dynasty. Water wheel was expertly used for water lifting and irrigation, namely Chinese noria was made by setting a thick bamboo tube on a light vertical water wheel. In addition to square pallet chain-pumps and Chinese noria, there were well wheels for vertical water lifting.

连机水碓（模型） 由一个水轮同时驱动一组碓，主要用于舂米或制粉状物，为晋代杜预创制。若干个碓锤井然有序地升落，将臼中的谷物或其他东西舂好。

Hydraulic Pestle Set (model): One water wheel is used to drive a set of pestles for rice pounding or powder making. It was created by Du Yu of the Jin Dynasty. Hydraulic Pestle Set rise and fall in good order to pound cereal or other things in the mortar.

连机水碓图

Picture of Hydraulic Pestle Set

筒车 （模型） 竹或木制成的轮型提水机械，竹筒或木筒在水中注满水，随轮转到上部时水自动泻入承水槽，输入田里。

Chinese Noria(model): It is a wheel waterlift machine made of bamboo or wood. It works in such as way that bamboo tubes or wood barrels are filled with water when immersed and rotate along with the wheel to the upper position to let water automatically pour down into water channels and flow into the fields.

井车 垂直提水机械。首尾相接的小水桶挂在直轮上，每个桶在井底充水，提到井口倾入水槽，实现连续提水。

Well Wheel: It is a machine for vertical water lifting. Water buckets end to end are hung on a straight wheel. Each bucket is filled with water at the bottom of the well and lifted up to the wellhead to let the water flow into channels so as to perform continuous water lifting.

第六章 古代兵器
Chapter 6 Ancient China's Weapons

原始社会晚期已有战争，有战争则有兵器，在中国漫长的历史发展过程中，无论是冷兵器还是火器，都在不断发展。

Wars occurred in the late primitive society. Where there are wars, there are weapons. In the long historical development process of China, both cold weapons and firearms kept consistent development.

第一节 冷兵器
Section 1 Cold Weapons

冷兵器是指用人力和机械力操持的直接用于斩击和刺杀的武器，如刀、矛、剑、弓箭等，它经历了石兵器、青铜兵器和钢铁兵器三个发展阶段。

Cold weapons refer to weapons that are held and operated by manpower and mechanical force，and directly used for beheading and stabbing, such as swords, spears，bows and arrows. Cold weapons'development underwent three stages of stone weapons, bronze weapons and iron and steel weapons.

石兵器 由原始社会晚期的生产工具发展而来，主要有石戈、石矛、石斧、石铲、石镞、石匕首以及玉刃矛、骨制标枪头等。石器时代的兵器虽然制作简单，但是已经形成了冷兵器的基本类型，为第一代金属兵器——青铜兵器的创制开了先河。弓箭，是旧石器时代人类最复杂的、科学技术含量最高的工具，中国在1万年前已经制作和使用弓箭，是世界上发明和使用弓箭最早地区之一。

54

Stone weapons：They were developed from production tools in the late primitive society with main categories of stone dagger-axe, stone spear, stone axe, stone spade, stone arrowhead and stone dagger, as well as jade-bladed spear and bone javelin head. Although weapons were easily made in Stone Age, basic types of cold weapons had been formed, which advocated creation and manufacture of bronze weapons, the first generation of metal weapons. Bows and arrows were the most complicated tool made by man with highest content of science and technology in the Paleolithic Age. Ten thousand years ago, bows and arrows had been made and used in China, which is one of the regions where bows and arrows were earliest invented and used in the world.

青铜兵器　大约在公元前21世纪建立的夏代已经问世，到了商代得到进一步发展。制造了戈、矛、斧等长杆格斗兵器，刀、剑等卫体兵器和弓箭等射远的综合兵器，以及胄、甲、盾等防护装具等。春秋战国时期还出现了青铜复合剑的制造技术，这种剑的脊部和刃部分别用含锡量不同的青铜铸成，这种脊韧刃坚的复合剑，标志着青铜兵器制造技术达到顶峰。

Bronze weapons：They had made appearance in the Xia Dynasty established around the 21st Century BC, and were further developed in the Shang Dynasty. People made pole battle weapons such as dagger-axe, spear and axe, defense weapons such as knives and swords and comprehensive weapons with long range such as bows and arrows, and protective devices such as helmet, armor and shield. Manufacturing technology of bimetallic bronze swords also occurred in the Spring and Autumn Period and the Warring States Period. Ridge and edge of the swords were cast by bronze with different content of tin. The bimetallic bronze swords with tough ridge and solid edge allowed manufacturing technology of bronze weapons to reach its summit.

钢铁兵器　中国虽然是在春秋晚期才进入铁器时代，但在商代已能够用陨铁制成铁刃铜钺。战国时期，由于钢铁冶炼技术的发展。为制造钢铁兵器提供原料，已经使用剑矛戟等钢铁兵器和用于防护的铁片兜鍪。到了西汉，淬火技术的发展导致钢铁兵器的使用相当普遍。从东汉到唐宋，钢铁兵器进入了全面发展时期。此时，除攻防兼备的刀盾等外，射远兵器弩，继西汉出现带刻度的望山后，三国、唐代创造了连弩、强弩等，杀伤力大大增强。晋代创造了马蹬，提高了骑兵的战斗力。宋代以后，钢铁兵器虽然仍在发展，但其战斗作用同逐渐发展的火器相比，退居次要地位。

Iron and steel weapons：Although the Chinese Iron Age began in the late Spring and Autumn Period, iron-bladed bronze tomahawk could be made by meteoric iron in the Shang Dynasty. In the Warring States Period, development of iron and steel smelting technology helped provide raw materials for making iron and steel weapons. Iron and steel weapons such as sword, spear and halberd and protective iron sheet helmet had been used. Up to the Western Han Dynasty, with development of quenching technology, iron and steel weapons had been universally used.

From the Eastern Han Dynasty to Tang and Song Dynasties, full development period of iron and steel weapons began. At that time, in addition to blade shield having both functions of attack and defense, for the weapon crossbow with long range, after occurrence of scaled Wangshan (aiming device in ancient China) in the Western Han Dynasty, repeating crossbow and heavy crossbow were created in the Three Kingdoms period and the Tang Dynasty to greatly strengthen killing capability. Saddle iron was created in the Jin Dynasty to improve fighting capacity of cavalryman. After the Song Dynasty, although iron and steel weapons kept developing, the function of fighting was inferior to firearms which were being gradually developed.

玉刃矛　（商后期）北京故宫博物院藏

Jade-Bladed Spear (of the late Shang Dynasty)：Collection of the Palace Museum, Beijing.

商代"妇好"钺　长39.5cm，刃宽37.5cm，重9kg，体形巨大，饰以双虎噬人纹，铭"妇好"二字。妇好是商王武丁的配偶，多次领兵出征，是著名的女统帅。河南安阳出土，中国国家博物馆藏。

"Fuhao" Tomahawk of the Shang Dynasty: It is large with length of 39.5 cm, weight of 9 kg and blade width of 37.5 cm. It was decorated with the pattern of two maneating tigers inscribing the words "Fuhao". Fuhao is one of wives of King Wuding of the Shang Dynasty. She was a famous female commander who led her soldiers in several military operations. It was unearthed in Anyang, Henan Province and collection of Museum of Chinese History.

商代铁刃铜钺　残长11.1cm，阑宽8.5cm。铁刃残存部分的后段夹于青铜钺身内。为约公元前14世纪器物。它表明3300多年前的商人已经熟悉了铁的热加工性能。此件是铁用于兵器制造的最早出土物之一。河北藁城台西村出土，河北省文物研究所藏。

Iron-Bladed Bronze Tomahawk of the Shang Dynasty: Its remainder length is 11.1 cm and peripheral width is 8.5 cm. The rear section of remained iron blade is interlaid in the bronze tomahawk body. It is an waref around the 14th Century BC. It reflects that people living in the Shang Dynasty more than 3300 years ago had been familiar with hot workability of iron. It is one of the earliest unearthed objects indicating application of iron to weapons manufacture. it was unearthed in Taixi Village, Gaocheng, Hebei Province. It is collection of Hebei Provincial Institute of Cultural Relics.

金柄铁剑　剑柄为黄金铸成，饰蟠螭纹，并嵌有宝石。长30.7cm。陕西宝鸡益门春秋墓葬出土。

Iron Sword with Golden Handle: The handle is cast by gold, decorated with coiled-dragon patterns and inlaid with precious stone. It is 30.7 cm long and was unearthed from the tomb of the Spring and Autumn Period in Yimen, Baoji, Shaanxi Province.

西周早期的青铜素面胄　通高23cm，素面，胄顶有一长脊，脊长18cm，作镂空网状纹。北京昌平出土。

Bronze Plain Helmet of the Early Western Zhou Dynasty: It is 23 cm high, plain. The helmet has a long ridge on the top. The ridge is 18 cm long with pierced net patterns. It was unearthed in Changping, Beijing.

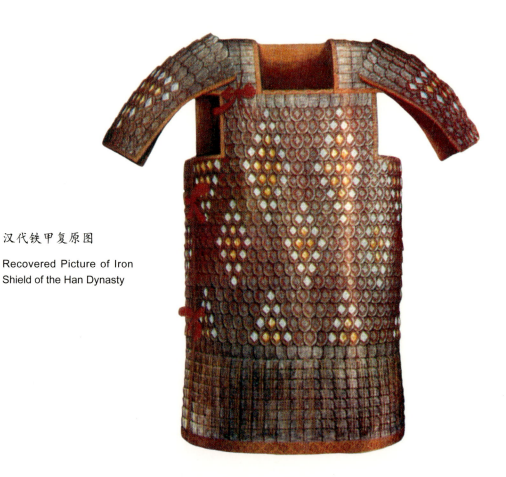

汉代铁甲复原图

Recovered Picture of Iron Shield of the Han Dynasty

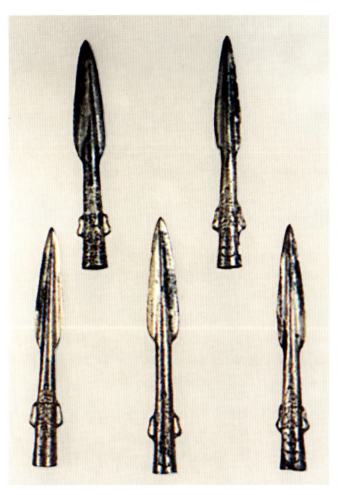

秦戟 秦戟多系戈头和矛头的联装戟，长度多在3m左右。

Halberd of the Qin Dynasty: Most halberds of the Qin Dynasty were assembled halberds of dagger-axe head and spear head in length of about 3m.

铜矛 战国兵器，四川新都马家出土。

Bronze Spear: weapon in the Warring States Period. It was unearthed in Majia, Xindu, Sichuan Province.

汉代弩机（模型）

Crossbow of the Han Dynasty (Model)

西汉铜弩机 1918年河北满城出土。

Bronze Arrow Projector of the Western Han Dynasty: unearthed in Mancheng, Heibei Province in 1918.

第二节 火器
Section 2 Firearms

　　黑色火药是中国的四大发明之一。以硝、硫、木炭为基本成分的黑色火药，在公元7世纪的隋唐时期才真正形成。公元10世纪北宋初年，火药武器开始用于战争，开创了人类战争史上火器和冷兵器并用的时代。北宋初年开始使用的是火球、火药箭等利用火药燃烧性火器，至南宋燃烧性火器过渡到管形射击火器。

　　Gunpowder is one of the four greatest inventions of ancient China. Gunpowder with basic ingredient of Saltpeter, sulfur and wood charcoal was actually formed in the Sui and Tang Dynasties in the 7th Century AD. In the early Northern Song Dynasty in the 10th Century AD, gunpowder-based weapons were initially used in wars, originating the age of firearms and cold-weapons in the war history of human beings. In the early Northern Song Dynasty, people initially used combustible firearms utilizing gunpowder such as fireball and exploding arrow. To the Southern Song Dynasty, combustible firearms were transited to tubular shooting firearms.

　　元代根据南宋火枪射击原理创制成火铳，经过改良并大量制造投入使用，成为明代军队制式装备，中国兵器从此进入以火器为主的历史阶段。中国发明的火药和创制的火器，在公元14世纪初叶传入欧洲，经过改进，在15世纪后期制成各种火绳枪炮。16世纪初，葡萄牙人东来又传入中国，因为当时国人把葡萄牙人称作佛朗机，所以也把这种枪炮称作佛朗机。明代万历年间大量仿制并发展了一些新的产品，戚继光（1528—1587年）编练的部队，使用火器的士兵已占总人数的一半左右。明熹宗天启元年（1621年）为抵御后金军的进攻，向澳门葡萄牙人购买了欧洲使用的早期加农炮进行仿制，当时国人叫它"红夷炮"，后改"夷"为"衣"，称"红衣炮"，后发展成为清军装备的系列火炮。

　　In the Yuan Dynasty, gun barrel was made as per shooting principle of firelock of the Southern Song Dynasty. It was modified and made and used in large quantities as standardized military equipment of the Ming Dynasty. Then the Chinese weapon historic period with predominant firearms began. Gunpowder invented and firearms created in China were transmitted to Europe in the early 14th Century AD, and then were modified, and used to make various match lock guns in the late 15th Century. In the early 16th Century, when the Portuguese came to China, the guns were transmitted to China. At that time, the Chinese people called the Portuguese Frankish, so the guns were also called Frankish. In Wanli Period of the Ming Dynasty, the guns were imitated in large quantities and some new products were developed. In troops trained by Qi Jiguang (1528—1587), cannon early used about a half of the soldiers had used firearm. In the first year of Tianqi period of Ming Emperor Xizong (1621 AD), to defend against troops of the Later Jin Dynasty, it was purchased from the Portuguese for imitation that was used in Europe; at that time, the Chinese people (in Macao) called it "Red-haired Barbarian Cannons"

which was then changed to "Red-coat Cannons". Red-coat Cannons developed to a series of gun equipment for Qing army.

　　明代火器制作已有较高水平，种类繁多，不仅有爆炸火器，而且有管状火器和喷射火器。最著名的热兵器有：世界最早的二级火箭"火龙出水"、32支火箭齐发的"一窝蜂"以及"架火战车"、"神火飞鸦"等。

铜火铳　元代创制了世界最早的金属管形火器。这个铜火铳为早期青铜火铳，属管状火器，是从梨花枪等火器发展而来。

Copper Gun Barrel: The world's earliest tubular metal firearm was created in the Yuan Dynasty. The copper gun barrel was early bronze gun barrel and tubular firearm developed from firearms such as Lihua Spear.

元代铜碗口铳

Bronze Bowl-Muzzle Bombard of the Yuan Dynasty

神威大将军特炮　1638年制，长2.86m、口径10.2cm，红夷炮型。

Shenwei Great General Special Gun: It was made in 1638 with length of 2.86m and caliber of 10.2cm. It is of Red-haired Barbarian Cannons.

Firearm manufacture had reached high level in the Ming Dynasty, with diverse types including not only explosive firearm but also tubular firearm and jet firearm. The most famous hot weapons included "Wild Water Dragon", the world's earliest two-stage rocket, "Hornetsu' Nest" shooting 32 fire arrows simultaneously as well as "Rockets-Carryier" and Rocket-Propelled Incendiary Called "Magic Flying Fiery Crow".

一窝蜂（模型）　一种筒形箭架。可同时发射32枚火箭的热兵器。装配时将火箭的导火索束在一起，点燃后同时射出，从而扩大了杀伤面，射程可达500m。据明《武备志》复原，中国历史博物馆藏。

Hornetsu' Nest (model): It is a cylindrical arrow rack as well as hot weapon which can shoot 32 fire arrows simultaneously. In assembly, igniter cords of arrows were bundled together. When the cords were ignited, the arrows would be shot simultaneously to expand killing range up to 500 m. It was recovered according to the *Wubeizhi* (Records of Armaments and Military Provisions) of the Ming Dynasty and is collection of Museum of Chinese History.

架火战车（模型）　在独轮车上载火铳、火箭及矛枪等，车前悬挂棉帘以作防护，可攻可守。常将数百辆车环列为营，称"车营"，在明代盛极一时。据明《武备志》复制。

Rockets-Carryier (model): It was made by loading wheelbarrow with gun barrel, fire arrows and spear. Cotton curtain was hung in front of the chariot for either attach or defense. Hundreds of chariots were usually arranged in a circle, which was called "chariot battalion". It was in fashion in the Ming Dynasty. The model was reproduced according to the *Wubeizhi* (Records of Armaments and military Provisions) of the Ming Dynasty.

火龙出水（模型） 世界上记载最早的二级火箭。龙体外四支火箭为动力火箭，使龙体前飞，然后引燃龙口内火箭，使口内杀伤火箭飞出击敌。据明《武备志》复制，中国历史博物馆藏。

Two-Stage Rocket Called Wild Water Dragon (model): It is the earliest recorded two-stage rocket in the world. Four fire arrows outside the dragon body are propelling arrows to push the dragon body to fly forward to ignite fire arrows in the dragon mouth and let killing fire arrows in the mouth fly to attack enemies. The model was reproduced according to the *Wubeizhi* （Records of Armaments and military Provisions） of the Ming Dynasty and is collection of Museum of Chinese History.

神火飞鸦（模型） 翅长60cm，身长56cm，以扎制风筝的形式结合火箭推动的原理发明的燃烧弹。内装火药，有4支火箭推动，可飞行300余米，多用于火战。中国历史博物馆藏。

Rocket-Propelled Incendiary Called Magic Flying Fiery Crow (model): The wings are 60 cm long and the body is 56 cm long. It was fire bomb invented as per the principle of combining kite making and fire arrow propelling. It was provided with gunpowder inside and four propelling fire arrows and its flying distance could reach 300 m. It was usually used in fire wars. It is collection of Museum of Chinese History.

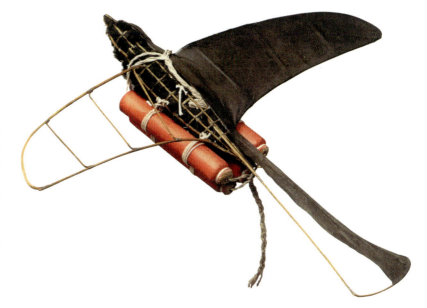

第七章　仪器仪表和度量衡
Chapter 7 Instrumentation, Weights and Measures

第一节　天文仪器
Section 1　Astronomical Instruments

我国古代设计和制造了各种精密而先进的天体测量仪器和装置。测量天体的仪器主要有浑仪、简仪等；表演天象的仪器主要是浑象等；还有集多种功能于一身的水运仪象台。

Various advanced precision astrometric instruments and devices were designed and manufactured in ancient China. Astrometric instruments mainly included armillary sphere and abridged armilla; sky phenomena projectors mainly included celestial globe; and there was water-driven astronomical tower which integrated multiple functions.

浑仪
Armillary Sphere

浑仪是以"浑天说"为理论基础制造的测量天体的仪器。浑，球也。"浑天说"是中国古代以地球为中心的宇宙理论。浑仪正是按这种理论而设计的，模拟天球，由多个同心圆环组合而成。中国浑仪大约在战国中期至秦汉时期(前4—前1世纪)出现，早期的浑仪比较简单，经过历代天文学家的不断完善，至唐代贞观七年(633年)李淳风设计了一架比较完善的浑天黄道仪。

It was an astrometric instrument made based on *Hun*, the "theory of sphere-heavens". *Hun* means sphere. The theory of sphere-heavens was the theory of space centering on the earth in ancient China. It was armillary sphere that was designed as per this theory. It was formed by assembling multiple concentric circular rings to simulate celestial sphere. Armillary sphere occurred around the middle Warring States Period to the Qin and Han Dynasties (the 4th Century BC to the 1st Century BC) in China. Early armillary sphere was simple and consistently improved by astronomers of the past dynasties. In the 7th years of Zhenguan Period of the Tang Dynasty, Li Chunfeng designed an almost perfect ecliptic armillary sphere.

浑仪在宋代(995—1162年)的百多年中, 共制作大型铜浑仪10座, 多座单重达2万斤。

Armillary sphere was made frequently in the Song Dynasty. In more than 100 years between 995 and 1162, 10 large armillary spheres were made in total. Several spheres had unit weight up to 10,000 kg.

简仪
Abridged Armilla

由于浑仪的圈环过于复杂, 北宋开始浑仪的改革。元代郭守敬加以革新简化, 于1276年制成简化的浑仪, 称简仪。它包括相互独立的赤道坐标式装置(世界上最早的大赤道仪)和地平坐标装置(与现代的地平经纬仪相似), 仪器运转灵活, 大大增强了仪器的适应性。简仪在窥管两端安有十字丝, 这是望远镜中十字丝的鼻祖; 为了减少仪器中环与环之间的摩擦, 安装了与近代滚柱轴承相似的小圆柱体, 是滚柱轴承的最早利用。简仪的创制, 是中国天文仪器制造史上的一大飞跃, 是当时世界上的一项先进技术。欧洲直到三百多年之后的1598年才由丹麦天文学家第谷发明与之类似的装置。

Since circular rings of armillary sphere were too complicated, alternation of armillary sphere had began since the Northern Song Dynasty. Guo Shoujing of the Yuan Dynasty innovated and simplified armillary sphere and invented simplified armillary sphere in 1276 which was called abridged armilla. It constituted of the equatorial mounting (the world's earliest large equatorial instrument) and the azimuth mounting (similar to modern altazimuth) which were separated each other. The instrument ran flexibly to greatly increase its adaptability. Abridged armilla was provided with hair cross at both ends of sighting-tube, which was the origin of hair cross for telescope. To reduce friction between rings in the instrument, small cylinder similar to recent roller bearing was installed. It was the earliest application of roller bearing. Creation of abridged armilla was a great forward leap in manufacture history of astronomical instruments in China and an advanced technology in the world at that time. In Europe, similar device was only invented by Tycho Brahe, Danish astronomer, in 1598 more than 300 years later.

现保存在南京紫金山天文台的浑仪是按照李淳风的办法制作的; 郭守敬创制的简仪, 清康熙五十四年(1715年)被传教士纪理安当作废铜熔化处理掉, 现保存在南京紫金山天文台的简仪是明代正统二年至七年(1437—1442年)间的复制品。清光绪二十六年(1900年)八国联军侵入北京时, 简仪被法军抢去, 运到法国大使馆, 过了几年才归还;

浑仪被德军抢去运往德国波茨坦，第一次世界大战结束后（1921年）才归还中国。1931年"九一八"事变，浑仪和简仪运往南京，1937年12月南京沦陷，两仪被日本侵略军损坏，新中国成立后修复布展。

Armillary sphere being kept in the purple mountain observatory in Nanjing was made by method of Li Chunfeng. Abridged armilla created by Guo Shoujing was disposed by smelting as copper scrap by a missionary Bernard-Kilian Stumpf in the 54th year of King Kangxi (1715) of the Qing Dynasty. Abridged armilla being kept in the Purple Mountain Observatory in Nanjing is a reproduction made between the 2nd and the 7th year of Zhengtong Period (1437—1442) of the Ming Dynasty. In the 26th year of King Guangxu of the Qing Dynasty (1900), when the Eight-Power Allied Forces invaded Beijing, the abridged armilla was robbed by the French aggressive troops and transported to French Embassy. It was returned only several years later. The armillary sphere was robbed by the German aggressive troops and transported to Potsdam, Germany, which was only returned to China in 1921 after World War I. Upon the "September 18th" Incident in 1931, the armillary sphere and the abridged armilla were transited to Nanjing. Upon the fall of Nanjing in December 1937, the two instruments were damaged by the Japanese aggressor troops and recovered for exhibition after establishment of the PRC.

浑象
Celestial Sphere

它是一种表演天体运行的仪器。它把太阳、月亮、二十八宿等天体以及赤道和黄道都绘制在一个球面上，能使人不受时间、气候条件的限制，随时观测当时的天象，相当于天球仪。中国的第一架浑象是西汉宣帝甘露二年（前52年）耿寿昌创制。后来历代都重视浑象的制作，张衡、一行、苏颂等天文学家都进行过设计，现存清代天体仪可算是古代浑象的仿制品。

It is an instrument to project sky phenomena. For the instrument, celestial bodies such as the sun, the moon and the twenty-eight lunar mansions as well as the equator and the ecliptic are drawn on a spherical surface to allow people to observe sky phenomena at the time at all times without being limited by time and climate conditions. It is equivalent to modern celestial globe. The first celestial Sphere of China was created by Geng Shouchang in the second year of Ganlu era of Emperor Xuan (52 BC) of the Western Han Dynasty. Stress had been laid on celestial globe manufacture in the following dynasties. Astronomers such as Zhang Heng, Yi Xing and Su Song performed design. The existing celestial globe of the Qing Dynasty can be regarded as imitation of celestial sphere in the ancient times.

水运浑象和机械日历
Water-Driven Celestial Sphere and Mechanical Calendar

东汉张衡(78—139年)以浑象配合漏壶，制造出漏水转动浑象。张衡制成大型浑象，在浑象内部设一套齿轮系统装置，以补偿式漏壶的流水为动力，驱动浑象每日均匀地绕轴旋转一周，使得浑象自动和近似准确演示天体周日活动。不仅如此，浑象还带动一组凸轮轴(当时名瑞轮萫荚)演示一个朔望月中日期的推移，是一种自动机械日历。张衡首创的这一水运浑象，是为后世得到进一步发展的机械天文钟的先声。

Zhang Heng (78—139) in the Eastern Han Dynasty manufactured water-driven celestial sphere by matching celestial sphere with water clock. Zhang Heng made large celestial sphere internally provided with a set of geared system devices. The celestial sphere uniformly completed one revolution around the axle by power of flowing water of compensatory water clock to automatically and approximately accurately demonstrate diurnal motion of celestial bodies. Furthermore, the celestial sphere also drove a set of camshafts (called *Ruilun Xuanjia* at that time) to demonstrate lapsc of time in one synodic month. It is an automatic mechanical calendar. The water-driven celestial sphere initiated by Zhang Heng is the herald of mechanical chronometer further developed in the later ages.

水运仪象台
Water-Driven Astronomical Tower

水运仪象台是以水为动力运转的天文钟。"仪"就是浑仪，"象"就是浑象，巧妙地将浑仪与水运浑象组合成一个整体，融漏壶、浑象、浑仪及报时机械于一体，集测时、守时、报时等功能于一仪，是一种大型综合性仪器，是天文仪器的一大发展。也是古代天文仪器和机械制造达到的一个高峰，至少领先于世界五六个世纪，成为中华民族的骄傲。

Water-driven astronomical tower is chronometer powered by water. In its Chinese name "*Shuiyun Yi Xiang Tai*", "*Yi*" means armillary sphere and "*Xiang*" means celestial globe. It was formed by skillfully assembling armillary sphere and water-powered celestial globe and by integrating water clock, celestial sphere, armillary sphere and time indicating machinery as well as functions of time determination, time keeping and timing dissemination. It was a large comprehensive instrument, emblemizing a great progress of astronomical instruments. It propelled ancient astronomical instruments and mechanical manufacture to reach the zenith at least five or six centuries earlier than in other countries all over the world. Therefore, it became the Chinese nation's pride.

苏颂和韩公廉等于北宋元祐元年(1086年)开始设计。到元祐七年全部完成。台高约12米，宽约7米；最上层设置浑仪且有可开闭的屋顶，这完全是现代天文台望远镜观测室活动屋顶的始祖。中层放置浑象，由机轮带动，使浑仪与浑象的转动与天体运动保持同步运转，是近代望远镜随天球同步运转的转仪钟的先驱；下层是报时系统，最为复杂(分为五个小层，首层朝南有门。第一小层有名为"正衡钟鼓楼"，分别有红衣、紫衣和绿衣木人报每个时辰的时初、时正和时刻；第二小层设24个司辰木人，报时初与时正；第三小层有24个木人报时初与时刻）。

Su Song and Han Gonglian et al started design in the first year of Yuanyou period of the Northern Song Dynasty (1086). It was completed in the seventh year of Yuanyou period. The tower is about 12 m high and 7 m wide. On the top layer is armillary sphere with openable roof. It is absolutely the origin of movable roof of sight chamber of telescope of modern observatory. On the middle layer is celestial sphere driven by mechanical wheel to allow armillary sphere and celestial sphere to rotate with motion of celestial bodies simultaneously. It is precursor of driving clock running along with celestial sphere for recent telescope. On the lower layer is time indicating system, which is most complicated (with five sub-layers, the first of which faces the south with door; the first sub-layer is named "Zheng Heng Bell and Clock Tower" and provided with red-coat, purple-coat and green-coat wooden men to announce the first four quarters, the second four quarters and quarter points of each one of the 12 two-hour periods of the day respectively;

郭守敬简仪（明代复制） 它突破了浑仪环圈交错不便观测的缺点，将环组分别架立，装置简便，而效用更广。现置放于南京紫金山天文馆。

Abridged Armilla by Guo Shoujing (reproduction of the Ming Dynasty): It overcame armillary sphere's disadvantage of inconvenience for observation due to alternating circular rings by erecting the ring sets separately. The device is convenient and easy with wider utilization. It is being placed in the Purple Mountain Observatory in Nanjing.

明代浑仪　明正统二年至七年（1437—1442年）制造。通高2.45m，装置有六合仪、三长仪、四游仪，用以观测全天恒星的入宿、去极度和日、月、五星的运行，是中国传统的天文仪器。原置北京观象台，1900年被德国掠置波茨坦宫前，至1921年才归还，1935年迁至南京紫金山天文台。

Armillary Sphere of the Ming Dynasty: It was made between the second year and the seventh year of Zhengtong period (1437—1442) of the Ming Dynasty. Its total height is 2.45 m. It was provided with component of the six cardinal points, three lengths and four displacements to observe determinative star distance and north polar distance of stars in the sky and running of the sun, the moon and the five visible planets. It was a traditional astronomical instrument in China. It was originally placed in Beijing Ancient Observatory. In 1900, it was robbed by the German aggressive troops and placed in front of Potsdam Palace and not returned until 1921. In 1935, it was transited to the Purple Mountain Observatory in Nanjing.

汉代铜漏壶 计时器具。大约出现在西周或稍晚些时候，以漏壶与浑象配合制造出水运浑象。圆筒形，下有三足，通高32.3cm，口径10.6cm，壶身近底处有一小流管，管长3.8cm，管口孔径0.25cm。壶盖上有方形提梁，壶盖和提梁上有正相对的长方形小孔各一，用以安插刻有时辰的沉箭。陕西兴平县茂陵附近西汉空心砖墓出土，陕西兴平县茂陵文物保管所藏。

Copper Clepsydra of the Han Dynasty: It is an instrument to record time and occurred in Western Zhou or a little later. The water-driven celestial sphere are made by matching celestial sphere with clepsydra. It is cylindrical with three legs at the bottom, total height of 32.3 cm and opening of 10.6 cm. There is a small flow pipe to the bottom of the body, with length of 3.8 cm and orifice aperture of 0.25 cm. The clepsydra cover has a rectangular hoop handle. Both the cover and the handle are provided with one respective rectangular hole opposite to one another for placing sinking arrow engraved with time. It was unearthed from the hollow brick tomb of the Western Han Dynasty near the Maoling Tomb in Xingping County, Shaanxi Province. It is collection of Maoling Cultural Relic Administrative Office in Xingping County, Shaanxi Province.

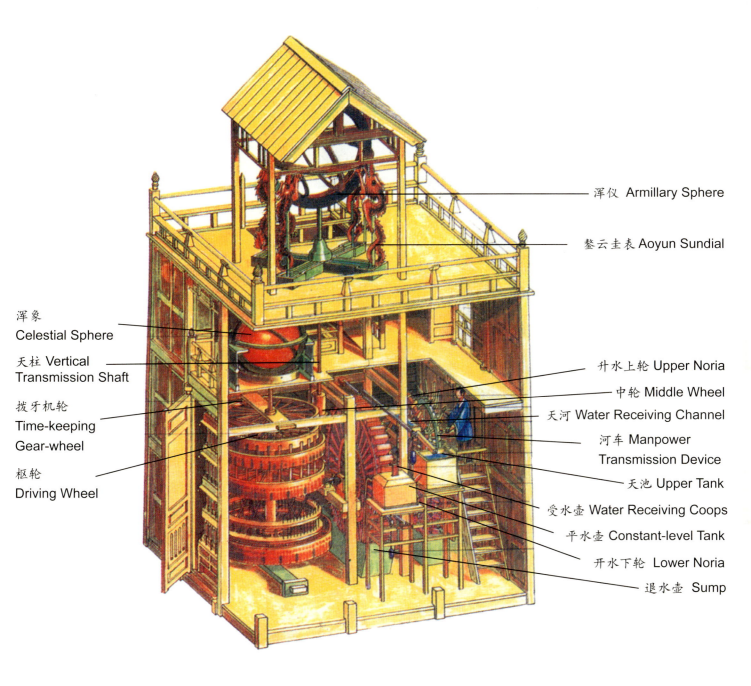

渾仪 Armillary Sphere

鳌云圭表 Aoyun Sundial

渾象
Celestial Sphere

天柱 Vertical
Transmission Shaft

拨牙机轮
Time-keeping
Gear-wheel

枢轮
Driving Wheel

升水上轮 Upper Noria

中轮 Middle Wheel

天河 Water Receiving Channel

河车 Manpower
Transmission Device

天池 Upper Tank

受水壶 Water Receiving Coops

平水壶 Constant-level Tank

开水下轮 Lower Noria

退水壶 Sump

水运仪象台结构示意图 北宋苏颂主持制成的木构水运仪象台，能用多种形式表现天体的运行。它由水力驱动，其中有一套擒纵机构。水运仪象台代表了当时机械制造的先进水平，是当时世界上先进的天文钟。

Structural Representation of Water-Driven Astronomical Tower: Wood structural water-driven astronomical tower made under charge of Su Song of the Northern Song Dynasty can represent running of celestial bodies in many ways. It is driven by water with a set of escapement mechanism. It represented advanced technical level of machinery manufacture at that time. It was the world's advanced chronometer at that time.

　　这三部分用一套传动装置和一组机轮连接起来，用漏壶水冲动机轮，带动浑仪、浑象、报时装置一起转动。可通过控制匀速流动的水来调节枢轮向某一方向等时转动，使浑仪和浑象的转动与天体运动保持同步。在报时装置中巧妙地利用了160多个小木人和钟、鼓、铃、钲四种乐器，不仅可以显示时刻，还能报昏、旦时刻和夜晚的更点。水运仪象台的机械传动装置，开始了现代钟表锚状擒纵器的先声，英国李约瑟认为"很可能是欧洲中世纪天文钟的直接祖先"。水运仪象台体现了中国古代天文仪器制作的高水平，尤其重要的是它体现出当时中国机械工程技术水平的卓越成就。

The three parts are coupled by a set of gear-drive equipment and a set of machine wheels. Water from the clepsydra propels machine wheels to drive armillary sphere, celestial sphere and the time signal system to rotate simultaneously. Water flowing at uniform speed can be controlled to regulate driving wheel to perform isochronous rotation towards a certain direction in order to allow armillary sphere and celestial sphere to rotate simultaneously with motion of celestial bodies. For the time signal system, more than 160 small wooden men and four musical instruments of bell, drum, ring and bell-shaped cymbals were skillfully used to not only indicate point of time but also report time of Hun and Dan (twilight before sunrise and after sunset) and the night watches. Mechanical transmission device of the Water-driven astrononical tower was the origin of anchor escape pinion of modern clocks. Joseph Needham from UK held that it is likely to be the direct progenitor of chronometer of the middle ages of Europe. It reflects high level of manufacturing astronomical instruments in ancient China. It is especially important that it reflects outstanding achievements in mechanical engineering level of China at that time.

　　水运仪象台在1127年金兵攻陷汴梁时被破坏。南宋时期，秦桧曾派人寻找苏颂后人并访求苏颂遗书，还请教过朱熹，想把水运仪象台恢复起来，结果始终没有成功。近年，科技部曾拨款某高校研究恢复水运仪象台的课题，尚未见到完成实物的报道。

Water-driven astrononical tower was damaged in 1127 AD when the Jin army captured Bianliang. In the Southern Song Dynasty, Qin Hui once sent for descendant of Su Song and paid a visit for last will of Su Song and consulted Zhu Xi to try to recover the Water-driven astrononical tower, but he failed. In recent years, the Ministry of Science and Technology of PRC appropriated money for a university to do research on the subject to recover the Water-driven astrononical tower, and completion of material objects has not been reported.

第二节　地动仪
Section 2　Seismometer

汉顺帝阳嘉元年(132年)张衡设计制造出了世界上第一台测定地震发生时间与方位的仪器——候风地动仪*。这种仪器利用地震波的传播和力学的惯性原理来探测地震震中的方向。虽然其功能只限于地震发生的时间和方位，但它比西方类似地震仪出现要早约1700年，李约瑟称它是世界地震仪之祖。

In the first year of Yangjia period of Emperor Shun of the Han Dynasty (132), Zhang Heng designed and made *Houfeng Didongyi* (seismometer), the world's first instrument to determine time and azimuth of an earthquake. *For this instrument, seismic wave propagation and mechanical principle of the inertia are utilized to determine epicenter direction. Although its function is limited to time and azimuth of an earthquake, it is about 1700 years earlier than similar seismograph in the western countries. Joseph Needham called it progenitor of the world's seismograph.

据《后汉书》载，东汉永和三年二月三日(138年3月1日)该仪器准确测知甘肃陕西临洮一带的一次六级以上的地震，这是世界上第一次由观测得知地震发生方位和时间的实录。

It was recorded by *The History of the Later Han* that on the third day of the second lunar month, the third year of Yonghe period of the Eastern Han Dynasty (March 1, 138), the instrument was used to accurately determine an earthquake with magnitude over six in Lintao areas of Shaanxi, Gansu Province. It is true record of knowing time and azimuth of an earthquake by observation for the first time in the world.

关于这架仪器，《后汉书》中记载："地动仪以精铜制成，圆径八尺，合盖隆起，形似酒樽。"(酒樽即酒坛)里面有精巧的机构，主要是中间的"都柱"(类似惯性运动中的摆)，四周有八组杠杆机械组合。如果发生地震，都柱受到震波作用，推动顺着地震波的一组杠杆，使仪器的龙首张口吐球，再由蟾蜍承接，由此可以观测到地震的方位。据记载，其灵敏度可测知人感觉不到的震幅。

---

*《后汉书》："张衡复造候风地动仪"。有人推测候风是"候风仪"，它与地动仪是两种东西；但也有人说"候风"是人名，张衡的地动仪是"复造候风"的；也有人认为，候风有候气的意思，古人以为地震是由地气所吊起的。因而以此为名。

* *The History of the Later Han* recorded that "Zhang Heng also invented *Houfeng Didongyi* (seismometer)". Some people concluded that "Houfeng" meant "Houfeng instrument", which was a different one from seismometer; some held that "Houfeng" was a person's name and seismograph of Zhang Heng was reproduction of Hou Feng; and others thought that "Houfeng" had the meaning of climate and ancient people believed that earthquakes were drawn by the *qi* of the earth and so it was taken as the name.

地动仪（王振铎复原）
张衡于132年首创了世界
上第一架地震仪——候
风地动仪。

Seismometer (recovered
by Wang Zhenduo): In 132,
Zhang Heng invented *Houfeng
Didongyi*, the world's first
seismograph.

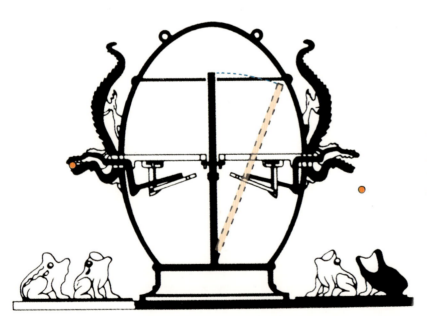

张衡地动仪原理示意图

Schematic Diagram of Principle of
Seismometer Invented by Zhang
Heng

For this instrument, it was recorded in *The History of the Later Han* that "Seismometer is made of refined copper with circular radius of 8 *chi* [a unit of length (3 *chi*=1 meter)]. When it is covered, it is high, like a wine vessel Zun." (Zun means wine jar.) It has elaborate mechanism inside, mainly including the central "*Duzhu* (thick column)" (similar to pendulum in inertial motion) surrounded by 8 sets of lever machanical assemblies. In case of an earthquake, the thick column is under the action of seismic wave to propel the set of levers along the direction of the wave to allow dragon head of the instrument to open its mouth and spit bead to be carried by bronze toad. Therefore, azimuth of the earthquake can be observed. It was recorded that it is sensitive enough to determine seismic amplitude that people are unable to perceive.

由于张衡地动仪是当时遥遥领先于世界的伟大发明，对其他国家也产生了深远的影响，有人认为张衡地动仪里面摆的构造设计，可能在隋唐时传到了伊朗和日本。《后汉书》中关于地动仪的记载，从19世纪以来，不断被译成多种外文，传播于世界，中外学者一致给予很高的评价。

Since Seismometer invented by Zhang Heng was far ahead of other great inventions in the world at that time and also had influence overseas, some people thought that architectonics of pendulum in the Seismometer by Zhang Heng might be transmitted to Iran and Japan in the Sui and Tang Dynasties. Records in *The History of the Later Han* on Seismometer have been consistently translated to Several foreign languages since the 19th Century for communication all over the world, winning high appraise from scholars in China and overseas uniformly.

第三节　指南针
Section 3　Compass

指南针是中国古代四大发明之一。它是利用磁铁在地球磁场中的南北极性而制成的一种指向仪器，它和齿轮结构的机械指南车不同。

Compass is one of the four greatest inventions of acient China. It is a pointing instrument made by utilizing phenomenon that a magnetic bar swinging freely in the earth's magnetic field will point towards the direction of the South Pole and the North Pole. It is different from mechanical South point carriage with toothed wheel.

现在所说的指南针是这类物品总的名称，在各个不同的历史发展时期，它有不同的形体，也有不同的名称，如司南、指南龟（鱼）、指南针和磁罗盘等。

Here Compass is a general name of this kind of objects. In different historical development periods, it had different shapes and different names, such as Sinan or Direction Guide, Tortoise-Shaped Compass or Fish-Shaped Compass, Compass Needle and Magnetic Compass.

采用天然磁石的司南，磁性较弱，效果不是很好。因此这种司南未得广泛的使用。北宋初年出现了更高一级有实用性的指南龟（鱼）和指南针，到19世纪现代电磁铁出现，才发展成为更加简便、更有使用价值的指向仪器。

Sinan made of natural magnet has weak magnetic properties and poor effect. Therefore, the Sinan was not widely used. In the early Northern Song Dynasty, superior practical Tortoise-Shaped Compass (Fish-Shaped Compass) and Compass Needle occurred. They developed into pointing instruments which was more convenient and valuable only in the 19th Century when modern electromagnet occurred.

司南——指南针的始祖
Sinan—Origin of Compass

司南，一种世界上最古老的磁性指向器，在战国时期已被用作指示方向的仪器。以天然磁石加工而成，形如勺。它可以自由旋转，当其静止时，勺柄就指向南方，故古人称之为司南。《韩非子·有度篇》载："先王立司南，以端朝夕"。"端朝夕"就是正四方、定方位的意思。《鬼谷子·谋篇》里也记载说："郑人取玉，必载司南，为其不惑也"。即郑国人采玉时就带了司南以确保不迷方向。在司南实践的基础上，才发明了可以实用的指南针。

Sinan, the world's earliest magnetic pointing instrument, had been used for pointing direction in the Warring States Period. It was made by processing natural magnet in the shape of spoon. It can freely rotate; when it is still, the spoon handle will point the south, so it was called Sinan (south pointing) by ancient people. It was recorded in *Hanfeizi, Youdu* that "*xianwang li Sinan, yi duan zhaoxi* (emperors in ancient times created Sinan to determine the four directions)." "*duan zhaoxi*" means to determine the four directions. It was also recorded in *Guiguzi, Mou* that "*zhengren quyu, bizai Sinan, wei qi buhuo ye*", meaning that the Zheng people pick jade with Sinan to ensure not to lose their ways. Practical compass was only invented based on practice with Sinan.

东汉时王充《论衡·是应篇》："司南之勺，投之于地，其柢指南。"依汉代制式复原，司南由青铜盘和天然磁体制成的磁勺组成。青铜盘外方内圆，四周刻有干支四维，合成二十四向，置勺于盘中心圆面上，静止时，勺尾指向为南。

It was recorded by Wangchong of the Eastern Han Dynasty in *Lunheng, Shiying* (Discourses Weighed in the Balance, Shiying), that "when spoon of Sinan is placed on the plate, its tail will point the south". It was recovered by method of the Han Dynasty. Sinan is composed of bronze plate and magnetic spoon made of natural magnet. The bronze plate has square outside and circular inside, surrounded by 24 azimuths consisting of all sides, celestial stems and earthly branches. When the spoon is placed on the central circular face and becomes still, its tail will point the south.

司南（模型） 司南被认为是世界上最早的磁性指南工具。当代学者王振铎先生复原的司南模型，由青铜地盘和磁勺组成。地盘外方内圆，中心圆面打磨光滑。圆外盘面上依次铸有四维、八天干、十二地支，共二十四方位，另有二十八宿。整个地盘寓天圆地方之意。磁勺依汉代制式，用铁铸成后磁化，置于地盘中心。由于地球磁场的作用，勺把指示南方。

Sinan (model): Sinan is regarded as the world's earliest magnetic south pointing tool. Sinan model recovered by Mr. Wang Zhenduo, a scholar of the day, is composed of bronze earth plate and magnetic spoon. The earth plate has square outside and circular inside. The central circular surface is polished smooth. On plate face around the circle, totally 24 azimuths including all sides of northeast, southeast, southwest and northwest, eight celestial stems and twelve earthly branches are cast successively as well as the twenty-eight lunar mansions. The whole earth plate has implied meaning of Round Heaven and Square Earth. Magnetic spoon is made by method of the Han Dynasty that it is cast with iron and magnetized and placed in the center of the earth plate. Under the action of the earth's magnetic field, the spoon handle will point the south.

指南针——伟大的发明
Compass Needle—Great Invention

宋代航海事业的发展，促进了对磁性指向器的探索，最终导致了指南针的发明和广泛应用。

Development of navigation in the Song Dynasty facilitated research on magnetic pointing instrument and eventually resulted in invention and wide application of Compass Needle.

北宋时，曾公亮在《武经总要》记载一种制造指南鱼的人工磁化方法：将薄铁片剪裁成鱼形，置炭火中将铁片烧红时，以铁钤钤鱼首出火。让鱼尾正对子位，蘸水盆中。在地球磁场作用下，铁片被磁化而显磁性；"用时，置水碗于无风处平放鱼在水面，会浮，其首常向午也"。沈括（1031—1095年）在《梦溪笔谈》中介绍了另一种人工磁化的方法："方家以磁石磨针锋，则能指南。"直到19世纪现代电磁铁出现以前，几乎所有的指南针都是采用这种人工磁化法制成的。人工磁化方法的发明，对指南针的应用和发展起了巨大的作用。这时，指南针在它的发展史上已经跨过了两个发展阶段——司南和指南鱼，发展成一种更加简便、更有实用价值的指向器，这些指向器都以这种磁针为主体，只是磁针的形状和装置有所变化而已。

In the Northern Song Dynasty, Zeng Gongliang in *Wujing Zongyao* recorded a manual magnetization method for making Fish-Shaped Compass as follows: cut out thin iron sheets into the shape of fish, burn it in charcoal fire until it becomes red, and clip the fish head out of fire with pincher; let fish tail be opposite to the position of *Zi* and soak it in water in basin. Under the action of the earth's magnetic field, iron sheet was magnetized to have magnetic properties. It was also recorded that "For use, when a blow with water is put in a windless place and the fish is placed on the water surface, the fish will float with head normally towards the south". Shen Kuo in *Mengxi Bitan* （Dream Pond Essays） introduced another manual magnetization method as follows:"Alchemists make needlepoint point the south by grinding it with magnet". By the 19th Century when modern electromagnet occurred, almost all Compass Needles had been made by such a manual magnetization method. Invention of the manual magnetization method played an important role in application and development of Compass Needle. Then Compass Needle had been developed to a more convenient and practically valuable pointer after its two historical development periods of Sinan and Fish-Shaped Compass with unchanged body of magnetic needle and different shape and position of the magnetic needle.

沈括在《梦溪笔谈》中记载了装置磁针的四种方法。一是缕悬法，将磁针用独根蚕丝悬挂起来，下置二十四方位盘，磁针两端所指即为南北方向；二是水浮法，将磁针横穿于灯芯草浮在水面就可以指示方向。这是两种比较实用的方法。另外两种方法稳定性差，不便实用，一是指甲旋定法，将磁针放在指甲上，磁针可以指南，二是碗唇旋定法，将磁针平放在瓷碗的口沿上，可以指南。

Shen Kuo (1031—1095) in *Mengxi Bitan*（Dream Pond Essays）recorded the following four methods for positioning magnetic needle: silk-suspension method-hanging magnetic needle with a single silk and placing 24-azimuth plate at the bottom so that the magnetic needle can indicate south-north direction at both ends; water-float method-pushing magnetic needle across aquatic grass and letting it float on water surface to indicate direction; both the two methods were practical. And the other two methods as follows were not steady and inconvenient: fingernail spin titration-placing magnetic needle on fingernail for south pointing; bowl lip and spin titration-placing magnetic needle on the edge of a ceramic bowl for south pointing.

沈括在做指南针的实验时发现，磁针所指方向，并非正南正北，而是"常微偏东，不全南也"，这是世界上关于磁偏角的首次发现；欧洲直至13世纪才发现磁偏角现象（有记载，欧洲人对磁偏角的发现是哥伦布在海上探险途中的1492年，系15世纪）。

缕悬法指南针（模型）　将不加拈的独根蚕丝系于木架上，蚕丝下端用蜡粘接于磁针中部，悬挂在无风的地方。木架下方置方位盘，以八天干、十二地支和四卦标示24方位。磁针在地磁场的作用下，即可指示方向。

Compass Needle Suspended with Silk Thread (model): It was made by tying a single untwisted silk on a wooden stand, bonding the lower end of the silk into magnetic needle center by wax and hanging in a windless place, and arranging azimuth plate at the bottom of the wooden stand, which indicates 24 azimuths by eight celestial stems, twelve earthly branches and four diagrams. Under the action of earth magnetic field, the magnetic needle can indicate direction.

When making experiments on Compass Needle, Shen Kuo found that magnetic needle did not indicate the exact north-south direction but "normally indicated north-south by east". It is the fist finding on magnetic declination in the world. The phenomenon of magnetic declination was not known until the 13rd Century in Europe (It was recorded that the European learnt about magnetic declination first in 1492 when Columbus was in maritime exploration, namely the 15th Century).

指南针用于航海，首见于北宋末（1119年）朱彧《萍州可谈》卷二："舟师识地理，夜则观星，昼则观日，阴晦则观指南针。"这是航海史上最早使用指南针的记载。

Application of Compass Needle to navigation was initially recorded in the late Northern Song Dynasty (1119) by Zhu Yu in *Pingzhou Ketan* (Pingzhou Table Talks), Volume 2 that "Marine technicians get geographical information by observing stars at night, observing the sun in the daylight and observing Compass Needle in darkness and gloom."It is the earliest recording on application of Compass Needle in the history of navigation.

到南宋咸淳时期（1265—1274年），文献记载始见"针盘"之名，即将磁针与方位盘组成完整的指南工具，称"地罗"或"子午盘"。地罗盘面分度法仍采用汉代地盘形制，以八干、十二支和四卦来表示24个方位。这种针盘已用于航海。

Up to Xianchun period (1265—1274) of the Southern Song Dynasty, designation of "Needle-Plate" was initially recorded in literature, namely magnetic needle and azimuth plate were assembled to form a complete south pointer called "*Diluo*" or "*Ziwupan*". For compass rose indexing, form and system of earth plate in the Han Dynasty was still used to indicate 24 azimuths by eight celestial stems, twelve earthly branches and four diagrams. This Needle-Plate had been used for navigation.

南宋陈元靓在《事林广记》（元初刊出）记载了支撑式指南仪器——指南龟的形制，以木雕成龟形，腹中嵌以磁体，将木龟置于竹制的尖顶立柱上，由于地磁场的作用，龟首尾指示南北。指南龟虽不具方位盘，但它是世界上第一具支撑式指南工具。这是后来出现的旱罗盘的先声。说明在12世纪末期以前，中国已有旱罗盘。

Chen Yuanliang of the Southern Song Dynasty recorded form and system of Tortoise-Shaped Compass (a supporting south-point device) in *Shilin Guangji* (published in the early Yuan Dynasty) as follows: carve the wood into the shape of tortoise, embed magnet to its abdomen and place the wooden tortoise on bamboo upright post with sharp top to allow tortoise tail to indicate north-south direction under the action of earth magnetic fields. Tortoise-Shaped Compass was not provided with azimuth plate, but it was the first supporting south pointer in the world. It is herald of non-water azimuth compass occurring later. It reflects that dry pivoted compass had occurred in China before the end of the 12th Century.

指南针发明后，人类全天候航行的能力得到了极大的提高。中国这一项卓越的发明创造，经丝绸之路传到了阿拉伯国家，在12世纪末到13世纪初又由阿拉伯人传入了欧洲。14—16世纪欧洲航海罗盘装上万向支架的常平架，形成了现代的航海罗盘乃至航空、航天罗盘。中国为全人类航行能力的提高，作出了不可磨灭的贡献。

Invention of Compass Needle greatly improved man's capability of all-weather navigation. This outstanding invention of China was transmitted to Arab countries via the Silk Road and then to Europe by the Arab between the end of the 12th Century and the 13th Century. Between the 14th Century and the 16th Century, marine compass was provided with gimbal mounting in Europe. Modern marine compass and even air compass and spaceflight compass were formed. The Chinese made irreplaceable contribution to improvement of navigation capability of human beings.

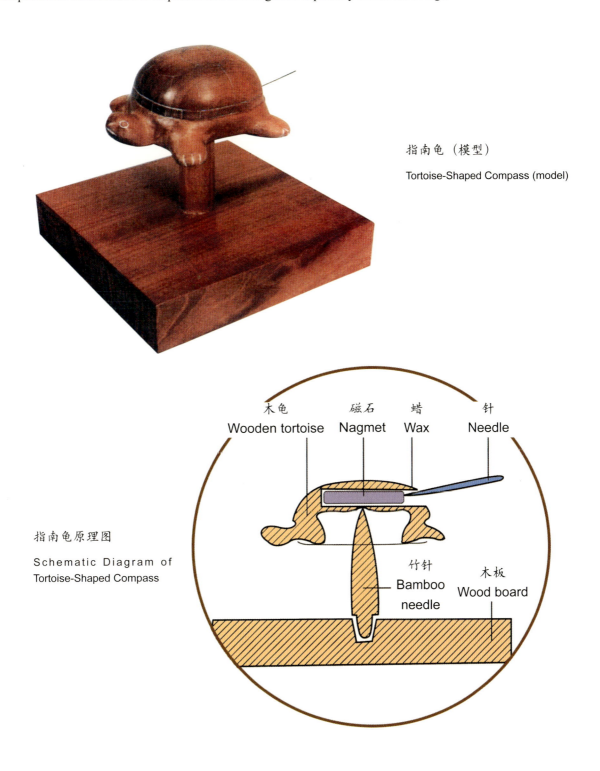

指南龟（模型）

Tortoise-Shaped Compass (model)

木龟　　　　磁石　　蜡　　　针
Wooden tortoise　Nagmet　Wax　Needle

指南龟原理图

Schematic Diagram of Tortoise-Shaped Compass

竹针
Bamboo needle

木板
Wood board

第四节 度量衡
Section 4　Weights and Measures

　　"度量衡"这一名称出自《尚书·虞书·舜典》。后来经《汉书·律历志》引用（"审度"、"嘉量"、"衡权"），因而固定下来，沿用至今。度量衡的概念可以追溯到遥远的古代。早在新石器时代，已有长度的测量。传说黄帝"设五量"（《大戴礼记·五帝德》），后人注释五量为"权衡、斗斛、尺丈、里步、十百"。

　　The designation weights and measures was from *Shangshu Yushu Shundian* (Documents of the Elder, The Book of Yu, The Canon of Shun). It was then cited in the *History of the Han Dynasty, the Studies of Music and the State of Calendar* as "*Shendu* (ruler)", "*Jialiang* (standard measures)"and "*Hengquan* (steelyard)" and fixed for continuous use till now. The concept of weights and measures can date back to primitive times. Early in the Neolithic Age, length measurement had occurred. It is said that the Yellow Emperor established the "Five Weights and Measures" [*Da Dai Liji·Wudi De* (Book of Rites with Commentaries of Dai De, The virtue of the Five Emperors)], which were explained as "*Quanheng* (scale), *Douhu* (measure for measuring decalities of grain), *Chizhang* (*chi*-ruler), *Libu* (*li*-step measure) and *Shibai* (measure in tens and hundreds)" by later generations.

　　早期度量衡计量单位相当粗糙。度量衡单位的形成，有人认为最初的一些规定直接取自人体的某些部位。如《孔子家语》"布指知寸，布手知尺，舒肘知寻"，《小尔雅》"一手之盛谓之溢，两手谓之掬"，以此确定长度及容量的标准。也有人认为与某些自然物有关，以积黍或丝、毛之类进行度量，而且因人因物而异。《世本·帝系》、《尚书》记载可能是在4000多年前的帝舜时代，进行过一次规模较大的统一度量衡的活动。在商周时代即已普遍使用度量器具，古遗址出土的商代骨尺和牙尺，已能进行较为准确的长度计量并使用了先进的十进位制。春秋战国时期，各国有各国的度量衡制，存在差异。秦始皇统一六国后，进行了统一度量衡的工作，颁布了统一度量衡的诏书，废除六国旧制，并将它铭刻在一批官定的度量衡器上，作为标准在全国推行，还规定了严格的管理制度。这些政策、措施，有利于繁荣社会经济，促进度量衡制度本身的完善和进步。[新]王莽始建国元年（公元9年），刘歆仿战国时代的栗式量制造了铜嘉量，集度、量、衡、律及数等多种标准于一身，并成为后世历代王朝修订度量衡制度的重要参考依据。

　　Since early measurement unit of weights and measures was rough, some people held that some initial regulations on establishment of unit of weights and measures were originated from some sites on human body. For example, it was recorded in *Kongzi Jiayu* (The School Sayings of Confucius) that "*cun* is equal to width of a finger, *chi* is equal to spacing between two stretching fingers and *xun* is equal to length between two stretching arms". It was recorded in *Xiao Erya* that "*Yi* refers to the volume that a hand can hold and *Ju* refer to the volume that two hands can hold". It was taken as the standards to determine length and volume. Other people also thought that it had something to do with some natural objects and used as measurement unit (*Si* and *Mao*). It was variable according to different people and different objects. It was recorded in *Shiben*, *Dixi* (The Book of Lineages, Emperor) and *Shangshu* that it might be in Emperor Shun's regime more than 4000 years ago，that a large-scale unification activity of weights and measures was conducted. Measuring instrumnets had been universally used in the Shang and Zhou Dynasties in China. Bone ruler and tooth ruler of the Shang Dynasty unearthed from ancient sites indicate that people had been able to perform relatively accurate length calculation and used advanced decimal system. In the Spring and Autumn Period and the Warring States Period, various countries had respective system of weights and measures, but different from each other. After the First Emperor of the Qin Dynasty unified the six countries, he carried out unification of weights and measures. He issued a decree for unification of weights and measures to abrogate the former systems of the six countries and engrave a batch of official measures and weights with the inscription as standard to be promoted in the Qin and established stringent management system. The policies and measures were favorable for obtaining prosperous social economy and facilitating improvement and advancement of measuring system. In the first year of establishment of Xin by Wang Mang (9 AD), Liu Xin made Bronze Standard Capacity Measure integrating multiple standards including weights and measures, music and maths by imitating Lishi Weight of the Warring States Period. The Bronze Standard Capacity Measure was the important reference for later dynasties to modify the measurement system.

战国秦商鞅铜方升　这是商鞅为统一秦国度量衡而制造的标准量器。以16.2立方寸的容积定为一升。上海博物馆藏。

Square Bronze Sheng Capacity Measure by Shang Yang of the Warring States Period: It was a standard measure made by Shang Yang for unification of weights and measures in the Qin Dynasty. One Sheng was defined as volume of 16.2 cubic *cun*. It is collection of Shanghai Museum.

秦始皇诏陶量　秦国量器。高9.4cm，口径20.4cm，容2000mL（小斗）。为一斗量。外壁刻有秦王政二十六年（前221年）的诏书："廿六年，皇帝尽并兼天下诸侯，黔首大安，立号为皇帝，乃诏丞相状、绾、法度量则不壹歉疑者，皆明壹之。"山东省博物馆藏。

Ceramic measure with a Decree by the First Emperor of the Qin Dynasty: It was a measure of the Qin. It is 9.4 cm high with aperture of 20.4 cm and can contain 2000 mL (millet). It is a decalitre-measure. It was engraved with imperial decree in the 26th year of the period of the First Emperor (221 BC) of the Qing Dynasty on the outer wall that "In the 26th year, the Emperor has conquered all vassal states to let people live in peace and established the title of emperor. Therefore, imperial edict is given to Prime Ministers Wei Zhuang and Wang Wan to definitely unify non-unified weights and measures by law". It is collection of Shandong Provincial Museum.

战国楚木衡和铜环权　木衡长27cm，中点穿丝提纽。距木衡两端各0.7cm处，用长9cm的丝线各系一个直径为4cm的铜盘。铜环权大小共9枚，重量大体以倍数递增，分别为一铢、二铢、三铢、六铢、十二铢、一两、二两、四两、半斤。总重约250g，为楚制一斤。湖南省博物馆藏。

Wooden measure and bronze-ring weight of Chu of the Warring States Period: The wooden measure is 27 cm long with rope through the center point to lift button. Two 9 cm-long threads are used to tie one bronze pan with diameter of 4 cm at position 0.7 cm from both ends of the wooden measure respectively. There are totally 9 bronze-ring weights of different sizes with weight approximately increasing by times, as one *zhu*, two *zhu*, three *zhu*, six *zhu*, twelve *zhu*, one *liang*, two *liang*, four *liang* and half *jin*. It has total weight of about 250g, equal to one *jin* in unit system of Chu. It is collection of Hunan Provincial Museum.

[新]王莽铜嘉量 青铜制，[新]王莽始建国元年（公元9年）铸。此器形制与《汉书·律历志》所记"上为斛，下为斗，左耳为升。右耳为合、龠"相符。器壁正面有81字总铭。每一种量器又各有分铭，记有五量的径、深、底面积和容积。按《汉书·律历志》记，以黄钟律管的容量作为一龠的容量标准，二龠为合，十合为升，十升为斗，十斗为斛。

Bronze Standard Capacity Measure of Xin Dynasty of Wangmang's regime: It was made of bronze by casting in the first year of establishment of Xin Dynasty (9 AD). Form and system of the measure is consistent with recording in the *History of the Han Dynasty, the Studies of Music and the State of Calendar* that "the upper part is Hu, the low part is *Dou*, the left side is *Sheng*, and the right side is *He* or *Yue*". General inscription of 81 characters is on the front face of the wall. Each weight is provided with respective inscription, indicating diameter, depth, surface area and volume of the five weights. According to recording in the *Hanshu·Lülizhi* of bronze bell is taken as volume standard of one Yue, and two Yue is equal to He, ten He is equal to Sheng, ten Sheng is equal to Dou, and ten Dou is equal to Hu.

王莽铜卡尺
Copper Caliper of Wang Mang's Regime

王莽新朝时一种铜制量具，其结构和功能相当于现代外卡尺。这个卡尺由固定尺、滑动尺等组成；竖用，滑动尺可上下移动，背面刻有铭文"始建国元年正月癸酉朔日制。"始建国元年即公元9年。是迄今发现的世界最早的游标量具，令人惊叹。

It was a copper measuring instrument in Xin Dynasty of Wang Mang's regime, with structure and function equivalent to modern outside calipers. The caliper consists of fixed ruler and sliding ruler, etc. It is used vertically with sliding ruler moving up and down. There is inscription of "made in the first day of Gui You of the first month of the lunar year of the first year of establishment of Xin" on the back. The first year of establishment of Xin Dynasty is 9 AD. It is the world's earliest vernier measuring instrument so far, marvelous.

[新]王莽始建国元年制造的外卡规

Outside Caliper Made in the First Year of
Establishment of Xin　Dynasty by Wang
Mang

铜卡尺示意图（王莽时期制造）

Copper Caliper (made in Wang Mang's
regime)

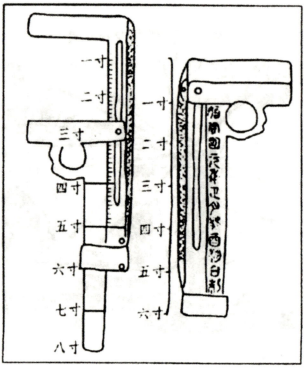

第八章 古代纺织机械
Chapter 8 Ancient Textile Machinery

中国的纺织技术，历史悠久，闻名于世。远在六七千年前，人们就会用麻、葛纤维为原料进行纺织，公元前16世纪（殷商时期），产生了织花工艺，公元前2世纪（西汉）以后，提花机发明，纺织技术迅速提高，不仅织出了薄如蝉翼的罗纱，还能织出构图千变万化的锦缎。织造技术的进步，直接与纺织机械的进步相关。

China has a long history of textile technology well known all over the world. Even six to seven thousand years ago, people could use raw materials of hemp and ko-hemp fibre for spinning. In the 16th Century BC (the Shang Dynasty), inweaving technology occurred. After the Second Century BC (the Western Han Dynasty), jacquard loom was invented to allow quick improvement of textile technology. Not only yarn as thin as cicada's wing can be woven, but also brocade with variant composition could be woven. Advancement of textile technology was directly related to advancement of textile machinery.

第一节 纺车和水力大纺车
Section 1 Spinning Wheel and Water Power Spinning Wheel

中国在汉代或更早些时候，完成了以手摇纺车对原始手工劳动"纺专"的替代。所谓"纺专"，是由骨质、陶质或石质制成的圆块，叫"专盘"，中间有一个孔，可插一个杆叫"专杆"，生产效率极低。手摇纺车的结构虽然比较简单，但是纺纱的效果比"纺专"提高约20倍。手摇纺车用绳轮传动，证明中国早在两千年前就在工具机上使用绳传动了。西汉杨雄（前53—18年）所著的《方言》就已提到叫"繀车"和"道轨"的这种手摇纺车。

In the Han Dynasty or earlier, substitution of cord wheel for primitive hand labor "Special Spinning Unit" was completed in China. The so-called "Special Spinning Unit" was circular block made of bone, ceramics or stone. It was also called "Special Plate" with a hole in the center to hold a bar named "Special Bar". It has extremely low productivity effect. The cord wheel has simple structure, but its spinning effect was about 20 times as that of "Special Spinning Unit". The cord wheel had been driven by rope pulley, proving that even two thousand years ago, ropes were used for driving machine tools in China. This cord wheel named "reeling machine" and "spin-orbit coupling" was mentioned in *Fangyan* (Dialects) written by Yang Xiong (53 BC—18 AD) of the Western Han Dynasty.

在手摇纺车的基础上不断前进，东晋著名画家顾恺之（约345—406年）的一幅画上已出现了脚踏纺车，特别是宋元时期，纺机有了大的改进。汉代的手摇纺车只能纺一个纱锭；东晋（3—4世纪）的脚踏纺车可纺3—5个纱锭，宋末元初（13世纪）发明的大纺车，纱锭增加到30多锭，它的传动已经采用和现在的龙带式传动相仿的集体传动了，特别是水转大纺车，其动力由人力、畜力改为水力推动，比用陆车既便且省。

纺车图　这幅汉墓壁画，反映了当时所用纺纱机具的状况。

Picture of Spinning Wheel: This picture from murals of tomb of the Han Dynasty reflects the situation of spinning machine tools used at that time.

宋末元初发明的水转大纺车（取自《纺织史话》）

Water Power Spinning Wheel Invented between the Late Song Dynasty and the Early Yuan Dynasty (from *Textile History*)

纺机的效率不断提高，汉代的手摇单绽纺车，一天能纺棉纱三到五两，脚踏纺车三锭也只七八两，纺麻五锭也不过二斤，而纺麻的大纺车一昼夜可纺一百斤。水转大纺车的发明，极大地提高了纺机效率，满足了宋元民间纺织专业户和大批量生产的需要，是纺织机械制造史上一个划时代的成就。在欧洲直到1769年才由英国人瑞恰德·阿克莱（Richard Arkwright）制造出水力纺机，建立了欧洲第一个水力纺纱厂。

Textile technology kept advancing based on cord wheel. Treadle-operated spindle-wheel occurred on a drawing of Gu Kaizhi (345—406 CA), famous painter in the Eastern Jin Dynasty. Especially in the Song and Yuan Dynasties, spinning wheel was greatly improved. For cord wheel of the Han Dynasty, only one spindle can be used for spinning. For treadle-operated spindle-wheel of the Eastern Jin Dynasty (3—4th Century), three to five spindles can be used for spinning. For Water Power Spinning Wheel invented between the late Song Dynasty and the early Yuan Dynasty (13th Century), the number of spindles was increased to more than 30. It was provided with collective drive similar to modern apron belt drive. In particular, Water Power Spinning Wheel was driven by water power instead of manpower and animal power, which was more convenient and

economical than land machines. Efficiency of spinning machine was continuously improved. For single-spindle cord wheel of the Han Dynasty, three to five *liang* of cotton yarn can be spun per day for cotton spinning, and only seven to eight *liang* of cotton yarn can be spun by treadle-operated spindle-wheel with three spindles per day; no more than two *jin* of cotton yarn can be spun by machine with five spindles for hemp spinning while Water Power Spinning Wheel for hemp spinning can be used to spin a hundred *jin* of cotton yarn in a whole day and night. Invention of Water Power Spinning Wheel helped greatly improve efficiency of spinning machine to meet demand of folk textile specialized households and mass production in the Song and Yuan Dynasties. It is an epochmaking achievement in manufacture history of textile machinery. Water power spinning machine was not made by Richard Arkwright from UK in Europe until 1769. Then the first water power spinning factory was established in Europe.

水转大纺车（模型）

Water Power Spinning Wheel（model）

第二节　织机和提花机
Section 2　Loom and Jacquard Loom

提花机，又称花机、花机子，是一种人力织造提花织物的机械，也是古代织造技术机械的最高成就。

Tihuaji (jacquard loom) was also called *Huaji* and *Huajizi*. It is a machine for manually weaving jacquard fabric as the top achievement of ancient weaving machinery.

1975年，在浙江余姚河姆渡新石器时代遗址出土了原始织机的工具，这种原始织机叫踞机或腰机。距今已有六千多年，是世界上发现最早的原始织布工具，它是现代织布机的始祖，至今仍可在某些少数民族地区见到。在河南安阳殷墟大司空村的殷商王族墓葬中发现了几何图纹的提花织品"绮"；到了周代，已经能织造多色提花的锦，表明中国的原始织机到周代已发展为提花机械。

In 1975, a primitive weaving machine tool was unearthed from Hemudu Neolithic Age site in Yuyao, Zhejiang Province. The primitive loom was called *Juji* (loom with the operator in a crouching position) or *Yaoji* (waist loom). It was used more than 6 thousand years ago as the earliest primitive weaving tool discovered in the world. It is the origin of modern looms and can be seen in some minority areas even now. Jacquard fabric "*Qi* (patterned fabric)" with geometrical patterns was found in tomb of imperial kinsman of the Shang Dynasty in Dasikong Village of Yinxu Site in Anyang, Henan Province. Up to the Zhou Dynasty, multicolor jacquard damask can be woven. This reflects development process from primitive loom to jacquard machinery in the Zhou Dynasty in China.

新石器时代出现的原始织机，至今仍可在某些少数民族地区看到。这是海南黎族妇女用原始织机织布的照片。

Primitive loom occurring in the Neolithic Age: It can be seen in some minority areas even now. The picture illustrates the scene that a woman of Li Nationality in Hainan is weaving by primitive loom.

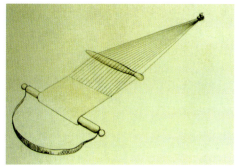

　　提花机装有分别升降各根经纱的提花机构，可用于织造复杂的大花纹织物。从商代使用手工提花法，发展为多踪多蹑及束综两种提花机。多踪多蹑提花机出现于战国时期。通常采用蹑（脚踏板）控制一综（吊起经线的装置）来织制花纹，为了织出花纹，就增加综框的数目，两片综框只能织出平纹组织，3—4片综框能织出斜纹组织，5片以上的综框才能织出缎纹组织。为织造复杂的、花形循环较大的花，多踪多蹑的花机逐步形成。据《西京杂记》载西汉昭帝末年，有巨鹿人陈宝光妻所织散花绫"机用一百二十蹑"，这样的多踪多蹑提花机织造起来十分繁琐，不能适应经济发展的需要。三国时曹魏初年，扶风（今陕西兴平）的马钧以"旧绫机丧功费日乃思绫机之变"，将多踪多蹑提花机改革成十二综蹑，采用束综提花的方法，既方便了操作，又提高了效率。这种提花机直到近代仍有使用。但从长沙马王堆汉墓出土的绒圈锦说

明，汉初已使用束综提花机。到宋代，这种提花机已发展得相当完善，南宋楼璹《耕织图》、元薛景石《梓人遗制》及明代宋应星的《天工开物·乃服篇》均有记述。此时提花机的结构已相当完善，织造时一人高跨机顶专管提花，另一人司织，两人密切合作，完成复杂的手工操作。这种提花机自战国秦汉出现以来，直到18世纪末，始终处于世界领先地位。提花机经丝绸之路传入西方。2010年"上海世博会"江苏馆还有陈列。

Jacquard loom was provided with pattern mechanism for ascending and descending of various warp yarns respectively. It can be used to weave complicated jacquard fabric. Manual jacquard weaving method used in the Shang Dynasty was developed to multi-heddle and step jacquard loom and draw loom. Multi-heddle and step jacquard loom occurred in the Warring States Period. Usually treadle was used to control one heddle (device for drawing up warp threads) to weave patterns. To weave patterns, the number of heald frames was increased for two heald frames can only be used to produce plain weave, three to four heald frames can be used to produce twill weave and only more than 5 heald frames can be used to produce satin weave. Multi-heddle and step jacquard loom was gradually formed in order to weave complicated patterns with large pattern design recurrence. According to recording in *Xijing Zaji* (Miscellaneous Records of the Western Capital), in the late period of Emperor Zhao of the Western Han Dynasty, wife of Chen Baoguang in Julu wove damask silk with design of scattered flowers by "loom with 120 treadles". Such a multi-heddle and step jacquard loom provided sophisticated operation for weaving, failing to meet requirements for economic development. In the early Wei Dynasty during the Three Kingdoms period, Ma Jun in Fufeng (present Xingping, Shaanxi Province) "thought of alternation of old damask loom which required great efforts and much time". He modified multi-heddle and step jacquard loom into 12-damask loom and also provided convenient operation and higher efficiency by draw jacquard weaving. This jacquard loom was still used in recent times. However, Pile-loop Brocade unearthed from the tombs of the Western Han Dynasty at Mawangdui indicates that jacquard loom was used in the early Han Dynasty. Up to the Song Dynasty, this jacquard loom had been fully developed. It was recorded and described by Lou Shu of the Southern Song Dynasty in his *Illustrations of Plowing and Weaving*, Xue Jingshi of the Yuan Dynasty in his *Ziren Yizhi* (Time-Honoured Institutions of Carpenters) and Song Yingxing of the Ming Dynasty in his *Tiangong Kaiwu*, *Weaving chapter*. At that time, jacquard loom had perfect structure. In weaving, one person took charge of jacquard weaving side sitting high on top of loom and the other person took charge of weaving to have close cooperation to complete sophisticated hand operation. This jacquard loom kept its leading position in the world from occurrence in the Warring States Period and Qin and Han Dynasties to the late 18th Century. Jacquard loom was transmitted to western countries via the Silk Road. It was still on display in the Jiangsu Pavilion of Expro 2010 Shanghai China.

另外，在提花技术中最难掌握的要算结花本。花本是提花机上贮纹样信息的一套程序。《天工开物》中说："凡工匠结花本者，心计最精巧。画师先画何等花色于纸上，结本者以丝线随画量度，算计分寸秒而结成之，张悬花楼之上。"就是说人们如果想把设计好的图案重现在织物上，得按图案使成千上万根经线有规律地交互上下提

综，几十种结线有次序地横穿排列，作成一整套花纹记忆装置。花本是古代纺织工匠的一项重要贡献，对现代电脑发展中程序控制与存储技术的发明有启示作用。

In addition, original design production can be considered the most difficult jacquard weaving technique. Original design is a set of programs on jacquard loom for storing information on pattern design. It was recorded in the *Tiangong Kaiwu* that "Where craftsman wants to produce original design, he must be specially careful. The painter draws some patterns on paper and the original designer measures with threads as per the pattern and produces the original design by concluding the law subtly and hangs it on the pattern sheet". It means that where people want to reproduce the designed pattern on the fabric, they have to make thousands of warp threads regularly and alternately lift heddles according to the pattern and arrange tens of tie lines in order crossing in order to make a complete set of pattern storage device. Original design is an important contribution of spinning craftsmen. It inspired invention of programmed control and storage technology in modern computer development.

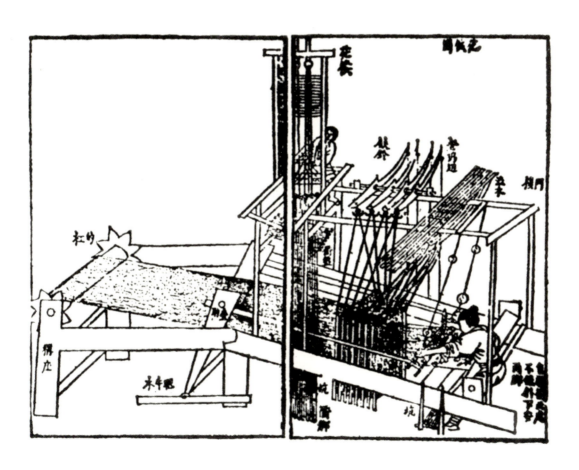

提花机图（《天工开物》）

Picture of Jacquard Loom from *Tiangong Kaiwu*

明代提花机（《中华科技五千年》）

Jacquard loom of the Ming Dynasty（from the *History of Science and Technology during Five Thousand Years in China*）

第九章 印刷术和古代印刷机械
Chapter 9 Printing and Ancient Printing Machinery

印刷术和火药、指南针、纸，并称中国古代科学技术的四大发明。印刷术的发明表现在学术方面，表现在推动中国和全世界文明发展中起了巨大作用，其对社会的影响，非任何其他古代发明所能比拟。

The four great inventions of ancient China are printing, gunpowder, compass, and papermaking. In terms of scientific learning, invention of printing played an important part in facilitating civilization development of China and the whole world. Its influence on the society is incomparable for any other ancient inventions.

第一节 雕版印刷
Section 1 Block Printing

自秦代统一文字后，汉字发展迅速，东汉《说文解字》收字9353个，南北朝成书的《玉篇》收字2.2万余个。著作也越来越多，《汉书·艺文志》收各类著作14994卷，《隋书·经籍志》收50889卷，隋内府藏书37万卷。西汉末年中国已有人口近6000万，东汉仅太学生就有5万多。这么多人，这么多著作，这么多文字，在印刷术发明前，文化的传播主要靠手工抄写书籍，实在是麻烦得很。因此，印刷术在中国发明有其时代背景。

Since unification of characters in the Qin Dynasty, the Chinese characters kept rapid development. 9353 characters were collected in *Shuo Wen Jie Zi* (exegesis of characters) of the Eastern Han Dynasty and about 22 thousand characters were collected in *Yupian* (Jade Chapters) written in the Southern and Northern Dynasty. As more and more works were written, 14994 volumes of various works were collected in the *History of the Han Dynasty, Record of Literature* and Arts; 50889 volumes of works were collected in the *History of the Sui Dynasty, Records of Confucian Classics* and 370 thousand volumes of books were collected in the imperial storehouse of the Sui Dynasty. In the late Western Han Dynasty, China had a population of nearly 60 million while there were more than 50 thousand imperial college students in the Eastern Han Dynasty without mentioning others. With such a large quantity of people, works and characters, it was complicated to transmit culture mainly by manually transcribing books before the printing was invented. Therefore, the printing was invented in China under special background of times.

印刷术首先是雕版印刷的发明，根据《隋书》和《北史》等文献记载，雕版印刷发明于隋代（598—618年）的可能性较大。距今已有1300多年历史。西汉时期发明了纸、东汉时期出现了松烟墨，为印刷术的产生准备了物质基础；战国时期出现的铸铜印、琢玉印和拍印技术，西汉时期成熟的印染工艺，为雕版印刷提供了技术准备。印章、拓印、印染技术三者相互启发、融合，雕版印刷技术应运而生。雕版印刷起源于隋朝至唐初，唐初的印刷品已有出土，636—637年唐太宗将

"牢阳司冠" 铜印
（战国）

Bronze stamp "*Lao Yang Si Guan*" (the Warring States Period)

其皇后的遗作《女则》刻印成书；1966年在韩国庆州佛国寺释迦石塔发现的《无垢净光大陀罗尼经》汉译本，因其经文中有武则天称帝时期推行的制字，可定为武周时期（690—704年）刻本；1907年甘肃敦煌石窟中发现的一本印刷精美的《金刚经》，末尾题有唐"咸通九年四月十五日"等字样（868年），这是目前世界上最早的有明确日期记载的印刷品。

For the printing, block printing was initially invented. According to recording in literatures such as the *History of the Sui Dynasty and the History of Northern Dynasties*, block printing was likely to be invented in the Sui Dynasty (598—618) more than 1300 years ago. Paper was invented in the Western Han Dynasty and pine-soot ink occurred in the Eastern Han Dynasty, providing material foundation for generation of printing. Techniques of cast bronze printing, carved jade printing and reprinting by beating occurred in the Warring States Period and dye printing became mature in the Western Han Dynasty, providing technical foundation for engraving printing. With inspiration and interfusion of techniques of stamp engraving, rubbing and dye printing to each other, block printing technology emerged as the times require. Block printing was originated between the Sui Dynasty and the early Tang Dynasty. There have

"齐官司丞"封泥（汉代）

Inkpad "*Qi Guan Si Cheng*" (the Han Dynasty)

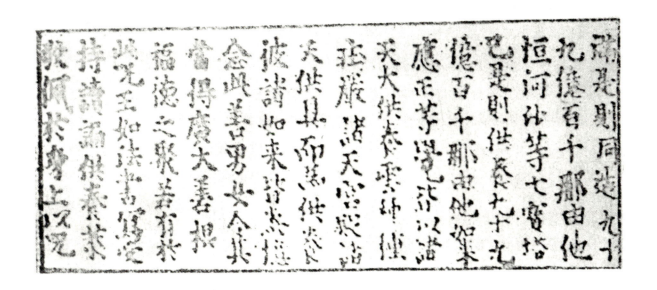

无垢净光大陀罗尼经（局部复制品）唐武周时期（690—704年）的雕版印刷品。1966年韩国庆州佛国寺释迦石塔内发现。

Aryarasmi–vimalvi Suddha–prabhā Nāma–dhārani Sutra (partial reproduction): It is engraving printed work of Wu-Zhou period of the Tang Dynasty (690—704). It was discovered in Sakyamuni Pagoda of Bulguksa Temple in Gyeongju, South Korea in 1966.

been unearthed printed works of the early Tang Dynasty. Between 636 and 637, Emperor Taizong of the Tang Dynasty block printed the empress's posthumous work *Nüze* (Examples for Women) into books. The Chinese translation of *Aryarasmi-vimalvi Suddha-prabh ā N ā ma-dh ā rani Sutra* discovered in Sakyamuni Pagoda of Bulguksa Temple in Gyeongju, South Korea in 1966 can be determined as block-printed edition of the Wu-Zhou period (690—704) for there were original characters promoted when Wu Zetian acted as the emperor. In 1907, a beautifully printed book *Diamond Sutra* was discovered in Dunhuang Grottoes in Gansu Province, with inscription of "April 15 of the 9th year of Xiantong period（868）" (of the Tang Dynasty) in the end. It is the world's earliest printed work with definitely recorded date so far.

第二节　活字印刷
Section 2　Movable-Type Printing

　　雕版印刷从出现到兴盛，经历了4个多世纪。11世纪中叶，中国发明了活字印刷术。雕版印刷对文化的传播起了很大作用，但耗费人力、物力和时间，活字印刷正好避免了雕版印刷的不足。

It was more than four centuries that block printing emerged and became prosperous. In the middle 11th Century, movable-type printing was invented in China. Block printing greatly facilitated cultural transmission, but required large quantities of human resources and material resources and much time. It was movable-type printing that overcame the shortcomings of block printing.

　　用活字印刷这种思想，很早就有了。秦始皇统一全国度量衡，陶量器上用木戳印四十字的诏书，考古学家认为，这是中国活字排印的开始，但当时未能广泛应用。古代的印章对活字印刷也有一定启示作用。沈括在《梦溪笔谈》中记叙了布衣（平民）毕昇在北宋庆历年间（1041—1048年）发明泥活字并用以印刷书籍的情况："庆历中，有布衣毕昇，又为活版。其法用胶泥刻字，薄如钱唇，每字为一印，火烧令坚。先设一铁板，其上以松脂蜡和纸灰之类冒之。欲印，则以一铁范置铁板上，乃密布字印。满铁范为一板，持就火炀之，药稍熔，则以一平板按其面，则字平如砥。若只印三二本，未为简易；若印数十百本，则极为神速。常作二铁板，一板印刷，一板已布字。此印者才毕，则第二板已具。更互用之，瞬息可就。"毕昇发明的这种泥活字印刷法，与雕版印刷比，工艺简单。使用方便，工效高，用材省，而且具备了制字、排版、印刷三个基本步骤，为近代活字印刷术的先驱。

The concept of movable-type printing occurred early. In nationwide unification of weights and measures by the first Emperor of the Qin Dynasty, the imperial decree of 40 characters was printed on ceramic measure by wood stamp, which was considered by archaeologists as the beginning of movable-type typesetting and printing in China but was not widely used at that time. Ancient stamp also inspired invention of movable-type printing. Shen Kuo in his *Mengxi Bitan* described invention of movable clay by simple-clothed person (common people) Bi Sheng in Qingli period (1041—1048) of the Northern Song Dynasty and application of it to book printing as follows: "In Qingli period, a simple-clothed person Bi Sheng made movable type by block characters with clay as thin as the edge of coins, each character being a stamp to be hardened by fire; placing an iron plate covered by pine resin wax and paper ash, etc.; and laying an iron mold on the iron plate immediately before printing to be densely covered by character stamps. When the iron mold was full of character stamps as one tablet, it was held close to flame; when the materials were slightly fused, a flat plate was used to press its surface to print characters as flat as whetstone. For printing several books, the method was not so easy; for printing tens or hundreds of books, it was marvelously quick. Usually two iron plates were prepared; when one is used for printing, the other one is being covered with arranged characters. When the printing is completed, the other plate was ready. Printing can be quickly completed by alternately using the two plates." Compared with block printing, the movable clay-type printing invented by Bi Sheng required simple processes. It was convenient, efficient and material saving. In addition, it was provided with three basic steps character making, typesetting and printing, and so is precursor of recent movable-type printing.

　　毕昇发明的活字印刷，当时未得到推广，但却流传下来了，1965年在浙江温州白

毕昇泥活字版
（模型）

Clay Type Plate
by Bi Sheng
(model)

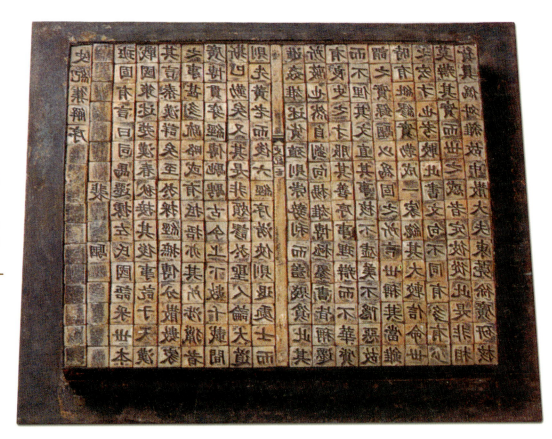

象塔内发现的刊本《佛说观无量寿佛经》经鉴定为北宋元符至崇宁（1100—1103年）年间的活字本。这是毕昇活字印刷术的最早历史见证。

Movable-type printing invented by Bi Sheng was not popularized at that time. However, his invention movable-type printing technology was handed down. Published version *Sutra on Visualization of the Buddha of Infinite Life* discovered in the White Elephant Pagoda in Wenzhou, Zhejiang Province in 1965 was determined as movable-type version between Yuanfu and Chongning periods (1100—1103) of the Northern Song Dynasty through identification. It is the earliest historical evidence for movable-type printing invented by Bi Sheng.

清道光年间（1821—1850年），安徽泾县翟金生根据《梦溪笔谈》关于泥活字的记载，制成泥活字10万多个，1844年印成了《泥版试用初编》。近年，北京图书馆发现用泥活字印的书；1962年于安徽徽州发现了翟式泥活字模。

Zhai Jinsheng in Jingxian County, Anhui Province of Daoguang period（1821—1850）of the Qing Dynasty, based on recording in the *Mengxi Bitan* on clay type, made more than 100 thousand clay types and printed the *First Compilation of Clay Tablet Probation* in 1844. In recent years, books printed with clay types have been discovered in Beijing Library; in 1962, the Zhai's clay type matrix was discovered in Huizhou, Anhui Province.

古维吾尔木活字　公元14世纪初元代的遗物，它说明木活字印书法已被维吾尔人熟练掌握。

Ancient Uigur Wooden Type: It is relic of the Yuan Dynasty in the 14th Century BC, reflecting that wooden-type printing technique had been well mastered by the Uigur at that time.

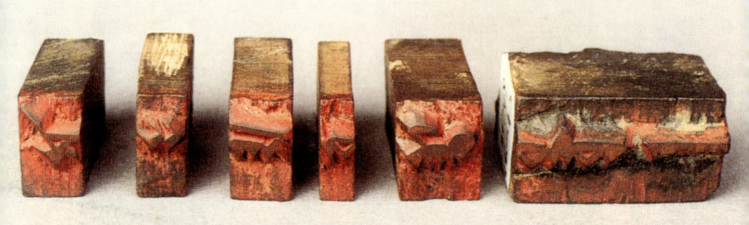

到了元代，农学家王祯创制木活字成功。皇庆年间（1312—1313年），王祯撰有《木活字印书法》；他还发明了转轮排字盘，又叫"韵盘"，用简单的机械，增加排字的效率。

Up to the Yuan Dynasty, agriculturist Wang Zhen successfully created wooden type. In Huangqing period (1312—1313), Wang Zhen wrote *Wooden-type Printing Technique* and invented rotating composing stick, which was also called "Yunpan" to use simple machines to prove type-setting efficiency.

甘肃敦煌莫高窟内曾发现元代维吾尔活字。这是迄今发现的年代最早的木活字遗物，说明维吾尔人已熟练掌握木活字印刷术。

Uigur type of the Yuan Dynasty was discovered in DunHuang MoGao Grottoes, Gansu Province. It was the earliest wooden type relic so far, indicating that the Uigur had well mastered wooden-type printing.

活字印刷的另一发展，是用金属材料制成活字，到明孝宗弘治年间（1488—1505年），铜活字正式流行于江南一带。

中国的活字印刷术经由我国新疆传入欧洲，1454年德国谷腾堡（J. Gutenberg，1398—1468年）受中国活字印刷的影响，用铅、锡、锑的合金制成活字来印书，比毕昇要晚400多年。活字印刷术是世界印刷术史上最重要的发明，是中国对世界文明所作出的伟大贡献。

Another development of movable-type printing was making type with metal materials Up to Hongzhi period of Emperor Xiaozong (1488—1505) of the Ming Dynasty, bronze type was formally popular in areas south of the Yangtze River. Movable-type printing of China was transmitted to Europe via Xinjiang Uyghur Autonomous Region. German J. Gutenberg (1398—1468), affected by movable-type printing of China, made type with alloy of lead, tin and stibium for printing books (1454), which was more than 400 years later than that by Bi Sheng. Movable-type printing is the most important invention in the world printing history as well as a great contribution made by China to the world civilization.

转轮排字盘（模型） 王祯研究制作的放置木活字的工具。排字者坐于两个转轮排字盘之间，木活字以音韵分类排列于字盘之上。拣字时转动字盘，依照稿本拣出所需木活字，排于书版之上。印刷完毕后，将活字还原在转轮排字盘上。这种转轮排字盘提高了拣排字效率。中国历史博物馆藏。

Rotating Composing Stick(Typesetting Disc) (model): It is a tool researched and made by Wang Zhen for placing wooden types. Type setter sits between two rotating composing sticks and arranges wooden types on the plates according to category by phonology. In selecting, the plates are rotated to pick out the wooden types required based on manuscript and arrange them on book printing plate. After completion of printing, the types will be returned to the rotating composing stick. The rotating composing stick helps improve character selecting and arranging efficiency. It is collection of the National Museum of Chinese History.

第十章 古代运输车辆
Chapter 10 Transport Vehicles in Ancient Times

　　上古时代的运输，全靠手提、肩杠、背负、撬引完成。后来又以马牛驮运。随着生产发展、社会进步，产品交易不断增多，产生了对运输工具的需求，创造出滚木、轮与轴，最后出现了陆地运输车辆。原始的车轮没有车辐，这种车轮在汉、唐时代著作中称之为"辁"。夏代前后出现了无辐条的辁和有辐条的车轮。由辁到轮，车辆的行走部件发生了一次大变革，为殷代造车奠定了基础。商代，我国已经能制造相当高级的两轮车，且车轮有辐条，结构精致华美；周代采用了油脂作为轴承的润滑材料；春秋战国时期出现了高架车辆、巢车等新型车辆。1980年出土的秦始皇陵铜车马，代表了当时车辆制造的最高工艺水平。汉代车辆种类很多，轺车是东汉时通用的交通工具，汉代马车上用的是先进的胸带式系驾法，当时欧洲采用的多是效率较低的颈带式系驾，而采用胸带式系驾法要晚于中国6个多世纪。汉朝以后出现了采用齿轮传动的指南车和记里鼓车，汉魏时期盛行独轮车，晋朝盛行牛车。

Transport was fully completed by hand holding, shouldering, back carrying and bar dragging in ancient times. Cattle and horses were used for pack later. With productivity development and social progression, product trade was continuously increased to require transport tools. Rolling log, wheel and axle were created and overland transport vehicles occurred eventually. Primitive vehicle wheel did not have any spoke. The wheel was called "*Quan* (the wooden wheel without spoke)" in works of the Han Dynasty and the Tang Dynasty. Around the Xia Dynasty, *Quan* without spoke and wheel with spoke occurred. From *Quan* to wheel, running parts of vehicles had been subject to a significant alternation. It provided solid foundation for vehicle manufacture in the Yin Dynasty. In the Shang Dynasty, advanced two wheels with spoke of elaborate structure had been manufactured in China. The Qin Shihuang Mausoleum copper combat chariots/horses unearthed in 1980 in China represents the highest technology level of vehicle manufacture at that time. There were diverse vehicles in the Han Dynasty. *Yaoche* (a light horse cart) is a universal vehicle in the Eastern Han Dynasty. Advanced chest-belt harness method was used for carriages in the Han Dynasty. In Europe, neck-strap harness with low efficiency was most used at that time, and application of chest-belt harness method was more than 6 centuries later than in China. Gear-

driven south-pointing carriage and *li*-recording drum carriage occurred after the Han Dynasty. Wheelbarrow prevailed in the Han and Wei Dynasties. Ox-cart prevailed in the Jin Dynasty.

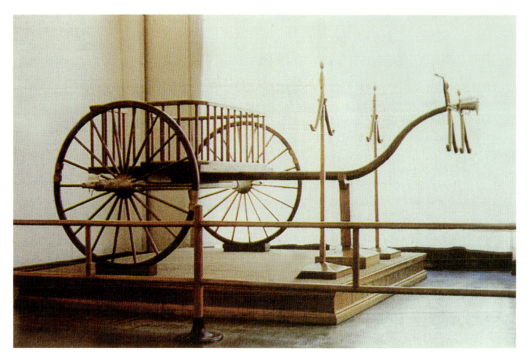

西周马车　这辆复原的车为独辕，一衡，四轭；轮大，车箱小，采用"轭式系驾法"，使四匹马曳引，可达到很高的速度。

Carriage of the Western Zhou Dynasty: The recovered carriage has a single shaft, one Weighting apparatus and four yokes with big wheels and small body. Driven by use of yoke and leather strap pulling technique, with four dragging horses of smooth breathing, it can reach a very high speed.

铜轺车　东汉时轺车已是通用的交通工具，甘肃武威擂台汉墓出土。

Copper *Yaoche*：*Yaoche* had been a universal vehicle in the Eastern Han Dynasty. It was unearthed from tomb of the Han Dynasty in Leitai, Wuwei, Gansu Province.

晋朝牛车 双轮双直辕，仅有9个轮辐，辕在轮轴之上较高处，车体较小。山西太原北齐墓出土。

Ox-cart of the Jin Dynasty: It has two wheels and two straight shafts with only 9 spokes. Shafts are high above wheel axles. The body is small. It was unearthed from tomb of the Northern Qi Dynasty in Taiyuan, Shanxi Province.

第一节　秦始皇陵铜车马
Section 1　The Qin Shihuang Mausoleum Copper Combat Chariots/Horses

秦始皇陵铜车马，公元前2世纪秦代制造，1980年出土于西安秦始皇陵墓西侧。

They were made in the Qin Dynasty in the 2nd Century BC and unearthed on the western side of Mausoleum of the First Emperor of the Qin Dynasty in Xi'an in 1980.

大型彩绘铜车马共两乘，一号铜车马是战车，二号铜车马是安车。车、马、驭手均为铸造成型，鞍上有金银错纹饰，均按1:2的比例制造，造型完全与真实车马相同，制作精良，外形美观，神情生动。它的制作体现了2200年前中国古代劳动人民精湛的铸造、金属加工和高水平的组装技术，是中国机械史的瑰宝，被誉为世界奇观之一，影响巨大。

There are two large painted copper chariots and harness in total. No. 1 copper chariot and harness was a chariot and No. 2 copper chariot and harness was a high-fronted, curtained carriage. Chariots, horses and drivers were formed by casting. Saddles were inlaid with gold and silver patterns. All were made as per scale of 1:2 in the shape identical to real chariots and horses, with elaborate workmanship, attractive appearance and vivid expression. Its manufacture reflects superb casting and metal working and advanced assembling technology of working people in ancient China 2200 years ago. It is a treasure in machinery history in China and famed Marvelous Spectacle of the World for its great influence.

铜车马制造工艺复杂，技术水平高，反映了秦代高度发达的车辆配置。更展示了精湛的铸造工艺、金属加工工艺和连接组装工艺。如热加工工艺方面，车辆篷盖的铸造，一号车的车篷盖面积很大，长178cm、宽129.5cm，但厚不足4mm，而且是拱形，形状复杂，其铸造极为困难，但成功地解决了这一难题，说明当时铸造水平之高。冷加工工艺，应用了钻、凿、锉、磨、雕刻等加工方法，做工精致。组装工艺，铜车马很复杂，仅二号车马就有3462个零部件（包括金银制零件1720件），采用了铸接、焊接、嵌接、插接、铆接、销接、活绞页连接及过盈配合等多种工艺，展示了很高的工艺技巧。

The copper chariots and harness was made by complicated processes which reflected high technology level and highly developed vehicle configuration in the Qin Dynasty and even superb casting technology, metal working technology and connection assembling technology. In terms of hot-working technology, for casting of ceiling cover of vehicles, No. 1 copper chariot and harness had a ceiling cover occupying a very large area with length of 178 cm and width of 129.5 cm, but the cover thickness was less than 4 mm in complicated arched shape; it is very difficult to successfully cast it, but the problem was well tackled at that time, indicating that casting technology was excellent at that time. In terms of cold-working technology, working methods were applied including drilling, chiseling, filing, grinding and engraving to provide elaborate workmanship. In terms of assembling technology, the copper chariots and harness was very complicated. Only for No. 2 copper chariot and harness, 3462 parts (including 1720 gold and silver parts) were used, and multiple techniques were applied including cast bonding, welding, scarfing, splicing, riveting, doweling, movable-hinge connection and interference fit, showing superb technological skills.

它的制作过程的标准化，反映在设计、取材、工艺各个方面的要求都极为严格。秦陵铜车马出土的零件误差都很小。主要零件都经过精铸、连接、修补、打磨、抛光大致相同的工艺过程，保证零件尺寸误差及表面粗糙度都很小。估计当时对零件的质量有明确要求，具备一定的工艺装备和生产技术及检验制度，保证了机械设计标准化的实施。铜车马设计的标准化也体现在所用材料上。铜、锡、铅等主要材料的成分配比都符合《考工记》中有关要求；有关零件均按不同要求选择适当材料配比。

For standardization of manufacturing process, stringent requirements were set in terms of various aspects design, material adoption and technology. Parts of The Qin Shihuang Mausoleum copper combat chariots/horses have small tolerance. Main parts were subject to approximately identical technological process of precision casting, connection, dressing, grinding and polishing to ensure small size tolerance and surface roughness of parts. It is estimated that there were definite requirements for quality of parts and certain technical equipment and production technology and inspection system, which ensured implementation of mechanical design standardization. Design standardization of the copper chariots and harness was also reflected by materials used. Component ingredient of main materials including bronze, tin and lead met relevant requirements in *Kaogongji* (The Records of Examination of Craftsman); proper material ingredient was selected for relevant parts according to different requirements.

秦始皇陵铜车马 上图为秦始皇的战车，下图为秦始皇的安车。安车前驾四马，单舆双轮，顶上有椭圆形车盖，秦始皇出游时乘坐。

The *Qin Shihuang* Mausoleum Copper Combat Chariots/Horses: The upper picture shows a chariot of the First Emperor of the Qin Dynasty and the lower picture shows a high-fronted, curtained carriage of the First Emperor of the Qin Dynasty. The high-fronted, curtained carriage is driven by four horses with a single cabin covered by elliptic ceiling on top and two wheels. by which the First Emperor of the Qin Dynasty went out for tour.

秦始皇陵铜车马，其结构设计合理、制作工艺精良、质量管理严格，是科技史上震惊世界的杰出成果。

The *Qin Shihuang* Mausoleum copper Combat chariots, with rational structural design, elaborate workmanship and stringent quality management, is a miraculous outstanding achievement in the history of science and technology.

第二节　指南车和记里鼓车
Section 2　South-Pointing Carriage and *Li*-Recording Drum Carriage

指南车
South-Pointing Carriage

指南车的结构有两种可能，利用机械系统之定向性或磁铁的指极性。其出现时间有多种说法：西晋崔豹《古今注》及《志林》等古籍说，黄帝与蚩尤作战，选指南车为雾中士兵引路；《西京杂记》认定指南车最早出现在西汉；《魏略》认为指南车是三国时马钧的发明。长时期以来传说指南车是黄帝时期的发明，但现今研究认为中国磁铁的发现时间为公元前3世纪，与五千多年前黄帝发明指南车，时间上有很大矛盾。现今的指南车（包括宋代的指南车）是齿轮传动并配有自动离合装置，依靠齿轮传动系统及离合装置来指向，此种指南车出现应在齿轮出现之后。西汉时出现了金属齿轮，而木齿轮的使用当更早些。因此，最早西汉时出现指南车比较可信。指南车起源很早，古代多次复制，但均未留下资料，直到宋代才有完整的资料。

South-pointing carriage has two possible structures by utilizing orientability of mechanical system or south pointing function of magnet. There are many sayings on its occurrence time: it was recorded by ancient books including *Gujinzhu* (Commentaries on Antiquity and Today) by Cui Bao of the Western Jin Dynasty and *Zhilin* that when the Yellow Emperor was fighting with Chi You, south-pointing carriage was selected to show the way for soldiers in fog; it was recorded by *Xijing Zaji* that south-pointing carriage occurred in the Western Han Dynasty; and it was recorded by *The Brief History of Wei* that south-pointing carriage was invented by Ma Jun of the Three Kingdoms period. It has been said that south-pointing carriage is an invention in the Yellow Emperor period for a long time, but now it is held that there is great conflict between invention of magnet in China in the 3rd Century BC and invention of south-pointing carriage in the Yellow Emperor period more than 5000 years ago based on research. Modern south-pointing carriage (including south-pointing carriage in the Song Dynasty) is driven by gear and provided with automatic clutch to indicating direction by transmission system and clutch. This south-pointing carriage must occur after gears. Metal gear occurred in the Western Han Dynasty and wooden gears must be used earlier.

Therefore, south-pointing carriage is more likely to occur in the Western Han Dynasty. South-pointing carriage occurred early and was reproduced many times in ancient times, but no data were left until the Song Dynasty when complete data were kept.

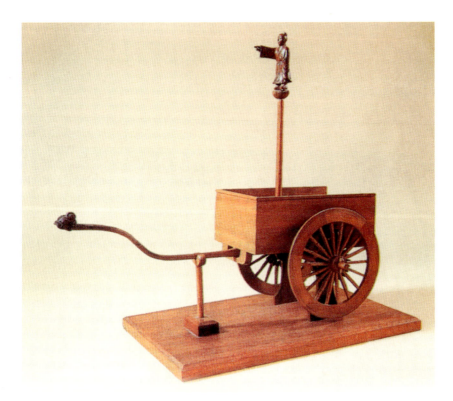

指南车(模型) 指南车利用齿轮传动原理保持原定所指方向不变，又叫定向车。三国魏明帝时（227—239年）马钧造出了指南车。此后指南车成为皇帝仪仗的组成部分。

South-Pointing Carriage （model）: It keeps the original direction indicated unchanged by utilizing gear driving principle and so is also called orientated chariot. South-pointing carriage was made by Ma Jun in Emperor Ming period of the Wei Dynasty (227—239). South-pointing carriage became part of imperial guard of honor afterwards.

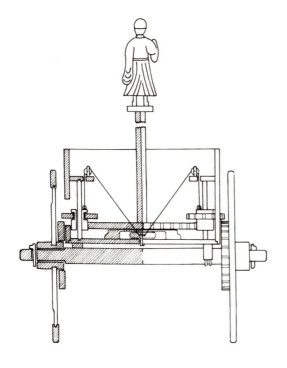

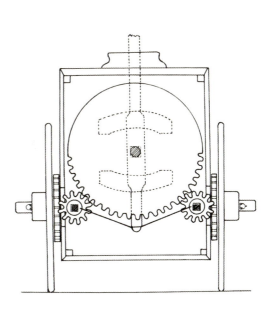

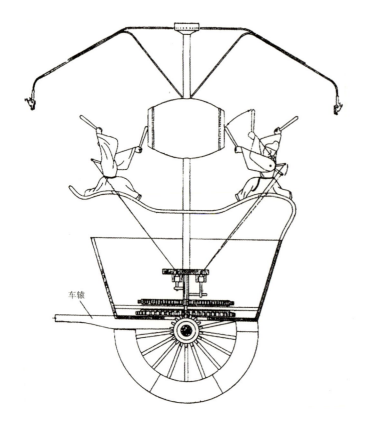

车辕

记里鼓车
Li-Recording Drum Carriage

西汉时出现记里鼓车。车中装有减速齿轮系统和凸轮杠杆等机械设置的古代车辆。利用车轮的转动，带动齿轮传动，变换为凸轮杠杆作用，使木人抬手击鼓，每行走一里击鼓一次，自报里程，与现代车辆上的里程表相似。

Li-recording drum carriage occurred in the Western Han Dynasty. It was ancient vehicle provided with mechanical devices such as speed reducing gear system and cam lever. It works in such way that along with wheels rotating, the gears begins to work, transforming into cam lever action to allow wooden men to raise hands and beat the drum once when the carriage runs over one *li* to

记里鼓车　车中装减速齿轮系和凸轮杠杆等机构。能自报行车里数，是近代里程表的先驱。

Li-Recording Drum Carriage: It is provided with mechanisms including speed reducing gear train and cam lever. It can automatically report the number of *li* the carriage has run over. It is precursor of odometer in recent times.

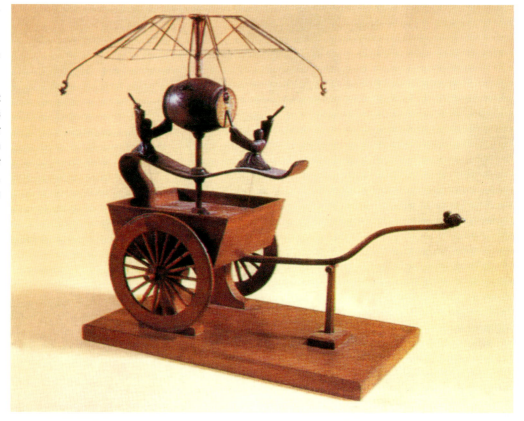

automatically report mileage. It is similar to odometer in modern cars.

指南车与记里鼓车是姐妹车，它们同为皇帝出行时的仪仗车。指南车以简单的结构，就能使木人的手臂始终指向南方，关键在于传动机构或连或断的设计；记里鼓车有一套减速齿轮系，始终与车辆同步转动，再经过传动机械，令木人击鼓以计所行里程。我国古代的指南车及记里鼓车是古代巧妙的自动化机械系统，构思灵巧，构造相当复杂，它体现了我国机械制造的高度水平，是我国古代机械制造技术的杰出代表。

South-pointing carriage and *li*-recording drum carriage were sister vehicles, both were vehicle for guard of honor when the emperor went out. South-pointing carriage can keep arm of wooden man pointing south with simple structure, for the key factor of switching design of transmission mechanism; *li*-recording drum carriage has a set of speed reducing gear train which always rotates with the carriage simultaneously and then allows wooden men to beat drum to record mileage by transmission machine. South-pointing carriage and *li*-recording drum carriage in ancient China are elaborate automatic mechanical systems in ancient times with fine design and very complicated construction, which reflect advanced mechanical manufacturing technology in ancient China as outstanding representatives thereof.

第三节　木牛流马——古代的独轮车
Section 3　Wooden Ox and Floating Horse—Ancient Wheelbarrow

根据《三国志·蒲元别传》的记载，诸葛亮率蜀汉军队伐魏时，为运军粮，由蒲元创出适用山地小道的木牛流马。关于这种运输工具的构造，后人说法大致有四：一是认为木牛流马是独轮车；二是认为是奇异发明，是"机器人"；三是认为木牛是独轮车，流马是四轮车；四是不明确木牛流马是什么。

According to recording in the *Records of the Three Kingdoms, Supplementary Biography of Pu Yuan*, when Zhu Geliang led Shu-Han troops to attack Wei Dynasty, for transporting army provisions, Pu Yuan created wooden ox and floating horse applicable to path in mountainous areas. On construction of this vehicle, there were about four sayings that wooden ox and floating horse was wheelbarrow; wooden ox and floating horse was marvelous invention as "robot"; wooden ox was wheelbarrow and floating horse is mule cart; and meaning of wooden ox and floating horse can not be determined.

现在经过考证研究，较多的学者认为是一种木制的独轮车。有适合于山地小道行走条件的结构设计特点，如车斗物料的装载使全车重心低；推送的结构方便省力；便于山地的刹车。独轮车盛行于汉魏时期，在当时是一种既经济又应用广泛的交通工具，在交通运输史上是一项十分重要的发明。

Nowadays, through textual research, most scholars consider it as wooden wheelbarrow. It is characterized by structural design suitable for running in path of mountainous areas; for example, the box is loaded to lower gravity center of the vehicle; propelling structure is convenient and labor saving; brake is convenient for running in mountainous areas. It prevailed in the Han and Wei Dynasties as an economical and most widely used vehicle at that time. It was a very important invention in the history of transportation.

独轮车（模型）　适用于山地小路使用，被称为"木牛流马"。

Wheelbarrow（model）: It was suitable for path in mountainous areas and called "wooden ox and floating horse".

第十一章 古代船舶
Chapter 11 Ancient Ships

　　中国是世界造船历史最悠久的国家之一，商周时期已经完成了从独木舟演变为木板船的转变。秦汉时期是中国船舶发展的一个重要时期，主要体现在两个方面：一是船舶制造向大型化发展，《后汉书·公孙述传》载"十层赤楼棉兰船"，即用丝棉装饰的高十层巨型楼船；《史记》卷三十也记有"治楼船，高十余丈"。这反映了当时造船技术已达到较高的水平。二是船舶设施不断完善提高，有许多突出成就，长期领先于世界。如船尾舵，在汉代出现，比西方早4个世纪。橹，出现于西汉初期或更早。水密隔舱，有记载公元5世纪初晋代卢循造槽舰，就是8个不漏水的舱（水密隔舱），并见于1973年6月在江苏如皋出土了造于唐代（649年）的九舱水密舱运输船，直到19世纪早期才传到欧洲，为世界各国采用。风帆，古代发明不会迟于商代（古埃及可能在公元前3100年出现帆，比中国早1500年）。大型船舶的制造，高效率推进工具橹的出现，控制方向的船尾舵的出现和充分、灵巧利用风力的帆的使用，说明我国古代造船技术到汉代已经成熟了。

　　China is one of the countries with the longest history of shipbuilding all over the world. In the Shang and Zhou Dynasties, transformation from dugout canoe to wooden boat had been completed. The Qin and Han Dynasties is an important period in the shipbuilding development of China mainly in the following two aspects: Ship enlargement—"Ten-floor magnolia ship decorated with floss silk", namely gigantic ten-storey towered ship decorated with floss silk, was recorded in *The History of the Later Han, Biography of Gongsun Shu*; it was also recorded in Volume 30 of *Shi Ji* (Historical Records) that "… constructed a towered ship with height of about 10 *zhang* [unit of length(=3.3 meters)]"; and this reflects that shipbuilding technology had achieved high level at that time; continuous improvement of ship facilities with many outstanding achievements ahead of other countries in the world: For example, stern rudder occurred in the Han Dynasty, four centuries earlier than in the western countries; yuloh occurred in the early Western Han Dynasty or earlier; for water-tight compartment, it was recorded that Lu Xun of the Jin Dynasty made compartment warship with eight water-tight compartments in the early 5th Century AD, and water-tight compartment was seen in the nine-watertight compartment transport ship made in the Tang Dynasty (649) unearthed in Rugao, Jiangsu Province in June 1973, and not transmitted to Europe and employed by countries all over the world until the early 19th Century; and wind sail was invented at latest in the Shang Dynasty in ancient times (sail may occur in Egypt in 3100 BC, which was 1500 years earlier than in China). Maturation of shipbuilding technology in the Han Dynasty in ancient China was reflected by manufacture of large ships, occurrence of efficient propelling tool yuloh, occurrence of stern rudder for direction control and application of sail by fully and skillfully utilizing wind power.

中国古代造船技术的特点是能创造出可以适应各种环境、不同性能要求的优良船型。例如：周代的方舟，是一种双体船。战国时期的舫船，也是一种稳性高的双体船。汉代的楼船非常高大雄壮。晋代卢循（？—411年）作八槽船。南北朝时期祖冲之（429—500年）造千里船，日行百多里；唐代李皋（733—792年）造桨轮船（即明轮船）是船舶技术上的一次重大进步，欧洲直到十五六世纪才出现，我国比之要早七八百年。唐代的宁波船，远航日本。其后宋代、明代的造船技术进一步发展，郑和七下西洋的宝船，达到木船制造的高峰。

Shipbuilding technology in ancient China was characterized by being capable of creating excellent ship types adaptable to various environments and different performance requirements. For example, square boat in the Zhou Dynasty was a twin-ship. Fang boat in the Warring States

沙船　中国古代的主要船型

Large Junk: main ship type in ancient China.

Period was also a twin-ship which has high stability. Towered ship in the Han Dynasty was very majestic. Lu Xun (? —411) of the Jin Dynasty made eight-compartment ship. Zu Chongzhi (429—500) of the Southern and Northern Dynasties made swift ship to run more than 100 *li* per day. Li Gao (733—792) of the Tang Dynasty made paddle wheel ship (namely paddle ship), which was a great progress in shipbuilding technology and 7 to 8 hundred years earlier than occurrence in Europe in the 15th Century to the 16th Century. Ningbo Ship in the Tang Dynasty was navigated to Japan far away. Shipbuilding technology was further developed in the Song Dynasty and the Ming Dynasty afterwards. Treasure Ship for Zheng He's maritime expeditions allowed wooden shipbuilding to reach its Summit.

福船　中国古代的另一种船型
Fujian Ship：another ship type in ancient China.

第一节　主要古船船型
Section 1　Main Acient Ship Types

中国木船船型十分丰富多样。到20世纪50年代有千种左右。古代航海木帆船中的沙船、乌船、福船、广船是很有名的船舶类型，尤以沙船和福船驰名中外。

There are diverse wooden ship types in China. By 1950s, there had been a thousand types. In navigation wooden sailing ships in ancient times, Large Junk, Beaky Ship, Fujian Ship and Guangdong Ship were very famous, among which Large Junk and Fujian Ship were well-known in China and overseas.

吴国大翼战船
Large-Sail Battleship of the Wu

春秋时代各诸侯国之间的兼并战争激烈而频繁，其中江南水战推动了造船业的发展。吴国的战船有大翼、中翼、小翼三种，另外还有楼船、突冒、桥船等。大翼战船长27.6m，宽3.68m，可容战士26人，棹（卒）50人，舳舻3人……共计91人。

In the Spring and Autumn period, fierce merging wars broke out among vassal states frequently. Sea-fight in areas south of the Yangtze River facilitated development of shipbuilding industry. Battleships in the Wu were classified as large-sail type, medium-sail type and small-sail type. In addition, there were towered ship, attack angle ship, bridge ship, etc. Large-sail battleship was 27.6 m long and 3.68 m wide and can contain 26 soldiers, 50 boatmen (servants), 3 stem and stern operators … totally 91 persons.

春秋吴国的大翼战船（模型）

Large-Sail Battleship of the Wu in the Spring and Autumn Period (model)

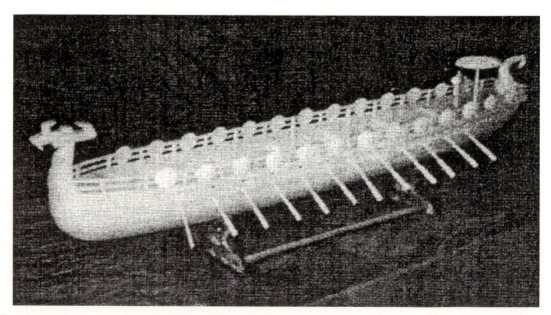

汉代战船（模型）　汉代已建成比较完备的水军。

Battleship of the Han Dynasty (model)：Complete navy had been established in the Han Dynasty.

汉代楼船

Towered Ship of the Han Dynasty

《史记》卷三十记有："治楼船，高十余丈，旗帜加其上，甚壮。"汉代兴起的楼船主要特征是具有多层上层建筑。汉代楼船的形制是：甲板之下为舱，供棹卒划桨之用；甲板上的战卒持刀剑，在短兵相接时作接弦战，舷边设半身高的防护墙，称为文楼，甲板上女墙之内设置第二层建筑即为庐，庐上战卒持长矛，有居高临下之势；再上有第三层建筑为飞庐，弓弩手藏此，是远距离的进攻力量；最高一层为爵室，正如现代的船桥，为驾驶室或指挥室。

It was recorded in Volume 30 of *Shi Ji* that "…made towered ship with height of about 10 *zhang* [unit of length (=3.3 meters)] and banners, magnificent". Towered ship emerging in the Han Dynasty was mainly characterized by multi-floor superstructure. Form and system of towered ship of the Han Dynasty are as follows: Below deck is compartment for boatmen (servants) to row oar; soldiers above deck hold swords for close hand-to-hand combat; protection wall as high as half a person is provided at the side and called Wenlou; inside parapet wall above deck, the second floor is provided and known as cottage, with soldiers holding lance in a commanding position; above is the third floor flying cottage to conceal crossbowmen who are attack force in the distance; and on the top floor is observation room, just like modern captain bridge of wheel house or operational room.

隋代五牙战舰
Wuya Warship of the Sui Dynasty

《隋书·杨素传》记载："素居永安，造大舰，名曰五牙。上起楼五层，前后置六柏竿，容战士八百人……"五牙舰舰长54.6m，型宽15m、甲板宽16m、型深4m、吃水2.2m。该舰建造于1400年前，总长为55m的大舰，当然了不起。

It was recorded in the *History of the Sui, Biography of Yang Su* that "Yang Su living in Yong'an made large ship named Wuya (five floors). There were five floors with six cypress poles in the front and at the rear. It can hold 800 soldiers…" Wuya Ship was 54.6 m long with molded breadth of 15 m, deck width of 16 m, molded depth of 4 m and draft of 2.2 m. The ship was made 1400 years ago with total length of 55 m, which was certainly amazing.

隋代五牙舰（模型）

Wuya Ship of the Sui Dynasty (model)

唐代车轮战舰
Wheel Warship of the Tang Dynasty

唐代的李皋（733—792年）对车轮战舰的发展起了承前启后的作用。魏、晋、南北朝时期，车轮船出现，文献中的"水车"出现，至宋代获得空前的发展。李皋造这种船，《旧唐书》、《新唐书》都有记载，清代《古今图书集成·经济汇编·成政典》载有车轮舸图。

Li Gao (733—792) of the Tang Dynasty served as a link between the preceding and the following wheel warships development. In the Wei, Jin, Southern and Northern Dynasties, wheel ship occurred as recorded in literature and called "water wheel"; up to the Song Dynasty, it had unprecedented development. This ship made by Li Gao were recorded in *Old Book of Tang and New Book of Tang*, and wheel barge picture was attached to *The Integration of Ancient and Modern Books, Economic Compilation, Military Affairs* of the Qing Dynasty.

在欧洲，车轮船的第一次试验，是1543年在巴塞罗那进行的，晚于中国约千年左右。李约瑟对李皋的技术成就很重视，他在1964年的"科学与中国对世界的影响"一文中提及。

In Europe, the first experiment on wheel ship was carried out in Barcelona in 1543, which was about a thousand years later than that in China. Joseph Needham paid special attention to technical achievements of Li Gao and mentioned in his Paper named "Influence of Science and China in the World" in 1964.

车船（采自《古今图书集成》） 以桨轮为推进器的明轮船，又称轮船、车轮舸，由桨船发展而来。李皋所制车船是由人力踏动的。与桨船相比，车船实现了连续推进，可提高航速。

Wheel Ship(from the *Integration of Ancient and Modern Books*): It was a paddle ship with paddle wheel as propeller. It was also called Lunchuan or Chelunge. It was developed from oar ship. Wheel ship made by Li Gao was driven by manually treading. Compared with oar sip, wheel ship was continuously propelled so that navigation speed can be improved.

唐代宁波船
Ningbo Ship of the Tang Dynasty

唐朝（618—907年）在中国历史上是极其昌盛和强大的，与阿拉伯、日本往来密切。唐代中国远洋航行的海船，以船身大、容积广、构造坚固、抵抗风浪力强而著称。在9世纪中叶，往来于中国和日本之间的，大体上完全是唐船，从宁波航行到日本嘉值岛，中国商船仅用3天时间。

In the Tang Dynasty (618—907), China was prosperous and powerful in the history. China had close communications with Arabia and Japan. In the Tang Dynasty, oceangoing ship of China was well-known for large body and volume, firm construction and strong resistance to heavy sea. In the middle 9th Century, most ships traveling between China and Japan were ships of the Tang Dynasty. It only took 3 days for the Chinese merchant ships to navigate from Ningbo to Jiazhi Island, Japan.

唐代宁波船图（原画藏日本）

Picture of Ningbo Ship of the Tang Dynasty (the original copy is collected in Japan)

第二节 郑和宝船
Section 2　Treasure Ship of Zheng He

　　明成祖永乐三年（1405年）至明宣宗宣德八年（1433年），郑和七次下"西洋"，十多年间访问了30多国，在世界航海史上写下了光辉的一页。每次出动船舰100—200艘，其中宝船40—60艘，共载27000多人。

From the third year of Yongle period of Emperor Chengzu (1405) to the eighth year of Xuande period of Emperor Xuanzong (1433) of the Ming Dynasty, Zheng He went on maritime expeditions seven times. During the ten years, he visited more than 30 countries as a brilliant page in navigation history of the world. Each time 100 to 200 ships were turned out to totally carry more than 27,000 persons, among which there were 40 to 60 treasure ships.

　　郑和航船船型有五种：一为宝船，9桅，长44.4丈、阔18丈；二为马船，8桅，长37丈，阔15丈；三是粮船，7桅，长28丈，阔12丈；四为坐船，6桅，长24丈，阔9.4丈；五为战船，5桅，长18丈，阔6.8丈。经中国航海史研究会召开的郑和宝船模型审定会审定，采用在福建出土的雕花黑漆木尺，比值为一尺等于28.3cm来换算，宝船总长为125.65m，宽50.94m，长宽比为2.466……型深12m，吃水8m，计算总排水量为14800t，载重量约在7000t以上。宝船舵杆长11.07m，是最大的沙船。"（全舟）体势巍然，巨无与敌，篷帆锚舵，非二三百人莫能举动"。航行时，"维销挂席，际天而行"。宝船载人超过千人。其船体规模，真可谓旷古盖世。牛津大学出版社于1994年出版的《中国曾控制公海——1405—1433期间的宝船队》一书，其第一章刊有美国作者J. 阿德金斯（Jan Adkins）所谓"郑和宝船与哥伦布旗舰圣·玛利亚号的对比图"，两者在尺度与规模上的对比，何其明显与生动。

There were five types of Zheng He's sailing ship: treasure ship with 9 masts which was 44.4 *zhang* [unit of length (=3.3 meters)] long and 18 *zhang* wide; equine ship with 8 masts which was 37 *zhang* long and 15 *zhang* wide; grain ship with 7 masts which was 28 *zhang* long and 12 *zhang* wide; passenger ship with 6 masts which was 24 *zhang* long and 9.4 *zhang* wide; and warship with 5 masts which was 18 *zhang* long and 6.8 *zhang* wide. Based on examination and approval at approving meeting for model of Treasure Ship of Zheng He held by China Research Society of Navigation History, according to conversion as per scale that one *chi* is equal to 28.3 cm with carved black-painted scale rule unearthed in Fujian Province, the treasure ship had total length of 125.65 m, width of 50.94 m (length to width ratio is 2.466...), molded depth of 12 m and draft of 8 m, with calculated total displacement of 14800 tons and deadweight of 7000 tons at least; rudder stock of the treasure ship was 11.07 m long; and it was the largest junk. "(The ship) was towering and so unparalleled gigantic with sail, anchor and rudder that it can not be held unless by two to three hundred people." In navigation, "it sailed for the horizon."

The Treasure Ship carried more than one thousand people. The hull size was unparalleled since the time immemorial. In book *China Ever Controlled High Sea, Treasure Ship Fleet between 1405 and 1433* published by Oxford University Press in 1994, the so-called "Comparison Diagram of Treasure Ship of Zheng He and Flagship Santa Maria of Christopher Columbus" by American author Jan. Adkins was published in Chapter 1, providing obvious and vivid comparison of size and scale between the two ships.

郑和宝船（模型）　郑和下西洋所乘帆船。《西洋番国志》称它"体势巍然，巨无与敌"。据推断，该宝船属沙船型。

Treasure Ship of Zheng He (model): It is the sailing ship by which Zheng He went on maritime expeditions. It was described to be "towering and unparalleled gigantic" in the Annals of the Foreign Countries in the Western Ocean. The Treasure Ship was concluded as large junk.

郑和下西洋仿古宝船 2006年在南京落成。

Inauguration Ceremony of Imitated Treasure Ship for Zheng He`s Maritime Expeditions: It was held in Nanjing in 2006.

明代木舵杆 1957年南京市文管会在明代宝船厂遗址发现的长度为11.07m的铁力木舵杆，现藏于中国国家博物馆。

Rudder Rod of Mesua Ferrea Linn of the Ming Dynasty: Its length was 11.07 m and discovered by Nanjing Cultural Relic Management Committee in Baochuanchang site of the Ming Dynasty in 1957, currently displayed in the National Museum of China.

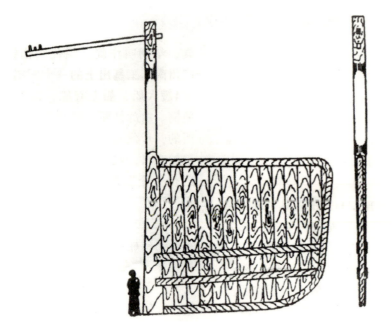

宝船厂舵复原图（据周世德） 舵叶高
6035mm、宽7041mm，面积为42.5m²。也有学
者认为"舵面积过大，又呈方形，则舵杆扭矩
太大，人力无法操作。11.07m舵杆，最大只能
配高6m、宽2.8m、面积16.8m²的舵"。"这根
舵杆只能配十七至十八丈的船"。

Picture of Recovered Rudder at Baochuanchang (by
Zhou Shide): Rudder blade is 6035 mm high and 7041
mm wide with area of 42.5 m². Some scholars hold that
"Rudder area is too large in square shape for manual
operation for consequent excessive torque of rudderstock.
For rudderstock of 11.07 m, rudder to be provided shall
have height of 6 m, width of 2.8 m and area of 16.8 m²
maximally." and that "This rudderstock can only be
provided to ship of 17 to 18 zhang."

郑和宝船与哥伦布旗舰的对比（采自Jan Adkins）

Comparison between Treasure Ship of Zheng He and Flagship of Christopher Columbus (from Jan Adkins)

第三节　舵、橹等船上设施
Section 3　Ship Facilities Including Rudder and Yuloh

中国发明的船上设施，除桨、帆、桅、碇等的不断成熟并定型外，最具有划时代意义的是舵和橹的发明及应用。

For ship facilities invented in China, in addition to consistent maturation and finalization of oar, sail, mast and anchor, invention and application of rudder and yuloh were epoch making.

舵
Rudder

舵是操纵与控制航向的工具，中国是世界上最早发明船尾舵的国家。舵的发明，同航海罗盘一样，是水运事业的一大进步。舵的出土文物最早见于东汉（25—220年），但从相关文物看，最早出现在西汉（前206—25年）。1976年广西贵县罗泊湾西汉一号墓中出土的铜鼓，上刻的龙舟竞渡纹饰，该舟已装有舵和碇（系泊工具，早期叫做碇，现代叫做锚）。1983年广州南越王墓出土的一个铜提梁，上刻绘有4艘大船，船上有舵，其时代当在西汉前期。由此推断，舵最先是由两广地区发明的，年代应在西汉以前。到公元1—2世纪的东汉，舵的使用已较为普遍。1954 年广州一个东汉墓葬中出土的陶船模型，已经有一个较为成熟的舵装置。

西汉铜鼓龙舟竞渡纹饰
广西贵县出土。

Dragon Boat Racing Decoration on Bronze Drum of the Western Han Dynasty：It was unearthed in Guixian County, Guangxi Zhuang Autonomous Region

铜提梁上刻的船及舵
纹饰　广州南越王墓
出土。

Boat and Rudder
Decoration Carved on
Bronze Handle：It was
unearthed from tomb of
the King of the Southern
Yue in Guangzhou

Rudder is used for manipulating and controlling course. The earliest stern rudder was invented in China all over the world. Invention of rudder, as sea compass, marked a great progress of shipping industry. The earliest unearthed relic of rudder occurred in the Eastern Han Dynasty (25—220), but according to relevant relics, it first occurred in the Western Han Dynasty (206BC—25). In 1976, a bronze drum was unearthed from Tomb 1 of the Western Han Dynasty in Luobowan, Guixian County, Guangxi Zhuang Autonomous Region, carved with dragon boat racing decoration. The boat was provided with rudder and *Ding* (a heavy stone used as an anchor, which was called Ding in early times and Mao (anchor) in modern times). In 1983, a bronze handle was unearthed from tomb of the King of the Southern Yue in Guangzhou, carved with four big boats with rudder which must be made in the early Western Han Dynasty. It can be concluded that rudder was first invented in Guangdong Province and Guangxi Zhuang Autonomous Region before the Western Han Dynasty. Up to the Eastern Han Dynasty between the First Century and the Second Century AD, rudder had been universally used. In 1954, a ceramic boat model was unearthed in tomb of the Eastern Han Dynasty in Guangzhou, which was provided with a mature rudder device.

在西方的一些船舶发展史著作中，认定最早的舵出现在1242年，在中国这一年是南宋淳祐二年。此时中国不仅普遍使用了舵，而且已经采用了现代意义的平衡舵。文物和文献都证明，中国舵的发明和应用，大约早于西方1000年，这是不争的事实。

In some western works on shipbuilding development history, it was firmly held that the earliest rudder occurred in 1242, namely the second year of Chunyou period of the Southern Song Dynasty in China. At that time, not only rudder had been universally used, but also balanced rudder similar to modern rudder had been used. Cultural relics and literature demonstrate that invention and application of rudder in China is about 1000 years earlier than in the western countries. It is a inarguable fact.

广州东汉带舵陶船（模型）

Ceramic Boat with Rudder of the Eastern Han Dynasty Unearthed in Guangzhou (model)

橹

Yuloh

在长沙出土的西汉船模上已经有橹。汉末刘熙撰《释名·释船》著作记载，并有诠释，表明至迟在公元前1世纪的西汉初期或稍前，橹已经出现，距今已有2000多年，有着"一橹三桨"的说法，意即橹的效率相当于桨的三倍。这种结构简单而又轻巧的船舶推进装置，是中国人在造船和航行技术上的一项带有突破性的杰出发明，也是中国对于世界造船和航行技术的一项重大历史贡献。橹的效率高是由于橹在水中以较小攻角滑动时阻力小而升力大，再加上橹对船是从桨的间歇推进到连续推进，而且有操纵船舶回转的功能，一直到现在仍为科技史学者所称道，甚至有人称它"可能是中国发明中最科学的一个"。现代广为应用的螺旋桨推进器，它的不间歇做旋转运动的叶片，实际上与水中滑动的橹板相似。螺旋桨的发明和改进，虽不能说源于橹，但其作用原理是一致的。

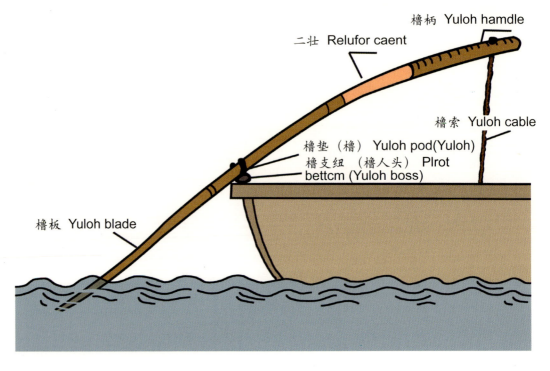

櫓柄 Yuloh hamdle
二壮 Relufor caent
櫓索 Yuloh cable
櫓垫（櫓）Yuloh pod(Yuloh)
櫓支纽（櫓人头）Plrot bettcm (Yuloh boss)
櫓板 Yuloh blade

櫓结构示意图

Yuloh Structural Representation

Boat model of the Western Han Dynasty unearthed in Changsha was provided with yuloh. It was recorded in work *Explanation of Names, Explanation of Ships* written by Liu Xi of the late Han Dynasty with explanatory notes that yuloh had occurred at latest in the early Western Han Dynasty in the First Century BC or earlier more than 2000 years ago and efficiency of yuloh was three times that of oar. This light ship propelling device with simple structure was a breakthrough invention by the Chinese in shipbuilding and navigation technology as well as a great historical contribution of China to the world shipbuilding and navigation technology. When yuloh was sliding in water with small attack angle, it was under small resistance and great ascending power; yuloh performed continuous propelling on ship while oar performed intermittent propelling; it had the function of operating ship for turning; so yuloh was efficient. These are still praised by scholars of the History of Science and Technology. Some people even said that it "may be the most scientific invention in China." For screw propeller being widely used in modern times, its blade continuously performing rotary motion is actually similar to yuloh blade sliding in water. It can not be said that invention and improvement of screw propeller were originated from yuloh, but the two have the same action principle.

第十二章 古代日用器物
Chapter 12 Articles of Daily Use in Ancient China

第一节 透光铜镜
Section 1 Light Penetrating Copper Mirror

中国古代造镜技术非常发达，并且对各种镜子成像原理有深入的研究。早在公元前11世纪前（商代末期），中国就已经使用铜镜。到了秦汉以后，铜镜更是得到进一步发展。中国古代铜镜至今仍旧被人们看作世界文明史上的珍品，特别是其中有2000多年历史的西汉透光镜，更引起人们极大兴趣。这种青铜制镜，它的镜面与普通铜镜一样可以照，但若将镜面置于日光下反射日光时，镜背面的图案文字悉映于墙壁，就像光线能够透过金属镜面，把背面的图案文字反射出来一样，故称"透光镜"。因为这一奇特现象，又被称为"汉代魔镜"。为了解开"透光镜"之谜，国内外花了几百年的时间进行研究探索，直到近代才发现，这是在铜镜铸造冷却与镜面研磨加工过程中所产生的铸造应力和弹性应变，使镜面发生肉眼不易察觉的和镜面纹饰相对应的变形，通过光程放大作用，产生了应对于镜背图案的明暗透光效应。这充分说明了中国古代高超的制镜技术和对光的反射特性的深刻认识。

Mirror manufacturing technology was highly developed in ancient China and deep researches were done on imaging principle of various mirrors. Early before the 11th Century BC (the late Shang Dynasty), copper mirror had been used in China. After the Qin and Han Dynasties, copper mirror was greatly developed. Copper mirror made in ancient China is still regarded as treasure in the world civilization history. In particular, people are quite interested in Light Penetrating Copper Mirror of the Western Han Dynasty with a history of more than 2000 years. For this copper mirror, its surface can be used as common copper mirror in which people can look at themselves. However, when the surface is placed in the sunlight to reflect sunlight, all patterns and words on mirror back will appear on the wall, as if the light could penetrate through the metal mirror surface to reflect the patterns and words on the back, so it was called "Light Penetrating Copper

Mirror". Due to this fancy phenomenon, it was also called "Witch Mirror of the Han Dynasty". To reveal the mystery of "Light Penetrating Copper Mirror", people in China and overseas spent hundreds of years on research and exploration. It was not found until recent times that it was casting stress and elastic strain produced in copper mirror casting cooling and surface grinding process that allowed the surface to produce microscopic deformation corresponding to decorations of the surface to produce shading transmission effect corresponding to patterns on the mirror back by optical path length amplification. It fully shows superb mirror manufacturing technology and profound understanding about reflection properties of light in ancient China.

西汉透光铜镜 镜背铭
文 "见日之光，天下大
明"。现藏上海博物馆。

Light Penetrating Copper Mirror
of the Western Han Dynasty:
Inscription "Jian Ri Zhi Guang,
Tianxia Da Ming (Exposed
to sunlight, clear reflection of
China)" on back, collection of
Shanghai Museum.

长信宫灯
Changxin Palace Lantern

第二节 长信宫灯
Section 2 Changxin Palace Lantern

　　河北满城刘胜墓出土的西汉长信宫灯，以宫女执灯造型，其右臂高举过灯，巧妙地起到烟道的作用。宫女形象生动真实，设计整体精巧，通体鎏金更为之增色，是一大特色。这种鎏金技术至迟始于战国时代，它是把液态汞金齐涂布于铜银等器物的表面。再经加热烘烤，令汞挥发而使金均匀地附着其上的工艺。长信宫灯至今仍金光耀目，足见西汉时鎏金技术之精湛。

Changxin Palace Lantern of the Western Han Dynasty unearthed from tomb of Liu Sheng in Mancheng, Hebei Province takes the shape of a maid of honor with lamp in hand. Her right arm is raised high above the lamp to serve as flue expertly. It is characterized by vivid image of a maid of honor, elaborate integrated design and through gold-plating as additional charm. The gold-plating technology at latest occurred in the Warring States Period and it was a process completed by applying liquid mercury-gold alloy to surface of bronze or silver articles and baking by heating to allow mercury to volatilize in order to evenly attach gold to the surface. Changxin Palace Lantern still glitters as gold, showing superb gold-plating technology in the Western Han Dynasty.

第三节　被中香炉
Section 3　Censer in Quilt

《西京杂记》卷一记载，西汉末年（公元1世纪）长安巧工丁缓制造"被中香炉"（银熏球），并说"被中香炉本出房风，其法后绝"。可知丁缓不是最初的发明人，房风何许人，已不可考，但据此可知，最晚汉代已有被中香炉。陕西西安唐代遗址曾出土制作精美的被中香炉实物。

It was recorded in Volume 1 of *Xijing Zaji* that in the Late Western Han Dynasty (the First Century AD), craftsman Ding Huan in Chang'an made "Censer in Quilt" (silver smoking ball), and "Censer in Quilt was initially made by Fang Feng and its manufacturing method had been lost". It can be seen that Ding Huan is not the original inventor, and the person named Fang Feng is not known. However, it can be concluded that Censer in Quilt occurred at latest in the Han Dynasty. True elaborate Censer in Quilt was unearthed at site of the Tang Dynasty in Xi'an, Shaanxi Province.

被中香炉　是中国能工巧匠充分运用重心及平衡等物理学知识创制的。

Censer in Quilt: It was created by the Chinese skillful artisan by fully applying physical knowledge including gravity center and balance.

被中香炉打开图

Picture of Unfolded Censer in Quilt

被中香炉利用回转仪原理制成，是世界上已知最早的常平支架装置。其构造精巧，无论球体香炉如何滚动，其中心位置的半球炉体都能始终保持水平状态。被中香炉镂空球内有两个环互相垂直，而可灵活转动，炉体可绕三个互相垂直的轴线转动。它是现代航天、航空、航海广泛应用的陀螺仪，是这些行业不可或缺的重要仪器。《西京杂记》的记载，表明陀螺仪在2000年前的汉代已在中国出现。而在欧洲直到16世纪才出现常平支架装置，相距1500年。

Censer in Quilt was made by utilizing principle of rotary gyroscope. It was the earliest known gimbal device in the world. With elaborate construction, no matter how sphere Censer rotates, hemispherical burner at the center can be kept in level position. There are two orthogonal rings in the pierced sphere of Censer in Quilt, which can freely rotate, and the burner can rotate around three axial lines perpendicular to each other. It is gyroscope widely applied to modern aerospace and navigation as an indispensable important instrument of the industries. Recording in *Xijing Zaji* indicates that gyroscope had occurred in the Han Dynasty of China two thousand years ago. Gimbal device did not occur until the 16th Century in Europe, which was 1500 years later than in China.

第四节 走马灯
Section 4 Revolving Scenic Lantern

走马灯利用热气流上升来推动叶轮转动，与现代的燃气轮机相比较，其基本原理是相同的。显然，走马灯已具有燃气轮机雏形。

For revolving scenic lantern, hot gas flow rise is utilized to propel impeller to rotate. Compared with modern gas turbine, it has the same fundamental principle. Obviously, revolving scenic lantern was an embryo of gas turbine.

据宋代的记载推断，走马灯的发明不晚于公元1000年左右的唐代。在《乾淳岁时记》和《武林旧事》中，以"马骑人物，旋转如飞"来形容"影灯"，影灯是走马灯的原名，《明皇杂录》记载"上在东都遇正月望夜，移仗上阳宫，大陈影灯"。

It can be concluded based on recording of the Song Dynasty that revolving scenic lantern was at latest invented in the Tang Dynasty around 1000 AD. It was described in *Qianchun Suishi Ji* (Records of Folk Customs in Qianchun Period) and *Wulin Jiushi* (The Past Things in Martial World) that "Shadow Lamp" was provided with horses and men which were rotating swiftly. "Shadow Lamp" was the original name of revolving scenic lantern. It was recorded in *Minghuang Za Lu* (Varia of Emperor Xuanzong of the Tang Dynasty) that "the emperor was in Dongdu (Luoyang) in the night of the 15th day of the 1st lunar month, and moved to Shangyang Palace with guard of honor for displaying luxurious shadow lamps".

走马灯 这是根据热学原理制造的极具观赏性的灯饰。它的上部有平装的叶轮，叶片沿一个转向斜置，立轴上挂装压纸剪成的骑马人物等。底板上的蜡烛点燃后，上升的热气流推动叶轮旋转，剪纸的影子映射在灯笼上，"奔驰马骤，团团不休"，颇具情趣。

Revolving Scenic Lantern: It is ornamental illumination made as per thermal principle. It has an upper flat impeller with blades inclined towards one turning direction and a vertical shaft on which horses and men cut with laminated paper were hung. When wax candle on the base plate is ignited, rising hot gas flow will propel the impeller to rotate to reflect shadow of the paper-cut on the lantern, which is quite appealing for "horses are running swiftly, round and round".

第五节　喷水鱼洗
Section 5　Splashing Fish Basin

　　古代称"洗"的东西，形状颇似今天的洗脸盆，有木洗、陶洗和铜洗。盆里刻鱼的称鱼洗，刻龙的称龙洗。这种器物在先秦时期已在人们生活中普遍使用。然而，在唐宋年间出现一种能喷水的铜质鱼洗，一般称它为喷水鱼洗。

　　喷水鱼洗，内底饰四条鱼纹，鳞尾毕具。洗里盛水后，用手沾水摩擦它外廓上的雨弦（双耳），立即发出响亮的嗡嗡声，继而盆里出现浪花，盆内底部所刻四条鱼的口沟处水珠四溅达尺余。摩擦越快，声音越响，波浪翻腾。这种奇妙的鱼洗曾多次在国内外展出，引人注目。这种器物的振动实为板振动，振动过程类似圆形钟的空气振动。表现中国古代人聪明才智的是，鱼洗中四条鱼的口须（又称喷水沟）总是刻在鱼洗基频推动（四节线）的波腹位置。这证明，古代工艺师了解掌握圆柱形壳体的基频振动，它的效果是能引起鱼在跳跃的错觉。这样一个小小的器皿，却能把科学技术、艺术欣赏和思辨推测三者结合在一起，不能不令人惊叹中国古代劳动人民深邃的智慧和精湛的技艺。

Articles called "*Xi*" in ancient times were in the shape similar to present wash basin, and classified as wooden basin, ceramic basin and bronze basin. Basin carved with fish was called fish

喷水鱼洗 当用手掌沾水摩擦鱼洗的双耳时，盆内水面会出现振动花纹，盆内底部所刻的四条鱼的口沟处水花喷溅达尺余。鱼洗亦发出震耳的嗡嗡声。

Splashing Fish Basin: When both ears of the fish basin are held and rubbed by hand with water, water surface in the basin will produce vibration patterns, and water will be sprayed at grooves of the four carved fishes at the bottom in a range of about one *chi*. In addition, the fish basin will produce deafening buzz.

basin, and that with dragon was called dragon basin. This kind of articles had been universally used in daily life in the pre-Qin period. A bronze fish basin which can spray water occurred in the Tang and Song Dynasties and was usually called splashing fish basin. For splashing fish basin, the inner bottom is decorated with four fishes with complete scale and tail. When the basin is filled with water and *Yuxian* (double ears) on its external edge was rubbed with water, it will buzz loudly at once, and spray will occur at the bottom at which globule will be sprayed around at grooves of the four carved fishes in a range of about one *chi*. The faster the ears are rubbed, the louder the buzz is, with wave rolling about. This wonderful fish basin has been showed in China and overseas many times, striking the eye. Vibration of this article is actually plate vibration, process of which is similar to air vibration of round bells. Tentaculum (also called spraying groove) of the four carved fishes in the basin is always at wave loop of (the fourth node line of) fundamental vibration of the fish basin, which really reflects acumen of the Chinese in ancient times. This shows that ancient craftsmen understood and mastered fundamental vibration of circular cylindrical shell. It has the effect to produce illusion that the fishes are leaping. Therefore, scientific technology, artistic appreciation and speculation are combined in such a small utensil. Great wisdom and superb workmanship of working people in ancient China are really marvelous.

第十三章 古代大型铜、铁铸件
Chapter 13 Large Bronze and Iron Castings in Ancient Times

大型和特大型铸件的制造，体现了隋唐五代和宋元时期中国金属铸造业的生产规模、高超的铸造技术和工艺水平。

Large and super large castings manufacture reflected production scale, superb casting technique and technology level of metal casting industry in the Sui, Tang and Five Dynasties and the Song and Yuan Dynasties of China.

晋阳铁佛 隋代曾在晋阳（现山西临汾）铸成铁佛，高70尺（唐代1尺约合0.306m）约21m。

Jinyang Iron Buddhist Sculpture: In the Sui Dynasty, an iron Buddhist sculpture was cast in Jinyang (present Linfen, Shanxi Province) with height of 70 *chi* (length unit, =0.306 m ca. in the Tang Dynasty) which was about 21 m.

唐代天枢 唐代武则天天册元年（695年）在洛阳铸造天"枢"，高105尺，用铜铁200万斤。

"Dubhe" of the Tang Dynasty: "Dubhe" was cast in Luoyang in the first year of Tiance period when Wu Zetian acted as the emperor of (695) the Tang Dynasty with 2 million *jin* of copper and iron, with height of 105 *chi*.

正定铜佛 隋开皇六年（586年）建正定龙藏寺（现名隆兴寺）并铸像，后毁。宋开宝四年（971年）重铸，总高22m，重约50t，铸造时用三千多人，分7段铸接。铸有42臂，故称千手千眼佛。

Zhengding Bronze Buddhist Sculpture: Zhengding Longcang Temple (present

正定铜佛　位于河北正定隆兴寺。初建于隋开皇六年（586年），后毁，宋开宝四年（971年）重铸，高22m。铸有42臂，故称千手千眼佛，后铜臂毁坏，改用木臂。

Zhengding Bronze Buddhist Sculpture: It is located in Longxing Temple in Zhengding, Hebei Province. It was initially built in the sixth year of Kaihuang period (586) of the Sui Dynasty and destroyed later. It was recast in the fourth year of Kaibao period (971) of the Song Dynasty with height of 22 m. It was cast with 42 arms and so called Thousand-hand and Thousand-eye Buddhist Sculpture. The bronze arms were destroyed afterwards and replaced by wooden arms.

Longxing Temple) was established in the sixth year of Kaihuang period (586) of the Sui Dynasty and a Buddhist sculpture was cast and destroyed later. It was recast in the fourth year of Kaibao period (971) of the Song Dynasty by more than 3000 people and cast bonded in seven sections, with height of 22 m and weight of about 50 tons. It was cast with 42 arms and so called Thousand-hand and Thousand-eye Buddhist Sculpture.

沧州铁狮　后周广顺三年（953年）铸。通高4.8m，加上足高0.5m，共达5.3m；长8m，宽3m许。约重40t。它是分段接铸而成，各段铸范共409块，泥芯是整体的。

Cangzhou Iron Lion: It has total height of 4.8 m and is 5.3 m high when added by foot height of 0.5 m. It is 8 m long and about 3m wide with weight of 40 tons. It was cast in the third year of Guangshun period (953) of the Later Zhou. It was cast bonded in sections with totally 409 casting molds with an integral clay core.

沧州铁狮　铸于953年，约重40t。

Cangzhou Iron Lion: It was cast in 953, with weight of about 40 tons.

当阳铁塔

Dangyang Iron Tower

当阳铁塔 位于湖北当阳玉泉寺，铸于宋嘉祐六年（1061年）。塔呈八角形，高17.90m，分13级，总重10.6万多斤。塔体分段铸造，由44个构件叠装而成。塔之各层尚铸有仪态不同的佛像。

Dangyang Iron Tower: It is located in Yuquan Temple in Dangyang, Hubei Province and was cast in the sixth year of Jiayou period (1061) of the Song Dynasty. The tower is octagonal with height of 17.90 m. It has 13 levels with total weight of more than 106 thousand *jin*. The tower body was cast in sections and formed by overlapping 44 structural members. Buddhist sculptures of different appearances were also cast on various levels of the tower.

永乐大钟 明永乐十五至十九年（1418—1422年）间铸制的大铜钟。初悬于汉经厂，清雍正时移至北京西郊觉生寺。通高6.75m，口外径3.3m，钟唇厚0.185m，总重约46.5t。用多个熔炉同时熔炼铜合金。一起浇铸。钟体内外满铸23万字的《华严经》、《金刚经》等。字体刚健雄劲，字迹清晰。大钟合金成分为铜80.54%、锡16.4%、铅1.12%。泥型铸造，大钟外范分七层，钟体与蒲牢分铸。其声宏亮，可闻数十里，是世界铸字最多的钟，也是世界上巨型古钟之一。

Yongle Bell: It is a big bronze bell cast between the 15th and 19th year of Yongle period (1418—1422) of the Ming Dynasty. It was initially suspended in the Han-Sutra Printing House and relocated to Juesheng Temple in the western suburb of Beijing in Emperor Yongzheng's regime of the Qing Dynasty. It has total height of 6.75 m, with outer diameter of the opening of 3.3 m, bell edge thickness of 0.185 m and total weight of about 46.5 tons. Copper alloy was smelt by multiple furnaces simultaneously for concurrent casting. The bell body was internally and externally cast with *Avatamsaka Sutra*, *Diamond Sutra*, etc. of 230 thousand powerful and clear cut characters.

永乐大钟　现存于北京大钟寺，高6.75 m、口径3.3m，重约46.5t。钟体内外铸有经文23万字，材质为青铜。

Yongle Bell: It is preserved in Dazhong Temple of Beijing. It is 6.75m high with opening diameter of 3.3 m, and weight of about 46.5 tons. It was internally and externally cast with sutra of 230 thousand characters. It was made of bronze.

Alloy of the bell was composed of 80.54% of copper, 16.4% of tin and 1.12% of lead. The bell was formed by clay-mold casting, with seven layers of external mold, and the body and button were separately cast. It can produce loud sound audible in a range of tens of *li*. It is the bell cast with most characters and one of ancient gigantic bells in the world.

武当山金殿 明成祖永乐十三年（1416年）铸制，仿木结构建筑，它用铜合金铸成各个构件，再以榫卯装配。除门扇外，通体鎏金，为现在最大的铜建筑物。

Golden Hall of Wudang Mountains: It was cast in the 13th year of Yongle period (1416) of Emperor Chengzu of the Ming Dynasty. It was an imitated wood structural building made by casting structural members with copper alloy and assembling them by mortise and tenon. It was plated by gold thoroughly except door leaves. It is the largest copper building now.

武当山金殿 位于武当山天柱峰顶。为现存最大的铜建筑物。除门扇外，通体鎏金。

Golden Hall of Wudang Mountains: It is located on top of Tianzhu Peak of Wudang Mountains. It is the largest existing copper building. It was plated by gold thoroughly except door leaves.

第二篇　中国近代机械史

Part 2
Modern History of Machinery in China

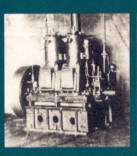

■ 晚清（鸦片战争）至中华人民共和国成立（1840—1949）

From the Late Qing Dynasty (the Opium War) to the Founding of People's Republic of China (1840—1949)

第一章 中国近代机械工业的诞生
Chapter 1 The Birth of Machinery Industry in Modern China

1840年鸦片战争爆发，帝国主义的炮舰轰开了中国的大门。愚昧自大的清王朝被迫认识到自己的落后，开始建设近代机械工业。建立近代机械工业（主要是兵器制造）是"维新运动"的主要内容。

The Opium War, first waged on China by imperialistic nations in 1840, ravaged the entire China. It compelled the central government of the Qing Dynasty to realize their inferiority to their western counterparts on all fronts, thus embarking on the endeavor of building modern machinery industry (largely weaponry making), which is the central theme of the "Reform Movement".

鸦片战争（1840—1842年）后，中国机械工业诞生。这个时期诞生的中国近代机械工业，从一开始就具有明显的半殖民地、半封建社会的特点：中国最早使用动力的机械工厂是随着外国侵略军而来的外商经营的船舶修造厂；中国人自己创办的机械工厂，最早是清政府的军火工厂；中国民族资本创办的机械工厂一直处于帝国主义、封建主义和官僚买办的压迫之下。

The period after the Opium War (1840—1842) witnessed the commencement of China's modern machinery industry, which is apparently marked with semi-colonial and semi-feudalistic characteristics. To be more specific, the earliest motive power machinery factories found in China were ship repair yards operated by foreign merchants that flocked to China along with foreign military invasions; the earliest known machine factories started up by Chinese people were munition factory run by the government of Qing Dynasty; machine factories funded by China's national capital were constantly oppressed by imperialistic, feudalistic and bureaucratic compradors.

1840—1949年，由晚清到中华人民共和国成立的100余年，中国机械由传统的手工作坊式小生产逐步向使用动力机器的生产方式发展，经历了诞生、发展和向现代机械工业的过渡，道路崎岖，创业维艰。

Over a span of over a century from the late Qing Dynasty to the founding of the People's Republic of China (1840—1949), China's machinery industry had gone through a gradual shift from traditional small-scale production characterized by labor-intensive manual workshops to machine-operated production—the journey of transition experiencing from commencement, development and to modern machinery industry is truly uneven and arduous beyond one's imagination at its inception.

第一节　19世纪40年代英美商人在我国建立船舶修造厂
Section 1　UK and US Merchants Set up Ship Repair Yards in China, in 1840s

1841年英军占领中国香港，英国人纳蒙随即在中国香港建立船坞，这是外国人在中国经营的第一家机械厂。

Immediately after the British Army seized Hong Kong in 1841, Namon, a Briton, set up docks and shipyards in Hong Kong, making the first machine factory operated by foreigners in China (Hong Kong).

鸦片战争结束后，1842年8月，中英《江宁条约》规定五口（广州、福州、厦门、宁波、上海）通商，帝国主义各国先后取得沿海和内河航行权，为适应航运发展的需要，外商在中国建立船舶修造厂。1845年，英国大英轮船公司（Peninsular and Oriental Shipping Co.）职员J.柯拜（John Couper），在广州黄埔建立柯拜船坞（Couper Dock），为有浮闸门的石坞，船坞水泵用蒸汽机带动，是当时远东首个石坞，具备承修当时世界一流船舶的能力。柯拜船坞是外资在中国内地经营的首家机械工厂。

Following the overwhelming defeat suffered by China in the Opium War, China and Britain signed "The Treaty of Nanking" in August 1842 that stipulated the opening-up of trading in five major harbors of China (Guangzhou, Fuzhou, Xiamen, Ningbo and Shanghai). Imperialistic nations successively seized control of coastal and internal navigational rights and overseas merchants, and in an effort to cope with the needs of shipping development, began establishing ship repair yards in China. In the year 1845, John Couper from Peninsular and Oriental Shipping Co, set up Couper Dock in Whampoa Harbor of Guangzhou, a stone dock with a floating sluice gate, the water pump powered by steam engine and a world-class ship repair capacity. It is the first stone dock in the Far East and the first foreign-owned machine factory operated in China mainland.

柯拜船坞　1861年重建

Couper Dock：Rebuilt in 1861

录顺石船坞　1861年建成

Lushunshi Dock：Built in 1861

　　1843年，上海开港后，很快取代广州成为中国对外贸易中心，外商在上海建立起一些船舶修造厂，19世纪40年代末英商A.密契尔（A. Mitchell）建立上海第一家外商修造厂浦东船厂（Pootung Dock）；1850年美商在上海建立伯维公司（Purvis&Co）修造船舶。

　　In 1843, Shanghai Harbor, shortly after it was opened to overseas trading, took the place of Guangzhou as China's overseas trading center, where foreign merchants set up some ship repair yards. The first foreign-built repair factory in Shanghai, Pootung Dock, was founded by the British merchant A. Mitchell at the end of 1840s; in 1850, the American merchants established Purvis & Co for ship repair business in Shanghai.

19世纪60年代末，外商在东南沿海口岸建立了22家船舶修理厂，雇用中国工人达9000人。

By the end of 1860s, a total of 22 ship repair yards, with as many as 9,000 Chinese employees, had been built by foreign business people along the southeast coast.

第二节　清政府设立近代军工企业的早期探索
Section 2　Early Exploration of Qing Dynasty in Establishing Modern Military Industry

清政府为了维护其政权和抵抗外国侵略的需要，着手建立自己的军事工业，19世纪60年代开始的洋务运动，建立军事工业是其主要内容之一。

In light of the increasing needs to safeguard its political regime and counter foreign military invasions, the government of Qing Dynasty commenced developing its own military industry, which is represented by the major component "Westernization Movement" launched in 1860s.

安庆内军械所
Anqing Internal Weapons Factory

安庆内军械所是由清政府洋务派曾国藩创办的中国第一座仿造西洋船、炮的机械工厂，系中国近代自行创办的第一座机械厂。清咸丰十一年（1861年）秋，湘军攻陷安庆，清同治元年（1862年）即兴办安庆内军械所，下设火药局以制造炸炮和子弹；设火药库以试制炮弹为主；设造船局主要试制火轮机（蒸汽机）和火轮船。由于曾国藩建所目的之一是"师夷长技以制夷"，所内"全用汉人，未雇洋匠"，各道工序主要以手工操作完成，但已是一个初具规模、有分工的手工工厂。由于缺乏机器设备，他命容闳赴美购置机器设备。由徐寿、华蘅芳等主持，1862年4月30日试制成功中国第一台小型蒸汽机（用现代眼光衡量，实际为一台蒸汽机模型），意义重大，给曾国藩以巨大鼓舞，决定"开始为小火轮之制造"。1864年试制的小火轮试航成功。

Anqing Internal Weapons Factory was the first machine factory that counterfeited western ships and cannons set up by Zeng Guofan, who was appointed by Foreign Affairs of the Qing Dynasty. It was also the frist machine factory independently setup by China in modern times. In the fall of the 11th year of the Emperor Xianfeng of the Qing Dynasty (1861), Hunan Army

148

besieged Anqing and Anqing Weapons Factory was then established in the first year of the Emperor Tongzhi of the Qing Dynasty (1862). The Bureau of Gunpowder, Powder Magazine and Bureau of Ship-building were introduced to take charge of producing cannons and bullets, cannonballs, as well as steam engines and steam boats on an experimental basis respectively. As one of the primary purposes of Zeng Guofan building the plant was to "learn the advanced technologies from the west in an effort to resist their invasions", all the employees were Chinese people of Han origin and none of them was foreign craftsman. Even though manual operations were required for each and every single procedure, the factory enjoyed a rudimentary scale and is characterized by division of labor. Yung Wing was dispatched to US to purchase machineries and equipments due to critical domestic shortage. On April 30th 1862, charged by Xu Shou and Hua Hengfang, China's first small-scale steam engine was successfully trial-produced (it was more of a prototype of steam engine by modern standard). This feat served of paramount significance that tremendously encouraged and inspired Zeng Guofan, who then determined to "manufacture steam engines". The trial navigation of the small steam engine trial-produced in 1864 was another huge success.

1864年7月19日清军镇压太平天国攻陷南京后,该所迁南京改称金陵内军械所,1865年后与外军械所合并改称金陵兵械所。徐寿、华蘅芳等在此自行设计和用手工制造了中国自制的第一艘大型轮船"黄鹄"号。

In the war of the Qing Military Army supressed the Taiping Rebellion, the Qing Military Army besieged and took over Nanjing on July 19th 1864. The plant was relocated to Nanjing and renamed Nanjing Internal Weapons Factory. In the year 1865, it was merged with external weapons factory and renamed Nanjing Weapon Machinery Plant. Xu Shou and Hua Hengfang independently designed and manually produced the first large-scale ship named "Huang He (Yellow Crane)" in China.

安庆内军械所的建立,有重要的历史意义,它不仅是中国第一家军事工业企业,从手工制造进入机器制造时代,而且推动了整个近代机械工业的发展。

The establishment of Anqing Internal Weapons Factory serves vital historical significance. It does not only symbolize the building of first military industrial enterprise in China—making the transition from manual productions to machine automations, but it promotes the development of the entire machinery industries in modern times.

苏州洋炮局（又名西洋机器局）

Suzhou Bureau of Western Cannon (also called as Bureau of Western Machines)

苏州洋炮局的前身是松江洋炮局（又名上海洋炮局）,创设于1863年4月,是李鸿章所部淮军中的一个随军修械所;1863年12月4日李鸿章镇压太平天国攻陷苏州,1864年1月6日随军移驻苏州,更名苏州洋炮局。苏州洋炮局的主要机械设备是购自被清政府遣散的"阿思本舰队"的制造及修理武器的机械设备,在当时是比较先进的。1864年7月19日清军攻陷南京,1865年5月李鸿章继曾国藩（派去镇压捻军）任两江总督。

李鸿章将苏州洋炮局的一部分（英人马柯里主持的西洋机器局）迁往南京，并入金陵制造局；另两部分（副将韩殿甲局和苏松太道丁日昌局）以后迁往上海成为江南制造总局的一部分。

Suzhou Bureau of Western Cannon was previously known as Sungkiang Bureau of Western Cannon (also referred to as Shanghai Bureau of Western Cannon) established in April 1863. It was a mobile machine repair unit that travelled with the Huai Army under the charge of Li Hongzhang and renamed when Li Hongzhang's army was stationed in Suzhou on January 6th 1864 following the capture of Suzhou On December 4th 1863 in the war of the Qing Military Army supressed the Taiping Rebellion. The majority of machineries and equipments available in Suzhou Bureau of Western Cannon were purchased from "Osborn Fleet" that had already been disbanded by the government of Qing Dynasty and they were pretty advanced back then. On July 19th 1864, the army of Qing Dynasty besieged Nanjing and in May the next year. Li Hongzhang succeeded to the post of Zeng Guofan, who was dispatched to crack down on the rebellious forces referred to as Nian Army, as the Viceroy of Liangjiang. Li Hongzhang split Suzhou Bureau of Western Cannon apart; the Bureau of Western Machines charged by the Briton Macartney Halliday was relocated to Nanjing and merged with Nanjing Production Bureau; the other two parts (bureaus charged by Adjutant Han Dianjia and Susongtai Dao Ding Richang respectively) were moved to Shanghai to be incorporated as an integral component of Jiangnan General Production Bureau.

第三节　民族资本经营的最早一批民营机器厂
Section 3　The Earliest Batch of Private Machine Factories Funded by National Capital

19世纪60年代后，为适应洋务运动逐渐拓展的需要，民族资本经营机械工业开始兴起。

In an effort to cope with the ever-growing needs for the expansion of Westernization Movement after 1860s, the machine factories funded by national capital started to emerge.

1866年方赞举在上海创办的发昌钢铁机器厂，是中国民族资本创办较早的机械厂，后发展成为早期上海最大的民营机器厂，1900年被英商耶松船厂兼并。同期还有广州陈联泰机器厂、上海甘章船坞等；1880年前后，上海均和安机器厂等相继开办，是中国最早的一批民办机械厂。这些厂创办时，一般只是一个铸造和小量修配船用零件的手工作坊，以后才逐步采用机器生产。如上海发昌厂开办时是一个手工打铁作坊，1869年开始使用车床，1876年开始制造"小火轮"。1872年开办的汉阳荣华昌翻砂厂，是中国最早的专业铸造厂。

Fachang Iron & Steel Machine Factory, set up by Fang Zanju in Shanghai in 1866, was among the earliest machine factories funded by China's national capital. It later evolved into the largest private-owned machine factory in early Shanghai, merged with S.C. Farnham & Co-a British Company-in 1900. Guangzhou Chenliantai Machine Factory and Shanghai Ganzhang Dock were also included in the same period; around 1880s, such factories as Shanghai Junhe'an Machine Factory successively set up, were among the earliest batch of private-owned machine factories. These factories were mostly small workshops that manufactured or repaired ship components at their beginnings and machine productions were phased in gradually afterwards. Shanghai Fachang Factory, for instance, was more of an iron-forging workshop at its nascence. In 1869, lathe was utilized and "small steam engines" were being manufactured from 1876 onwards. Hanyang Ronghuachang Foundry Factory set up in 1872 was the earliest professional foundry factory found in China.

第二章　晚清、民国北洋政府时代的中国机械工业

Chapter 2　China's Machinery Industry in the Era of Late Qing Dynasty and Beiyang Government of Republic of China

这一时期，外商、清政府军工和民办机械工业企业都有一定发展。

This particular period witnessed the notable development of machinery enterprises operated by foreign merchants, the military department of Qing Dynasty and private individuals.

第一节　外商经营的机械厂和"洋行"垄断中国机械市场

Section 1　Machinery Factories Run by Foreign Merchants and "Foreign Firms" Monopolized China's Machinery Market

据统计，1908年外商经营的34个主要机器厂中（船舶修造厂28家，占82%；铁路车辆工厂3家，占9%），英国人经营的占2/3。上海耶松船舶公司（上海造船厂前身）为英商在华最大投资企业，其资金超过当时中国全部民族资本机械工业资金总和的4倍；广州黄埔船坞公司兼并了港穗各船厂，分别垄断了上海和中国南方修造船业。1880年英商在胥各庄（1899年迁唐山）建修车厂，这是中国第一个铁道车辆修造厂。

Statistics collected in 1908 shows that two thirds of the 34 major machinery factories operated by foreign merchants (of which 28 were ship repair yards, accounting for 82% of the total; 3 were railway locomotive factories, accounting for 9%) were operated by British merchants. Shanghai S.C. Farnham & Co (the predecessor of Shanghai Ship-building Factory), with over four times the total national capital of Chinese machinery industries, was the largest enterprise invested by British merchants in China, while Guangzhou Whampoa Dock Company merged with all the ship factories in Hong Kong and Guangzhou, monopolizing ship repair and ship building industries in Shanghai and south China respectively. In 1880, British merchants set up the first locomotive

repair and manufacturing factory of China in Xugezhuang (relocated to Tangshan in 1899).

日俄战争（1904—1905年）后，日本在中国东北加快对中国的经济侵略步伐，至
20世纪20年代已有20多家较大的铁路、造船和机械厂。

After the Russo-Japanese War (1904—1905), Japan speeded up its economic invasion in the
northeast of China and by the 1920s, there had been already over 20 relatively large-scale railways,
ship-building and machinery factories.

当时中国所需机器主要靠进口，机器进口贸易由各国在华洋行垄断。著名的洋行有
慎昌洋行（美国）、祥和洋行（德国）、怡和洋行（英国）、三井洋行（日本）等。

Back then, the machines in China were largely reliant on import; however, the import trade
of machines was dominated by foreign firms in China, among which famous ones including
Anderson-Meyer & Co.Ltd (US), Xianghe Co., Ltd (Germany), Jardine, Matheson & Co., Ltd (UK),
and Mitsui & Co., Ltd (Japan).

第二节 晚清政府加速军工企业的设立
Section 2 The Government of the Late Qing Dynasty Expedited the Establishment of Military Industrial Enterprises

晚清兵工厂是在当时特定的国内和国际背景下加快发展的，"师夷之长技以制
夷"是"洋务运动"的重要内容之一。兴办兵工厂作为国策于19世纪60年代初开始推
行。从清咸丰十一年到宣统二年（1861—1910年）的50年中，清王朝先后兴办了一批
军工厂，具有一定规模的30多个，分布在21个行省，详见下页表。

The arsenals in Late Qing Dynasty experienced rapid development at the special domestic and international background. "Learning advanced technologies from western countries to resist their military invasions" had always been an essential component of "Westernization Movement". Setting up arsenals was gradually promoted and introduced as a nationwide policy in the beginning of 1860s. Over a span of 50 years from the 11th year in the reign of the Emperor Xianfeng to the second year in the reign of the Emperor Xuantong（1861—1910）, the government of the Qing Dynasty had successively constructed a number of arsenals, of which more than 30 already had a considerable scale, distributed in 21 administrative provinces all over the country as shown in the following table.

清政府经营的重点近代军事工厂简表
Table of major modern military factories run by the government of Qing Dynasty

厂 名 Name	地址 Address	设立年份 Year of Establi–shment	创办人 Founder	简 介 Brief Introduction
安庆内军械所 Anqing Internal Weapons Factory	安庆 Anqing	1861	曾国藩 Zeng Guofan	规模很小，以手工制造为主，生产子弹、火药、炸炮、轮船等 Very small in scale; chiefly manual productions; manufacturing bullets, gunpowder, cannons and ships
上海洋炮局 Shanghai Bureau of Western Cannon	上海 Shanghai	1863	李鸿章 Li Hongzhang	规模很小，以手工制造为主，年末迁苏州，生产子弹、火药 Very small in scale, chiefly manual productions; relocated to Suzhou at the end of year; manufacturing bullets and gunpowder
苏州洋炮局 Suzhou Bureau of Western Cannon	苏州 Suzhou	1864	李鸿章 Li Hongzhang	自上海移至苏州，1865年移至金陵，生产子弹、火药 Relocated to Suzhou from Shanghai and then relocated to Nanjing in 1865; manufacturing bullets and gunpowder
江南制造总局 Jiangnan General Production Bureau	上海 Shanghai	1865	曾国藩 Zeng Guofan 李鸿章 Li Hongzhang	清政府所办规模最大的军用工业，造轮船、军火与机器、钢材 The largest military enterprise set up by the government of Qing Dynasty; manufacturing ships, munitions, machines and steel products
金陵制造局 Nanjing Production Bureau	南京 Nanjing	1865	李鸿章 Li Hongzhang	苏州洋炮局迁至南京成为金陵厂的基础，1881年扩建金陵火药局，生产子弹、火药、枪炮 The relocation of Suzhou Bureau of Western Firearm to Nanjing laid the foundation of Nanjing Factory, which was expanded to Nanjing Bureau of Gunpowder in 1881; manufacturing bullets, gunpowder and firearms

（续表）

厂　名 Name	地址 Address	设立年份 Year of Establi-shment	创办人 Founder	简　介 Brief Introduction
福州船政局 Fuzhou Administrative Bureau of Ship	福州 Fuzhou	1866	左宗棠 Zuo Zongtang	清政府所办规模最大的船舰制造厂 The largest factory set up by the Qing Dynasty that manufactured ships and fleet
天津机器局 Tianjin Bureau of Machine	天津 Tianjin	1867	崇　厚 Chong Hou 李鸿章 Li Hongzhang	规模仅次于江南制造局，1900年毁于八国联军，生产子弹、火药、枪炮、水雷及钢材 The scale is only second to Jiangnan Production Bureau; unfortunately, it was destroyed in the year 1900 by the Eight-Power Allied Forces; manufacturing bullets, gunpowder, firearms, torpedo and steel products
西安机器局 Xi'an Bureau of Machine	西安 Xi'an	1869	左宗棠 Zuo Zongtang	1872年迁至兰州，生产子弹、火药 Relocated to Lanzhou in 1872; manufacturing bullets and gunpowder
福建机器局 Fujian Bureau of Machine	福州 Fuzhou	1869	英　桂 Ying Gui	生产子弹、火药 Manufacturing bullets and gunpowder
兰州机器局 Lanzhou Bureau of Machine	兰州 Lanzhou	1872	左宗棠 Zuo Zongtang	1880年停办 Closed in 1880
云南机器局 Yunnan Bureau of Machine	昆明 Kunming	1872	岑毓英 Cen Yuying	曾停办，1884年再建，生产子弹、火药 Suspended temporarily and resumed operation in 1884; manufacturing bullets and gunpowder
广州机器局 Guangzhou Bureau of Machine	广州 Guangzhou	1874	瑞　麟 Rui Lin	生产子弹、火药、小轮船 Manufacturing bullets, gunpowder and small ships
广州火药局 Guangzhou Bureau of Gunpowder	广州 Guangzhou	1875	刘坤一 Liu Kunyi	生产火药 Manufacturing gunpowder
山东机器局 Shandong Bureau of Machine	济南 Jinan	1875	丁宝桢 Ding Baozhen	生产子弹、火药、枪炮 Manufacturing bullets, gunpowder and firearms
湖南机器局 Hunan Bureau of Machine	长沙 Changsha	1875	王文韶 Wang Wenshao	生产火药、枪、开花炮弹 Manufacturing gunpowder, guns and Shrapnel
四川机器局 Sichuan Bureau of Machine	成都 Chengdu	1877	丁宝桢 Ding Baozhen	生产子弹、火药、枪炮 Manufacturing bullets, gunpowder and firearms

厂 名 Name	地址 Address	设立年份 Year of Establi-shment	创办人 Founder	简 介 Brief Introduction
大沽造船所 Dagu Ship-building Factory	大沽 Dagu	1880	李鸿章 Li Hongzhang	
吉林机器局 Jilin Bureau of Machine	吉林 Jilin	1881	吴大澂 Wu Dacheng	生产子弹、火药、枪 Manufacturing bullets, gunpowder and guns
金陵火药局 Nanjing Bureau of Gunpowder	南京 Nanjing	1881	刘坤一 Liu Kunyi	生产火药 Manufacturing gunpowder
浙江机器局 Zhejiang Bureau of Machine	杭州 Hangzhou	1883	刘秉璋 Liu Bingzhang	生产子弹、火药、水雷 Manufacturing bullets, gunpowder and torpedo
神机营机器局 Shenjiying Bureau of Machine	北京 Beijing	1883	奕 譞 Yi Xuan	1890年冬毁于火 Ruined in a fire in the winter of 1890
广东枪弹厂 Guangdong Bullet Factory	广州 Guangzhou	1885	张之洞 Zhang Zhidong	生产子弹、枪炮 Manufacturing bullets and firearms
台湾机器局 Taiwan Bureau of Machine	基隆 Keelung	1885	刘铭传 Liu Mingchuan	
贵州机器局 Guizhou Bureau of Machine	贵阳 Guiyang	1886	潘 霨 Pan Wei	生产子弹、火药 Manufacturing bullets and gunpowder
湖北枪炮厂 Hubei Firearms Factory	汉阳 Hanyang	1890	张之洞 Zhang Zhidong	1893年正式开工。原设广州。1908年改称汉阳兵工厂，抗日战争时内迁湘、川，生产子弹、火药、枪炮 Officially launched in 1983; it was originally based in Guangzhou and renamed Hanyang Arsenal in 1908. It was relocated to Hunan and Sichuan provinces during the Sino-Japanese war; manufacturing bullets, gunpowder and firearms
陕西机器局 Shaanxi Bureau of Machine	西安 Xi'an	1894	鹿传麟 Lu Chuanlin	生产枪弹、修理机器 Manufacturing bullets and repairing machines
奉天制造局 Mukden Production Bureau	沈阳 Shenyang	1897	依克唐阿 Yike Tanga	又称盛京机器局，生产子弹、火药，张作霖在此基础扩建成有名的"东三省兵工厂" Also known as Shengjing Bureau of Machine; manufacturing bullets and gunpowder; Zhang Zuolin expanded it into what was famously known as "Arsenal of the Three Northeastern Provinces"

（续表）

厂 名 Name	地址 Address	设立年份 Year of Establi-shment	创办人 Founder	简 介 Brief Introduction
河南机器局 Henan Bureau of Machine	开封 Kaifeng	1897	刘树棠 Liu Shutang	
山西制造局 Shanxi Production Bureau	太原 Taiyuan	1898	胡聘之 Hu Pinzhi	
新疆机器厂 Xinjiang Machine Factory	乌鲁木齐 Urumqi	1898	饶应祺 Rao Yingqi	生产枪弹 Manufacturing bullets
黑龙江机器局 Heilongjiang Bureau of Machine	黑龙江 Heilongjiang	1899	恩泽 En Ze	生产枪弹 Manufacturing bullets
江西子弹厂 Jiangxi Bullet Factory	南昌 Nanchang	1903	麦特 Mai Te	生产子弹、毛瑟枪 Manufacturing bullets and Mauser guns
北洋机器局 Beiyang Bureau of Machine	德州 Dezhou	1904	袁世凯 Yuan Shikai	天津机器局被毁后迁去建立，生产子弹、火药 Relocated and established after Tianjin Bureau of Machine was destroyed; manufacturing bullets and gunpowder
安徽机器局 Anhui Bureau of Machine	安庆 Anqing	1907	冯煦 Feng Xu	生产子弹、火药 Manufacturing bullets and gunpowder
四川兵工厂 Sichuan Arsenal	成都 Chengdu	1910	赵尔巽 Zhao ErXun	生产子弹、火药 Manufacturing bullets and gunpowder

在30多个主要军工厂中，安庆内军械所在中国兵工史、机械史上有重要意义，它的兴办，是中国机械工业、军事工业，从手工制造向机械制造过渡的标志，对整个机械工业的建立发展走出了第一步。江南制造总局（制造枪炮、轮船）、福州船政局（专业修造兵船）、金陵机器制造局（生产大炮）和天津机器制造局（火药及子弹），任务各有侧重，它们集合在一起，构成中国早期军事工业的主干。还有后起之秀的湖北枪炮厂，此工厂是当时除了外人在华所办工厂外，设备先进、规模最大的机械制造厂。这些工厂各有其重要历史地位。

Among over 30 major weapons factories, Anqing Internal Weapons Factory had served utmost significance in China's ordnance and machinery history. Its establishment and development marked the transition from manual production to machine production in China's machinery and military industry; it represented the first step forward to the establishment and development of the entire machinery industry. Jiangnan General Production Bureau (manufacturing firearms and ships), Fuzhou Administrative Bureau of Ship (exclusively repairing and building warships), Nanjing Machine Production Bureau (manufacturing cannons) and Tianjin Machine Production Bureau (manufacturing gunpowder and bullets), with their own unique focus, had constituted the backbone of China's early military industry. Hubei Firearms Factory of tremendous promise was the largest, advanced-equipped machinery factory back then, apart from factories operated by foreigners in China. Each had demonstrated essential historical significance.

江南机器制造总局
Jiangnan General Production Bureau

1865年，曾国藩会同李鸿章奏准设立，将苏州洋炮局的韩、丁两局迁上海，与收购的美商旗记铁工厂合并，将曾国藩命容闳为安庆内军械所在美国采购的百余台机器并入，1865年6月3日成立。江南局建立之初，中国的机器工业几乎为零，故江南机器制造总局集舰船、枪炮、弹药、水雷等制造于一身，形成了大生产、细分工、产品多样的现代化机器生产的特点。经不断扩建，至1895年，有轮船厂、机器厂、枪厂、炮厂、无烟药厂、铸造厂、锻造厂、炼钢厂等近20个工厂，拥有职工3592人，各种机床662台，还有3000t水压机，15t马丁炼钢炉，当时公认其设备是世界第一流的。19世纪90年代，它已发展成为中国乃至东亚技术最先进、设备最齐全的机器工厂，被誉为"中国第一厂"。1867—1904年该局除生产枪炮、兵船外，还制造了各种机器设备591台，其中金切机床249台。1868年8月建成中国近代自行建造的第一艘蒸汽兵船"恬吉"号。

In 1865, Zeng Guofan and Li Hongzhang were authorized to relocate the two bureaus headed by Han and Ding of Suzhou Bureau of Western Cannon to Shanghai and merge them with acquired US company Thomas Hunt & Co. Hundreds of machines purchased from US by Yung Wing appointed by Zeng Guofan, were phased in to Anqing Internal Weapons Factory and Jiangnan General Production Bureau was officially established on June 3rd 1865. During its nascent phase, the machinery industry of China was almost in square one. In light of this, manufacturing of fleets and ships, cannons, arms and torpedo, undertaken by Jiangnan General Production Bureau, had collectively incorporated characteristics of modern machine production: large-scale production, fine division of labor and a wide variety of products. Through constant expansion and constructions, there were nearly 20 factories by the year 1895, including shipbuilding factories, machine factories, gun factories, cannon factories, smoke-free pharmaceutical factories, casting factories, forging factories and steel refineries. There were a total of 3,592 employees, as well as 662 of all sorts of machine tools, 3,000t hydraulic press and 15t Martin steel-smelting furnace, which was believed to be world-class equipment back then. In 1890s, it had already had the most advanced technologies and fullest range of equipments in China and even across the entire East Asia, for which it was renowned the "No.1 factory in China". From 1867 to 1904, apart from

cannons and warships, a total of 591 machines and equipments of all sorts were manufactured by this bureau, among which 249 were metal-cutting machine tools. In August 1868, the first steam-powered warship by the name of "Tianji" was independently built in modern China.

江南机器制造总局大门

Gate of Jiangnan General Production Bureau

江南制造局翻译处的主要中国译员徐寿、华蘅芳和徐建寅

The Main Chinese Translators of Translation Office of Jiangnan General Production Bureau including Xu Shou, Hua Hengfang and Xu Jianyin

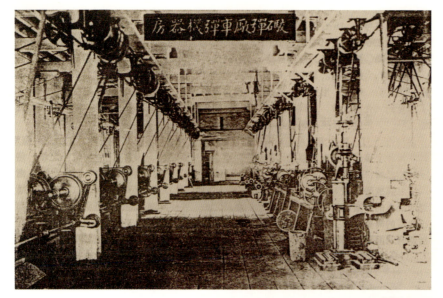

江南制造局炮弹厂车弹机器房

Vehicle and Bullet Machine Room of
Cannonball Factory of Jiangnan General
Production Bureau

江南制造局机器正厂

Main Machine Factory of Jiangnan General
Production Bureau

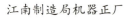

江南制造局炮厂房

Cannon Factory of Jiangnan General
Production Bureau

江南制造局钻炮管机
（深孔钻床）

Gun Barrel Drill Machine
(deep hole drilling
machine) of Jiangnan
General Production
Bureau

1905年4月，该局分为江南船坞和上海兵工厂。上海兵工厂由于经营不善，1928年停产。江南船坞更名为江南造船所，后发展为江南造船厂。

In April 1905, Jiangnan General Production Bureau was split into Jiangnan Dock and Shanghai Arsenal. Shanghai Arsenal was shut down in 1928 due to poor management while Jiangnan Dock was renamed Jiangnan Shipbuilding Plant, which later evolved into Jiangnan Shipbuilding Factory.

江南机器制造局在中国近代机械史上创造了许多"中国第一"。除"恬吉"号外，1876年建造中国第一艘铁甲螺旋桨驱动军舰"金瓯"号；1878年制造出第一架钢制火炮，第一支后装线镗步枪；1891年造出第一台车床，炼出中国第一炉钢水，第一磅无烟火药；举办了中国第一个机械工业制造学校；最早从西方引进先进技术，1917年冬以1万美元引进美国人高伦发明的5hp以上汽油机制造技术；1920年，为美国承造万吨级运输舰，是中国制造的第一条万吨级舰轮。

Jiangnan General Production Bureau has accomplished many "No.1 in China" in modern machinery history of China. Apart from "Tianji", the bureau built the first warship "Jinou" characterized by steel armors and powered by screw propellers in 1876, the first steel artillery and the first breech-loading rifle in 1878. The first lathe was constructed in 1891, producing the first furnace of molten steel; the first pound of smoke-free gunpowder. The bureau established the first machinery industry manufacturing institute in China, and took the lead to import advanced technologies from western countries-importing manufacturing technologies of gasoline engine measuring 5hp and above in capacity which was invented by an American named Galon for the price of USD 10,000 in the winter of 1917, and the first fleet of transport ships with a capacity measuring ten thousands of tons in China for US in 1920.

1869年江南制造局所造第1艘木
壳暗轮兵船"操江"号

The First Warship Named "Caojiang"
with Wooden Shell and Hidden Wheels
Manufactured by Jiangnan General
Production Bureau in 1869

1912年江南造船所制造的"江
华"号客轮

"Jianghua" Passenger Liner
Manufactured by Jiangnan Ship-yard
in 1912

江南船坞于1921年为美国建
造的14750t远洋货船"官府"
（Mandarin）号

"Mandarin" 14,750 Tons Ocean
Cargo Ship Jiangnan Dock Built by
Jiangnan Dock for US in 1921

1920年江南造船所为万吨级运输舰制造的3000hp主机

3,000hp-Main Engine Manufactured by Jiangnan Ship-yard for the Transport Ship With Capacity of Ten Thousand Tons in 1920

1918年江南造船所仿造的"高伦"汽油机

Mimic "Galon" gasoline engine Manufactured by Jiangnan Ship-yard in 1918

1867—1904年（清同治六年五月至清光绪三十年）江南制造局制造的机器设备
Machines and equipments manufactured by Jiangnan General Production Bureau from 1867 to 1904 (May of the 6th year of the Emperor Tongzhi of the Qing Dynasty until the 30th year during the Emperor Guangxu of the Qing Dynasty)

机器名称 Name of Machine	数量（台） Quantity (Unit)	开始制造的时间 Starting Year of Manufacturing
车床 Lathe	138	至迟清同治十二年（1873） Delayed to the 12th year of the Emperor Tongzhi of the Qing Dynasty (1873)
刨床 Planer	47	至迟清同治十二年（1873） Delayed to the 12th year of the Emperor Tongzhi of the Qing Dynasty (1873)
钻床 Driller	55	至迟清同治十二年（1873） Delayed to the 12th year of the Emperor Tongzhi of the Qing Dynasty (1873)
锯床 Hacksaw Machine	9	清同治十三年（1874） 13th year of the Emperor Tongzhi of the Qing Dynasty (1874)
齿轮机床 Gear Machine Tool	8	至迟清同治十二年（1873） Delayed to the 12th year of the Emperor Tongzhi of the Qing Dynasty (1873)
卷铁板机 Iron Sheet Rolling Machine	5	至迟清同治十二年（1873） Delayed to the 12th year of the Emperor Tongzhi of the Qing Dynasty (1873)
卷炮弹机器 Cannonball Rolling Machine	3	至迟清同治十二年（1873） Delayed to the 12th year of the Emperor Tongzhi of the Qing Dynasty (1873)
汽锤 Steam Hammer	4	至迟清同治十二年（1873） Delayed to the 12th year of the Emperor Tongzhi of the Qing Dynasty (1873)
大锤机器 Large Hammering Machine	3	至迟清同治十二年（1873） Delayed to the 12th year of the Emperor Tongzhi of the Qing Dynasty (1873)
印锤机器 Striking Hammering Machine	4	至迟清同治十二年（1873） Delayed to the 12th year of the Emperor Tongzhi of the Qing Dynasty (1873)
砂轮 Grinding Abrasive Wheel	10	至迟清同治十二年（1873） Delayed to the 12th year of the Emperor Tongzhi of the Qing Dynasty (1873)
磨石机器 Stone Grinding Machine	16	至迟清同治十二年（1873） Delayed to the 12th year of the Emperor Tongzhi of the Qing Dynasty (1873)
挖泥机器及挖泥船 Dredger and Dredging Ship	2	至迟清同治十二年（1873） Delayed to the 12th year of the Emperor Tongzhi of the Qing Dynasty (1873)

（续表）

机器名称 Name of Machine	数量（台） Quantity (Unit)	开始制造的时间 Starting Year of Manufacturing
绞螺丝机器 Screw Reaming Machine	3	清同治十三年（1874） 13th year of the Emperor Tongzhi of the Qing Dynasty (1874)
剪刀冲眼机器 Shear-punching Machine	3	清同治十三年（1874） 13th year of the Emperor Tongzhi of the Qing Dynasty (1874)
翻砂机器 Molding Machine	28	清光绪元年（1875） 1st year of the Emperor Guangxu of the Qing Dynasty (1875)
造炮子泥心机器 Cannon Clay-core Making Machine	3	清光绪元年（1875） 1st year of the Emperor Guangxu of the Qing Dynasty (1875)
舂药引机器 Mortor Powder Detonator Machine	5	清光绪三年（1877） 3rd year of the Emperor Guangxu of the Qing Dynasty (1877)
起重机器 Craning Machine	84	清光绪三年（1877） 3rd year of the Emperor Guangxu of the Qing Dynasty (1877)
筛砂机器 Sand Screening Machine	5	清光绪四年（1878） 4th year of the Emperor Guangxu of the Qing Dynasty (1878)
试铁力机器 Iron Strength Testing Machine Testing	2	清光绪四年（1878） 4th year of the Emperor Guangxu of the Qing Dynasty (1878)
造枪准星机器 Gun Sight Beads Machine	5	清光绪五年（1879） 5th year of the Emperor Guangxu of the Qing Dynasty (1879)
剪铁机器 Iron-shearing Machine	4	清光绪七年（1881） 7th year of the Emperor Guangxu of the Qing Dynasty (1881)
轧机 Rolling Mill	5	清光绪七年（1881） 7th year of the Emperor Guangxu of the Qing Dynasty (1881)
抽水机 Lift Pump	77	清光绪八年（1882） 8th year of the Emperor Guangxu of the Qing Dynasty (1882)
造皮带机器 Belt Machine	4	清光绪十一年（1885） 11th year of the Emperor Guangxu of the Qing Dynasty (1885)
压铅条机器 Lead-pressing Machine	1	清光绪十一年（1885） 11th year of the Emperor Guangxu of the Qing Dynasty (1885)

机器名称 Name of Machine	数量（台） Quantity (Unit)	开始制造的时间 Starting Year of Manufacturing
蒸汽机 Steamer	32	清光绪十一年（1885） 11th year of the Emperor Guangxu of the Qing Dynasty (1885)
磨刀机器 Sharpening Machine	2	清光绪十二年（1886） 12th year of the Emperor Guangxu of the Qing Dynasty (1886)
锅炉 Boiler	15	清光绪十二年（1886） 12th year of the Emperor Guangxu of the Qing Dynasty (1886)
磨枪头炮子机器 Bullet and Shell Grinding Machine	4	清光绪十三年（1887） 13th year of the Emperor Guangxu of the Qing Dynasty (1887)
压模机器 Mould Pressing Machine	3	清光绪十三年（1887） 13th year of the Emperor Guangxu of the Qing Dynasty (1887)
压铁机器 Iron Pressing Machine	1	清光绪十八年（1892） 18th year of the Emperor Guangxu of the Qing Dynasty (1892)
压钢机器 Steel Pressing Machine	1	清光绪十九年（1893） 19th year of the Emperor Guangxu of the Qing Dynasty (1893)
锯钢机器 Steel-sawing Machine	1	清光绪十九年（1893） 19th year of the Emperor Guangxu of the Qing Dynasty (1893)
炼钢炉 Steel Furnace	9	清光绪二十年（1894） 20th year of the Emperor Guangxu of the Qing Dynasty (1894)
水力压机 Hydraulic Pressing Machine	1	清光绪二十一年（1895） 21st year of the Emperor Guangxu of the Qing Dynasty (1895)
装铜帽机器 Copper Cap Installing Machine	4	清光绪二十一年（1895） 21st year of the Emperor Guangxu of the Qing Dynasty (1895)
造铜引机器 Copper Detonator Making Machine	1	清光绪二十三年（1897） 23rd year of the Emperor Guangxu of the Qing Dynasty (1897)
敲铁机器 Iron Hammering Machine	2	清光绪二十三年（1897） 23rd year of the Emperor Guangxu of the Qing Dynasty (1897)
试煤机器 Coal Testing Machine	1	清光绪二十八年（1902） 28th year of the Emperor Guangxu of the Qing Dynasty (1902)
发电机器 Power Generating Equipment	1	
压书机器 Book Press Machine	1	

福州船政局
Fuzhou Administrative Bureau of Ship

福州船政局是晚清洋务运动领袖之一左宗棠一手规划并创办的，是中国近代第一座建造轮船的专业机械厂。它于1866年12月开工，1868年基本建成，占地39.4万平方米，设有铸铁厂（翻砂车间）、轮机厂（动力车间）、合拢机器厂（机器安装车间）、钟表厂（仪表车间）、捶铁厂（锻造车间）等18个主要工厂。是当时远东最大近代造船厂，日本横滨、横须贺铁工厂的规模无法与之相比。1869年9月建造成功第一艘兵商两用轮船"万年清"号，排水量1370t，主机功率432kW，螺旋桨推进，功率和吨位都大大超过日本同期仿造的"千代"号或"清辉"号。福建船政局自1866年创建到清末共建造了40艘兵船，占同期国内58艘自制兵船的70%，其中有"平远"号等多艘巡洋舰。

Fuzhou Administrative Bureau of Ship was the first specialized machine factory that built ships in modern China. It was planned and set up by Zuo Zongtang, one of the leading pioneers of the Westernization Movement in the late Qing Dynasty. The construction was started in December, 1866 and roughly completed in 1868. With an area of 394,000 m^2, the bureau covered 18 major factories, such as cast iron factories (molding floor), turbine factory (motive power plant), machine jointing factory (machine installation room), clock factory (meter shop), and iron hammering factory (forging shop). It was back then the largest modern ship-building factory in China, overshadowing Japanese Yokohama and Yokosuka iron factories in terms of scale. The first ship named "Wannianqing" (Qing Dynasty Forever) that served both military and commercial purposes was successfully built in September 1869. It was powered by propellers and had a displacement of 1,370 t and host power of 432 kW, which far surpassed the counterfeit "Qiandai" or "Qinghui" manufactured by Japan. Over the period from 1866 to the late Qing Dynasty, Fuzhou Administrative Bureau of Ship constructed 40 warships, among which are "Pingyuan"(safe and far) and many other cruisers, accounting for 70% of the total 58 warships built nationwide.

1877年始，连续派出多批学生赴英、法留学，多数成为其后中国造船工业的重要技术力量。

From the year 1877 onwards, batches of students had been continuously sent to UK and France to further their education. The majority later constituted the major technical forces behind China's ship-building industry.

福州船政局建局30多年曾有过造船的辉煌，终因体制结构问题（经费由国家拨发，所造船舰无偿调拨给三洋"北洋、南洋、粤洋"海军），于1907年停办。

Fuzhou Administrative Bureau of Ship had accomplished great achievements during the 30 years since its establishment. However, it was suspended and shut down in 1907 on account of problems in its system structure. (The funds were channeled by the national government and ships built were handed out for free to the navy in the "three oceans": "North Ocean, South Ocean and Guangdong Ocean".)

福州船政局办公厅
正门

Main Entrance of
the General Office of
Fuzhou Administrative
Bureau of Ship

1871年福州船政局建成的"伏波"号兵轮

"Fubo" (subduing the waves) War Liner Built by
Fuzhou Administrative Bureau of Ship in 1871

福州船政局1889年
竣工的装甲巡洋舰"龙
威"号（编入北洋海军
后改为"平远"号）

The Armored Cruiser
"Longwei" (Dragon
Might) built by Fuzhou
Administrative Bureau of
Ship in 1889 (Renamed
"Pingyuan" (peace and
far) after being incorporated
into Beiyang Navy)

福州船政局制造的"建安"号鱼雷快舰

"Jian'an" (safe and sound) Torpedo Rapid Naval Vessel Manufactured by Fuzhou Administrative Bureau of Ship

"扬武"号（三桅）及"伏波"号（二桅）兵船在停泊中

"Yangwu" (demonstrating power) (three masts) and "Fubo" (two masts) on the Berth

天津机器制造局（后改称北洋机器制造局）
Tianjin Bureau of Machine Production (Renamed Beiyang Bureau of Machine Production)

1867年崇厚创办天津机器制造局，1870年投产。建局时仿效江南制造局模式，主要制造军火，还承修兵商轮船。19世纪90年代成为当时中国的近代军火总汇，规模仅次于江南制造总局。1875年开始造船，曾先后制造了中国第一艘挖泥船、潜水艇、游艇等特种船。该局毁于1900年八国联军侵华战争中，1903年迁移山东德州重建，但规模不复当年。

Tianjin Bureau of Machine Production was set up by Chonghou in 1867 and put into production in 1870. During the nascent phase, it emulated the mode of Jiangnan General Production Bureau, which mainly manufactured firearms and undertook the repair of ships that served both military and commercial purposes. It developed into the repository of arms in modern China in 1890s, with a scale that was only second to that of Jiangnan General Production Bureau. Since it started to build ships in 1875, the bureau had successively produced the first dredger, submarine and yacht as well as other special ships. It was ruined during the military invasion mounted by the Eight-Power Allied Forces in 1900, and restored in Dezhou of Shandong Province in 1903, but with a much smaller scale.

在八国联军铁蹄下被毁的天津机器局

Tianjin Bureau of Machine Ruined by the Invasion of the Eight-Power Allied Forces

金陵机器制造局
Nanjing Bureau of Machine Production

1865年李鸿章创建，先后将苏州洋炮局、安庆内军械所并入，其后又经曾国藩、李鸿章扩建。建局之初仅能制造枪弹、炮弹、引信等，1869年开始制造轻型火炮，至1874年已发展成为拥有机器厂、翻砂厂、枪厂、火药厂等10余个工厂。1928年改称金陵兵工厂，抗日战争时内迁重庆，改名兵工署二十一厂，国民党制式武器"中正式"步枪主要由该厂生产。1945年员工达15201人。

First set up by Li Hongzhang in 1865, Nanjing Bureau of Machine Production incorporated Suzhou Bureau of Western Cannon and Anqing Internal Weapons Factory and later was expanded by Zeng Guofan and Li Hongzhang. At the beginning of the establishment, it was only capable of producing bullets, cannonballs and detonators. From the year 1869 onwards, it started to make light cannons, and had developed into a scale of over 10 factories including machine factories, sand-casting factories, gun factories, and gunpowder factories by the year 1874. It was successively renamed Nanjing Arsenal in 1928 and 21st Factory of Arsenal Office when was relocated to Chongqing during the Anti-Japanese War. Standard arm Mauser M1924 Gewehrs used by Kuomintang were mainly produced by this particular factory. In the year 1945, the number of its employees reached 15,201.

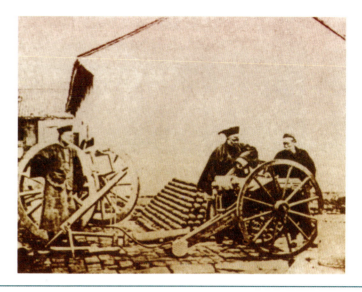

金陵机器局制造的火炮

Artillery Manufactured by Nanjing Bureau of Machine

湖北枪炮厂
Hubei Firearm Factory

　　张之洞于1893年创建的大型综合性兵工厂，与江南、天津二局并称为清朝三大兵工厂。以白银30万两从德国利弗（Lever）机器厂购买一套日产十连发毛瑟枪50支，年产25—120mm口径山炮50门的全套设备，另有1套制造刺刀设备。前后建设有炼钢厂、无烟火药厂等9个分厂，1904年更名湖北兵工厂，1908年又更名汉阳枪炮厂。该局是当时造枪造炮最多的兵工厂之一，至1910年共制造7.9mm口径的毛瑟枪（即抗日战争前著名的"汉阳造"步枪）13.61万支，57mm格鲁森式火炮988门及大量枪弹炮弹。

湖北兵工厂的大门，张之洞在湖北汉阳创办

The Entrance of Hubei Arsenal Set up by Zhang Zhidong in Hanyang, Hubei Province

The large-scale comprehensive arsenal set up by Zhang Zhidong in 1893 was dubbed the "Three Largest Arsenals", along with Jiangnan and Tianjin Bureaus. Apart from a set of bayonet equipments, the factory was equipped a comprehensive set of equipments, which was purchased from German Lever Machine factory at the price of 300,000 Tael of silver dollars (the then currency) and capable of producing 50 Mauser guns with a running fire of ten shots daily and 50 mountain artilleries with a caliber of 25—120 mm. With a total of 9 branch factories including steel refineries and smokeless gunpowder factories constructed successively, the factory was renamed Hubei Arsenal in 1904 and Hanyang Firearm Factory in 1908. As one of the arsenals that manufactured the largest number of guns and cannons at the time, the factory had manufactured a total of 136,100 Mauser guns with a caliber of 7.9 mm (a rifle well-known as "Made in Hanyang" prior to Anti-Japanese War), 988 Grusen artillery with a caliber of 57mm and a large number of bullets and cannonballs.

第三节 民国北洋政府时期（1912—1927年）中国机械工业的发展

Section 3 The Development of Chinese Machinery Industry in the Reign of Beiyang Government(1912—1927) of Republic of China

1911年辛亥革命爆发，1912年中华民国临时政府（历史上称为北洋政府）成立，到1927年国民政府定都南京，这一时期，历史上称为北洋政府时期。

The reign of Beiyang Government began from the Revolution of 1911 (the Chinese bourgeois democratic revolution led by Dr. Sun Yat-sen which overthrew the Qing Dynasty) and the establishment of the provisional government of Republic of China (known as Beiyang government in history) in 1912, till 1927 when the government made Nanjing as the capital city.

这一时期，各地军阀为扩大其军事实力，新建和扩建一些军工厂。汉阳兵工厂、太原兵工厂得到较大发展，至1926年分别拥有员工4500余人和11000余人，1913年新建南苑飞机修造厂，1915年新建巩县兵工厂，1916年新建奉天（沈阳）军械厂。奉天厂在1922年更名为东三省兵工厂，投资2亿多银元大规模扩建，员工由建厂初的300人，发展为1925年的21000多人，除生产枪炮外，还生产机床等机械产品，是当时全国最大的机械厂。

During this particular period, warlords in various places started to construct and expand some arsenals or weapons factories in an effort to enhance their military strength. Hanyang Arsenal and Taiyuan Arsenal had gained considerable development, with over 4,500 and 11,000 employees respectively by the year of 1926. Nanyuan Plane Repair Factory and Gong Township Arsenal were built in 1913 and 1915 respectively. Besides, Mukden (Shenyang) Weapons Factory built in

1916 was renamed the Arsenal of the Three Northeastern Provinces in 1922 and expanded in large scale with an investment of more than 200 million silver dollars (the then currency). The number of its employees increased from merely 300 shortly after the factory was founded to over 21,000 in 1925. With ability to manufacture firearms and such mechanical products as machine tools, it developed into the largest machine factory back then.

1913年，全国共有23个兵工厂，拥有员工2.85万人、资金1.28亿元，分别占中国工业的10.5%和38.7%，占中国机械工业的60.7%和80.4%，至1927年，兵工厂增至47个。

There were altogether 23 arsenals in China in 1913, with 28,500 employees and a capital of RMB128 million, accounting for 10.5% and 38.7% of China's industries, and 60.7% and 80.4% of China's machinery industry respectively. By the year 1927, the number of arsenals had increased to 47.

1914年，第一次世界大战爆发，西方工业国家无力东顾。1915年以后的几年，是中国民族资本发展机械工业的"黄金时期"，上海民营机械厂由1914年的91家增至1924年的284家，湖北由19家增至33家。但1918年第一次世界大战结束后至1926年北伐战争前，由于内战频繁和外资厂商挤压，民营机械企业又重新陷入困境。

The First World War which broke out in 1914 undermined the efforts invested by western industrialized countries in their military invasions in China, and contributed to the development of machinery industry funded by China's national capital in following several years after 1915, known as "golden period". The private-owned machine factories in Shanghai increased considerably in number from 91 in 1914 to 284 in 1924; the number experienced similar explosive growth from 19 to 33 in Hubei Province. However, during the period spanning from the end of the First World War in 1918 to the time before the Northern Expedition in 1926, private-owned machine enterprises got again in hot water due to frequent internal conflicts and squeeze of foreign-owned factories and merchants.

此一时期，机械工业的生产技术有所提高。兵工厂仿造第一次世界大战前后出现的新兵器，如抗战时期国民党部队的制式武器7.9mm中正式步枪就是此时由巩县兵工厂研制定型的；日军侵华战争使用"三八式"步枪由太原兵工厂仿制大量生产。民机产品市场需求旺盛，发展了万吨运输舰，成套纺织机械等。

During this period, the production technique in machinery industry had made tremendous progress. Inspired by the new weapons appearing around the First World War, Gong Township Arsenal designed and made Mauser M1924 Gewehrs with a caliber of 7.9 mm which were widely used by Kuomintang during the Sino-Japanese War; Taiyuan Arsenal mass produced the Japanese Rifles named Sanpati-shiki hoheijyuu utilized by the Japanese army during the Anti-Japanese War. The huge demand for civil machine products stimulated the development of transport ships with a tonnage of ten thousand tons and full sets of textile machineries.

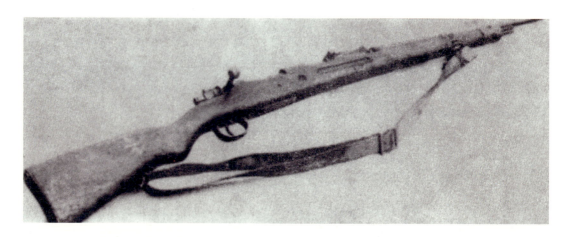

巩县兵工厂造7.9mm中正式步枪

Mauser M1924 Gewehr with a Caliber of 7.9mm made by Gong Township Arsenal

太原兵工厂造仿日6.5mm三八式步枪

Japanese Rifle Named Sanpati-shiki Hoheijyuu with a Caliber of 6.5mm Counterfeited by Taiyuan Arsenal

沈阳兵工厂大门

Entrance of Shenyang
Arsenal

汉阳兵工厂外貌
Exterior Appearance of
Hanyang Arsenal

第四节 民营机械工业在艰难中发展
Section 4 Private-Owned Machinery Industry was Developing through Difficult Periods

　　清政府对机械工业的态度，从一开始的被动到后来的鼓励。19世纪60年代中期开始，左宗棠、张之洞、郭嵩涛、丁日昌等有识之士都曾建议清廷设厂制造民用机器，但未被接受，直到1894年中日甲午战争清政府战败，1895年4月签订屈辱的中日《马关条约》，清政府迫于形势，不得不改弦更张。1895年7月清政府颁布上谕，宣称要"力行实政"，要"造机器"，与原来洋务派只限于"坚船利炮"、"造船制炮"相比，有了较大进步。同时制定、实施了一系列奖励发展民族工商业的法令措施。1898年7月13日颁布《振兴工艺给奖章程》，首次以专利、官衔的方式鼓励发明创造；1903年颁布《公司注册试办章程》，奖励设立公司；1906年颁发《奖给商勋章程》，鼓励研制新机器；1907年颁发《华商办理实业爵赏章程》，鼓励投资办实业；清政府并于1903年设立工商部，倡办实业和学堂，引进技术。

The government of Qing Dynasty tended to encourage machine manufacturing rather than originally being passive. From mid-1860s, quite a number of scholars including Zuo Zongtang, Zhang Zhidong, Guo Songtao and Ding Richang had made suggestions to the Qing Dynasty for establishing factories that manufacture civil machines, but they were all invariably rejected. The situation didn't change until then when China suffered a defeat of Sino-Japanese War in 1894 and signed the humiliating *Treaty of Shimonoseki* in April 1895. Given this pressing situation, the government of Qing Dynasty had no choice but to change tunes. In July 1895, the government of Qing Dynasty issued orders, proclaiming the desire to "implement real politics" and intention to "make machines". Compared with the original westernization faction that emphasized "solid ships and cannons", and "producing ships and cannons", it had made great progress. A series of incentives and legal measures in developing national industry and commerce had been devised and implemented. *Regulations of Incentives in Reviving Industry* rolled out on July 13th 1898, encouraged invention and creation by means of patent and awarding official rankings for the first time. The *Trial Regulations of Company Registration* promulgated out in 1903 were intended to award the establishment of more companies. *Regulations of Awarding Businesses* were introduced in 1906, encouraging research and manufacturing of new machines. *Regulations Encouraging Chinese Merchants to Set up Companies* were issued in the year 1907 to encourage investment in setting up more businesses. The government of Qing Dynasty set up Ministry of Industry and Commerce in the year 1903 in a gesture to advocate establishing businesses and schools and importation of technologies.

早期民族资本经营的机械工厂多数是由手工作坊逐步发展起来的，或萌芽于轻工产品制造业的机修车间；1901年创办的协记机器厂、1911年创办的美昌机器厂，都是由卷烟厂机修力量发展的烟机修造厂。一些曾在外资工厂或官办机器局工作过的技术工人、手工业的铜铁匠们成为民办机器厂的技术力量。1852年创办的上海甘章船坞，1866年创办的上海发昌机器厂，1876年的广州陈联泰机器厂等都是创办较早、规模较大的民办机械厂。

The majority of early machine factories funded by national capital were evolved from early manual workshops or originated from light industrial machine repair shop; Both Xieji Machine Factory established in 1901 and Meichang Machine Factory were repair shops for cigarette machine and developed by cigarette machine maintenance staff. Some technicians, coppersmiths and blacksmiths who once worked in foreign-owned factories or government-run machine bureaus had become the major technological force driving the development of private-owned machine factories. Shanghai Ganzhang Shipyard set up in 1852, Shanghai Fachang Machine Factory set up in 1866, and Guangzhou Chen Liantai Machine Factory established in 1876 were among the earliest and largest private-owned machine factories.

随着机械产品修造市场需求的增加，民办机械工业有一定的发展，逐步形成船舶、纺织、印刷等民用机械及公用事业修配专业。1913年与1895年比较，全国民办机械工业的职工由4457人增至18450人；工厂由96家增至182家。当时规模较大的有1895年创办的汉口周恒顺机器厂、1902年创办的上海大隆机器厂、1904年创办的上海求新制造机器轮船厂及1907年创办的汉口扬子机器厂等。但其规模远不及外资机械厂，如当时华人创办最大的求新厂和扬子厂，资本分别为70万元和49万元，而英商的耶松和瑞镕两厂资本分别为770万元和105万元。由于技术力量薄弱，市场为外国人控制，民营机械厂处境艰难。

With increasing market demand in machinery production and repair, private-owned machinery industry had achieved certain improvements. Specialized field of repair and replacements in civil machinery industry and public services, such as ships, textile and printing, gradually took shape.

As compared with that in 1895, the number of employees in private-owned machinery industry nationwide increased from 4,457 to 18,450 in 1913; the number of factories rose from 96 to 182. The large-scale factories at the time included Hankou Zhouhengshun Machine Factory set up in 1895, Shanghai Dalong Machine Factory set up in 1902 and Shanghai Qiuxin Machine Ship Factory established in 1904 and Hankou Yangzi Machine Factory set up in 1907. However, they were far overshadowed by foreign-owned machine factories in scale. For example, Qiuxin Machine Ship Factory and Yangzi Machine Factory, the largest factories established by Chinese people had a capital of RMB 700,000 and 490,000 respectively, while the capital of S.C. Farnham Co. and Ruirong Factory, two British companies, totaled RMB 7.7 million and 1.05 million respectively. Moreover, weak technological power and market dominated by foreign people made the situation even tougher for private-owned machine factories.

尽管处境艰难，民办机械工业的动力机械和交通机械还是具有一定制造水平。约在1908年广州均和安机器厂仿制出单缸8hp煤气机，1910年求新机器轮船厂仿制出25hp火油发动机，此前1909年还造成了配大型水泵的200hp以上蒸汽机。1909年冯如在美国试飞成功自制的飞机，1910年谭根在美国制成水上飞机，与1903年美国的莱特兄弟研制成飞机相差不过6年。

冯如回国后装配的飞机

Plane Assembled by Feng Ru after Coming Back to China

In despite of difficult situation, the manufacturing of motive power machinery and transportation machinery of private-owned machinery industry had already attained a certain level. Guangzhou Junheàn Machine Factory managed to manufacture single-cylinder 8hp gas engine in 1908, while Qiuxin Machine Ship Factory managed to imitate and manufacture 25hp kerosene engine in 1910, following the production of steamers with over 200hp for large-scale water pumps in 1909. What is more, Feng Ru successfully trial-flied independently designed plane in US in 1909, only 6 years after 1903 when the Wright Brothers from US successfully researched and built planes. In the next year, Tan Gen built seaplane in US.

冯如

Feng Ru

1911年1月18日，冯如驾机在奥克兰海湾附近进行了完美的试飞

On January 18th 1911, Feng Ru completed a successful and perfect trial flight in the vicinity of Oakland Bay

第三章　国民政府定都南京到"七七"事变前的中国机械工业

Chapter 3　China's Machinery Industry from Deciding on Nanjing as the Capital by the National Government to the "July 7 Incident"

1927年国民政府定都南京到1937年"七七"事变前，这一时期军阀混战基本结束，中国步入了近代相对快速的发展时期。国民政府着手发展机械工业，国营机械工厂的建设开始起步，民营机械工厂有所发展，取得了一些成绩。

Over the period from choosing Nanjing for its capital by the national government in 1927 to the "July 7 Incident" in 1937, the chaotic internal conflicts among different warlords had come to end, China stepped into relative rapid developmenr period. The national government started to develop machinery industry, embarking on the endeavor of building state-run machine factories. Private-run machine factories had achieved some developments and accomplishments.

1927年后，国民政府制定实施了一些鼓励民族工业发展和鼓励技术进步的政策措施。1928年颁布《奖励工业品暂行条例》，1929年7月颁布《特种工业奖励法》，1932年颁布《奖励工业技术暂行条例》，这些措施对机械工业的发展有积极影响。

After 1927, the national government introduced and implemented a series of policies and measures to encourage the development of national industries and technological progress, among which were *Provisional Regulations on Awarding Industrial Products* issued in 1928, *Methods of Incentives for Special Industries* in July 1929, *Provisional Regulations on Awarding Industrial Technologies* in 1932. These measures exerted positive influences on the development of machinery industry.

据1934年统计，全国共有民用机械厂1781个、工人45767人，主要集中在上海，占工厂数的90%，工人数的69%（统计不完整，按地区计缺东北、杭州、广州，按部门计缺电力、矿山、交通等专业部门的修配厂）。

According to statistics compiled in 1934, there were 1,781 civil machinery factories with 45,767 employees in total, the majority of which, accounting for 69% and 90% respectively, were concentrated in Shanghai. (The statistics were incomplete; figures from northeast China, Hangzhou and Guangzhou were not taken into account in terms of areas; numbers of repair factories in electrical, mining and transportation were not taken into consideration as well in terms of sector.)

为了应对不可避免的日本帝国主义的入侵，国民政府于1932年11月1日成立国防设计委员会，1935年4月更名为资源委员会，1936年3月资源委员会拟定为期5年的《重工业建设计划》，计划建设一批大型国营机械厂。1936年资源委员会在株洲建设中国汽车制造公司，在湘潭筹建中央电工器材厂；兵工系统重点扩建南京、汉阳兵工厂；航空委员会在杭州建飞机制造厂，在南昌建轰炸机制造厂；1936年铁道部在株洲筹建铁路总机厂等。可惜由于对日本帝国主义侵华野心、时间和能力估计不足，这些项目在日寇进逼下于1937年底大都被迫停建或迁址。

To counter the inevitable Japanese imperialistic invasions, Kuomintang government set up National Committee of Defense Design on November 1st 1932, which was renamed to Resource Committee in April 1935. In March 1936, Resource Committee drew up the five-year's *Heavy Industries Construction Plan* to set up a number of large-scale state-run machine factories. In 1936, Resource Committee established China Automobile Manufacturing Company in Zhuzhou and prepared to set up Central Electrical Equipment Factory in Xiangtan; the emphasis was put on expanding Nanking and Hanyang Arsenals for arsenal system; Aviation Committee established Plane Manufacturing Plant and Bomber Manufacturing Plant in Hangzhou and Nanchang respectively; Ministry of Railways prepared to establish Railway General Machine Factory in Zhuzhou in 1936. Unfortunately, due to Japan's imperialistic ambition of launching military invasions into China, and the inadequate estimation of time and capability, the majority of these projects were compelled to be suspended or relocated by the end of 1937, upon the invasions of Japanese army.

到1937年"七七"事变前，中国机械工业具有一定修造能力的工厂，在民用机器制造方面，主要有新中工程公司，永利宁化学公司机器厂，大隆、环球、周恒顺、新民等机器厂；在修造船方面，主要有江南、马尾、求新、大沽、黄埔等厂；在铁路机械修造方面，主要有长辛店、唐山、四方、江岸等厂。有的机械厂已形成较大规模并采用现代化管理办法。如上海大隆机器厂1937年已有机床231台，工人1300名，一年可制造整套棉纺设备4万锭左右；又如广州协同和机器厂，1932年即建立制造工票、记录工时制度；新中工程公司1935年开始在图纸上加注尺寸公差。

By the "July 7 Incident" in 1937, China's machinery industry had already built some factories with certain repair capability. In terms of civil machine manufacturing, there were Xinzhong Engineering Company, machine factory of Yonglining Chemical Company, as well as Dalong, Global, Zhouhengshuan, Xinmin machine factories etc; in ship building and repair, there were Jiangnan, Mawei, Qiuxin, Dagu and Whampoa factories; in railway machine repair, there were factories in Changxindian, Tangshan, Sifang and Jiangàn. Some machine factories had already had relatively larger scale and adopted modern management. For example, with 231 machine tools and 1,300 employees in 1937, Shanghai Dalong Machine Factory was capable of complete set of textile equipments with 40,000 spindles annually; Guangzhou Xietonghe Machine Factory had already introduced systems of manufacturing work tickets and recording working hours in 1932; Xinzhong Engineering Company began to mark tolerance in dimension on their blueprints in 1935.

此时，也有一些具有一定规模和实力的机械厂，因不敌外商的竞争和刻意打击被兼并，如最大的民营求新制造机器轮船厂，被耶松船厂兼并；扬子机器厂被迫加入日本控制的汉冶萍公司。

However, some machine factories, despite certain scale or power at that moment, were unable to survive the competitions and intentional attack launched by foreign merchants and companies. The largest private-owned Qiuxin Machine Ship Yard was merged with S.C. Farnham Co.; Yangzi Machine Factory was compelled to join Hanyeping Company controlled by Japan.

1931年"九一八"事变时，东北已有几十家机器厂，沈阳兵工厂和大连机械制作所已是大型机械厂。事变后，日军为了把东北建成侵略中国的基地，大举建设机械厂，至1938年止，新设机械厂180多家，飞机、汽车、兵工、仪表、金属加工等行业俱全，形成了完整的机械工业体系，可惜战后被苏军拆掉一空。

When the Mukden Incident broke out on September 18th 1931, there were already dozens of machine factories in northeast China, among which Shenyang Arsenal and Dalian Machine Manufacturing Factory had already become a large scale. After the incident, Japan massively built machine factories in an effort to make the northeast China a base of military attacks on China. By the end of 1938, a comprehensive machine industrial system took shape, covering over 180 newly built machine factories that engaged in plane, automobile, arsenal, instruments and metal working industries. Unfortunately, everything was dismantled and looted by the Russians after the War.

总的看来，此时中国机械工业基础仍很薄弱，技术装备水平不高。据战前对上海248家民营机械厂的调查，有磨床的只七八家，基本上没有较精密的计量、测量仪器。包括军工企业在内，全国有铸钢能力的只有9个厂，共拥有电弧炉12座、总公称能力13.65容量吨，最大的2t。广大的民营机械厂，只有上海的大隆、新中、新民，济南的陆大，汉阳的周恒顺，重庆的华兴等少数机械厂有工程师。战前，国民政府实业部核准的工程师，民营厂累计只有52人。

In general, the foundation of China's machinery industry was still relatively weak and the technological facilities were far from being advanced. According to investigations on 248 private-owned machine factories in China before the Sino-Japanese War, grinding machines were only equipped in seven or eight factories, and barely instruments and devices could perform precise measurements. Only 9 factories including military enterprises were capable of steel casting nationwide, with collectively 12 electric arc furnaces and a total nominal capacity of 13.65 t, the largest being 2 t. Among private-owned machine factories, only a few had engineers, such as Dalong, Xinzhong and Xinmin in Shanghai, Luda in Jinan, Zhouhengshun in Hanyang and Huaxing in Chongqing. The number of engineers stood at 52 qualified by Department of Industries of the National Government in private-owned factories before the War.

这个时期的装备主要靠进口，1936年前几年，年均需机械设备近8000万元，国产设备及配件只有2200万元。

During this period, equipment was largely reliant on import. The average annual demand for machines and equipment were worth nearly RMB 80 million a few years before 1936, but domestically manufactured equipment and components were only worth RMB 22 million.

1930年7月成立的中央工业试验所机械组，是中国首家机械工程研究机构。

Machinery Team of Central Industrial Laboratory established in July 1930 was the first research institute of mechanical engineering in China.

1936年10月统计，全国有19所高等院校办了机械工程院系或专业。

According to statistics in October of 1936, 19 learning higher institutes nationwide introduced Mechanical Engineering department or major.

上海求新制造机器轮船厂的机器厂

Machine Factory of Shanghai Qiuxin Factory that Manufactured Machines and Ships

大隆机器厂制造的织布机
Looms Manufactured by Dalong
Machine Factory

大隆机器厂制造的初纺机

Primary Textile Machine Manufactured
by Dalong Machine Factory

大隆机器厂制造的高速绕纱机

High-speed Winding Machine Manufactured by Dalong Machine Factory

1931年5月，沈阳民生工厂试制成功的民生牌75型1.8t载货汽车，为国产第一辆汽车。除汽油机、后桥、电气设备、轮胎外购外，其他自制。

Shenyang Minsheng Factory successfully trial-produced "Minsheng" 75-model trucks that had a capacity of 1.8 t in May 1931, which was the first automobile domestically manufactured. Everything, except gasoline engine, rear axle, electric equipment and tyres that were purchased from overseas, was independently designed and manufactured.

1932年12月，山西汽车修理厂试制成功的山西牌1.5t载货汽车。除火花塞、喇叭、电机、轴承外购外，其他均由工厂自制。左上角为监制者姜寿亭。

"Shanxi" truck with a capacity of 1.5 t was trial-produced successfully in Shanxi Automobile Repair Factory in December 1932. Everything, except spark plug, horn, electric machines and bearings that were purchased overseas, was independently designed and manufactured by the factory. On the top left corner is Jiang Shouting, the supervisor.

1935年清华大学装配的载货汽车（庄前鼎称"除引擎、接合器、变速轮、车架、后轴转向器及电池等向美国购买外，其他各件均在中国制造"。）

The truck assembled by Tsinghua University in 1935 (It was claimed by Mr. Zhuang Qianding that except engine, clutch, gearbox, framework, steering gear of rear axle and batteries that were purchased from the US, other components were all invariably made in China.)

清华大学机械工程系热力工程实验室

Thermal Engineering Laboratory of Mechanical Engineering

Department of Tsinghua University

第四章 抗日战争时期的中国机械工业
Chapter 4 China's Machinery Industry during the Anti-Japanese War

第一节 沿海沿江机械工厂大规模内迁
Section 1 Massive Inland Relocation of Machine Factories in Coastal Regions and along the Changjiang River

　　1931年在平津告急的情况下，国民政府行政院即开始调研工厂内迁问题。"七七"事变爆发，1937年8月9日，资源委员会向行政院建议，内迁2000台工作母机，次日行政院批准迁厂计划；8月11日，上海工厂迁移委员会成立，8月13日，日军开始进攻上海，22日，顺时机器厂在炮火下强行拆迁。至12月10日，上海共迁出机器厂66家，沿海其他地区的工厂也开始内迁。至1941年12月，上海、江苏、山东、山西等地内迁民营机器厂230家，复工198家，主要迁往川、渝、湘、桂、陕等省市，以重庆最多，是中国机械工业史上一次大迁移，这些机器厂为后方机械工业的中坚，对抗日战争作出重要贡献。

Given the fact that Beijing and Tianjin were under an imminent threat in 1931, the Administrative Office of National government launched investigation on inland internal relocation of factories. Following the breakout of "July 7 Incident", Resource Committee proposed relocating 2,000 machine tools internally to Administrative office on August 9th 1937, and was approved by the latter on the following day. On August 11th, Shanghai Factory Relocation Committee was officially set up. Nine days after the invasions upon Shanghai from Japanese army on August 13th Shunshi Machine Factory was compelled to be demolished and relocated, given the ever-increasing intensity of war. By December 10th, a total of 66 factories had been relocated elsewhere outside Shanghai and inland relocation was underway in other coastal areas as well. By December 1941, a total of 230 private-owned machine factories have been inland relocated from Shanghai, Jiangsu, Shandong and Shanxi, 198 of which resumed operations afterwards. The majority of these factories were relocated to Sichuan, Chongqing, Hunan, Guangxi and Shaanxi, particularly Chongqing, making a large-scale relocation in China's machinery industry history and a significant contribution later during the Anti-Japanese War as the backbone of machinery industry in home front.

另外，兵工署、资委会、航委会、铁道部自行安排所属工厂内迁。如南昌飞机厂迁南川，杭州飞机公司迁云南瑞丽的垒允（1940年10月为日机炸毁）、韶关飞机厂迁昆明，金陵兵工厂、汉阳兵工厂和巩县兵工厂迁重庆、湖南和兰州；有的工厂只迁出一小部分，多数被炸毁或落入日寇之手，如江南造船所只迁出叶在馥等20人和20多台机床，马尾造船所只有小部分设备运到南平，西北实业公司也迁出很少，组成了仅有20余台机床的机器厂。

Besides, Bureau of Arsenal, Resource Committee, Aviation Committee and Railway Department arranged and deployed independently inland-relocation of factories under their administration. Nanchang Aircraft Factory, for instance, was relocated to Nanchuan; Hangzhou Aircraft Company was moved to Leiyun in Ruili of Yunnan Province (destroyed in the air raid by Japanese army in October 1940); Shaoguan Aircraft Factory, Jinling Arsenal, Hanyang Arsenal and Gong Township Arsenal were moved to Kunming, Chongqing, Hunan and Lanzhou respectively. Some factories, unfortunately, were already ravaged by the bombing or seized by Japanese army, leaving only a small proportion of them could be salvaged. For example, Jiangnan Ship-building Plant was almost destroyed except that 20 people including Ye Zaifu and over a score of machine tools that were successfully relocated; a very limited percentage of equipments in Mawei Ship-building Plant were managed to be transported to Nanping; Northwest Industrial Company suffered a similar fate-being scaled down to a machine factory consisting of slightly over 20 machine tools.

由于对日寇侵华深入内地的能力估计不足，一些机器厂多次转移，损失很大，如上海新中工程公司、华成电器厂，一迁武汉、再迁湖南、三迁重庆，1944年到达重庆时设备几乎损毁殆尽。

Owning to underestimation of the ability of Japanese army to invade into inner parts of China, a huge loss was incurred during the time and again relocations of factories. Both Shanghai Xinzhong Engineering Company and Huacheng Electrical Appliance Factory were successively relocated to Wuhan, Hunan and Chongqing, but by 1944 when they arrived in Chongqing, the equipment was almost entirely damaged.

第二节　抗战时期国民党"大后方"的机械工业
Section 2　Machinery Industry in "Home Front" of Kuomintang during Anti-Japanese War

1937年抗战前，西部地区机械工业极为薄弱，战时有了很大发展。在政府扶持、政策支持和职工抗战热情高涨的情况下，内迁民营厂有了很大发展。如上海新中工程公司内迁湖南的五年，由1个厂发展到6个厂、职工由700多人发展到2000多人，生产增长10倍以上（但在国民党军湘桂大撤退中损失殆尽）。内迁的国营工厂，虽在搬迁过程中，元气大伤，但其后仍有发展。在这一时期，国民政府也新建了一批机械厂，大多数设在昆明、重庆。如在昆明新建中央机器厂、中央电工器材厂，在重庆新建汽车配件厂、农业机械公司，在贵州建设的大定飞机厂、贵阳农机公司等。

The machinery industry in western China was extremely weak before the breakout of Anti-Japanese War in 1937, but gained tremendous development in times of the war. The inland relocation of private-owned factories made headways given the government subsidies, policy support and employees'ever-growing passion for fighting the war. Within the period of five years after Shanghai Xinzhong Engineering Company, for instance, was relocated to Hunan Province, it expanded rapidly in scale from one factory to six and the number of employees soared from slightly over 700 to more than 2,000, sustaining an exceptional over tenfold growth (unfortunately, it was ruined during the retreat of Kuomintang army from Hunan and Guangxi). Despite a considerable loss during inland relocation, private-owned factories still managed to make visible developments. During this particular period, national government set up a new batch of machine factories, mostly in Kunming and Chongqing. Among them, Central Machine Factory and Central Electrical Equipment Factory were built in Kunming, Automobile Component Factory and Agricultural Machinery Company in Chongqing, Dading Aircraft Factory in Guizhou and Agricultural Machinery Company in Guiyang.

因战争需要，促使机械工业有一定发展。1943年，国民党"大后方"，除近百家军工厂外，共有机械厂1477家，工人69508人。机械工业在工业中已成三大行业（纺织、化工、机械）之一，企业、资金、工人数分别占全部工业的28.05%，22.7%和19.33%。1941年，生产了机床2615台、交流电动机2.2万kW、变压器1.6万kVA、内燃机3900hp、蒸汽机4500hp。

The rising demand as a result of war had considerably promoted the development of machinery industry. By 1943, apart from hundreds of arsenals, there were a total of 1,477 machine factories with 69,508 workers in the home front of Kuomintang. Machinery industry had risen to be one of the three major industries (textile, chemical and machinery industry), accounting for 28.05%, 19.33% and 22.7% of that of all industries in terms of the number of enterprises and employees and amount of capital respectively. A total of 2,615 machine tools, 22,000 kW of alternating current motors, 16,000 kVA of transformers, 3,900 hp of internal combustion engines and 4,500 hp of steam engines were produced in 1944.

抗战时期中央机器厂制造的250hp的VG25
煤气机及配套的发电机

250hp of VG25 Coal Gas Engine and Supplementary
Generator Manufactured by Central Machine Factory
in Anti-Japanese War

1939年新中工程公司仿制出的
65hp M.A.N柴油汽车发动机

65hp M.A.N Diesel Engine for
Automobiles Counterfeited by Xinzhong
Engineering Company in 1939

抗战时期新中工程公司试制的汽车

Automobiles Trialmanufactured by Xinzhong Engineering Company in Anti-Japanese War

抗战时期中央机器厂制造的立铣床

Vertical Milling Machine Manufactured by Central Machine Factory in Anti-Japanese War

抗战时期中央机器厂制造的8ft车床

8-feet-long Lathe Manufactured by Central Machine Factory in Anti-Japanese War

抗战时期中央机器厂制造的
2000kW汽轮发电机及从瑞士进
口的汽轮机

2000 kW Steam Turbine Generator
Manufactured by Central Machine
Factory and Steam Turbine Imported
from Switzerland in Anti-Japanese War

新中工程公司仿制的
36hp狄塞尔柴油机

36hp Diesel Engine
Counterfeited by Xinzhong
Engineering Company

第三节 苏区、解放区的机械工业
Section 3 Machinery Industry in Soviet and Liberated Regions

1927年秋收起义后，中国共产党领导的中国工农红军在井冈山建立了第一个修械所，1931年10月在江西省兴国县官田镇建立中央苏区兵工厂，第二方面军在湖南永顺建兵工厂，1932年第四方面军在四川道江、1933年红25军和26军在陕北吴起镇成立兵工厂或修械所。中央红军到陕北后，在延安成立兵工厂，是边区军工基础。

After the Autumn Harvest Uprising in 1927, the Red Army set up the first machine repair plant in Mountain Jinggang, followed by the establishment of Central Soviet Region Arsenal in Guantian Township of Xingguo County of Jiangxi Province and the arsenal by the Second Front Army in Yongshun of Hunan Province in October 1931. In 1932, the Red Four Front and 25th & 26th Red Army set up arsenals or machine repair plants in Daojiang of Sichuan Province and Wuqi Township of north Shaanxi Province respectively. After the Central Red Army arrived in north Shaanxi Province, they set up arsenals in Yan'an, which laid a solid foundation for war industry in border regions.

抗日战争爆发后，1938年3月中央军委成立军事工业局，决定在安塞县茶坊镇建立陕甘宁边区机器厂，沈鸿带来的上海利用五金厂7名青工和10台机床并入该厂。1938年11月6日，中共六大六中全会号召"每个游击战争根据地都必须尽量设法建立小的兵工厂"。除陕甘宁边区机器厂扩充至4个厂，从修配枪炮发展到修造枪炮外，各个解放区都建立了大小不等的一系列兵工厂，其中涌现了如著名的设在山西黎城县的黄崖洞兵工厂等。抗战胜利前后，各根据地拥有工人100人以上、设备10台以上有固定厂房的兵工厂50余个、职工3万余人。这些厂除制造武器外，还制造了一些民用机器，在抗日战争和解放战争中都发挥了重要作用。

After the Anti-Japanese War broke out, the Military Commission of CPC Central Committee set up Bureau of Military Industry in March 1938 and determined to build Shaanxi-Gansu-Ningxia Border Machine Factory in Chafang Township of Anzhai County. Seven young workers and ten machine tools from Shanghai Liyong Hardware Factory, brought by Shen Hong, were incorporated in the factory. The Sixth Plenary Session of the Sixth CPC Central Committee held on November 6th 1938 encouraged "every guerilla war base to set up small arsenal". Apart from the expansion of Shaanxi-Gansu-Ningxia Border Machine Factory into four factories which were able to repair and manufacture firearms than just components, a series of arsenals of an assortment of scales were set up in each liberated area, among which Huangyadong Arsenal set up in Licheng County of Shanxi Province was quite well known. Around the time of clenching victory in Anti-Japanese War, there were already over 30,000 workers and 50 arsenals that had more than 100 workers and 10 sets of equipment in each military base. They manufactured weapons but also civil machines, which served a vital role in Anti-Japanese War and War of Liberation.

江西兴国县官田兵工厂修械工房

Machine Repair Factory of Guantian Arsenal in Xingguo County of Jiangxi Province

1940年10月，朱德总司令参加了在延安王家坪召开的军工生产会议。
自左至右：李涛、叶剑英、朱德、叶季壮、李强

In October 1940, Zhu De, Commander-in-Chief, attended the meeting of military productions in Wangjiaping of Yan' an.
From left to right: Li Tao, Ye Jianying, Zhu De, Ye Jizhuang, Li Qiang

边区机器厂（即茶坊兵工厂）手
榴弹厂的工人在浇铸手榴弹弹体

Workers in Grenade Plant of Border
Machine Factory (i.e. Chafang Arsenal)
Were Molding Grenade Body

茶坊兵工厂子弹厂
用道轨钢自制的切
口机

Cutting Machine
Independently Made
by Bullet Factory of
Chafang Arsenal out of
Rail Steel

黄崖洞兵工厂造
"五〇"掷弹筒
和弹

50 Grenade Launcher
Manufactured by
Huangyadong Arsenal

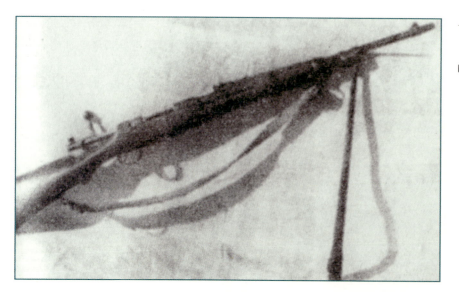

黄崖洞兵工厂造"八一"式步枪

"Bayi" Rifle Manufactured by Huangyadong Arsenal

修复后的黄崖洞兵工厂部分厂房

Part of the Restored Huangyadong Arsenal

华北兵工一厂铸造迫击炮弹的焖火炉

Normalizing Furnace Used for Mortar Projectiles Manufactured by No.1 Factory of North China Arsenal

晋冀鲁豫解放区彭庄子弹厂
动力工房一角

A Snapshot of Power Barrack of
Pengzhuang Bullet Factory in
Liberated Area of Shanxi-Tianjin-
Shandong-Henan

1947年春，山西长治附城兵
工十五厂，用火车机车轴车
制150mm迫击炮管组装的
150mm迫击炮及其炮鞍

In the spring of 1947, No. 15
Factory of Changzhi Fucheng
Arsenal in Shanxi Province were
manufacturing 150 mm mortars and
saddles that were assembled from
150 mm mortar barrel made out of
locomotive axle

新四军修械所的修配车间

Repair and Assembly Workshop of Machine Repair Works of the New Fourth Army

彭庄子弹厂大工房

The Large Barrack of
Pengzhuang Bullet Factory

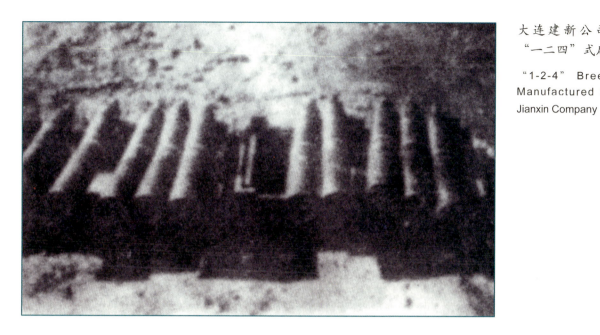

大连建新公司生产的
"一二四"式后膛炮弹

"1-2-4" Breechloader
Manufactured by Dalian
Jianxin Company

茶坊兵工厂研制成功的落
尺式炮弹初速仪

Muzzle Velocity Meter of
Cannonball Successfully
Developed and Manufactured
by Chafang Arsenal

山西武乡县柳沟兵工厂机工房、钳工房外景

Exterior View of Machining Shop and Benchwork Room of Liugou Arsenal in
Wuxiang County of Shanxi Province

第四节 沦陷区的机械工业
Section 4 Machinery Industry in Enemy-Occupied Region

抗战初期，沿海省市机械工业遭到巨大损失。如上海，1937年"七七"事变之初，有民办机械厂570家，"八·一三"战争爆发后，除内迁66家外，直接毁于炮火的360家，设在浦东、杨树浦的船舶修造厂，全被日军占领，设在租界内的百余家机械厂生产全部停顿。嗣后租界内的机械工业陆续恢复生产并发展至784家。但1941年12月太平洋战争爆发后，日军占领上海租界，强行征购物资和装备，被掠夺的机床即在5000台以上，多数机械工厂陷于瘫痪。沦陷区其他省市情况类似。

At the initial phase of Anti-Japanese War, the machinery industry in coastal provinces and cities suffered tremendous loss. For instance, there were 570 private-owned machine factories in Shanghai before the "July 7th Incident". However, after the breakout of "August 13th Event", expect for 66 that had already been inland relocated, 360 machine factories were destroyed; ship repair yards in Pudong and Yangshupu were all seized by Japanese army; hundreds of machinery factories in foreign concessions were compelled to suspend their productions. Machinery industries in leased territories gradually resumed productions thereafter, expanding to 784 in number. Following the breakout of the Pacific War in December 1941, Japanese army seized the leased territories in Shanghai, compulsively procured supplies and equipment. Over 5,000 machine tools were looted as a result incapacitating most of the machine factories. Similar picture could be seen in enemy-occupied regions in other provinces and cities.

关内沦陷区机械工厂，较大的多被征用生产军需用品。如上海大隆机器厂，日军改为大陆铁工厂转向军火生产；江南造船所，被日军占用，先后改名"朝日工作部江南工场"、"三菱重工业株式会社江南造船所"，加速造修军用船舰，工人最多时超过万人。

The majority of large machine factories in enemy-occupied area inside the Shanhaiguan Pass were requisitioned to produce military products. Shanghai Dalong Machine Factory, for instance, were converted by Japanese army into Mainland Iron Factory that manufactured weapons; Jiangnan Ship-yard was controlled by Japanese army, and later renamed successively "Jiangnan Workshop of Asahi Department of Work" and "Jiangnan Ship-yard of Mitsubishi Heavy Industry Corporation" to speed up the building of military fleets and the employees numbered over ten thousands at the maximum.

东北沦陷区，日军为将其建设成侵略战争的基地，无论是1937年关东军的满洲国"产业开发五年计划"，还是1943年的"新产业五年计划"，重点都要扩充机械工业，机床、汽车、飞机均是重点发展对象。到1940年，东北共有机械厂968家，员工44980人。有的机械工厂已扩至相当规模，如大连机械制作所，职工由战前五六百人至1945年增至6800多人，机器设备1295台，年产机、客、货车分别60辆、150辆和400辆；住友金属工业株式会社奉天工场，1944年有职工2072人，拥有4000t锻造液压机、30t平炉（3座）和4m立车等重型设备。可惜在东北光复后，苏军于1945年9月至1946年3月将东北机器设备拆走，按"二战"前币值约20亿美元。致使新中国成立后我国重建东北机械工业基本上从零开始。

The enemy-occupied area in northeast China was transformed by Japanese army into base for military invasions. No matter in "Five-year Plan of Industrial Development" of Manchukuo of Japan's Kwantung Army in the year 1937 or in "New Industrial Five-year Plan" in 1943, the key laid in expanding machinery industry, in which machine tools, automobiles and planes were as the main. By the year of 1940, there had already been totally 968 machine factories with 44,980 employees, some of which even gained a sizeable scale, such as Dalian Machine Production Plant. The number of employees soared sharply from less than 600 prior to the war to over 6,800 in the year 1945. The machines and equipment numbered 1,295 units, with an annual production of 60 locomotives, 150 passenger vehicles and 400 trucks; there were 2,072 employees, 4,000 t hydraulic forging press, 30 t open-hearth furnace (3 sets) and 4m vertical lathe and other heavy equipment in Mukden Workshop of Sumitomo Metal Industry Co., Ltd in 1944. Unfortunately, the Soviet army dismantled and removed machines in northeast China from September 1945 to March 1946 after its recovery, which were worth USD 2 billion in terms of currency value before the Second World War. The machinery industry in northeast China had to start from scratch after liberation.

第五章 抗战胜利后到新中国成立前的中国机械工业

Chapter 5 China's Machinery Industry from the Victory of Anti-Japanese War to the Founding of People's Republic of China

抗战胜利后，国民党政府集中力量接收沦陷区的日伪工厂，几乎停止了对后方机械工业的扶持，同时由于内迁职工纷纷返回原籍，后方工厂很难维持生产。

After achieving victory of Anti-Japanese War, Kuomintang government concentrated their power on accepting the puppet factories in the enemy-occupied area and halted its efforts to support machinery industry in the home front; meanwhile, workers coming due to inland relocation started to migrate back to their hometowns , which made it tough for those factories to maintain production.

在上海，国民党政府接收了160多家日伪控制的机械厂，其中规模最大的原英、美、法商经营的机器厂，如：英联、马勒、求新等造船厂交还外商；原属民族资本家经营的机器厂如大隆、振隆等发还原主；有7家日伪经营的机器厂改组为官僚资本机器厂；有的小厂停工拍卖。在其他收复区，由于日军撤退时的严重破坏和不良分子的盗卖，特别是东北地区的机器设备被苏联军队劫掠一空，基本上丧失生产能力。

In Shanghai, Kuomintang government took over more than 160 machine factories controlled by Japanese puppet regime, among which machine factories originally operated by British, American and French merchants were of the largest scale. For instance, British United, Moller and Qiuxin ship-building factories were returned to foreign merchants; while machine factories originally funded by national capital such as Dalong and Zhenlong were returned to their owners; seven machine factories run by Japanese puppet regime were reshuffled to bureaucratic capital machine factories. Smaller factories were subject to production suspension or auction. In some other regions recovered, due to severe destruction inflicted while Japanese army was retreating and illegal robbery and sales, especially the robbery of machines and equipments by the Soviet army in northeast China, factories were basically deprived of production capability.

抗战胜利后，全国机械工业公营企业，由资源委员会组建成一批专业托拉斯，结合"战后经济建设计划"，欲图有所振兴，可惜1946年内战全面爆发而无法实现。

After the war, the public-owned enterprises in machinery industry nationwide were converted to trust by Resource Committee and "Postwar Economic Construction Plan" was adopted in a hope to revive the industry, which, unfortunately, failed to be realized when the Chinese Civil War broke out on a comprehensive scale in the year 1946.

第二次世界大战后，盟国原规定令日本赔偿机器设备，由于美国占领日本的盟军总部别有他图，只获得少量赔偿设备，随后即停止赔偿。总起来看，抗战胜利后的这几年，一个令人充满希望的中国机械工业，每况愈下，生产经营日渐衰败，至新中国成立前夕，中国机械工业已成为一个残缺不全的烂摊子。

After World War Two, it was originally stipulated by the Allies that Japan shall compensate for all the machines and equipment to China. However, only a small amount was realized before the compensation stopped because the US Allies'headquarter had ulterior motives when they conquered Japan. Afterwards, compensation was halted. In general, the greatly promising China's machinery industry was weakening everyday after the victory of Anti-Japanese War, and turned out to be in a terrible mess on the eve of liberation .

抗战胜利后大隆机器厂制造的10ft重型全齿车床

10ft Heavy Full-gear Lathe Manufactured by Dalong Machine
Factory after the Victory of Anti-Japanese War

抗战胜利后上海恒新股份两合公司制造的14ft高速龙门刨床

14-feet High-speed Double Housing Planer Manufactured by Shanghai Hengxin Holdings Joint Liability Corporation after the Victory of Anti-Japanese War

结 语
Conclusion

从1840年鸦片战争到1949年新中国成立，百余年中国近代机械工业，发展道路艰难、曲折，但写就了一部发展民族机械工业的奋斗史。

For over a hundred years' time spanning from the breakout of the Opium War in 1840 to the founding of the People's Republic of China in 1949, China's modern machinery industry underwent an arduous and bumpy journey, making a struggling history of national machinery industry.

虽经全国人民的努力，仁人志士的奋斗，中国机械取得了历史上的最大进步，从传统手工业作坊走向近代机械工业，生产技术都取得一些成绩，但备受帝国主义侵略者摧残打击和资本主义、封建主义的压抑，中国机械工业始终远远落后于工业化国家，始终没有摆脱修配性质，但仍为新中国现代机械工业的发展准备了条件，特别是培养和储备了许多优秀人才，为新中国现代机械工业建设，发挥了至关重要的作用。

Thanks to the concerted efforts of the people around the country. China's machinery industry witnessed the greatest improvements and underwent the transition from traditional manual workshops to modern machinery industry with notable achievements in production technologies. However, ravaged by imperialistic invaders and suppressed by capitalism and feudalism, machinery industry in China still lagged far behind than counterparts in other industrialized nations and could get rid of the nature of repair and assembly. Despite that, it still provided conditions for the development of China's modern machinery industry, particularly in the cultivation and reserves of outstanding talents, thus playing a vital role in the construction of modern machinery industry for new China.

附表　中国近代机械工业发展进程概况
Appendix: Development Briefing on China's Modern Machinery Industry

年份 Year		机械工程大事 Important Events of Mechanical Engineering	国内外相关政治经济要事 Key Relevant Economic and Political Events at home and abroad
公元 A.D.	中国年代 In Feudalistic Years		
1840	清道光二十年 20th year of Daoguang of the Qing Dynasty		鸦片战争爆发 The first Opium War broke out
1841	清道光二十一年 21st year of Daoguang of the Qing Dynasty	英军占领香港，英商纳蒙在港建立船坞，是外商在中国经营的第一家机械工业企业 丁拱辰刊刻《演炮图说》 魏源在《四洲志》的基础上，编著《海国图志》，出版了50卷，提出"师夷之长技以制夷"，并有专文介绍火轮船 The British Army seized control of Hong Kong. Namon, a British merchant, established dockyard in Hongkong, which was the first machine industrial enterprise set up by foreign businessmen in China. Ding Gongchen inscribed *Illustrations of Cannons*; WeiYuan, based on *Si Zhou Zhi* (the Chinese version of *The Encyclopaedia of Geography*), compiled *World Geography Records*, which consisted of 50 volumes that were published. He proposed the notion of "learning advanced technologies from western countries to resist their invasions" and there were special articles introducing steamer.	

206

年份 Year		机械工程大事 Important Events of Mechanical Engineering	国内外相关政治经济要事 Key Relevant Economic and Political Events at home and abroad
公元 A.D.	中国年代 In Feudalistic Years		
1842	清道光 二十二年 22nd year of Daoguang of the Qing Dynasty	广东潘世荣制造了一艘小轮船，但"不甚灵便"；嘉兴县丞龚振麟也仿造了明轮船 Pan Shirong, from Guangdong Province, built a small ship; unfortunately, it was "inconvenient and cumbersome"; Jiaxing County magistrate Gong Zhenlin, also counterfeited a paddle wheel steamer.	8月29日签订中英《江宁条约》，规定开放广州、福州、厦门、宁波、上海为通商口岸，并割让香港 China and UK signed "The Treaty of Nanking" on August 29th, in which Guangzhou, Fuzhou, Xiamen, Ningbo and Shanghai were compelled to open up to foreign merchants and businesses and meanwhile, the government ceded Hong Kong to UK.
1843	清道光 二十三年 23th year of Daoguang of the Qing Dynasty	丁拱辰的《演炮图说辑要》出版，其中《西洋火轮车火轮图说》记载了他制成的小蒸汽机、小机车和小轮船，是中国对西方轮船、蒸汽机车进行探索的先行者 香港纳蒙船坞建造了一艘80吨的小轮船"中国"号 *Summary of Illustrations of Cannon* written by Ding Gongchen was published, in which a small steam engine, a small locomotive and a small ship he built were documented in *Illustrations of Western Trains*; he was the vanguard of China's exploration of western ships and steam locomotive. A small ship known as "China" measuring 80 tons in capacity was built in Hong Kong Namon Dock.	10月签订中英《五口通商章程：海关税则》，中国开始丧失关税自主权 In October, China and Britain signed "Regulation of Opening up of Business at Five Ports: Tariff Policies"; China started to lose customs autonomy.
1845	清道光 二十五年 25th year of Daoguang of the Qing Dynasty	苏格兰人柯拜在广州黄埔开办柯拜船坞，是中国境内开办的第一家船舶修造厂，也是中国境内首先使用蒸汽机、机床等近代机器的机械厂 John Couper, a Scot, set up John Couper Dock in Whampoa of Guangzhou, which was the first ship repair and building factory in China, and was also the first machine factory to utilize steam engine and machine tools as well as other modern machines in China.	
1846	清道光 二十六年 26th year of Daoguang of the Qing Dynasty	安徽歙县人郑复光撰写了《火轮船图说》、《镜镜泠痴》是中国最早的有关火轮船设计和制造的专著 Zheng Fuguang, from Xi Township of Anhui Province, wrote *Illustrations of Steaming Ship* and *Jing Jing Ling Chi*, which were the earliest masterpieces in China about the design and manufacturing of steam boat.	

（续表）

年份 Year		机械工程大事 Important Events of Mechanical Engineering	国内外相关政治经济要事 Key Relevant Economic and Political Events at home and abroad
公元 A.D.	中国年代 In Feudalistic Years		
1847	清道光 二十七年 27th year of Daoguang of the Qing Dynasty	魏源的《海国图志》增为100卷 *World Geography Records* written by Wei Yuan were increased to 100 volumes.	
1850	清道光 三十年 30th year of Daoguang of the Qing Dynasty	容闳赴美留学，1854年毕业于耶鲁大学，1863年与曾国藩见面，提出建设西式机器厂的建议 美商在上海建立修船厂伯雄公司 Yung Wing pursued further studies in the US, graduating from Yale University in 1854. In the year 1863, he met with Zeng Guofan, proposing establishing western machine factories. US merchants set up Boxiong Company that repaired ships in Shanghai.	
1852	清咸丰二年 2nd year of Xianfeng of the Qing Dynasty	郭甘章在上海经营甘章船坞，修理外国轮船 Guo Ganzhang operated Ganzhang Dock in Shanghai, repairing foreign ships.	
1856	清咸丰六年 6th year of Xianfeng of the Qing Dynasty	柯拜船坞建造了一艘由柯拜自行设计的总长54m、宽6.7m的"百合花"号轮船，是最早在中国境内建造的最大轮船 7月，美商贝立斯在上海开设的船厂制造了一艘载重40 t的轮船"先驱"号，这是外国人在上海制成的第一艘轮船，不久，另一艘姊妹船也相继下水 Couper Dock built a "Lily" Ship measuring 54 meters long and 6.7 meters wide. It was independently designed by John Couper and the largest ship built in China. In July, Belisce an American merchant, built the first ship by foreigners in Shanghai "Pioneer" with a carrying capacity of 40 t in the ship company set up in Shanghai. It wasn't long before another similar ship was launched out.	第二次鸦片战争爆发（英法联军） The Second Opium War broke out (between China and British and French Allied Forces).
1860	清咸丰十年 10th year of Xianfeng of the Qing Dynasty	曾国藩上奏清廷："将来师夷智能造炮制船尤可期永远之利。"最早提出自力更生造炮制船，发展中国船炮工业的主张 Zeng Guofan was the first person in China that made the suggestion to the government of the Qing Dynasty to independently build cannons and ships and develop China's ship and cannon industry which would bring long benefit.	第二次鸦片战争中国战败 China suffered a defeat in the Second Opium War.

208

（续表）

年份 Year		机械工程大事 Important Events of Mechanical Engineering	国内外相关政治经济要事 Key Relevant Economic and Political Events at home and abroad
公元 A.D.	中国年代 In Feudalistic Years		
1861	清咸丰十一年 11th year of Xianfeng of the Qing Dynasty	奕訢等人奏请购买外国船炮获准 曾国藩创办安庆内军械所 The proposal of Yi Xin to purchase foreign ships and cannons was approved. Zeng Guofan set up Anqing Internal Weapons Factory.	总理各国事务衙门成立 Offices of Foreign Affairs under Prime Minister were established.
1862	清同治一年 1st year of Tongzhi of the Qing Dynasty	李鸿章接受英国人马格里的建议，在上海开办松江洋炮局 徐寿、华蘅芳等人在安庆内军械所试制成一台小蒸汽机 合信翻译《蒸汽机简述》 美商在上海、广州设旗记铁工厂 Li Hongzhang accepted the advice offered by Macartney Halliday, a Briton, to set up Song River Bureau of Western Cannon in Shanghai. Xu Shou and Huang Hengfang trial–built a small steam engine in Anqing Internal Weapons Factory; He Xin translated *A Brief Introduction of Steam Engine*; US merchants set up Thomas Hunt & Co in Shanghai and Guangzhou.	
1863	清同治二年 2nd year of Tongzhi of the Qing Dynasty	徐寿、华蘅芳等人制造出螺旋桨推进的轮船，于11月试航，"行驶迟钝，不甚得法" 容闳向曾国藩建议采用"制造机器之机器"，建立机器母厂，以立一切制造之基础，最早提出建立机器制造厂 Xu Shou and Hua Hengfang manufactured ships powered by propellers; the testing navigation was conducted in November; however, the "speed was slow due to technology constraints"; Yung Wing suggested to Zeng Guofan adopting "machines that manufactured machines", establishing machine factories to build the foundation for all productions. He was the earliest person raising the notion of setting up machine manufacturing factories.	
1864	清同治三年 3rd year of Tongzhi of the Qing Dynasty	李鸿章将位于上海松江的洋炮局迁苏州，更名苏州洋炮局，并接受马格里建议，买下被清政府遣散的阿斯本舰队中所配备的全套修理用机器，装备了苏州洋炮局 受曾国藩委派，容闳去美国购买机器 左宗棠在杭州招募工匠仿造轮船 Li Hongzhang relocated Song River Bureau of Western Cannon from Shanghai to Suzhou, and renamed it "Suzhou Bureau of Western Cannon". Besides, he took the advice of Macartney Halliday to purchase the comprehensive set of repair machines of "Osborn Fleet" to equip Suzhou Bureau of Western Cannon; Yung Wing was dispatched by Zeng Guofan to purchase machines from the US; Zuo Zongtang was recruiting carpenters in Hangzhou to counterfeit ships.	7月19日清军攻陷太平天国都城南京 On July 19th, the army of the Qing Dynasty captured Nanjing, the capital city of the Taiping Heavenly Kingdom (1851–1864).

（续表）

年份 Year		机械工程大事 Important Events of Mechanical Engineering	国内外相关政治经济要事 Key Relevant Economic and Political Events at home and abroad
公元 A.D.	中国年代 In Feudalistic Years		
1865	清同治四年 4th year of Tongzhi of the Qing Dynasty	徐寿、华蘅芳等在南京内军械所制成木质明轮轮船"黄鹄"号，1866年春试航成功，在中国近代造船史上具有划时代的意义，同时造出所配蒸汽机 李鸿章会同曾国藩奏设江南制造局，并由丁日昌筹办，该局成立之初，曾仿制"制器之器" 容闳买回的100余台机器运到上海，装备了江南制造局 金陵机器局成立 英国人杜兰德在北京演试小火车，随即被拆除 Xu Shou and Hua Hengfang successfully built wooden paddle wheel steamer known as "Huang Hu (Yellow Crane)" in Nanjing Internal Weapons Factory, which was successfully tested in the spring of 1866. It served landmark significance in modern ship-building history of China; meanwhile, steam engine was built; Li Hongzhang and Zeng Guofan jointly set up Jiangnan Production Bureau, which was hosted and organized by Ding Richang. "Machine for Machine Production" was counterfeited at the inception of the bureau. Over 100 machines purchased by Yung Wing were shipped back to Shanghai to furnish Jiangnan Production Bureau; Nanjing Bureau of Machine was established; Durand, a Briton, tested and displayed a small train in Beijing, which was then immediately dismantled.	
1866	清同治五年 5th year of Tongzhi of the Qing Dynasty	左宗棠创办福州船政局，12月23日在马尾动工，聘法国人日意格为监督 左宗棠创办中国近代海军学校——求是堂艺局（后改名福建船政学堂） 方赞举在上海创办发昌机器厂，是我国第一个民族资本开办的机器厂 Zuo Zongtang set up Fuzhou Administrative Bureau of Ship, of which the construction commenced in Mawei on December 23rd and a Frenchman by the name of Prosper Giguel was hired as the supervisor. Zuo Zongtang set up Modern Navy Institute of China - Truth-seeking Machine Bureau of (later renamed Fujian Administrative Institute of Ship. Fang Zanju set up Fachang Machine Factory in Shanghai, which was the first machine factory funded by national capital.	
1867	清同治六年 6th year of Tongzhi of the Qing Dynasty	福州船政局前学堂开学，设造船、设计专业和学徒班（艺圃） 1867—1873年，江南制造局仿制出车床、刨床、钻床、开齿轮机器、卷铁板机器、汽锤、大锤机器等 Fuzhou Administrative Institute of Ship was officially launched, opening up ship-building, and design majors and apprenticeship class (Yipu) From 1867—1873, Jiangnan Production Bureau counterfeited machine tools, planer, drilling machine, open gear machine, iron plate rolling machine, steam hammering and large hammering machines.	

（续表）

年份 Year		机械工程大事 Important Events of Mechanical Engineering	国内外相关政治经济要事 Key Relevant Economic and Political Events at home and abroad
公元 A.D.	中国年代 In Feudalistic Years		
1868	清同治七年 7th year of Tongzhi of the Qing Dynasty	8月，江南制造局制成明轮兵船"恬吉"号，9月15日试航成功，是中国建造的第一艘明轮军舰 Paddle wheel steamer named "Tianji" manufactured by Jiangnan Production Bureau in August was on trial navigation on September 15th. It is the first paddle warship made in China.	1867—1868年日本明治维新（1867—1912年称明治时代） Meiji Restoration from 1867 to 1868 (the period from 1867 to 1912 is known as Meiji Era)
1869	清同治八年 8th year of Tongzhi of the Qing Dynasty	江南制造局制成螺旋桨推进的轮船"操江"号，是中国建造的第一艘由螺旋桨推进的木壳兵舰，其配套的400马力蒸汽机自行生产 6月，福州船政局制造的第一艘轮船"万年清"号运输船下水，9月完成 The first propeller-powered wooden warship built in China was named "Caojiang" and built by Jiangnan Production Bureau and the 400hp steam engine equipped was independently manufactured. In June, the first transport ship known as "Qing Dynasty Forever" manufactured by Fuzhou Administrative Bureau of Ship was launched out for the first time and completed in September.	
1870	清同治九年 9th year of Tongzhi of the Qing Dynasty	福州船政局8月开始仿制580马力蒸汽机，经10个月完成，在中国机械制造史上有重要意义；以后安装于福州船政局建造的"安澜"号上，1871年下水 江南制造局创办翻译学馆 Fuzhou Administrative Bureau of Ship started to counterfeit 580hp steam engine in August, which was completed after 10 months, serving paramount significance in the history of China's machine productions; it was later installed in "Anlan" Ship built by Fuzhou Administrative Bureau of Ship launched in waters in 1871; Jiangnan Production Bureau set up translation institute.	
1871	清同治十年 10th year of Tongzhi of the Qing Dynasty	福州船政局用机器轧制钢板、圆钢、方钢；首先采用新的冶炼技术，铸造大型汽缸，安装3t汽锤，锻造大轴，为中国最早的大型铸锻车间 江南制造局出版译著《汽机新制》 Fuzhou Administrative Bureau of Ship utilized machine rolling steel plate, round steel, square steel, adopted new metallurgical techniques for the very first time cast large cylinder installed 3t steam hammer, forged large axle, making it the earliest large forging factory. Jiangnan Production Bureau published the translation *New Machine Manufacturing*.	

年份 Year		机械工程大事 Important Events of Mechanical Engineering	国内外相关政治经济要事 Key Relevant Economic and Political Events at home and abroad
公元 A.D.	中国年代 In Feudalistic Years		
1872	清同治十一年 11th year of Tongzhi of the Qing Dynasty	江南制造局出版译著《汽机必以》 Jiangnan Production Bureau published the translation *Machine Knowledge*.	容闳带第一批30名幼童赴美国留学 Yung Wing took a batch of 30 children to US to further their education.
1873	清同治十二年 12th year of Tongzhi of the Qing Dynasty	按陈启沅的设计，陈联泰号制造出缫丝机 中国工程技术人员开始在福州船政局监造轮船 Based on the design of Chen Qiyuan, "Chen Liantai" manufactured silk filature; China's engineering technicians started to supervise the production of ships in Fuzhou Administrative Bureau of Ship.	日本建立工学寮，设有机械科 Japan set up Industrial Institute, with department of machine.
1874	清同治十三年 13th year of Tongzhi of the Qing Dynasty	福州船政局使用自制的单锻压力为7t的汽锤 丁日昌建议设厂制造"耕织机器"，遭非议，未被清政府采纳 Fuzhou Administrative Bureau of Ship utilized self-made steam hammer with a single-forging pressure of 7 tons; Ding Richang suggested setting up factories to build "farming and weaving machine", which raised intense controversies and failed to be accepted by the government of the Qing Dynasty.	
1875	清光绪一年 1st year of Guangxu of the Qing Dynasty	福州船政局派魏瀚、陈北翱、陈季同三人赴法国学习制造技术 Fuzhou Administrative Bureau of Ship dispatched Wei Han, Chen Beiao and Chen Jitong to learn manufacturing technologies in France.	
1876	清光绪二年 2nd year of Guangxu of the Qing Dynasty	福州船政局仿制750hp复式高压蒸汽机 江南制造局制成铁甲螺旋桨推进的军舰"金瓯"号，载重250t，航速10节 发昌机器厂制造并出售小轮船，仿制车床 Fuzhou Administrative Bureau of Ship counterfeited 750hp high-pressure compound steam engine; Jiangnan Production Bureau built "Jin'ou" iron-armored warship powered by propellers; it had a carrying capacity of 250 t and the speed was 10 knots; Fachang Machine Factory built and sold small ships as well as counterfeited lathe.	

（续表）

年份 Year		机械工程大事 Important Events of Mechanical Engineering	国内外相关政治经济要事 Key Relevant Economic and Political Events at home and abroad
公元 A.D.	中国年代 In Feudalistic Years		
1877	清光绪三年 3rd year of Guangxu of the Qing Dynasty	江南制造局制造起重机 福州船政局正式往欧洲派留学生 Jiangnan Production Bureau built cranes; Fuzhou Administrative Bureau of Ship officially dispatched students to Europe.	
1879	清光绪五年 5th year of Guangxu of the Qing Dynasty	曾昭吉在四川机器局试制成水轮机 Zeng Zhaoji successfully trial-built water turbine in Sichuan Bureau of Machine.	
1880	清光绪六年 6th year of Guangxu of the Qing Dynasty	英国人创办胥各庄修车厂，1899年迁唐山 天津机器局试制出一艘式如橄榄的潜水艇 The Briton set up machine repair factory in Xuge Village which is relocated to Tangshan in 1899; Tianjin Bureau of Machine trial-built an olive-shaped submarine.	
1881	清光绪七年 7th year of Guangxu of the Qing Dynasty	胥各庄修车厂制成0-3-0型蒸汽机车"中国火箭"号（龙号） Machine repair factory of Xuge Village built 0-3-0 model steam turbine locomotive known as "China's Rocket" (aka dragon).	清政府撤回留美幼童 The government of the Qing Dynasty called back the young kids studying in US.
1882	清光绪八年 8th year of Guangxu of the Qing Dynasty	江南制造局制成抽水机 Jiangnan Production Bureau built water pump.	
1883	清光绪九年 9th year of Guangxu of the Qing Dynasty	福州船政局杨廉臣、李寿田、魏瀚监造的中国第一艘巡洋舰"开济"号下水，自行配套1788kW（2400hp）大功率康邦卧式蒸汽机 The first cruiser known as "Kaiji" in China, supervised by Yang Lianchen, Li Shoutian, and Wei Han in Fuzhou Administrative Bureau of Ship, was launched out on a virgin voyage; the 1788 kW (2400hp) large-power Cambon horizontal steam engine was independently equipped by China.	
1887	清光绪十三年 13th year of Guangxu of the Qing Dynasty	上海张万祥锡记铁工厂开始仿造日本式轧花机 上海永昌机器厂开始仿制意大利式缫丝机 Shanghai Zhang Wanxiang Xi Iron Factory started to counterfeit Japanese-styled cotton gin; Shanghai Yongchang Machine Factory began to counterfeit Italian silk filature.	

年份 Year		机械工程大事 Important Events of Mechanical Engineering	国内外相关政治经济要事 Key Relevant Economic and Political Events at home and abroad
公元 A.D.	中国年代 In Feudalistic Years		
1888	清光绪 十四年 14th year of Guangxu of the Qing Dynasty	福州船政局1888年1月，"龙威"号铁甲铁壳舰下水，排水量2100t，功率1788kW（2400hp），航速14节，首次。采用铆接工艺，为中国当时自己建造武器装备最优良的兵轮。以其优良的性能，编入北洋海军，改名"平远"号，成为北洋海军"八大远"中唯一的一艘国产巡洋舰 Iron-armored and iron-covered "Long Wei (Dragon Power)" fleet built by Fuzhou Administrative Bureau of Ship was launched out on a virgin voyage in January 1888; the displacement was 2,100 t; power was 1,788 kW (2400hp) and the speed was 14 knots; for the very first time, it adopted riveting technique and was the best warship manufactured independently by China; it was incorporated into Beiyang Navy due to its outstanding performance and was renamed "Pingyuan", becoming the only domestically built cruiser among the eight in Beiyang Navy.	
1890	清光绪 十六年 16th year of Guangxu of the Qing Dynasty	江南制造局15t平炉投产 发昌机器厂被耶松船厂吞并 汉阳铁厂引进高炉、转炉、平炉、轧钢机 15-ton open hearth was put into production by Jiangnan Production Bureau; Fachang Machine Factory was acquired by S.C. Farnham & Co.; Hanyang Iron Factory imported blast furnace, converter, open hearth and steel rolling mill.	
1891	清光绪 十七年 17th year of Guangxu of the Qing Dynasty	江南制造局的炼钢厂冶炼出中国第一炉钢 China's first furnace of steel was smelted by steel refinery of Jiangnan Production Bureau	
1894	清光绪 二十年 20th year of Guangxu of the Qing Dynasty		中日甲午之战 The Sino-Japanese War of 1894–1895 broke out

（续表）

年份 Year		机械工程大事 Important Events of Mechanical Engineering	国内外相关政治经济要事 Key Relevant Economic and Political Events at home and abroad
公元 A.D.	中国年代 In Feudalistic Years		
1895	清光绪 二十一年 21st year of Guangxu of the Qing Dynasty	盛宣怀在天津创办中西学堂，设有机械工程科，是为最早的机械专科学校 因屈辱的《马关条约》，引起全民强烈不满，7月，清政府迫于形势，宣称要"力行实政"、"造机器" Sheng Xuanhuai established Sino-western institute, introducing the course of mechanical engineering and it was the earliest institute with the major of mechanics. The humiliating "Treaty of Shimonoseki" evoked widespread dissatisfaction; in July, the government of the Qing Dynasty was forced by the then situation, to proclaim the "pressing forward with implementation of industrial policies" and "making machines".	中国在中日甲午战争战败，4月签订《马关条约》 China suffered an overwhelming defeat in Sino-Japanese War of 1894-1895 and signed the "Treaty of Shimonoseki" in April
1896	清光绪 二十二年 22nd year of Guangxu of the Qing Dynasty	江南制造局创办工艺学堂，设化学工艺、机器工艺科 朱志尧设计出棉籽轧油机 Jiangnan Production Bureau set up Institute of Industry, with majors of chemical industry and machinery industry. Zhu Zhiyao successfully designed cottonseed oil press.	
1897	清光绪 二十三年 23rd year of Guangxu of the Qing Dynasty	江苏南通张謇办厂制造面粉机、榨油机、碾米机等 Zhang Jian, from Nantong city of Jiangsu Province, set up factories to manufacture flour manufacturing machine, oil press, and rice mill.	
1898	清光绪 二十四年 24th year of Guangxu of the Qing Dynasty	耶松船厂与祥生船厂合并为耶松船厂公司，资金557万两白银，为英帝国在华最大企业 S.C. Farnham merged with Xiangsheng Dock to form S.C. Farnham & Co, with a capital of 5.57 million liang (the then currency); it was the largest British enterprise in China.	戊戌政变；清政府颁布《振兴工艺给奖章程》 Hundred Days' Reform (1898); the government of the Qing Dynasty worked out "Regulations of Incentives in Reviving Industry"
1900	清光绪 二十六年 26th year of Guangxu of the Qing Dynasty	上海开始仿制印刷机 Shanghai started to counterfeit printing machines	庚子之乱、八国联军侵华 Chaos of Gengzi and the Eight-Power Allies invaded China

年份 Year		机械工程大事 Important Events of Mechanical Engineering	国内外相关政治经济要事 Key Relevant Economic and Political Events at home and abroad
公元 A.D.	中国年代 In Feudalistic Years		
1901	清光绪 二十七年 27th year of Guangxu of the Qing Dynasty	德国人在青岛四方村创办铁路机厂 Germans started to build railway machine factories in Sifang Village of Qingdao.	
1902	清光绪 二十八年 28th year of Guangxu of the Qing Dynasty	严裕棠在上海创办大隆机器厂 俄国人办大连铁路机厂 Yan Yutang set up Dalong Machine Factory in Shanghai; Russians established Dalian Railway Machine Factory.	
1903	清光绪 二十九年 29th year of Guangxu of the Qing Dynasty	清政府制定《大学学堂章程》，其中规定了机器工业课程 京师高等实业学堂成立，设有机械科 唐山修车厂（胥各庄厂迁来）建成2-6-0中型机车 The government of the Qing Dynasty devised "University Regulations", which covered machinery industry course Metropolitan Higher Industrial Institute with the machine major was set up Tangshan Automobile Repair Factory (relocated from Xuge Village) built 2-6-0 medium-size vehicle	清政府设商部，颁布《奖励公司章程》 The government of the Qing Dynasty introduced Department of Commerce, issuing "Business Incentives Regulations"
1904	清光绪 三十年 30th year of Guangxu of the Qing Dynasty	朱志尧在上海创办求新制造机器轮船厂，资本70万元 Zhu Zhiyao set up Qiuxin Factory that manufactures machines and ships in Shanghai, with a capital of RMB700,000.	1904—1905年，日本和沙俄为重新瓜分中国东北和朝鲜而进行的日俄战争在中国境内展开 From 1904-1905, Russo-Japanese War for carving up northeast China and North Korea went on within China's territory.
1905	清光绪 三十一年 31st year of Guangxu of the Qing Dynasty	江南制造局改为官督商办，分成江南船坞和上海兵工厂 Jiangnan Production Bureau was converted to being commercially-run and supervised by the government, consisting of Jiangnan Dock and Shanghai Arsenal	

（续表）

年份 Year		机械工程大事 Important Events of Mechanical Engineering	国内外相关政治经济要事 Key Relevant Economic and Political Events at home and abroad
公元 A.D.	中国年代 In Feudalistic Years		
1906	清光绪 三十二年 32nd year of Guangxu of the Qing Dynasty	清政府颁发《奖给商勋章程》，鼓励制造新机器 日本人在大连成立南满铁道株式会社 The government of the Qing Dynasty issued "Regulations of Awarding Businesses", encouraging manufacturing of new machines; Japanese set up South Manchuria Railways Corporation in Dalian.	商部令各省设工艺局厂和劝工陈列所 Department of Commerce orders each province to set up industrial factories and exhibition units.
1907	清光绪 三十三年 33rd year of Guangxu of the Qing Dynasty	福州船政局因经营体制问题，造船难以为继，6月清廷批准停办 日本人在大连办沙河口铁路机厂 广东侨商陈国圻在黑龙江使用蒸汽拖拉机、耕作机械、收割机 王光、李维格创办汉口扬子机器厂，资本35万两白银（1915年增资至100万两白银） Fuzhou Administrative Bureau of Ship was unable to sustain ship-building business on account of its operational system and was authorized to suspend its operation by the Qing Dynasty; Japanese set up Shahekou Railway Machine Factory in Dalian; Chen Guoqi, an overseas Cantonese businessman, utilized steam tractor, farming machines and harvester in Heilongjiang; Wang Guang and Li Weige set up Hankou Yangtze Machine Factory, with a capital of 350 thousand liang (increased to 1 million by the year 1915).	清政府改订奖励公司章程；颁发爵赏章程，规定凡办1000万两银元以上之实业者赏男爵，2000万两银元以上者赏子爵 The government of Qing Dynasty revised business incentives regulations and issued regulations on awarding royal rankings; those who set up an industrial business worth more than 10 million and 20 million silver dollars would be awarded baron and viscount respectively.
1908	清光绪 三十四年 34th year of Guangxu of the Qing Dynasty	广州市成立民间"机器研究社"，是为中国最早的民办机械研究机构 "Research Institute of Machine" was set up in Guangzhou, which was the first private-owned research institute of machine in China.	
1909	清宣统一年 1st year of Xuantong of the Qing Dynasty	广州均和安机器厂仿制成功8hp煤气机，是中国最早的内燃机产品 冯如在美国设计制造出飞机，并试飞成功 23名中国学生去英美学习飞机和潜艇制造 Junhe'an Machine Factory in Guangzhou successfully counterfeited 8hp coal gas engine, which was the earliest internal combustion engine in China. Feng Ru made a successful trial flight with the aircraft designed and manufactured by himself in US. 23 Chinese students went to UK and US to learn aircraft and submarine manufacturing.	农工商部成立工业试验所，化验工业原料 Department of Agriculture, Industry and Commerce set up industrial laboratory to carry out chemical analysis of industrial raw materials.

（续表）

年份 Year		机械工程大事 Important Events of Mechanical Engineering	国内外相关政治经济要事 Key Relevant Economic and Political Events at home and abroad
公元 A.D.	中国年代 In Feudalistic Years		
1910	清宣统二年 2nd year of Xuantong of the Qing Dynasty	求新制造机器轮船厂仿制成25hp火油发动机、铁木脚踏织机、轧光机 上海泰记机器厂仿制钻床 谭根在美国创造了性能先进的水上飞机 清政府在北京南苑建厂制造飞机 Qiuxin Machine and Ship-building Factory designed 25hp kerosene engine, ironwood treadle loom and calendar. Shanghai Taiji Machine Factory manufactured drilling machine; Tan Gen invented advanced seaplane in US; The government of the Qing Dynasty set up factories in Nanyuan District (Southview Villas) in Beijing to manufacture aircrafts.	
1911	清宣统三年 3rd year of Xuantong of the Qing Dynasty	冯如携自制的双翼飞机从美国回到广州，翌年试飞时牺牲 Feng Ru brought the self-made double-winged aircraft from US to Guangzhou and unfortunately died in the trial flight the next year	辛亥革命胜利，结束了清朝的封建专制统治 Xinhai Revolution (the first civil revolutionary against feudalism in China in 1911) ended in triumph, putting an end to the authoritarian rule of the Qing Dynasty
1912	民国1年 1st year of Republic of China	江南船坞改称江南造船所，所造的 "江华" 号客轮下水，该轮排水量4130t、3000hp、时速14nmile，是当时长江最好的客轮 Jiangnan Dock was renamed Jiangnan Ship-building Plant; the passenger ship known as "Jianghua" went on a virgin voyage; the displacement was 4,130 t, 3,000hp and the speed was 14nmile, which was the best passenger ship in Yangtze River.	中华民国成立 北京政府颁布实施《奖励工艺品暂行章程》 詹天佑发起成立中华工程学会，后发展成为中国工程师学会 National Republic of China was founded. Beijing government worked out and implemented "Provisional Regulations of Awarding Industrial Products"; Zhan Tianyou proposed and set up Engineering Society of China, which later developed into Society of Chinese Engineers.
1913	民国2年 2nd year of Republic of China	中宝时钟厂在烟台成立 广州协同和机器厂仿制成烧球式40hp柴油机 Zhongbao Clock Factory was set up in Yantai Guangzhou Xietonghe Machine Factory counterfeited 40hp hot bulb diesel engine	日本制造飞机发动机 Japan manufactured aircraft engines.

（续表）

年份 Year		机械工程大事 Important Events of Mechanical Engineering	国内外相关政治经济要事 Key Relevant Economic and Political Events at home and abroad
公元 A.D.	中国年代 In Feudalistic Years		
1914	民国3年 3rd year of Republic of China		第一次世界大战爆发 The World War I broke out.
1915	民国4年 4th year of Republic of China	祁暄发明中国打字机 Qi Xuan invented Chinese typewriter	
1916	民国5年 5th year of Republic of China	华生电器厂成立，初期制造直流电动机、发电机 Huasheng Electrical Machinery Factory was founded, specified in manufacturing direct current motors and alternating generators.	
1917	民国6年 6th year of Republic of China	江南造船所购买"高伦"汽油机专利权，是为中国机械工业首次购买外国技术 Jiangnan Ship-building Plant purchased patent for "Galon" petrol engine, which was the first time for China machinery industry ever to purchase foreign technologies.	交通部成立"铁路技术标准委员会"，詹天佑为会长 Department of Communications set up "Committee for Railway Technical Standards", headed by Zhan Tianyou
1918	民国7年 7th year of Republic of China	北洋政府海军部在福州马尾设立海军飞机工程处及海军飞潜学校，建有一个装配车间，是中国第一个正规的飞机制造厂 江南造船厂承造美国商务部运输舰12艘，其中载重量万吨的4艘于1920—1921年完成 华生电器厂开始造交流电动机 上海鸿昌机器造船厂仿制12hp及60hp柴油机 上海邓顺昌机器厂仿制针织横机 日本人开办大连机械制作所 Department of Navy of Beiyang Government set up Navy Aircraft Engineering Plant and Navy Institute of Aircraft and Submarine, with an assembly factory; it was the first official aircraft manufacturing factory in China; Jiangnan Production Bureau undertook the production of 12 transport ships as ordered by Department of Commerce of US; four of them with a loading capacity of over ten thousand tons were completed between 1920 and 1921. Huasheng Electrical Machinery Factory started to manufacture alternating current motors; Shanghai Hongchang Machine and Shipbuilding Factory produced 12hp and 60hp diesel engines; Shanghai Dengshunchang Machine Factory counterfeited flat knitting machine; Japanese set up Dalian Machine Production Plant.	

年份 Year		机械工程大事 Important Events of Mechanical Engineering	国内外相关政治经济要事 Key Relevant Economic and Political Events at home and abroad
公元 A.D.	中国年代 In Feudalistic Years		
1919	民国8年 8th year of Republic of China	福建马尾海军飞机工程处制造出水上飞机 Navy Aircraft Engineering Plant at Mawei of Fujian manufactured seaplane.	孙中山著《实业计划》 Sun Yat-sen wrote "Industrial Plan"
1920	民国9年 9th year of Republic of China	江南造船所制造出14000余吨级运输舰"官府"号，主机3670hp（4台）蒸汽机自行配套 王岳记仿造出3号万能铣床 Jiangnan Ship-building Plant manufactured "Government" transport ship of over 14 thousand tons; 3,670hp steam engines (four in all) in the main machine were independently supplemented. Wang Yueji counterfeited No.3 universal milling machine.	
1921	民国10年 10th year of Republic of China	交通大学、东南大学设中国最早的机械工程系，系主任分别为周仁和李世琼 刘仙洲编著的《机械学》出版 University of Communications and Southeast University were the earliest universities with machine engineering majors with Zhou Ren and Li Shiqiong as the deans respectively; *Mechanics* written and compiled by Liu Xianzhou was published.	
1922	民国11年 11th year of Republic of China	大隆机器厂仿照日本丰田式产品，试制出织布机 Dalong Machine Factory test-manufactured weaving machine by emulating Toyota products in Japan.	
1923	民国12年 12th year of Republic of China	上海中国铁工厂仿造日本丰田式自动织布机 大隆机器厂开始制造棉织机 Shanghai China Iron Factory manufactured automatic weaving machine by emulating Toyota products in Japan; Dalong Machine Factory started manufacturing cotton weaving machine.	
1924	民国13年 13th year of Republic of China	上海益中公司试制成交流电动机 刘仙洲编著的《内燃机关》出版 Shanghai Yizhong Company trial-manufactured alternating current motor; *Internal Combustion Engine* written and compiled by Liu Xianzhou was published.	
1925	民国14年 14th year of Republic of China	支秉渊等人在上海创办中国新中工程公司 张荫麟译著有关中国古代机械的论文 Zhi Bingyuan set up China Xinzhong Engineering Company in Shanghai; Zhang Yinlin translated articles about China's ancient machines.	
1926	民国15年 15th year of Republic of China	福州船政局改为海军马尾造船所 Fuzhou Administrative Bureau of Ship was converted to Navy Mawei Ship-building Plant.	

（续表）

年份 Year		机械工程大事 Important Events of Mechanical Engineering	国内外相关政治经济要事 Key Relevant Economic and Political Events at home and abroad
公元 A.D.	中国年代 In Feudalistic Years		
1928	民国17年 17th year of Republic of China	东北当局创办皇姑屯机厂 程瀛章、张济翔编订《机械工程名词草案》 Northeast authorities established Huanggutun Machine Factory; Cheng Yingzhang and Zhang Jixiang compiled "Draft of Technical Jargons of Mechanical Engineering"	6月，中央研究院成立，下设工程研究所 国民政府颁布《奖励工业品暂行条例》 In June, Central Research Institute was founded, with engineering research institute established; National government issued "Provisional Regulations of Awarding Industrial Products"
1929	民国18年 18th year of Republic of China	建设委员会在上海经营电机制造厂 新中工程公司制成双缸狄塞尔柴油机 Construction Committee operated electric machine manufacturing plants in Shanghai; Xinzhong Engineering Company manufactured double-cylinder Rudolf Diesel engine.	国民政府颁布《特种工业奖励法》 National government worked out "Method of Awarding Special Industries"
1930	民国19年 19th year of Republic of China	中央工业试验所在南京成立，设化学、机械两个组。机械组是中国最早的机械工程科学试验研究机构 何乃民编著的《汽车学纲要》出版 China Central Industrial Laboratory was set up in Nanjing, with chemistry and machine groups. Machine group was the earliest research institute involving scientific experiments of mechanical engineering; *Overview of Automobile* compiled by He Naimin was published.	
1931	民国20年 20th year of Republic of China	红军在江西兴国官田镇建中央苏区兵工厂，二方面军在湖南永顺建兵工厂 沈阳民生工厂生产出一辆民生牌载货汽车，这是国产第一辆汽车 实业部筹办中央机器制造厂（抗战前停办） 大隆机器厂20世纪30年代中期能制造整套棉纺机 The Red Army set up Central Soviet Arsenal in Guantian Township, Xingguo of Jiangxi and the Second Front Army set up arsenal in Yongshun of Hunan; Shenyang Minsheng Arsenal built the first "Minsheng" truck, which was the first automobile manufactured by China; Industrial Department was planning to set up Central Machine Production Factory (suspended prior to the Anti-Japanese War); Dalong Machine Factory manufactured the comprehensive set of cotton weaving machine in mid-1930s.	"九·一八"事变，日本占领东北 Mukden Incident broke out; Japan seized control of northeast China

（续表）

年份 Year		机械工程大事 Important Events of Mechanical Engineering	国内外相关政治经济要事 Key Relevant Economic and Political Events at home and abroad
公元 A.D.	中国年代 In Feudalistic Years		
1932	民国21年 21st year of Republic of China	实业部工业标准委员会正式成立，设有机械组 河南的汤仲明、湖南的向德等人改装出木炭汽车 大隆机器厂推广高速钢刀具，试用硬质合金刀具、块规等，1932—1935年仿制出Novton磨床 Industrial Standard Committee of Industrial Department was set up, and machine group was introduced. Tang Zhongming from Henan and Xiang De from Hunan designed charcoal-powered automobiles; Dalong Machine Factory promoted high speed steel tools and used carbide cutting tools and measuring blocks on a trial basis; Novton grinding machine was counterfeited from 1932 to 1935.	国民政府颁布《奖励工业技术暂行条例》 因九·一八事变后日军侵华形势，11月1日，国民政府组织成立国防设计委员会（资源委员会前身）其任务是对全国的军事、国际关系、财政经济、教育文化进行调研 National government issued "Provisional Regulations of Awarding Industrial Techniques"; Given the Japanese invasion into China after the Mukden Incident, national government set up National Defense Design Committee (the predecessor of Resource Committee) which was responsible for the investigation and research into national military, international relations, finance and economy and education and culture
1933	民国22年 22nd year of Republic of China	山西汽车修理厂生产了3辆载货汽车 中央工业试验所试用酒精代替汽油作发动机燃料 Shanxi Automobile Repair Factory produced three trucks; Central Industrial Laboratory tested on substituting petroleum with ethanol as the fuel for engine;	
1934	民国23年 23rd year of Republic of China	中美合办中央飞机制造公司，在杭州笕桥建成投产，抗战前曾生产全金属轰炸机 航空委员会第一飞机修理厂制成"爪哇"号飞机 江南造船所造了柴油机护航舰 北洋大学机械系邓日谟开始仿制飞机发动机 刘仙洲编著的《英汉对照机械工程名词》在清华大学出版 China and US jointly founded Central Aircraft Manufacturing Company; launching production in Jian bridge of Hangzhou; the company manufactured metal bomber before the Anti-Japanese War; No. 1 Aircraft Repair Factory of Aviation Committee manufactured "Java" aircraft Jiangnan Ship-building Plant manufactured escort with diesel engine. Deng Rimo from Department of Machine in Beiyang University started to counterfeit the aircraft engine; *English-Chinese Translation of Technical Jargons of Mechanical Engineering* compiled by Liu Xianzhou was published in Tsinghua University	

（续表）

	年份 Year	机械工程大事 Important Events of Mechanical Engineering	国内外相关政治经济要事 Key Relevant Economic and Political Events at home and abroad
公元 A.D.	中国年代 In Feudalistic Years		
1935	民国24年 24th year of Republic of China	新中工程公司开始在图纸上标注尺寸公差 红军在陕北瓦窑堡创建红色兵工厂，1938年迁到安塞县茶坊镇 刘仙洲编著的《机械原理》、《中国机械工程史料》出版 伪满成立大陆科学院，下设机械方面的研究机构 满洲机器股份公司在沈阳成立 Xinzhong Engineering Company started to denote the measurement tolerance on the blueprint The Red Army set up Red Arsenal in Wayaobao of north Shaanxi Province, relocated to Chafang Township of Ansai County in 1938; *Principle of Mechanics* and *History of China's Mechanical Engineering* compiled by Liu Xianzhou were published; Puppet Manchu set up Mainland Institute of Science, with research institute regarding machines; Manchu Machine Holdings Corporation was set up in Shenyang.	4月，国防设计委员会易名资源委员会，主要执掌资源的调查、开发及动员等 工业标准委员会开始编订中国工业标准 In April, National Defense Design Committee was renamed Resource Committee; mainly in charge of investigation, development and encouragement of resources, etc. Industrial Standard Committee started to devise industrial standards in China.
1936	民国25年 25th year of Republic of China	中国机械工程学会在杭州成立。此前，1934年成立中国航空工程学会和电机工程学会，1935年成立中国自动机工程学会 王守竞博士主持在湘潭筹建机器制造厂，拟制造飞机发动机、原动机、机床及工具、汽车 曾养甫等人筹建中国汽车制造公司，拟仿造德国Benz牌汽车 铁道部在杭州筹建铁路总机厂，1938年因战事停建 清华大学制成中国第一个航空风洞，成立航空研究所 中国机械自给率约为23.5%，车辆船舶自给率16.5%，钢铁自给率为5% Chinese Mechanical Engineering Society was founded in Hangzhou. Earlier on, China Aviation Engineering Society and Electrical Engineering Society were set up in 1934. China Automatic machine Engineering Society was set up in 1935; Doctor Wang Shoujing was in charge of building machine manufacturing plants in Xiangtan, planning to manufacture aircraft engine, prime motor, machine tools and automobiles; Zeng Yangfu was planning to set up China Automobile Manufacturing Company, planning to counterfeit Benz automobiles from Germany; Department of Railway was planning to establish Railway General Factory in Hangzhou, which was suspended in 1938 on account of warfare; Tsinghua University made the first aviation wind tunnel in China, and set up aviation research institute; The self-sufficiency rate of China's machinery was approximately 23.5%; self-sufficiency rate of vehicles and ships was 16.5%; self-sufficiency rate of iron and steel was 5%.	资源委员会编发《重工业建设计划》兴建冶金、化工、机械、能源、电器等重工业厂矿，先后上马了钢铁厂、机械、电工器材厂等一批企业 Resource Committee drafted *Construction Plan of Heavy Industry* to revive the construction of industrial mines related to metallurgy, chemical, machinery, energy sources and electrical appliances, rolling out a batch of enterprises like iron and steel factories, machinery and electrical appliances factories.

年份 Year		机械工程大事 Important Events of Mechanical Engineering	国内外相关政治经济要事 Key Relevant Economic and Political Events at home and abroad
公元 A.D.	中国年代 In Feudalistic Years		
1937	民国26年 26th year of Republic of China	中国机械工程学会出版《机械工程》季刊 新中工程公司仿制出35hp的Perkins高速柴油汽车发动机 中国汽车制造公司在上海建装配厂，组装Benz牌载货汽车 张世钢试验用植物油代替柴油作为汽车燃料，获成功 中意合办中央南昌飞机制造厂 日本全面侵华，上海等地机器厂开始内迁 中共中央军委成立军事工业局，滕代远任局长 11月6日，中共六大六中全会号召："每个游击战争根据地都必须尽量设法建立小的兵工厂，办到自制弹药、步枪、手榴弹等程度，使游击战争无军火缺乏之虞。"抗战胜利前后各根据地共拥有工人100人以上、设备10台以上、有固定厂房的兵工厂50余个，职工3万余人 Chinese Mechanical Engineering Society published a quarterly magazine of *Mechanical Engineering*; Xinzhong Engineering Company counterfeited 35hp Perkins high-speed diesel automobile engine; China Automobile Manufacturing Company set up assembly factory in Shanghai, assembling Benz trucks; Zhang Shigang experimented on the replacement of diesel with vegetable oil as automobile fuel ended in success. China and Italy jointly set up Central Nanchang Aircraft Manufacturing Factory; Japan launched a full-throttle attack on China; machines factories in Shanghai and other cities started to be relocated internally after the Lugouqiao Incident; The Military Commission of the CPC Central Committee of set up Military Industrial Bureau, headed by Teng Daiyuan; On November 6th, the Sixth Plenary Session of the Sixth CPC Central Committee encouraged "every guerilla war base shall do their best to set up small arsenals so that they could independently manufacture bullets, rifles, and grenades, sparing guerilla war from the shortage of weapons". Around the victory of Anti-Japanese War, each base had a total of more than 100 workers, over 10 equipments, more than 50 arsenals with factories at fixed locations and over 30 thousand employees.	7月7日，日本侵略者制造了卢沟桥事件，抗日战争全面爆发 8月9日，资源委员会向行政院提出工厂内迁方案，次日行政院批准；11日，上海工厂联合迁移委员会成立；13日，日军开始进攻上海；22日，顺时机器厂在炮火下第一家拆迁 抗战初期，146家上海民营企业西迁，占上海民营工厂的10% On July 7th, Japanese invaders created Lugouqiao Incident, unveiling the Anti-Japanese War that lasted for eight years; On August 9th, Resource Committee submitted the proposal of internally relocating factories to Executive Office, which was approved and authorized the next day; on 11th, Shanghai Factory Union Relocation Committee was set up; on 13th, Japanese army started to invade Shanghai; on 22nd, Shunshi Machine Factory was the first to be demolished and relocated given the gunfire. During the initial phase of Anti-Japanese War, 146 private-owned enterprises were relocated westward, accounting for 10% of private-owned factories in Shanghai.

（续表）

年份 Year		机械工程大事 Important Events of Mechanical Engineering	国内外相关政治经济要事 Key Relevant Economic and Political Events at home and abroad
公元 A.D.	中国年代 In Feudalistic Years		
1938	民国27年 27th year of Republic of China	纺织机试验所在重庆成立 江南造船所被日寇占用 满洲飞行机械制造株式会社成立 Weaving Machine Laboratory was founded in Chongqing; Jiangnan Ship-building Plant was seized by Japanese army; Manchu Air Machine Production Corporation was established.	国民政府先后颁布《工业奖励法》、《工矿业奖助暂行条例》 National government worked out "Method of Industrial Incentives" and "Provisional Regulations of Industrial and Mining Incentives"
1939	民国28年 28th year of Republic of China	资源委员会机器制造厂在昆明建成投产，定名为中央机器厂，下设几个分厂，总经理为王守竞 航空委员会在西南筹办飞机发动机厂 中央工业试验所先后在重庆成立机械设计室、机械实验工厂、动力试验室、材料试验室、热工试验室等 新中工程公司在湖南祁阳仿制成65hp的MAN柴油汽车发动机，不久改型为45hp煤气机 航空委员会在成都设航空研究所 中央大学机械工程系首次招收一名攻读硕士学位的研究生，该生1941年毕业 Machine Production Factory of Resource Committee was set up and put into production in Kunming; it was named Central Machine Factory, with a number of branch factories; the general manager was Wang Shoujing; Aviation Committee was planning to set up aircraft engine factory in southwest China; Central Industrial Laboratory successively set up Machine Design Room, Machine Test Factory, Dynamic Lab, Material Lab , and Thermodynamic engineering Lab; Xinzhong Engineering Company built 65hp MAN diesel automobile engine in Qiyang in Hunan, which was later transformed into 45hp coal gas engine; Aviation Committee set up Aviation Research Institute in Chengdu; Mechanical Engineering Department of China Central University recruited a postgraduate student pursuing master's degree for the first time, who graduated in 1941.	
1941	民国30年 30th year of Republic of China	中国工程师学会设立工程标准协进会 航空委员会在贵州大定乌鸦洞建成飞机发动机厂 The Chinese Engineers Society set up Engineering Standard Association; Aviation Committee set up factories manufacturing aircraft engines in Wuyadong of Dading in Guizhou	12月8日，日军偷袭美国珍珠港，太平洋战争爆发 On December 8th, Japanese army raided Pearl Harbor in US; the Pacific War broke out

（续表）

年份 Year		机械工程大事 Important Events of Mechanical Engineering	国内外相关政治经济要事 Key Relevant Economic and Political Events at home and abroad
公元 A.D.	中国年代 In Feudalistic Years		
1942	民国31年 31st year of Republic of China	度量衡局成立机械工业标准起草委员会，分组制定标准 中央机器厂试制出齿轮滚刀，仿制成瑞士的精密铣床、250hp煤气机 支秉渊驾驶煤气汽车从祁阳赶到重庆，其发动机为新中公司自制 1942—1943年，中国兴业公司机器厂制造轧钢机 1942—1944年，航空委员会南川第二飞机制造厂设计制造出中运-1式运输机 满洲工作机械株式会社生产单轴自动车床、磨床等 Bureau of Weights and Measures set up Committee drafting mechanical industrial standards and laying out standards by groups; Central Machine Factory test-produced gear hobbing cutter, counterfeited Swiss precision milling machines and 250 hp coal gas engine; Zhi Bingyuan drove a coal gas automobile from Qiyang to Chongqing; with the engine manufactured independently by Xinzhong Company; From 1942—1943, machine factory of China Xingye Corporation manufactured steel rolling machine; From 1942—1944, Nanchuan No.2 Aircraft Manufacturing Factory of Aviation Committee designed and manufactured Zhongyun-I transport plane; Manchu Work and Machine Corporation manufactured single-axle automatic lathe and grinding machines.	
1943	民国32年 32nd year of Republic of China	中央机器厂制成150hp混流式水轮发电机组、30kW转桨式水轮机、显微镜、钻夹头等，并在1943年前后试制出块规 中国汽车制造公司华西分厂（重庆）成功地用桐油代替柴油作为汽车燃料 中国工程师学会对支秉渊煤气汽车研制成果授予金质奖章荣誉 1943—1944年间，吴震寰设计了2000kW水轮机 Central Machine Factory manufactured 150hp mixed flow hydro-turbine generators, 30 kW rolling-oar hydro-turbine, microscope, drill chuck and tested and manufactured measuring blocks around 1943; West China Branch Factory (Chongqing) of China Automobile Manufacturing Company successfully substituted diesel with tung oil as automobile fuel; The Chinese Engineers Society awarded Gold Medal of Honor to the results of Zhi Bingyuan's research and productions in coal-gas automobiles; From 1943—1944, Wu Zhenhuan designed 2000 kW hydro-turbine.	国民政府召集各方代表，讨论通过《战后经济建设计划》 National government summoned representatives of each party and passed "Postwar Economic Construction Plan"

（续表）

年份 Year		机械工程大事 Important Events of Mechanical Engineering	国内外相关政治经济要事 Key Relevant Economic and Political Events at home and abroad
公元 A.D.	中国年代 In Feudalistic Years		
1944	民国33年 33rd year of Republic of China	大定飞机发动机厂装成两台G105B式飞机发动机 中央机器厂制成150hp柴油机，又在四川泸县安装2000kW汽轮发电机组，其中汽轮机、发电机转子为瑞士制造，其余均为自制 1944—1945年，新中工程公司仿制一台卧式镗床 上海亚中铁工厂仿制了一台10ft液压万能磨床 满洲轴承制造株式会社月产轴承7万套 延安自然科学研究院的物理系改为机械工程系 Dading Aircraft Engine Factory assembled two G1058 aircraft engines; Central Machine Factory manufactured 150hp diesel engine; installed 2000 kW steam turbine generating set in Lu Township of Sichuan, which was independently developed apart from steam turbine and generating rotor that were manufactured in Switzerland; From 1944—1945, Xinzhong Engineering Company counterfeited a horizontal boring lathe; Shanghai Yazhong Iron Factory counterfeited a 10-inch hydraulic universal grinding machine; Manchu Bearing Production Corporation had a monthly production capacity of 70 thousand sets of bearings; Department of Physics of Yan'an Research Institute of Natural Science was renamed Department of Mechanical Engineering.	
1945	民国34年 34th year of Republic of China	上海公用电机厂制造300hp电动机 中国开始索要日本的赔偿机器，实际上得到很少 交通部开始筹建株洲机车厂 1945—1948年，朱家仁试制成"蜂鸟"号直升机 Shanghai Public Electrical Machinery Factory manufactured 300hp electric motor; China began to claim compensation for machines from Japan, but ended up receiving little; Department of Communications began to plan the construction of Zhuzhou Locomotive Factory; From 1945—1948, Zhu Jiaren trial-manufactured "Humming Bird" Helicopter.	美国将原子弹投向日本广岛、长崎 日本战败投降 国民政府中央设计局会同资源委员会提出《重工业五年计划》 Atomic bombs exploded in Hiroshima and Nagasaki; Japan was defeated and surrendered; Central Design Bureau of National Government and Resource Committee jointly proposed "Five-year Plan for Heavy Industry".

年份 Year		机械工程大事 Important Events of Mechanical Engineering	国内外相关政治经济要事 Key Relevant Economic and Political Events at home and abroad
公元 A.D.	中国年代 In Feudalistic Years		
1946	民国35年 35th year of Republic of China	日本投降后，苏军大规模拆运东北的机器设备，按"二战"前币值至少20亿美元 中央机器有限公司成立，原中央机器厂改称昆明机器厂 中国农业机械特种股份有限公司改组为中国农业机械公司 中国纺织机械制造公司在上海成立 大定飞机发动机厂在广州设立分厂 After Japan surrendered, Soviet army dismantled and robbed machines and equipment in northeast China on a massive scale, which were worth at least USD 2 billion according to the currency value before the World War II; Central Machine Co., Ltd. was founded and the original Central Machine Factory was renamed Kunming Machine Factory; China Agricultural Machine Special Holdings Co., Ltd. was reshuffled to become China Agricultural Machine Corporation; China Textile Machinery Manufacture Corporation was founded in Shanghai; The branch of Dading Aircraft Engine Factory was set up in Guangzhou.	内战爆发 The Chinese Civil War broke out.
1947	民国36年 36th year of Republic of China	国民政府中央标准局成立 1947年是1946—1949年间机械工业生产状况最好的一年 Central Bureau of Standard of National Government was founded. The year 1947 witnessed the best production status of machinery industry during the period from 1946 to 1949.	
1948	民国37年 37th year of Republic of China	中央机器公司昆明机器厂制成500hp滑环式交流电动机 Kunming Machine Factory of Central Machine Corporation manufactured 500hp slip-ring alternating current motor.	
1949	民国38年 38th year of Republic of China	资源委员会从美国西屋公司得到汽轮机、发电设备的图纸和技术资料 Resource Committee acquired blueprint and technical materials on steam turbine and generating equipment from Westinghouse Electric in US.	中华人民共和国成立 The People's Republic of China was founded.

第三篇　中国现代机械史

Part 3
Contemporary History of
Machinery in China

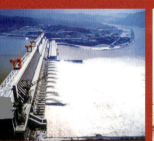   

■ 1949年新中国成立至2008年（1949—2008年）

From the founding of the People's Republic of China in 1949 to 2008 (1949—2008年)

综　述
General

机械是发展了的工具，是现代社会进行生产和服务的六大要素(人、资金、能源、信息、材料和机械)之一，并参与能量和材料的生产。机械工业的服务领域很广，现代机械工业有五大服务领域：

Machinery is a developed tool and one of six elements (people, fund, energy, information, materials and machinery) for production and services in modern society. It applies to production of energy and materials. With a wide scope of services, modern machinery industry mainly serves the following five sectors:

（1）研制和提供能量转换机械，包括将热能、化学能、原子能、电能、流体压力能和天然机械能转换为适合于应用的机械能的各种动力机械，以及将机械能转换为所需要的其他形式的能量。

Research and production of machinery for energy conversion, including various power machines converting thermal energy, chemical energy, atomic energy, electrical energy, liquid pressure energy and natural mechanical energy into applicable mechanical energy, and machines converting mechanical energy into other necessary forms.

（2）研制和提供用以生产各种产品的机械，包括农、林、牧、渔业机械和矿山机械以及各种重工业机械和轻工业机械等。

Research and production of machines for producing various products, including machines for agriculture, forestry, animal husbandry and fishery, mining machines and various machines for heavy industry and light industry, etc.

（3）研制和提供从事各种服务的机械，如物料搬运机械，交通运输机械，医疗机械，办公机械，通风、采暖和空调设备以及除尘、净化、消声等环境保护设备等。

Research and production of machines for various services, like machines for material handling, transportation, medical appliances and office apparatus, ventilation, heating and air-conditioning equipment, and environmental protection equipment for dust removal, purification and noise elimination.

（4）研制和提供家庭和个人生活用的机械，如洗衣机、电冰箱、钟表、照相机、运动器械和娱乐器械等。

Research and production of machines for domestic and daily use, like washing machines, refrigerators, clocks, cameras and equipment for sports and entertainment, etc.

（5）研制和提供各种军事装备。

Research and production of all kinds of military equipment.

1949年10月1日，中华人民共和国成立。当时，中国的农业基本上仍然是以手工个体劳动为主的传统农业，而此时的工业，则比世界上主要的资本主义国家落后100余年。当时，中国的机械工业企业只有3000多个，职工10万多人，拥有金属切削机床3万台左右。大多数机械厂只能从事修理和装配业务。1954年毛泽东同志对此有过一段形象的描绘："现在我们能造什么？能造桌子、椅子，能造茶壶、茶碗，能种粮食还能磨成面粉，还能造纸，但是一辆汽车、一架飞机、一辆坦克、一辆拖拉机都不能造。"

The People's Republic of China was founded on Oct. 1, 1949. At that time, China's agriculture was still mostly traditional agriculture depending on individual manual labor, and the industry was at such a level as major capitalist countries were at more than 100 years ago. There were only over 3,000 enterprises dealing with machinery industry in China, with over 100,000 employees and about 30,000 metal-cutting machine tools. Most of these machinery works are only capable of repair and assembly. Chairman Mao made a vivid description in 1954"what can we produce now? We can produce tables, chairs, teapots, bowls, food, flour and paper, but we are not capable of making a car, an airplane, a tank and even a tractor. "

党中央对机械工业发展寄予殷切的期望，给予很大支持。1956年4月，毛泽东在作《论十大关系》报告时感叹："什么时候我们能坐自己生产的小汽车就好了。"1951年4月17日，中央就颁发了《关于航空工业建设的决定》。1953年，毛泽东亲自签发了《中共中央关于力争三年建设长春汽车厂的指示》。1959年，毛泽东针对苏联中止对华援助研制核潜艇时说："核潜艇，一万年也要搞出来。"

The Central Government expects a lot out of the machinery industry and gave great support. In April 1956, when Chairman Mao was giving the report of "On Ten Relationships", he said, "If only we could go for meetings in cars developed by our people..." The Central Government issued *Decision on Construction of Aircraft Industry on April* 17, 1951, Chairman Mao signed *The Central Government's Instruction on Building Changchun Automobile Factory in Three Years* in the year 1953. When Soviet Union ceased assistance to China in terms of research and production of nuclear submarines, Chairman Mao said in 1959, "No matter how long it will take, we will finally work out nuclear submarines."

第一个五年计划时期，当时的第一机械工业部就按中央要求在中南海办了汇报性的机械展，毛泽东、刘少奇、邓小平等中央领导都观看了展览，仅毛泽东就看了六次。1958年，毛泽东曾说，我是想对发展机床工业的重要性作些调查，但一到工厂，变成大家看我。因此他指示在中南海瀛台举办小型机床工具展览。1958年7月2日，他在此详细地观看了机床操作表演，而且用哲学、政治经济学的观点说，原材料按照人们的意愿，通过了机床与工具、改变成需要的机器零件，充分体现了工业生产中人、机、物三者的关系。1958年9月5日，毛泽东在最高国务会议讲话中说："机械里头有个工作母机，什么矿山，什么炼油，什么电子，什么化学，什么建筑，什么农业，什么交通运输，这些机器都要有个工作母机，无非是车、铣、刨、钻之类，这些东西是根本的。"1959年冬，机械工业部按照毛泽东的要求，在中南海瀛台又一次组织机床工具展览，1960年4月24日，毛泽东又用3个小时观看机床操作表演，了解机床各种性能。

During the first five-year planning period, the First Ministry of Machine-building Industry held a machinery exhibition for report purpose in Zhongnanhai as required by the Central Government. State leaders including Mao Zedong, Liu Shaoqi and Deng Xiaoping inspected the exhibition. What's more，Mao inspected for 6 times. In 1958, Mao said that he wanted to do survey on the significance of developing machine tool industry, but every time when he inspected some factory he became the focus. So he required a small-sized machine tool exhibition at Yingtai in Zhongnanhai. He watched operation of machine tools in the exhibition on July 2, 1958, and said with a view of philosophy and political economics that raw materials were made into machine parts by machine tools to people's need and this fully embodied the relations between people, machines and materials in industrial production. Mao addressed at the supreme state conference on Sept. 5, 1958, "There is a major machine tool for mining, refinery, electronics, chemistry, architecture, agriculture and transportation. Turning, milling, planning and drilling are the basic methods." The Ministry of Machine-building Industry held another machine tool exhibition at Yingtai as required by Mao in the winter of 1959. Mao watched operation of machine tools for 3 hours to learn various functions of the tools on April 24, 1960.

以上提及的毛泽东说过的话至今已有五六十年。甲子回望，中国已从"农业经济大国"变为"工业经济大国"。中国机械工业没有让中央领导失望，2008年中国机械工业总产值是1949年的2.2万倍，职工数量则是200多倍。

Mao gave the aforesaid opinions more than 50 to 60 years ago. Now China is a big power of industry instead of agriculture. The machinery industry never gets state leaders down. The output of China's machinery industry and the employees thereof in the year 2008 were 22,000 times and over 200 times of those in 1949 respectively.

中国机械工业发展概况表(1949—2008年)

Development of machinery industry in China (1949—2008)

	1949	1952	1978	2008	2008/1949（倍）(times)	1950—2008年平均年增（%）1950—2008 mean annual growth (%)	1978/1949（倍）(times)	1950—1978年平均年增（%）1950—1978 mean annual growth (%)	2008/1978（倍）(times)	1979—2008年平均年增（%）1979—2008 mean annual growth (%)
工业总产值（亿元）Gross industrial output (RMB 100 million)	5.59	25.86	1082.28	123047.08	22012	18.90	193.61	19.91	113.69	17.09
企业数（个）Number of enterprises			10890	130306					11.97	8.65
职工人数（万人）Number of employees (10,000)	10.7		499.13	2246.22	209.93	9.5	46.65	14.15	4.50	5.22
大型拖拉机（万台）Large-sized tractors (10,000)			11.43	21.71					1.91	2.19
金属切削机床（万台）Metal-cutting machine (10,000)	0.16	1.37	18.33	61.73	385.81	10.62	114.56	17.76	3.37	4.13

（续表）

	1949	1952	1978	2008	2008/1949（倍）(times) 1950—2008年平均年增（%）1950—2008 mean annual growth (%)	1978/1949（倍）(times) 1950—1978年平均年增（%）1950—1978 mean annual growth (%)	2008/1978（倍）(times)	1979—2008年平均年增（%）1979—2008 mean annual growth (%)
数控机床（台）Numerical control machine (sets)			581	122211			210.35	19.52
汽车（万辆）Automobiles (10,000)			14.91	934.51			64.49	14.90
轿车（万辆）Sedans (10,000)			0.26	503.73			2049.27	28.94
发电设备（万kW）Power generating equipment (10,000 kW)		0.54	483.83	13319.4			27.58	11.69
水电设备（万kW）Hydropower equipment (10,000 kW)		0.54	144.56	2418.16			16.73	9.85
内燃机（万kW）Inter-combustion engines (10,000 kW)	0.74	2.94	2905.67	54977.08	74293.35 20.94	3926.58 33.02	18.92	10.30

拖拉机、汽车、发电设备产量已居全球第一。中国已进入全球机械大国的前列，正向现代机械强国挺进。

Production of tractors, automobiles and power generating equipment ranked the first in the world. China becomes a big power of machinery and is heading toward a strong power of modern machinery.

汽车　1956年，中国造出第一辆载货车；1958年，造出第一辆轿车。2009年，中国汽车产量已超过1300多万辆，居全球第一，从具有自主知识产权的0.6升微型轿车到5.6升红旗高级轿车，应有尽有。

Automobiles: China produced its first truck in 1956 and its first sedan in 1958. Production of automobiles exceeded 13 million in 2009, ranking the first in the world. Products range from 0.6L mini-car to 5.6L HQ limousine, all with proprietary intellectual property rights.

飞机　1956年9月8日成功制造了第一架喷气式歼击机"歼-5"飞机，现在自行研制并批量装备空军的"歼-10"飞机，其性能不亚于美国"F-16"和法国"幻影-2000"飞机。

Airplane: China made its first jet fighter (J-5) successfully on Sept. 8, 1956. Performance of "J-10" fighter, which is researched and produced by China independently and with which the Chinese air force is now equipped, is as good as that of "F-16" (by U.S.A.) and "Mirage-2000" (by France).

坦克　1958年12月成功制造了第一辆"59式"中型坦克，现在生产的"99式"主战坦克，可与世界先进坦克抗衡。

Tank: the first "59-type" medium tank was successfully manufactured in Dec. 1958. "99-type" main battle tank produced at present can resist advanced equipment in the world.

拖拉机　1958年制造了第一台拖拉机，现在已能生产300马力的大型轮式拖拉机；2009年生产大中型拖拉机39.19万台，占全球产量的30%以上。

Tractor: China manufactured its first tractor in 1958. Now, China can produce 300hp large-sized wheeled tractors. About 391,900 large and medium-sized tractors were manufactured in 2009, accounting for more than 30% of global production.

60年来，中国机械工业从落后于发达国家100余年，迅速提高到21世纪世界先进水平。

The machinery industry in China was at such a level as developed countries were at more than 100 years ago, when the P.R.C. was founded. It has grown to the worldwide leading level in the 21st century over 60 years. Let the whole world see this unprecedented historic progress.

东方红-2884大功率
(288 hp)轮式拖拉机

YTO-2884 Heavy Duty
(288 hp) Wheeled Tractor

红旗检阅车

Hongqi HQE（"Red
Flag" brand limousine）

中国第一种自主设计的第三代战斗机——歼-10

J-10, the First Type of the Third-Generation Fighter Independently Designed by China

99式主战坦克

"99-type" Main Battle Tank

第一节　艰苦创业，初步奠定基础的机械工业
Section 1　Initial Base of Machinery Industry Established through Hard Work

（一）恢复生产，着手新厂建设准备工作
Production resumed and preparation for construction of new factories commenced

1949—1952年国民经济恢复时期，国家对饱受战争创伤的机械修配工业进行了一系列的改革、改组工作，建立起初步生产秩序，还仿制一些机械产品，旧中国那种以修配为主的局面开始有所改变。

During the recovery period of national economy from 1949 to 1952, China carried out a series of reform and restructuring in the war-worn machine repair industry to establish the primary sequence of production. Some mechanical products were also copied. The situation mainly focusing on reparing in the old China began to change.

中华人民共和国建立初期，我国机械工业企业使用的主要工艺设备——皮带车床

Pulley Lathes—the major manufacturing equipment applied to machinery industry in early years of the P.R.C.

中华人民共和国成立
前，潍坊华丰机器厂仿
制的12 hp卧式柴油机

12 hp horizontal diesel
engine copied by Weifang
Huafeng Machinery Factory
before founding of the
P.R.C.

20世纪50年代初期，济南柴油
机厂生产的第一批12 hp柴油机

The first batch of 12 hp diesel engine
produced by Jinan Diesel Engine
Plant in the early 1950s

1950年，济南第一机床厂生产的
第一台五尺车床

The first 5 ft. lathe produced by Jinan First
Machine-tools Plant in 1950

1950年9月，上海虬江机器厂（上海机床厂前身）制造的"虬13式万能工具磨床"

In Sept of 1950,"Qiu13 universal tool grinder" made by Shanghal QiuJiang Machine Works(the predecessor of Shanghai Machine Tool Works)

新中国成立伊始，就开始启动大规模建设新的大型骨干企业，如第一个重机厂——太原重型机器制造厂，1951年10月就破土动工，1950年初决定在沈阳筹建重电机厂（因"抗美援朝"改在哈尔滨建设，即后来的哈尔滨电机厂），1952年决定在上海建设三大动力设备厂。"156项"在东北的机械项目，从1950年开始相继成立筹备组，进行前期准备工作，沈阳风动工具厂在1952年即开始建设。

New large-sized key enterprises were constructed. Large-sized construction commenced after the foundation of the P.R.C. Construction of Taiyuan Heavy Machinery Factory, the first heavy machine factory in the P.R.C., began in Oct. 1951. It was decided to build a heavy electric machinery factory in Shenyang at the beginning of 1950 (the factory was finally built in Harbin, known as Harbin Electric Machinery Factory, due to the war to resist U.S. aggression and aid Korea). It was decided to build three major power equipment factories in Shanghai in 1952. Preparatory groups were organized one after another from 1950 on, for 156 mechanical projects in Northeastern China. Construction of Shenyang Pneumatic Tools Factory began in 1952.

（二）实行"计划经济"体制，全力建设"156项"
"Planned Economy" began with efforts to construct "156 Projects"

1953—1957年是国民经济第一个五年计划时期，机械工业主要方面是对原有老厂进行组织调整和技术改造，与新企业的建设很好地结合起来，使机械工业逐渐成为独立而完整的机械制造业。这时，开始实行计划经济体制，还对私营经济进行社会主义改造。

The first 5-year planning period of national economy was from 1953 to 1957. The major task of machinery industry was organization adjustment and technical reform of the original factories combined with construction of new enterprises, to shape an independent and complete machinery industry gradually. The system of "planned economy" was adopted at that time, with socialist transformation of private sectors of economy.

太原重型机器制造厂是"一五"时期我国自行设计、建设的重点工程项目；图为1951年正在兴建的冷作车间施工工地

Taiyuan Heavy Machinery Factory was a key engineering project designed and constructed by China itself during the first 5-year planning period. The picture Shows the construction site for cold-working workshop under construction in 1951.

这一时期，进一步确定了企业的产品专业方向，实行计划管理，加强技术管理和经济管理并进行企业的技术改造，以改变老厂的生产技术落后面貌，充分发挥老厂的作用。这一时期，机械工业的生产总值，老厂占80%以上，机械产品国内自给率为62%。苏联援建的"156项"所需设备，交由国内供应的比重，按重量计为52.3%，按金额计为45.9%，鞍山钢铁公司、武汉钢铁公司、第一汽车制造厂、洛阳拖拉机厂等重要项目有50%左右的设备，分交由国内供应。

In this period, product orientation of enterprises was further specified, planning management was implemented, technical and economic management was reinforced and technical reform of enterprises was executed, to change the backward production technologies of old factories and to leverage the functions of the factories. 80% of the gross product of the machinery industry was attributable to these old factories. 62% of mechanical products were supplied by domestic enterprises. The equipment supplied by domestic enterprises for "156 projects" aided by Soviet Union accounted for 52.3% of all the equipment necessary for these projects by weight and 45.9% by amount of money. About 50% of equipment for important projects, involving Anshan Iron and Steel Group Corporation, Wuhan Iron and Steel (Group) Corp., FAW Group and YTO Group, etc., were supplied by domestic enterprises.

（三）"一五"时期"156项"工程设备国内供应设备比例

Proportion of equipment supplied by domestic enterprises in all the equipment for "156 Projects" in the first 5-year planning period

项目 Item	国内供应设备比重（%） Proportion of equipment supplied by domestic enterprises (%)	
	按设备重量计 By weight of equipment	按设备价值计 By value of equipment
"156项"总计 Total of "156 projects"	52.3	45.9
其中：鞍山钢铁公司 Including: Anshan Iron and Steel Group Corporation	49	43
武汉钢铁公司 Wuhan Iron and Steel (Group) Corp.	58	54
第一汽车制造厂 FAW Group	62.4	65.6
洛阳拖拉机厂 YTO Group	53.5	44.6

这一时期，发挥自己的技术能力，在苏联的援助下，发展了大量新产品，技术水平显著提高。如在机械装备方面：116型多刀自动车床、主轴直径110mm镗床、ck371型平面磨床、工作台直径2m立车等，3m³挖掘机、930m³高炉，100万t洗煤设备，

2500kW、6000kW、12000kW成套火电设备，10000kW水电设备和110 kV高压输变电设备等，在交通运输设备方面：4t载货汽车，1-5-1型货运机车和夂丅6客运机车，军用舰艇和多种内河及沿海客货轮船，"初教-5"教练机、"歼-5"喷气式歼击机等。

In this period, a lot of new products were developed and technologies were remarkably advanced with China's own technologies and the assistance of Soviet Union. Examples of machinery equipment: "116" multi-tools auto lathe, boring mill with 10 mm spindle diameter, "ck371" surface grinder, vertical lathe with 2m-diameter bench, 3m^3 excavator, 930 m^3 blast furnace, 1 million ton coal washer, complete sets of 2500kW, 6000kW and 12000kW thermal power equipment, 10,000kW hydropower equipment and 110 kV high-voltage transmission and distribution equipment, etc. Examples of transportation equipment: 4t truck, "1-5-1" freight locomotive, "夂丅6" passenger locomotive, naval vessels for military purpose, diverse passenger and freight ships for use on inland rivers and along coast, "CJ-5" trainer and "J-5" jet fighter, etc.

以苏联帮助中国设计的156项工业建设工程为中心，集中力量建设一批大型现代化的机械工业骨干企业。在"156项"中的机械工业建设项目60项，（其中民用机器行业25项、轻工1项、航空航天14项、兵器16项、船舶4项）以此为中心，建立中国机械工业的初步基础。这些重大项目的建设，从无到有地建立了飞机、坦克、汽车、拖拉机、发电设备、石油化工设备、冶金矿山设备、新式机床、精密仪表等机械制造行业，船舶、兵器等行业也得到了加强。这批项目，绝大部分在"一五"时期开始建设，大多在1955年到1962年之间陆续建成投产。尔后都成为各行业的骨干排头兵企业，在国民经济发展和国防建设中发挥了重要作用。

A group of large-sized key modern machinery enterprises were constructed, with the focus being the 156 engineering projects designed with the assistance of Soviet Union. Among these "156 projects", 60 projects were engaged in machinery industry (including 25 projects dealing with machines for civilian use, 1 project with light industry, 14 projects with aviation and space flight, 16 projects with weapons and 4 projects with ships), based on which the initial base of China's machinery industry was established. By constructing these key projects, China shaped its machinery industry for the first time, with products covering airplanes, tanks, automobiles, tractors, power generating equipment, petrochemical equipment, metallurgical and mining equipment, new machine tools and precision instrument, etc. Furthermore, the industries of ships and weapons grew stronger. Most of these projects were started in the first 5-year planning period and put into service one after another from 1955 to 1962, which later became leading enterprises in various industries and played key roles in national economic development and national defense construction.

1953年7月15日，第一汽车制造厂举行隆重奠基典礼

Foundation stone laying ceremony for the First Automobile Works
(FAW) on July 15, 1953

"In commemoration of the foundation laying for the FAW",
an inscription by Mao Zedong

245

第一汽车制造厂工地雨季施工

Construction on the site of FAW in rainy season

安装3000 t大压床

Installation of 3000 t large-sized press machine

1956年10月15日，一汽举行汽车投产开工典礼

Production commencement ceremony for FAW on Oct. 15, 1956

第一机械工业部部长黄敬在一汽投产开工典礼大会上讲话

Huang Jing, Minister of the First Ministry of Machine-building Industry, addressing at the production commencement ceremony for FAW

新车出厂报捷

A triumphant announcement of new trucks going off production lines

1956年7月13日，第一辆解放牌汽车下线

The first FAW Jiefang brand truck going off the production line on July 13, 1956

1959年10月26日，周恩来总理在农机部部长陈正人关于第一拖拉机制造厂落成典礼报告上的批示："请谭副总理主持剪彩典礼"

"Vice Premier Tan, please preside over the Ribbon-cutting Ceremony"，replied by Premier Zhou Enlai on the report of inaugural ceremony for YTO submitted by Chen Zhengren, the Minister of Agricultural Machinery Minstry, on Oct. 26, 1959.

第一拖拉机制造厂
落成典礼大会会场

The meeting place for the inaugural ceremony of the First Tractor Factory

国务院副总理谭震林在第一拖拉机制造厂落成典礼大会上讲话

Tan Zhenlin, Vice Premier of the State Council, was addressing at the inaugural ceremony of the First Tractor Factory.

第一台东方红牌拖拉机诞生出厂

The first YTO tractor leaving the factory

第一台东方红牌拖拉机开进农村，受到农民的热烈欢迎

The first YTO tractor was greatly welcomed by villagers.

1956年6月28日，哈尔滨汽轮机厂举行开工典礼

Commencement ceremony for Harbin Steam Turbine Works on June 28, 1956

1957年，正在施工的哈尔滨汽轮机厂主机厂房

Main workshop of Harbin Steam Turbine Works under construction in 1957

1958年4月，哈尔滨汽轮机厂生产的首台2.5万kW汽轮机组

The first 25,000kW steam turbine unit produced by Harbin Steam Turbine Factory in April, 1958

1959年，哈尔滨汽轮机厂制造的5万kW单轴式汽轮机组

50,000kW single-shaft steam turbine unit produced by Harbin Steam Turbine Factory in 1959

第二节 "大跃进"和国民经济调整中的机械工业
Section 2　Machinery Industry during "Great Leap Forward" and National Economy Regulation

(一)"大跃进"给中国机械工业发展带来很大破坏
Development of machinery industry in China was seriously damaged due to "Great Leap Forward"

"大跃进"始于1957年下半年，毛泽东1957年11月访苏回来提出"15年赶英国"；1958年5月"八大"提出只要七八年时间就可以在钢铁和其他主要工业产品产量上追上英国，只要15年或者更长一点时间就可以赶上美国。"大跃进"的局面完全脱离了当时我国经济发展的实际情况。

"Great Leap Forward" began in the second half year of 1957. Chairman Mao commented after his visit to Soviet Union in Nov. 1957, that China could catch up with the level of UK in 15 years. It was commented at the eighth National Congress in May 1958 that, it would only take 7 or 8 years for China to catch up with UK by iron and steel and other major industrial products, and only 15 years or a little longer to catch up with USA. The situation of "Great Leap Forward" totally deviated from China's economic fact.

1958年8月，中共中央在北戴河召开的政治局扩大会议，"大跃进"运动在全国范围内大规模地展开。机械工业被提到了重要的位置。当时的说法是"一为粮，二为钢，加上机器，叫三大元帅，三大元帅升帐，就有胜利的希望"。国民经济大跃进，迫切需要大量机械设备，当时机械工业提出的口号是"全民动手，快马加鞭，提供更多更好的机器，保证社会主义建设的高速发展"。机械工业在"大跃进"中出现一系列问题。一是违反科学规律大搞群众运动，正常生产秩序被打乱，造成设备严重损坏，给机械的生产、发展带来很大破坏。二是全民大办机械工业，虽产量大幅增长，但粗制滥造，造成很大浪费。如冶金设备，1957年产量1.38万t，1958—1960年总计产量66万t，其中包括300多套简易轧机、上千套简易炼焦设备、上万套简易小高炉、小转炉；又如金属切削机床，1957年产量2.8万台，1958—1960年累计生产35万台，其中简易土机床和皮带机床就有28万台，有的就是在板凳上加一个电动机，多数不能使用。三是基本建设失控，浪费严重。当时办厂的方针是各级办厂，遍地开花。1958—1960年，仅民机系统建设投资即达75亿元，平均每年25亿元，为1957年投资8.9亿元的2.8倍；三年内完工的厂房1100万m²，为第一个五年计划时期164万m²的6倍，三年安装1000 t以上自由锻水压机15台，而第一个五年计划时期只有2台。由于赶进度，工程质量极差，有的厂房未及投产，就须进行修理、加固、降级使用，大多报废，肥梁胖柱，随处可见。四是发展了一些重大新产品，但质量上存在不同程度问题，能通过验收、鉴定保存下来的，大都是"一五"计划时期着手安排的一些重大新产品。如5万kW火电设备、220 kV高压输变电设备、3350 m³/h制氧机、3200 m石油钻机、"东风牌"万吨级远洋货轮、内燃机车、韶山型电力机车、400 mm×560 mm双柱坐标镗床、φ80 mm×2500 mm精密丝杠车床等。还自行设计制造了万吨自由锻造水压机、1.2万kW双水内冷汽轮发电机、135系列柴油机、医用核子同位素设备等。

The Central Committee of the Communist Party of China held an enlarged session of the Political Bureau at Beidaihe in August 1958. "Great Leap Forward" movement began vigorously all over China. The machinery industry was highly valued. It was said at that time that "food, steel and machines are three most important products. Development of the three products indicates a bright future." "Great Leap Forward" of national economy required plenty of machinery equipment. A slogan for the machinery industry said that, "the whole nation should be devoted to machinery to provide more and better machines for ensuring swift socialist construction." Some problems occurred in the machinery industry during "Great Leap Forward". Firstly, excessive mass movements were carried out against scientific rules, normal sequence of production was disturbed, equipment was seriously damaged and production and development of machinery were heavily harmed. Secondly, the whole nation was devoted into the machinery industry, as a result of which, the volume of production increased remarkably but products were poor causing serious waste. For example: the production of metallurgic equipment was 13,800 t in the year 1957, and the total production was 660,000 t from 1958 to 1960, including more than 300 sets of simple rolling mills, over 1,000 sets of simple coking equipment and over 10,000 sets of simple small blast furnaces and small converters; the production of metal-cutting machine tools was 28,000 sets in 1957, and the total production was 350,000 sets from 1958 to 1960, including 280,000 sets of simple self-made machine tools and belt-driven machine tools. However, some products were just motors on stools and most products were unusable. Thirdly, capital construction was out of control and waste was serious. The policy of factory construction at that time was to set up factories at each level and everywhere. Investment in construction of machinery system for civilian use was RMB 7.5 billion from 1958 to 1960, with the annual mean investment being RMB 2.5 billion, which was 2.8 times of the investment of RMB 890 million in 1957. Workshops of 11 million m² were completed within three years, which was 6 times of 1.64 million m² completed during the first 5-year planning period. There were 15 sets of free-forging hydraulic press above 1,000 t installed within three years, while only 2 sets installed during the first 5-year planning period. Some workshops must be repaired, reinforced or degraded for use even before they were put into service, due to short construction period and poor quality. Most of the workshops were unusable and buildings of poor quality were everywhere. Fourthly, some new key products were developed, but they all had quality problems more or less. Most of the products accepted and reserved were new key products planned during the first 5-year planning period. Examples include

50,000kW thermal power equipment, 220 kV high-voltage electric transmission and distribution equipment, 3,350 m³/h oxygenator, 3,200 m oil rig, "Dongfeng" 10,000 t ocean vessel, diesel locomotive, SS-series electric locomotives, 400 mm×560 mm double-column jig boring machine and ϕ 80 mm×2500 mm precision leading screw lathe, etc. 10,000 t free-forging hydraulic press, 12,000 kW turbo-generator with double internal water-cooling system, 135-series diesel engines and nucleon isotope equipment for medical use, etc.

(二) 机械工业贯彻"调整、巩固、充实、提高"方针
The policy of "regulation, consolidation, substantiality and improvement" was adopted for machinery industry

"大跃进"的严重失误使中国国民经济遭遇严重困难，1961年1月中共八届九中全会决定从1961年起对国民经济实行"调整、巩固、充实、提高"的方针，国民经济进入调整时期。机械工业认真贯彻了这一方针，进行了大量工作。

The serious mistake of "Great Leap Forward" harmed China's national economy seriously. In Jan. 1961, the 9th plenary session of the 8th CPC Central Committee decided to adopt the policy of "regulation, consolidation, substantiality and improvement" for national economy as from 1961, when regulation of national economy began. This policy was seriously followed in the machinery industry and lots of works were done.

机械工业"大跃进"中问题比其他部门更加突出。1961年全国工业产值增长速度比上年下降38%，机械工业下降64.5%；1962年机械工业不少主要产品产量低于1957年水平。

The machinery industry during "Great Leap Forward" saw more serious problems than other sectors. The national rate of industry development was lower than the last year by 38% and the machinery industry dropped by 64.5% in 1961. For many major mechanical products, the volume of production in 1962 was lower than the level in 1957.

主要机械产品产量(1957—1962年)
Quantity of major mechanical products (1957—1962)

产品名称 Name of product	单位 Unit	1957	1960	1962
矿山设备 Mining equipment	万吨 10,000 ton	5.29	25.2	3.5
冶金设备 Metallurgic equipment	万吨 10,000 ton	1.38	23.2	2.2
起重设备 Lifting equipment	万吨 10,000 ton	3.2	16.7	2.0
工业泵 Industrial pump	万台 10,000 sets	4.6	19.4	2.4
金属切削机床 Metal-cutting machine	万台 10,000 sets	2.8	15.4	2.3
发电设备 Power generating equipment	万千瓦 10,000 kW	19.7	338.8	15.2
汽车 Automobile	万辆 10,000 sets	0.79	2.26	0.97
拖拉机 Tractor	万台 10,000 sets	—	1.16	0.71

当时，机械工业一方面任务不足，严重吃不饱。另一方面，国民经济和"两弹一星"等国防尖端需要的关键产品，要由国内供应，特别是苏联撕毁合同，很多重点项目原来由苏联供应的关键设备，我国机械工业无法提供。如高精度机床、原子能设备、新型材料所需大型设备、精密仪器仪表、化肥设备、石油设备等，相关企业管理混乱，产品质量差，经济效果差，基建战线太长等问题都亟须解决。

At that time, supply exceeded demand in the machinery industry. What's more, key products for national economy and those requiring sophisticated technologies for national defense such as "Two Bombs and One Satellite", especially the key equipment that should be supplied by Soviet Union for many significant projects but relevant contracts were broken by Soviet Union, had to be supplied by domestic enterprises. However, the domestic machinery industry was incapable of providing such equipment as high-precision machine tool, atomic equipment, large-sized equipment for new materials, precision instrumentation, fertilizer equipment and oil equipment, etc. Problems to be solved included disordered enterprise management, poor product quality and poor economic benefits and excessively long front of capital construction.

当时，为了加强国防工业，重新将军工部门和民用机械部门分开；1961年1月，国防工业整风会议召开，贯彻中央军委提出的"军品第一、质量第一，在确保质量的基础上求数量"的方针。

The department of military industry was independent of the department of machinery for civilian use to promote the defense industry. A rectification meeting of the defense industry was held in Jan. 1961. The policy of "Military Products First, Quality First; Expanding Production with Acceptable Quality" formulated by the Military Commission of the Central Committee of CPC was applied.

民用机械工业方面，全面贯彻调整时期的方针。一是精简队伍。如一机部系统，1960年底有企业2442个，1963年减为1475个，同期职工人数由161万人减为85万人，但保留了骨干力量。调整力量加强军工配套设备、原子能设备、氮肥设备、石油设备、精密机床的制造能力，例如原子能设备，就是以发电设备厂为核心，组织了工艺相近的100多个企业，大力协同搞出来的；石油设备定点生产企业66个；氮肥设备，定点生产企业100个；等等。二是压缩在建规模。如一机部系统1960年在建的国家安排项目500多个（另有地方安排项目1500个左右），至1962年压缩到107个，停缓建4/5，投资主要用于发展缺口短线产品。当时还从日本、法国等引进了液压件、电动量仪，重型汽车等成套项目，这是新中国成立以来，中国机械工业第一次从西方国家引进的制造技术。三是为"两弹一星"的研制，发展大型关键装备。机械工业在极端困难和国际严密封锁下，全靠国内自己力量完成了"两弹一星"及其生产装备和试验研究装备，如精密机床、"九套大型设备"的研制；完成了航天、航空、舰船、兵器等国防军工任务。其中最为突出的如原子能设备，充分发挥现有企业潜力，只用了二三年时间陆续研制出第一套原子能反应堆和核原料加工设备及核物理试验设备（加速器），为中国独立自主发展原子能工业作出了贡献。还有包括为发展冶金工业、航天工业、航空工业所需的3万t模锻水压机、12500 t卧式挤压水压机、2800 mm冷轧和热轧铝板轧机、80—200 mm钢管冷轧机等9套大型关键设备。这个时期还研制了两台1.2万t水压机、10万kW成套水力及火力发电设备和车轮轮箍轧机等重大新产品（其中有些设备延至1980年才完成），标志着中国机械工业在技术上与工业国家的差距开始缩小。这个时期的工作主要还有贯彻《工业企业七十条》，整顿企业管理秩序，改进工业管理，发展工业协作，试行经济办法管理工业。

As for the industry of machinery for civilian use, policies in the regulation period were fully followed. Firstly, the organization was streamlined. For example, enterprises under the First Ministry of Machinery Industry decreased from 2,442 by the end of 1960 to 1,475 in 1963, and employees thereof decreased from 1.61 million to 0.85 million in the same period, with the backbone preserved. Resources were reallocated for better capability of manufacturing auxiliary equipment for military use, atomic equipment, nitrogen fertilizer equipment, oil equipment and precision machine tool. For example, atomic equipment was developed by joint efforts of over 100 enterprises with similar processes, with the focus on power generating equipment factories.

There were 66 production enterprises designated for oil equipment and 100 production enterprises designated for nitrogen fertilizer equipment. Secondly, the scale of construction was cut down. For example, with the First Ministry of Machinery Industry, the projects under construction planned by the state were reduced from over 500 (in addition, there were 1500 projects planned by local government) in 1960 to 107 in 1962. Construction of four fifths of the projects were ceased or suspended. Investment was mainly for developing products in short supply. Projects of complete sets of machinery and equipment, like hydraulic parts, electric micrometers and heavy duty trucks, were introduced from Japan, France and other countries. This was the first time that manufacturing technologies were introduced from western countries for China's machinery industry after foundation of the P.R.C. Thirdly, large-sized key equipment were developed for research and manufacture of "Two Bombs and One Satellite". Against plenty of difficulties and strict blockade by other countries, China accomplished "Two Bombs and One Satellite" and equipment for relevant production, tests and research independently, like precision machine tools and "nine sets of large-sized equipment". Tasks of military industry for national defense were accomplished, involving aviation, space flight, ships and weapon. The most striking products include atomic equipment, for which potentials of existing enterprises were leveraged. As a result, the first set of atomic reactor, nuclear raw materials processing equipment and nuclear physical testing equipment (accelerator) were developed within 3 years, which made a contribution to China's independent development of atomic energy industry. The nine sets of large-sized key equipment included 30,000 t hydraulic die press, 12500 t horizontal hydraulic extrusion press, 2800 mm aluminum sheet cold-rolling and hot-rolling mills and 80—200 mm tube cold-rolling mills, etc. In this period, some other new key products were developed (some were not finished until 1980), such as two 12,000 t hydraulic presses, complete sets of 100,000kW thermal and hydraulic power generating equipment and wheel and hub mill. This indicated a small technical gap in machinery industry between China and industrial countries. Other major works in this period included implementation of *Seventy Regulations for Industrial Enterprises*, regulation of enterprise management order, improvement of industrial management, development of industrial cooperation and trial application of economic measures to manage enterprises.

1961年12月，由太原重型机器制造厂为马鞍山钢铁公司制造的我国第一套火车车轮压轧生产线成套设备及产品；是中国机械工业首次为冶金工业提供的大型成套设备。

Complete sets of equipment and products of China's first set of locomotive wheel mill production line, produced by Taiyuan Heavy Machinery Factory for Maanshan Iron & Steel Company Limited in Dec. 1961. It was the first time that Chinese machinery industry provided complete sets of equipment for metallurgical industry.

沈阳重型机器厂为西南铝加工厂研制的12500 t有色金属卧式挤压水压机(九大设备之一)，1967年制造完成，1978年获全国科学大会奖

12,500 t nonferrous metal horizontal hydraulic extrusion press (one of the nine sets of equipment) was developed by Shenyang Heavy Machinery Factory for Southwest Aluminum Fabrication Plant; it was finished in 1967 and won the National Science Conference Prize in 1978.

第一重型机器厂、太原重型机器厂为西南铝加工厂联合研制的2800 mm铝板轧机(九大设备之一)，1970年制造完成，1978年获全国科学大会奖

2800 mm aluminum sheet mill (one of the nine sets of equipment) was developed by First Heavy Machinery Works and Taiyuan Heavy Machinery Factory for Southwest Aluminum Fabrication Plant; it was finished in 1970 and won the National Science Conference Prize in 1978.

第一重型机器厂、机械科学研究院为西南铝加工厂联合研制的30000 t模锻水压机(九大设备之一)，1970年完成全部制造任务，1978年获全国科学大会奖

30,000 t hydraulic die forging press (one of the nine sets of equipment) was developed by First Heavy Machinery Works and China Academy of Machinery Science & Technology for Southwest Aluminum Fabrication Plant; it was finished in 1970 and won the National Science Conference Prize in 1978.

1962年，第一机械工业部部长刘鼎主持完成了12500 t锻造水压机。该水压机立柱采用钢锭锻后电渣焊焊接，上中下横梁采用四包钢水合浇，沈阳重型机器厂和第一重型机器厂为主设计制造。

12500 t forging hydraulic press was designed and manufactured mainly by Shenyang Heavy Machinery Factory and First Heavy Machinery Works, which was organized by Liu Ding, the Vice Minister of the First Ministry of Machine-building Industry and finished in 1962; the stand column was made of forged ingots welded by electroslag welding, the upper, middle and lower cross beams were poured with four steel ladles.

1962年，第一机械工业部副部长沈鸿任总设计师，以上海江南造船厂为主制造了12000 t级自由锻造水压机。该水压机采用全焊接结构、"蚂蚁啃骨头"加工、枕木和油压千斤顶起吊。

12000 t free-forging hydraulic press was mainly manufactured by Shanghai Jiangnan Shipbuilding Plant and finished in 1962, for which the chief designer was Shen Hong, who was the Vice Minister of the First Ministry of Machine-building Industry; all welded structure was used; large-sized work pieces were fabricated section by section with existing small machine tools; hydraulic jack and sleepers were used for hoisting.

第三节 "文化大革命"时期的机械工业
Section 3 Machinery Industry during the "Great Proletarian Cultural Revolution"

1966年5月至1976年10月，中国进行了一场"文化大革命"。"文化大革命"给机械工业造成了重大损失，许多方面不仅停滞不前，反而倒退，机械工业生产技术之前与工业发达国家日益缩小的差距，又拉大了。但是由于广大职工坚持生产与建设，仍取得一定成绩。

"The Great Proletarian Cultural Revolution" ("the Revolution" for short) was improperly launched in China from May 1966 to Oct. 1976. The Revolution harmed the machinery industry seriously. Many sectors saw regression instead of progress. The gap in production technology of machinery industry between China and industrially developed countries was widened again. However, some achievements were still made because workers insisted hard work.

(一) 工业管理受到猛烈冲击
Industrial management was violently shocked

不合理的重复建设和生产问题极为严重。汽车，是宜于集中大批量生产的产品，1977年由"文化大革命"前的10个汽车厂发展到130个厂点，车型大都是"解放"、"跃进"、"北京130"等老产品，产品质次价高，其中年产量1000辆以上的工厂只有9个，不少厂年产量仅100—200辆。1977年解放牌汽车的成本，第一汽车厂为9862元，很多小厂高达20000元以上。机床生产方面，仅浙江省即有生产机床的厂点625个，而1965年全国只有100多个机床厂。轴承生产方面，由44个厂发展到600多个。许多技术要求高、需要量不大的产品也有同样情况，如万马力柴油机制造厂仅上海一地即有3个，6135型160 hp柴油机全国有18个厂生产，除上海、贵阳两厂外，其他厂技术上都没有过关。还有当时为"1980年全国基本实现农业机械化"的目标，各地大办农业机械，到1978年，全国共有大中型拖拉机厂65个，小型拖拉机厂143个。

Irrational repeated construction and production were serious problems. Centralized mass production of automobiles was applicable. The number of automobile factories grew from 10 before the Revolution to 130 in 1977. Most of the automobile types were old products like "Jiefang", "Yuejin" and "Beijing 130", with poor quality but high prices. Only 9 out of these factories were capable of producing more than 1,000 automobiles every year. A lot of other factories could produce only 100—200 automobiles every year. The cost of a "Jiefang" truck was RMB 9,862 for FAW but more than RMB 20,000 for many small factories in the year 1977. There were 625 machine tool factories in Zhejiang Province, while there were only over 100 machine tool factories all over China in 1965. The number of bearing factories grew from 44 to over 600. Similar situation was found for many products with high technical requirements and small demand. For example, there were 3 factories producing 1 million hp diesels in Shanghai; there were 18 factories producing 6135-type 160hp diesel engines in China, but, except for one factory in Shanghai and one in Guiyang, the other factories were technically unacceptable. In addition, agricultural machines were vigorously developed all over China with the goal of "mostly realizing agricultural mechanization all over China by 1980". There were 65 large and medium-sized tractor factories and 143 small-sized tractor factories in China by 1978.

企业管理混乱，机械产品质量下降。1972年年初，据20个省、自治区、直辖市的调查，产品抽查合格率下降到45%；1976年，调查了全国铲车行业的11个企业，只有1个企业产品整机性能合格；调往唐山震区的汽车，到现场有20%开不动；1972年援越汽车被越方拒收，宁肯要苏制老旧汽车。周恩来批评："质量这样下降，如何援外？如何备战？这是路线问题。"

Enterprise management was disordered and quality of mechanical products degraded. The acceptability of products dropped to 45%, according to random checks in 20 provinces, autonomous regions and municipalities under direct administration of the Central Government at the beginning of 1972. In 1976, all over the country, 11 enterprises dealing with forklift were surveyed, but only 1 enterprise was found with acceptable performance of whole machine produced. Out of the automobiles sending to Tangshan earthquake stricken area, 20% could not run on the site. Automobiles produced as an aid to Vietnam were refused by Vietnam in 1972, and Vietnam would rather take old trucks made by Soviet Union. Premier Zhou Enlai said critically, "With such poor quality, how can we aid other countries? How can we prepare for any possible war? It's a problem of policy."

生产指挥系统指挥失灵，不少企业处于瘫痪状态。"文化大革命"期间，第一机械工业部系统250个骨干企业中，有59个企业生产极不正常，其中25个长期瘫痪，34个半瘫痪。如洛阳轴承厂，1976年计划生产轴承1600万套，只完成448万套，而且成品合格率只有20%；武汉锅炉厂，长期停产；大足汽车厂长期停工停产，从法国引进的重型汽车技术资料，一直不能利用；重庆机床厂，1973—1976年，四年三次停产，每次长达10个月以上。

Commanding system for production was out of order, where a lot of enterprises were down. During the Revolution, 59 out of 250 key enterprises under the First Ministry of Machine-building Industry were with extremely abnormal production, among which, 25 enterprises were in a state of paralysis for a long time and the other 34 were in a state of half paralysis. For example, Luoyang Bearing Factory planned to produce 1.6 million sets of bearings but only accomplished 4.48 million sets in 1976, and the acceptability of finished products was only 20%. Wuhan Boiler Factory stopped production for a long time. Dazu Automobile Factory stopped production for a long time, and technical data introduced from France for heavy-duty trucks found no scope.

Chongqing Machine Tool Works stopped production for three times from 1973 to 1976, with each stop lasting for more than 10 months.

科研、教育工作遭到巨大破坏。一些学有专长的知识分子和专家受批判、遭迫害，变相劳改，无法开展教学、科研工作，形成了人才、科研断层；一些骨干科研基地被强制解散或搬迁，如上海汽轮机锅炉研究所，是全国唯一的比较完整的电站设备研究基地，被强迫撤掉。

Scientific research and education were pulled down. Some intellectuals and experts were oppressed or reformed through labor, as a result of which, scientific research and education were obstructed, leading to shortage in talents and scientific research. Some key bases of scientific research were forced to dissolve or relocate. Shanghai Turbine & Boiler Research Institute was dissolved, which was the only complete research base for power station equipment in China.

拉大了与国外机械工业水平的差距。由于执行"闭关锁国"的政策，加上"文化大革命"的冲击破坏，而国外此时却在飞速发展，原来与国外水平缩小的差距又拉大了。如解放牌载货汽车，是仿制苏联20世纪50年代初期产品，至1965年苏联已两次改型，而第一汽车制造厂一直到20世纪80年代才作改进；北京第一机床厂的万能铣床，也是仿制苏联20世纪50年代初期产品，20年来改进不多。又如合成氨设备，国外的30万t设备，采用透平压缩机，能反复回收生产过程余热，吨氨能耗1000万大卡，而国内设备，主压缩机为往复式压缩机，吨氨能耗1800万大卡以上。

As a result, gap between China and other countries was widened again, because China secluded itself from the outside world and was harmed by the Revolution while other countries made great progress. For example, FAW did not improve "Jiefang" truck until 1980s, which was a copy of a product made by Soviet Union in early 1950s, but Soviet Union had improved the product twice by 1965. Universal milling machine made by Beijing No.1 Machine Tool Plant saw little improvement over 20 years, which was also a copy of a product made by Soviet Union in early 1950s. The energy consumption per ton of ammonia by domestically-made 300,000t synthetic ammonia equipment was more than 18 million kcal, with its main compressor being reciprocating compressor, while that by overseas-made 300,000t synthetic ammonia equipment was only 10 million kcal with turbine compressor to recover waste heat in production again and again.

(二) 为国家发展尖端技术产品完成了一批重大设备和科研成果
A group of significant equipment was developed and important achievements were made in scientific research for China to develop cutting-edge products

机械装备。这一时期完成了年产150万t钢铁的攀枝花钢铁公司从矿山开采到轧制钢材的全套设备，第二汽车厂的冷加工成套设备，年产150万吨炼油成套设备，20万—

30万kW水力、火力发电设备和330 kV高压输变电设备等。还有许多国防专用设备，如核材料用扩散机、航天工业用20 t振动台、航空工业用风洞设备等。

Mechanical equipment: Machinery equipment accomplished in this period included complete sets of equipment for a range from mining to steel rolling for Pangang Group Company Ltd. with an annual production of 1.5 million ton iron and steel, complete sets of cold working equipment for the Second Automobile Works, complete sets of refinery equipment with an annual production of 1.5 million ton 200,000—300,000 kW thermal and hydraulic power generating equipment and 330 kV high-voltage electric transmission and distribution equipment, etc. Much equipment dedicated to national defense were also developed, like nuclear materials diffusion machines, 20t vibrating table for space industry and wind tunnel equipment for aviation, etc.

国防装备。取得许多历史性突破，如1970年成功发射了第一颗人造卫星，第一艘核潜艇研制成功等。

National defense equipment: Great historic breakthrough was made in terms of national defense equipment . China's first man-made satellite was successfully launched and its first nuclear submarine was developed successfully in 1970.

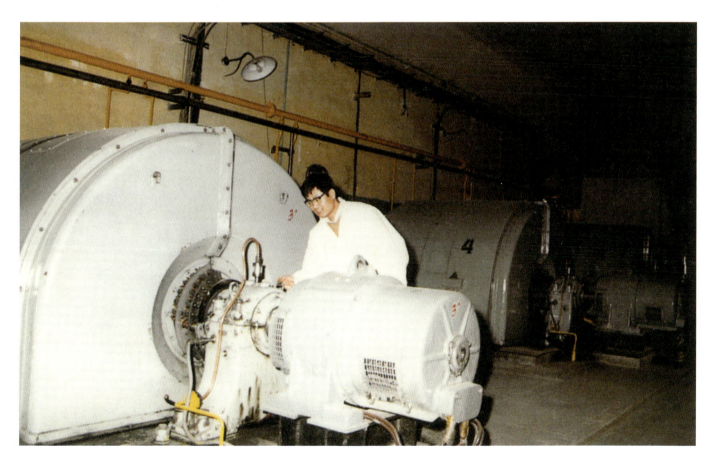

1965年，沈阳水泵厂、哈尔滨电机厂制造的石墨轻水反应堆主循环泵及5000kW电机

Main circulating pump and 5000kW electrical machine, manufactured by Shenyang Pump Manufactory and Harbin Electric Machinery Factory for Light Water graphite Reactor in 1965

1972年，上海电机厂、北京重型电机厂等单位制造组装的气体扩散机机组

Gas diffusion machine unit manufactured and assembled by enterprises including Shanghai Electric Machine Factory and Beijing Heavy Electrical Machinery Works in 1972

1972年，东风电机厂制造的四号气体扩散机机组

#4 gas diffusion machine unit manufactured by Dongfeng Electric Machinery Works in 1972

1974年，兰州石油化工机器厂制造的地下核试验用钻机塔架

Drill tower manufactured by Lanzhou Petroleum & Chemical Machinery Works for underground nuclear test in 1974

1977年，第二重型机器制造厂
等单位制造的高通量工程试验堆
堆内构件栅格板

Grid plate for internals of High Flux
Engineering Test Reactor, manufactured
by enterprises including The Second
Heavy Machinery Plant in 1977

1966年，哈尔滨锅炉厂制造的导
弹驱逐舰主锅炉

Main boiler manufactured by Harbin Boiler
Plant for guided missile destroyer in 1966

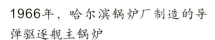

1968年，哈尔滨汽轮机厂制
造的导弹驱逐舰主汽轮机齿轮
联合机组正在总装

General assembly of main steam
turbine gear unit for guided missile
destroyer, manufactured by Harbin
Steam Turbine Works in 1968

第一重型机器制造
厂制造的核潜艇反
应堆压力壳

Reactor pressure vessel
for nuclear submarine,
manufactured by First
Heavy Machinery Works

1968年，北京机械自动化研究所等单位研制的
20 t电液伺服振动试验台(正在进行卫星试验)

20 t electro-hydraulic servo shaking table developed
by institutes including Beijing Research Institute of
Automation for Machinery Industry in 1968 (in satellite
test)

1968年，太原重型机器厂制造的酒泉卫星发射中心移动式发射塔架及脐带塔

Traveling launch tower and umbilical at Jiuquan Satellite Launch Center, manufactured by Taiyuan Heavy Machinery Factory in 1968

1980年，太原重型机器厂制造的西昌卫星发射中心固定式发射塔架

Fixed launch tower at Xichang Satellite Launch Center, manufactured by Taiyuan Heavy Machinery Factory in 1980

1980年，东风电机厂等制造的6 m×8 m风洞

Wind tunnels (6 m×8 m) manufactured by enterprises including Dongfeng Electric Machinery Works in 1980

(三)"三线建设"
"Third-line Construction"

从1964年开始，不包括新疆、西藏和内蒙古在内的中西部的13个省、自治区进行了一场以战备为指导思想的大规模国防、科技工业和交通基本设施建设，史称"三线建设"。"三线建设"重要工作是迁移沿海工业到内地，对机械工业来说，兴建大批军事工业和民用机械工业，从1965年到1980年，在三线地区建成了中国一大批国防科研基地，形成了门类齐全、各方配套的国防工业生产基地。

"Third-line Construction" began in 1964 with the view of preparation for war, referring to large-scale construction of infrastructures for national defense, scientific technology, industry and traffic in 13 provinces and autonomous regions in the Midwest of China, excluding Xinjiang Uygur Autonomous Region, Tibet Autonomous Region and Inner Mongolia Autonomous Region. A major task of "Third-line Construction" was to transfer industries in coastal areas to inland areas. For machinery industry, it was to vigorously develop military industry and the industry of machines for civilian use. A lot of scientific research bases for national defense and production bases with complete facilities for national defense were built in "Third-line" areas from 1965 to 1980.

在军工方面，这里不仅能生产轻武器，而且能生产先进的重武器。至1975年，西南以重庆为中心的常规兵器工业基地产量已经占全国的一半左右。建成了四川和陕西的战略武器科研生产基地，四川、陕西、贵州和鄂西北等地的航空工业基地，长江中上游地区的船舶研究和生产基地，酒泉和西昌卫星发射基地。到1975年，中国三线地区国防工业的生产能力、技术力量和装备水平都超过一、二线地区，改变了中国的国防工业布局。

Military industry: both light arms and advanced heavy weapons could be produced in these areas. The production of the conventional weapon industrial base centering on Chongqing in the Southwest of China accounted for half of the national production by 1975. Bases for scientific research and production of strategic weapons were built in Sichuan and Shaanxi, aviation industrial bases were built in Sichuan, Shaanxi, Guizhou and the northwest of Hubei, ship research and production base were built in areas along the middle and upper reaches of Yangtze River and Jiuquan Satellite Launch Center and Xichang Satellite Launch Center were set up. The production capacity, technical level and equipment of defense industry in the "Third-line" areas exceeded those in the "First-line" and the "Second-line" areas by the year 1975. Layout of China's defense industry was changed.

民用机械方面，在三线地区也进行了大规模的建设。1965—1979年，在三线地区共投资93.39亿元，相当于1949—1965年机械工业全部投资的70%以上，其中1966—1970年占全部投资超过2/3。1965—1979年三线地区机械工业施工项目1623个；建筑竣工面积2129万m²，其中生产建筑面积834万m²；安装金属切削机床35119台，锻压设备5633台；新增固定资产64.4亿元。三线建设，主要采用了沿海老厂迁建或援建的形式，共援建或迁建了241个

270

工厂、研究所，内迁职工62679人，设备17727台。三线地区机械工业拥有的职工、固定资产和设备，1979年比1965年分别增长了3.3倍、3.7倍和2.7倍；产值、职工人数固定资产和机床拥有量在全国的比重，1965年约为1/4，到1975年提高到1/3。初步形成了以重庆为中心的包括川、贵、滇在内的比较完整的西南机械工业基地；在西北初步建成了汉中、关中、天水、银川、西宁等一批各有特色的机械工业集中的城市，其中佼佼者如在鄂西的第二汽车厂、四川的东方电机、汽轮机、锅炉厂等。

Machines for civilian use: investment in the "Third-line" areas totaled RMB 9,339 million from 1965 to 1979, accounting for more than 70% of the total investment in machinery industry from 1949 to 1965. Investment from 1966 to 1970 accounted for over 2/3 of the total investment. From 1965 to 1979, for machinery industry in the "Third-line" areas, there were 1,623 construction projects; floor space of buildings completed was 21.29 million m^2, including 8.34 million m^2 for production purpose; 35,119 sets of metal-cutting machine tools and 5,633 sets of forging and pressing equipment were installed; fixed assets increased by RMB 6.44 billion. "Third-line Construction" was carried out mainly by means of relocating old factories from coastal areas

"三线建设"图

The map of "Third-line Construction"

to inland areas or building new factories in inland areas with the help of old factories in coastal areas. In total, 241 factories and research institutes were relocated or newly built, with 62,679 employees and 17,727 sets of equipment moving to inland areas. The numbers of employees, fixed assets and equipment in machinery industry in the "Third-line" areas increased by 330%, 370% and 270% respectively in 1979, compared with the numbers in 1965. Output value, employees, fixed assets and machine tools accounted for one fourth in the national volume in 1965 and one third in 1975. Complete machinery industrial bases in the Southwest of China covering Sichuan, Guizhou and Yunnan were preliminarily set up, centering on Chongqing. Machinery industry was developed in a centralized way with different focuses in different cities in the Northwest of China, including Hanzhong, Guanzhong, Tianshui, Yinchuan and Xining; key enterprises thereof included the Second Automobile Works in the west of Hubei, and Dongfang Electrical Machinery Works, Dongfang Steam Turbine Works and Dongfang Boiler Works in Sichuan.

经过"三线建设"，机械工业基本上做到了品种上沿海能生产的，内地都有生产点。汽车厂、机车车辆厂、飞机厂、战略武器厂、船用配套厂、拖拉机厂、内燃机厂、冶金矿山及大型铸锻件厂、机床厂、基础零部件厂、发电设备及电器厂，都建成了与沿海骨干企业相类似的能力。机械工业完成了内地、沿海的战略布局。

After "Third-line Construction", almost all the mechanical products that could be produced in coastal areas could be produced in inland areas. Factories, which dealt with automobiles, locomotives, airplane, strategic weapon, auxiliary equipment for ships, tractors, internal-combustion engine, mining & metallurgical machinery, large-sized casting and forging, machine tools, basic parts and components, power generating equipment and electrical equipment, were as capable as key enterprises in coastal areas. The strategic layout of machinery industry in inland and coastal areas was completed.

三线地区与沿海地区部分民机产品骨干企业对照表
Comparison of key enterprises of civil machinery between "Third-line" areas and coastal areas

行业 Industry	三线地区 "Third-line" areas	沿海地区 Coastal areas
汽车 Automobiles	第二汽车厂、大足汽车厂 The Second Automobile Works, Dazu Automobile Factory	第一汽车厂，上海、南京和济南汽车厂 FAW, and automobile factories in Shanghai, Nanjing and Jinan
发电设备 Power generating equipment	四川东方（锅炉、汽轮机、发电机及水电） Dongfang factories in Sichuan (dealing with boiler, steam turbine, generator and hydropower)	哈尔滨、上海（锅炉、汽轮机、发电机及水电） Harbin and Shanghai (dealing with boiler, steam turbine, generator and hydropower)
输变电 Electric transmission and distribution	西安1套 One set in Xi'an	沈阳1套 One set in Shenyang

272

（续表）

行业 Industry	三线地区 "Third-line" areas	沿海地区 Coastal areas
电机、电器、电材 Eletric machine, electric apparatus and materials	四川、湖南、贵阳、天水各厂 Factories in Sichuan, Hunan, Guiyang and Tianshui	上海、辽宁、天津、北京各厂 Factories in Shanghai, Liaoning, Tianjin and Beijing
大型机床、精密机床、 Large-size machine tools and precision machine tools	昆明、武汉、汉中、西宁、重庆各厂 Factories in Kunming, Wuhan, Hanzhong, Xining and Chongqing	上海、北京、沈阳、大连、济南、南京、齐齐哈尔各厂 Factories in Shanghai, Beijing, Shenyang, Dalian, Jinan, Nanjing and Qiqihar
工具砂轮 Tools and abrasive wheels	重庆、成都、郑州、贵州各厂 Factories in Chongqing, Chengdu, Zhengzhou and Guizhou	哈尔滨、上海、沈阳、山东各厂 Factories in Harbin, Shanghai, Shenyang and Shandong
冶金、矿山等重型机械和大型铸锻件 Heavy machinery for metallurgy and mining, and large-sized casting and forging	德阳、太原、洛阳等厂 Factories in Deyang, Taiyuan and Luoyang	富拉尔基、沈阳、大连、上海、北京等厂 Factories in Fula'erji, Shenyang, Dalian, Shanghai and Beijing
石化设备及通用机械 Petrochemical equipment and general machinery	兰州、宝鸡、开封、四川、长沙、武汉各厂 Factories in Lanzhou, Baoji, Kaifeng, Sichuan, Changsha and Wuhan	上海、沈阳、杭州、天津各厂 Factories in Shanghai, Shenyang, Hangzhou and Tianjin
轴承 Bearings	洛阳、襄阳、贵州、汉中、西北等厂 Factories in Luoyang, Xiangyang, Guizhou, Hanzhong and the Northwest of China	哈尔滨、瓦房店、上海等厂 Factories in Harbin, Wafangdian and Shanghai
仪器仪表 Instruments & meters	西安、重庆、贵州、湘西、贵阳、银川等厂 Factories in Xi'an, Chongqing, Guizhou, Guiyang, Yinchuan and the West of Hunan	上海、北京、天津、沈阳、哈尔滨、长春、苏州、南京等厂 Factories in Shanghai, Beijing, Tianjin, Shenyang, Harbin, Changchun, Suzhou and Nanjing
拖拉机 Tractors	洛阳、西宁（20世纪80年代改工程机械）等厂 Factories in Luoyang and Xining (the factory in Xining began to deal with engineering machinery in 1980s)	天津、上海、长春、鞍山等厂 Factories in Tianjin, Shanghai, Changchun and Anshan
内燃机 Internal-combustion engines	重庆、贵阳等厂 Factories in Chongqing and Guiyang	上海、杭州、无锡、北京、潍坊等厂 Factories in Shanghai, Hangzhou, Wuxi, Beijing and Weifang
农机和配套 Agricultural machines and auxiliary machines	四川、陕西、河南、湖北、湖南各厂 Factories in Sichuan, Shaanxi, Hunan, Hebei and Hubei	江苏、山东、北京、天津、上海、四平各厂 Factories in Jiangsu, Shandong, Beijing, Tianjin, Shanghai and Siping

第二汽车制造厂厂址选定在湖北省郧阳县十堰镇一带，图为十堰镇原貌(1966年)

The Second Automobile Works was located near Shiyan Town, Yunyang County, Hubei Province. The picture shows an original view of Shiyan Town (In 1966).

1967年4月1日，第二汽车制造厂在湖北郧阳县十堰大炉子沟举行开工典礼

Commencement ceremony for The Second Automobile Works in Daluzigou, Shiyan, Yunyang County, Hubei Province on April 1, 1967

1975年7月1日，第二汽车厂第一个基型车——两吨半越野车正式投产，饶斌厂长驾驶第一辆车下线

The first basic model produced by The Second Automobile Works, which was a kind of 2.5t off-road vehicle, was formally put into production on July 1, 1975. Rao Bin, the factory manager, was driving the first truck off the line.

第二汽车厂部分专业厂鸟瞰

A bird's-eye view of some specialized plants under The Second Automobile Works

第二汽车厂生产的东风牌5 t载货车

"Dongfeng" 5 t trucks produced by The Second Automobile Works

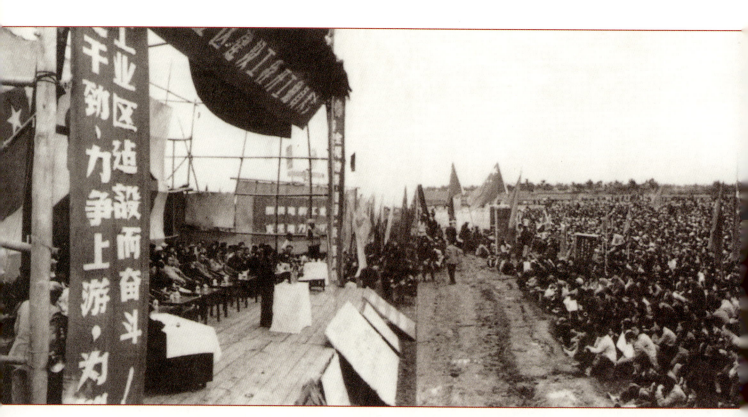

"大跃进"时期，1958年10月13日，德阳水力发电设备厂(现东方电机股份有限公司)开工动员大会会场

Kick-off Meeting for Deyang Hydroelectric Generating Equipment Factory (currently Dongfang Electric Machinery Co., Ltd.) on Oct. 13, 1958 during "Great Leap Forward" period

1959年，德阳水力发电设备厂生产的第一台7 kW小电机

The first 7kW small electric machine produced by Deyang Hydroelectric Generating Equipment Factory in 1959

德阳水力发电设备厂建厂时安装15 m立车车床底盘

15 m vertical lathe stand installed at construction of Deyang Hydropower Generating Equipment Factory

"大跃进"时期，1959年第二重型机器制造厂动工兴建大会会场

Kick-off Meeting for construction of The Second Heavy Machinery Plant in 1959 during "Great Leap Forward" period

第二重型机器制造厂建厂初期的
基建兵团

Capital Construction Corp in the early
construction period of The Second Heavy
Machinery Plant

第二重型机器制造厂建
厂施工工地

Construction site of The
Second Heavy Machinery
Plant

"三线建设"时期,1968年9月25日,陕西鼓风机厂搭起的简
易值勤窝棚,保护第一批建厂物资

A simple duty shed set up at Shaanxi Blower Factory to protect the first group
of materials for plant construction, on Sept. 25, 1968 during "Third-line
Construction" period

施工中的陕鼓金工二车间

No. 2 Machining Workshop of
Shaanxi Blower Factory under
construction

陕鼓第一炉铁水

The first furnace of molten iron
produced by Shaanxi Blower
Factory

"三线建设"时期，1966年8
月29日，由北京第二机床厂包
建的汉川机床厂破土动工

Construction of Hanchuan Machine
Tool Factory began on Aug. 29, 1966
during "Third-line Construction"
period, which was constructed by
Beijing No.2 Machine Tool Plant.

汉川机床厂职工组成的突击连，开赴施工工地

A group composed of employees of Hanchuan Machine Tool Factory going to the construction site to finish work quickly

第四节　改革开放以来的机械工业
Section 4　Machinery Industry after Reform and Opening-Up

　　1978年12月18日召开的中共十一届三中全会，确定了在新的历史条件下实行"改革开放"的总方针。由此也启动了中国机械工业改革开放、创新发展的新时期。

The 3rd plenary session of the 11th CPC Central Committee held on Dec. 18, 1978, defined the general policy of "reform and opening-up" in new conditions, by which a new period of reform, opening-up, innovation and development began for China's machinery industry.

(一) 成功实现了计划经济体制向社会主义市场经济体制的转变
Successful change from planned economy to socialist market economy

　　首先是适时推动产供销管理模式及价格体系的改革。率先突破了多年来计划经济体制下的产品分配方式。十一届三中全会闭幕不久，宁江机床厂于1979年6月25日在《人民日报》上刊登"承接国内外用户直接订货"的广告，突破了过去生产资料不是商品的束缚；1980年8月在长沙举办了具有里程碑意义的产需直接见面交易会，改变了计划经济时期那种"任务靠上级安排，材料靠上级供应，产品靠上级收购"的局面。1982年之后，随着中共十二大精神的贯彻，市场经济在机械工业发展中的主导作用更为突出，指令性计划产品的范围和数量进一步减少，到20世纪90年代初期，只有发电设备和汽车尚有少量国家订货。绝大部分机械产品已经由企业根据市场需求自主经营、按照市场规则自主参与市场竞争，中国机械工业平稳地实现了已实施40年计划经济体制的大变革。与此配套，进行机械产品的价格体系改革，逐步缩小国家统一定价范围，机械产品价格放开，使价格能够比较灵活反映社会劳动生产率和市场关系的变化。

Firstly, reform was carried out in the management of production, supply and marketing and the price system in proper time. The form of product distribution adopted for planned economy for many years was changed for the first time. Soon after the plenary session, Ningjiang Machine Tool Factory issued an advertisement on *People's Daily* on June 25, 1979, saying "We welcome orders directly from users at home and abroad", which was the first time to say means of production were commodities. A historic trade fair for direct contact between producers and suppliers was held in Changsha in Aug. 1980, which changed the old pattern under planned economy that "tasks were assigned, materials were supplied and products were purchased by the superior". Market economy played a more predominant role in developing machinery industry, and there were less varieties and amounts of products manufactured under mandatory order, as the spirit of the 12th CPC

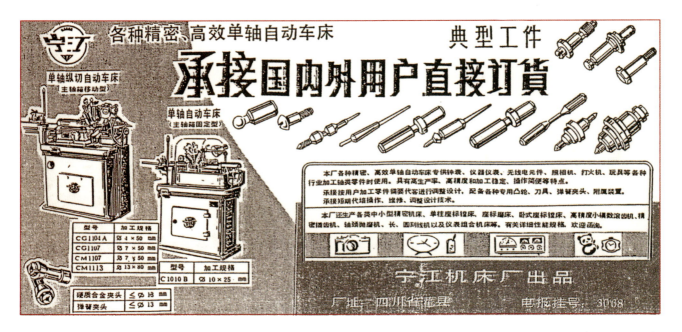

1979年6月25日宁江机床厂在《人民日报》刊登的承接国内外用户直接订货广告全版图（这是新中国成立后中国机械工业突破计划经济体制下"生产资料不是商品的束缚"的第一份广告，影响巨大）

Advertisement of Ningjiang Machine Tool Factory to invite orders directly from users at home and abroad was published on the *People's Daily* on June 25th 1979. It was the first advertisement after founding of the PRC in Chinese machinery industry, breaking through the bonds of "Production means weren't commodities" under the planned economy system and had significant influence.

Central Committee was followed through after 1982. In early 1990s, a few government purchase orders remained for power generating equipment and automobiles. Most types of mechanical products were managed by enterprises themselves to participate in market competition, according to rules and demand of market. The system of planned economy running for 40 years was steadily reformed in China's machinery industry. The price system of mechanical products was also reformed to gradually cut down the scope of government uniform pricing and to adopt free pricing policies for mechanical products, "so that prices can better reflect fluctuations in the relation between market and productivity of social labor".

　　第二是国有企业改革成效显著和民营经济快速崛起。机械工业国有企业经过扩大企业自主权、推行承包经营责任制和推进现代企业制度、推进公司制和股份制改造、推进大型企业上市，改革的着力点始终围绕着搞活企业并提高其市场竞争力。国有企业通过改革、改制和改组，机制性不利因素已经明显减少，相对优越于民营企业的较强科研开发实力和规模效应逐步凸现，运行质量和发展速度大幅提高。国民经济发展和国防建设所需的关系国家经济安全的重大装备主要由国有企业承担，是参与国际竞争的主要力量。如上海、东方和哈尔滨三大动力设备公司生产的发电设备，一汽、上汽、东风、长安、北汽等大型集团生产的轿车都占全国总产量的70%以上，冷热连轧板设备主要由一重、二重制造。国有企业成为我国重大技术装备自主研发的主体力量，700 MW水电机组、超超临界1000 MW火电机组、大型冷热连轧板机、大型舰船和海洋工程装备、航天和各种飞机等高精技术装备，均由国有和国有控股企业开发研制。国有经济在中国机械工业发展中仍居极为重要地位，特别是一些重大技术装备地位更为突出。

Secondly, the reform of state-owned enterprises saw great achievements and private economy rose swiftly. Reform measures for state-owned enterprises engaged in machinery industry included expansion of the enterprises' decision-making powers, execution of contractual management responsibility system, further implementation of modern enterprise system and corporate system, shareholding reform and listing of large-sized enterprises. The central point of reform was prosperity of enterprises with improvement in their competitive edges. Adverse factors due to system decreased remarkably by reform, restructuring and reorganization of state-owned enterprises, which gradually showed stronger capabilities in scientific research and development and better scale effect than private enterprises with much better operation quality and development speed. Significant equipment, which were necessary for national economic development and national defense construction and related to national economic security, were mainly provided by state-owned enterprises that played a major role in international competition. Power generating equipment produced by three power equipment companies including Shanghai, Dongfang and Harbin accounted for over 70% of China's total output of such equipment; so were the sedan cars produced by large-scale groups including FAW, SAIC, Dongfeng, Changan and BAW. Cold & hot continuous plate rolling equipment were mainly produced by China First Heavy Industries and China National Erzhong Group Co. State-owned enterprises became the major force for China's independent research and development of significant technical equipment. 700 MW hydropower generating units, 1000 MW ultra-supercritical thermal power generating units, large-sized cold & hot continuous slab rolling machines, large equipment for ships and oceaneering, hi-tech and precision technical equipment for space flight and various aircrafts were developed by state-owned enterprises and state-held enterprises. State-owned economy, especially some significant technical equipment, played a critical role in the development of machinery in China.

2000—2007年国有企业在机械工业中的比重(%)
Proportion of state-owned enterprises in machinery industry from 2000 to 2007 (%)

	2000	2005	2007
工业增加值 Industrial value	42.16	30.67	23.71
销售收入 Sales revenue	43.58	31.77	25.93
利润总额 Total profits	30.65	26.75	28.30

民营经济，民营企业特别是个体、私营企业，在20世纪50年代中期社会主义改造时退出市场。改革开放以来对其有了新的认识、新的定位，至90年代承认其为社会主义市场经济的"重要组成部分"，对非公经济认识的重大突破，揭开了民营经济发展的新篇章。经过不断改制、创新、发展，一批民营强势机械企业已经崛起，特变电工、中联重科、三一重工、正泰、德力西、华立、万向、吉利、长城、宗申、力帆等机械、汽车集团公司，已具有立足国内，走出国门的实力，在国内外市场有较强的竞争优势。特别是进入21世纪以来，随着混合所有制的出现，一批强势民营企业，积极参与国有企业的改革，调整产业结构，获得巨大成功。新疆特变电工并购了大型国有企业沈阳变压器厂，一跃成为研制1000 kV特高压交流输变电和±800 kV直流输电线路装备的明星企业；中联重科与国有浦沅工程机械集团强强联合，走上国际化发展的道路，成为全球混凝土机械制造的强者；万向集团在成为国际知名汽车零件公司后，又投巨资控股汉中的几个机床企业，进入数控机床领域。各种所有制企业平等竞争，特别是民营企业在机械工业发展中的地位更显突出。民营机械工业企业的主要经济指标占规模以上机械工业企业的比重，2000年近40%，2005年已提高到50%左右。

Private economy and enterprises, especially individually owned enterprises and private enterprises, exited market during socialist transformation in middle 1950s, but were reoriented after reform and opening-up and be recognized as a "key component" of socialist market economy in 1990s. The breakthrough in cognition of private economy was the start of a new development stage of private economy. Some excellent private machinery enterprises emerged along with continuous restructuring, innovation and development, including mechanical and automobile groups or companies like Tebian Electric Apparatus Stock Co., Ltd., Changsha Zoomlion Heavy Industry Science & Technology Development Co., Ltd., Sany Group Co., Ltd., CHINT, DELIXI Group, Holley Metering Limited, Wanxiang Group, Geely Holding Group, Great Wall Motor Company Limited, Zongshen Industrial Group and Lifan Group, which were capable of participating in international competition with great competitive edge in domestic and overseas markets. Especially, in the 21st century, as diversified ownership was adopted, some strong private enterprises played an active and successful role in the reform of state-owned enterprises and in the adjustment of industrial structure. Shenyang Transformer Works, a large-sized state-owned enterprise, was merged into Tebian Electric Apparatus Stock Co., Ltd., which made Tebian a hot spot enterprise developing equipment for 1000 kV extra-high voltage AC electric transmission and transformation and ±800 kV DC electric transmission lines. Puyuan Engineering Machinery Group was merged into Changsha Zoomlion Heavy Industry Science & Technology Development Co., Ltd. which hereby started international development and played a dominant role in global manufacturing of concrete machinery. Wanxiang Group, after becoming internationally famous for automobile parts, held shares in several machine tool enterprises in Hanzhong by means of huge investment to get engaged in the field of numerical control machine tools. Enterprises with different ownerships competed on an equal basis. Private enterprises played a more dominant role in the development of machinery. Major economic indices of private machinery enterprises accounted for almost 40% of those of machinery enterprises above designated scale in 2000 and 50% in 2005.

机械工业各经济类型企业主要指标比重情况(%)
Proportions of machinery enterprises with different ownerships by economic indices (%)

	2000			2007		
	国有 State-owned	民营 Private	三资 Three types of foreign-funded enterprises	国有 State-owned	民营 Private	三资 Three types of foreign-funded enterprises
工业增加值 Industrial value added	42.16	39.49	18.35	23.71	51.45	24.84
销售收入 Sales revenue	43.58	37.15	19.27	25.93	48.21	25.86
利润总额 Total profits	30.65	43.69	25.66	28.30	45.97	25.73

(二) 对外开放，融入国际机械市场

Opening up to enter international machinery market

1. 对外贸易

Foreign trade

1840年鸦片战争后的近160年来，中国机械产品对外贸易一直是"进口大于出口"，20世纪80年代以来，成为中国对外贸易逆差最大的行业，逆差最多时达300多亿美元。2001年"入世"后，出口增速大步加快，中国机械产品外贸从逆差大户发展成为顺差大户。以民用机械产品为例，2006年开始少量顺差，2007年顺差达到241.4亿元；外贸净出口率不断提高，1978年为12.06%，1990年为34.97%，2000年为40.97%，2005年为46.87%，2006年为50.13%，首次超过50%成为净出口，实现了历史性改变；2007年达53.34%。

China's mechanical products had been with adverse trade balance for 160 years after the First Opium War in 1840, and had seen the greatest adverse trade balance being USD 30 billion among all the industries in China since 1980s. Export growth soared after China became a member of the World Trade Organization in 2001, and adverse trade balance in China's mechanical products turned into surplus. Take mechanical products for civilian use for example: surplus occurred at small scale in 2006 and reached RMB 24.14 billion in 2007; the rate of net export kept rising from 12.06% in 1978 to 34.97% in 1990, 40.97% in 2000, 46.87% in 2005 and to 50.13% in 2006, which was the first time to be net export by exceeding 50% and was a historic change, and further reached 53.34% in 2007.

(1) 中国已成为机械贸易大国

China became a big trading country by machinery

按《联合国贸易统计》，中国机械工业全行业的进出口贸易，2008年仅次于美国、德国，居全球第三位，占总量的10.1%，2006年为8.5%；其中出口额和进口额分别居全球第四位和第二位。

According to *Trade Statistics of UN*, import & export trade of China's machinery industry ranked the third in the world, next to that of USA and Germany in 2008, when it accounted for 10.1% of the gross (8.5% in 2006); the export volume and the import volume ranked the fourth and the second largest in the world respectively.

2008年世界机械工业主要贸易国家
Major trading countries by machinery in 2008

	进出口总额 Total import & export volume		进口总额 Total import volume		出口总额 Total export volume	
	亿美元 USD 100 million	比重（%） Proportion (%)	亿美元 USD 100 million	比重（%） Proportion (%)	亿美元 USD 100 million	比重（%） Proportion (%)
全世界贸易总额 Total global trade volume	86827	100.0	42688	100.0	44139	100.0
美国 USA	11445	13.2	5945	13.9	5500	12.5
德国 Germany	10775	12.4	3643	8.5	7132	16.2
中国 China	8806	10.1	4463	10.5	4343	9.8
日本 Japan	6094	7.0	1404	3.3	4690	10.6
法国 France	4619	5.3	2227	5.2	2392	5.4
英国 UK	3239	3.7	1755	4.1	1484	3.4

资料来源：《联合国贸易统计》。统计范围：全部机械工业。
Source: *Trade Statistics of UN*. Scope: the whole machinery industry.

(2) 21世纪以来机械产品外贸出口快速发展
Export of mechanical products grew swiftly in the 21st century

　　1956年中国就开始出口机械产品，但在20世纪60年代，中国机械产品主要是按国家间的协定，以无偿援外的形式出口，70年代才开始商务贸易出口。改革开放初期，机械产品整体出口水平很低，主要是劳动密集型和材料密集型、工艺简单的标准件，手用工具等，主要面向无须进行售后服务的维修市场；出口贸易伙伴主要是亚洲的发展中国家。1985年，亚洲市场占出口贸易的75%；对美、日、西欧等世界外贸主市场只占10.8%。1984年中国机械产品出口额居世界第30位，占当时世界机械产品出口总额的3.4%。

China began to export mechanical products in 1956. In 1960s, China exported mechanical products mainly as free aid to foreign countries according to agreements among countries. China did not start commercial export until 1970s. In early years of reform and opening up, the overall export of mechanical products was at low level, which mainly involved labor-intensive and material-intensive standard parts and hand tools made through simple process; the export was mainly to maintenance market not requiring after-sale services, and major export trade partners were developing countries in Asia. About 75% of export trade was to the Asian market in 1985, and only 10.8% was to major foreign trade markets in the world like USA, Japan and Western Europe. The export volume ranked the 30th in the world in 1984, accounting for 3.4% of global total export volume of mechanical products.

1985年和2001年是中国机械工业扩大外贸出口的两个转折点。1985年，国务院发出扩大机电产品出口的号召，机械产品出口贸易进入新阶段，中国机械产品出口迅速发展；在2001年加入世贸组织后，中国机械出口更是迈开大步，按《联合国贸易统计》，2008年全球机械产品外贸出口总额44139亿美元，其中中国4343亿美元，占9.84%，居世界第四位(日本有关外贸分析报告，2008年出口外贸中国超过日本，仅次于德国、美国，居第三位)。

Two turning points for China's machinery industry to expand export came in 1985 and 2001. The State Council required expansion of export of mechanical and electrical products in 1985. So the export trade of mechanical products entered a new stage, and China's export of mechanical products grew swiftly. China's machinery export soared after the country became a member of the WTO in 2001. According to *Trade Statistics of UN*, global total export volume of mechanical products was USD 4413.9 billion in 2008, among which, China's volume was USD 434.3 billion accounting for 9.84% and ranking the 4th in the world. (According to relevant trade analysis reports of Japan, the export of China surpassed Japan to be the 3rd, only next to Germany and USA in 2008.)

2004—2008年主要国家机械产品出口额
Export volumes of mechanical products of major countries from 2004 to 2008

	国家 Country	2004 出口额（亿美元）Export volume (USD 100 million)	比重（%）Proportion (%)	2006 出口额（亿美元）Export volume (USD 100 million)	比重（%）Proportion (%)	2008 出口额（亿美元）Export volume (USD 100 million)	比重（%）Proportion (%)	2005—2008平均年增（%）2005—2008 mean annual growth (%)
	全世界总计 Global total	27681	100	39121	100	44139	100	12.4
1	德国 Germany	4513	16.3	5740	14.82	7132	16.16	12.1
2	美国 USA	3232	11.7	4902	12.53	5500	12.46	14.2
3	日本 Japan	3092	11.2	4095	10.47	4690	10.63	11.0
4	中国 China	1351	4.9	2612	6.68	4343	9.84	33.9
5	法国 France	1666	6.0	1418	3.62	2392	5.42	9.5
6	英国 UK	1207	4.4	1982	5.07	1484	3.36	5.3

资料来源：《联合国贸易统计》，统计范围：全部机械工业。
Source: *Trade Statistics of UN*; scope: the whole machinery industry.

出口机械产品结构不断优化。从20世纪90年代中期机械产品出口逐步向技术含量和附加值较高的产品和成套设备转变。大型远洋船舶、民用飞机、地铁车辆、汽车、成套设备等已批量出口。如船舶工业已成为外向型产业，70%的产量出口，从中小型一般散货轮向万吨级集装箱船、滚装船、超深海洋钻探平台等高技术船和海洋工程装备发展；民用飞机出口1500架；汽车出口发展很快，2002年2万辆，2007年61万辆，出口车型由商用车向轿车转变；大型发电设备已成为重要出口产品，2007年出口53套/498.9万kW，2009年增至287套/1648.13万kW，国产超临界600 MW机组已出口土耳其、印度和俄罗斯；日产水泥熟料1万t的世界最大水泥生产线装备，已向阿联酋等中东国家出口多套，3万m³/h级以上大型制氧机、9000 m深井石油钻机均已多台出口。

The structure of mechanical products exported was improved again and again. The types of mechanical products exported were gradually changed to hi-tech products and complete sets of equipment with high value added as from the middle 1990s. Large-sized ocean ships, civil aircrafts, subway vehicles, automobiles and complete sets of equipment were exported in large batches. Ship-building industry became export-oriented, 70% of production of which was exported. Products developed from medium and small-sized general bulk freighters to 10,000 TEU container vessels, roll on/roll off ships, hi-tech vessels and oceaneering equipment. 1,500 civil aircrafts were exported. Automobile export grew swiftly; 20,000 cars were exported in 2002 and 610,000 in 2007; types of automobiles exported changed from commercial vehicles to sedan cars. Large-sized power generating equipment played an important role in export; 53 sets /4.989 million kW were exported in 2007 and 287 sets /16.4813 million kW in 2009; domestically made supercritical 600 MW units were exported to Turkey, India and Russia. Many sets of the largest cement production line equipment in the world with a daily production of 10,000 t cement clinker were exported to countries in the Middle East like United Arab Emirates. Many sets of large-sized oxygenerators above 30,000 m^3/h and 9000 m deep oil drilling rig were exported.

对外贸易伙伴。21世纪初，贸易伙伴已达216个，市场多元化已经形成。主要伙伴是欧盟、日本和美国，占2007年进出口总额的56.2%，出口主要去向是欧盟、美国、日本和我国香港特别行政区，共占出口总量的61.5%。从贸易平衡看，2007年我国香港特别行政区、美国顺差最多，仅民机产品，分别为198亿美元和181.8亿美元；日本、德国逆差最多，2007年分别为271.1亿美元和201.8亿美元。

Trading partners: China had 216 trading partners in early 21st century, where market diversification formed. Major trading partners were the European Union, Japan and USA, which contributed 56.2% of the total volume of export and import in 2007. As the main destinations of export, the European Union, USA, Hong Kong and Japan jointly contributed 61.5% of the total volume of export. In a view of trade balance, the largest surplus was with Hong Kong and USA in 2007, being USD 19.8 billion and 18.18 billion respectively for machinery for civilian use; the largest adverse trade balance was with Japan and Germany, being USD 27.11 billion and 20.18 billion respectively in 2007.

出口贸易方式发生变化。20世纪80年代末，民机出口额中，加工贸易比重近70%，一般贸易占不到30%。"入世"以来，情况发生了变化，2007年一般贸易比重占49.68%，加工贸易占44.91%，一般贸易出口超过加工贸易出口，发生了历史性变化。

Mode of export trade: processing trade accounted for nearly 70% while general trade for less than 30% of the export volume of machinery for civilian use in late 1980s. Things changed after China became a member of the WTO. General trade accounted for 49.68% while processing trade for 44.91% in 2007. General trade export exceeded processing trade export, which was a historic change.

2. 利用外资

Utilization of foreign funds

1981年12月，湖北汽车公司与美国合资经营的武汉派克密封件厂开业，是中国机械工业最早签约的中外合资经营项目。随后，1984年1月15日北京汽车制造厂与美国汽车公司合营的北京吉普车有限公司开业，这是中外合资经营的第一家汽车公司。当年10月10日上海汽车厂与联邦德国大众汽车公司合营项目合同正式签字，为中国机械工业较大规模利用外资迈出了重要的一步。90年代以来机械工业利用外资增长迅速，以原机械工业部系统为例，1995年有三资企业10303个，到2007年底达21317个，且2007年三资企业在机械工业部系统主要经济指标的比重，企业数7.37%，产值25.64%，利润25.73%，资产总额26.7%。

Parker-Hubei Seals Co., Ltd., a joint venture of Hubei Automobile Company and an American company, started business in Dec. 1981, which was the project of Sino-foreign joint venture firstly signed in China's machinery industry. Later, Beijing Jeep Corporation Ltd., a joint venture of BAW and Daimler-Chrysler AG (an American automobile company), started business on Jan. 15, 1984, which was the first Sino-foreign joint venture dealing with automobiles. The contract for the joint venture project of Shanghai Automobile Factory and Germany Volkswagen was formally signed on Oct. 10, 1984, which was a significant step for China in application of large-scale foreign funds to

湖北派克密封件有限公司是机械行业第一家中外合资企业，其产品主要为汽车、摩托车、电器开关、液压气动、石油化工、板式换热器等行业配套，图为该公司生产现场

As the first Sino-foreign joint venture in machinery industry, Parker-Hubei Seals Co., Ltd. mainly produced automobiles, motorcycles, electric switches, hydraulic & pneumatic equipment, petrochemical equipment, plate heat exchangers and other auxiliary equipment. The picture above was the production field of this company.

美国派克•汉尼汾公司到湖北派克密
封件有限公司访问(右为公司总经理
周沛岳)
Visitors from Parker Hannifin Corporation to
Parker-Hubei Seals Co., Ltd. (Zhou Peiyue
(right), General Manager of this company)

machinery industry. Foreign funds applied to machinery industry grew swiftly as from 1990s. Take the system of the original ministry of machinery industry for example, there were 10,303 foreign-funded enterprises (of three types) in 1995, and 21,317 by the end of 2007. The proportions of foreign-funded enterprises (of three types) in the system of machinery industry were 7.37% by number of enterprises, 25.64% by output value, 25.73% by profits and 26.7% by total assets in the year 2007.

大量吸收外资，对促进机械工业的发展发挥了十分重要的作用。一是相当程度上弥补了建设资金的不足，20世纪90年代民用机械工业使用的外资相当于同期行业固定资产投资的一半左右。二是提高了产品的档次和水平，如轿车、电梯、文化办公设备、自动化控制装置等，三资企业的产品，填补了产品的技术空白。三是扩大了机械产品的出口，2008年三资企业出口额为1308.40亿美元，占总量的53.95%。

Introduction of foreign funds at large scale impelled the development of machinery. On the one hand, shortage of construction funds was made up considerably. Foreign funds applied to the industry of machinery for civilian use was about half of the investment in fixed assets of the industry in 1990s. On the other hand, products were upgraded, including sedan cars, elevators, office supplies and automatic control devices, etc. Products made by the three types of foreign-funded enterprises (Sino-foreign joint ventures, Sino-foreign cooperative enterprises, and wholly foreign-owned enterprises) filled technical gap. Furthermore, export of mechanical products was expanded. The export volume of the three types of foreign-funded enterprises was USD 130.84 billion accounting for 53.95% of the gross volume in 2008.

利用外资作为我国对外开放基本国策的重要内容，对推动中国机械工业持续快速发展功不可没，2001—2007年，三资企业对机械发展的贡献率，工业增加值为26.35%、销售收入27.5%、出口交货值为59.8%，直接就业人员340万人，占总人数的1/4。

Utilization of foreign funds, as a key element of China's basic state policy of reform and opening up, contributed a lot to the continuously swift growth of machinery industry in China. The rate of contribution by the three types of foreign-funded enterprises to the development of machinery was 26.35% by industrial value added, 27.5% by sales revenue and 59.8% by export delivery value from 2001 to 2007, where the number of persons in direct employment was 3.4 million accounting for one fourth of the total number.

利用外资在为中国机械工业发展注入活力的同时，也出现了一些负面影响和教训。如外资企业对洛阳轴承集团公司、徐工集团机械有限公司被质疑为外资恶意并购，"斩首行动"影响"国家经济安全，国防安全"以及贱卖问题，引发公众的关注，催生了国家有关部门《外国投资者并购境内企业的规定》出台。《华尔街日报》评论外资收购徐工案是外国投资基金进入中国的 "分水岭"。在此以后，中国对待外资的态度从盲从转变为审慎。

Adverse effects and cases occurred along with injection of new strength by applying foreign funds in China's machinery industry. The merger cases of LYC Bearing Corporation and Xuzhou Construction Machinery Group Co., Ltd. (XCMG) were questioned about hostile takeover by foreign funds. "Decapitation Strike" related to foreign funds involved "national economic

上海三菱电梯有限公司是1987年1月组建的合资企业，先后利用引进技术国产化和自行开发研制了20多种电梯产品，并为用户提供各类电梯39500余台，图为该公司高120 m的三菱电梯试验塔，为亚洲之最

As a joint venture, Shanghai Mitsubishi Elevator Co., Ltd. was founded in Jan. 1987. It developed over 20 types of elevator products by localization of imported technologies and independent development, and provided over 39,500 elevators of different kinds to users. The picture above showed the 120 m-high testing tower of this company for its elevators, which was the No.1 testing tower in Asia.

security", "defense security" and sale at a sacrifice, being concerned by the public. As a result, *Regulations for Merger with and Acquisition of Domestic Enterprises by Foreign Investors* was issued by relevant state departments. It was commented by *Wall Street Journal* that, acquisition of XCMG by foreign funds was the "watershed" for foreign investment funds entering China. After that, China's attitude towards foreign funds changed from blind follow to a cautious view.

(三) 创新能力提高，重大技术装备跨越式发展
Key technical equipment developed in a leap-forward way, with better innovation capability

技术创新能力不断提升。据机械科学研究院等有关单位调查，机械工业主导产品的技术来源中，国内占比从20世纪80年代的24.5%，90年代的43%，上升到21世纪初的60%。长期以来，国家高度重视机械装备制造业的发展，特别是2006年2月，国务院颁布了《关于加快振兴装备制造业的若干意见》以后，机械工业结合重大工程建设，引进消化吸收国外先进技术，通过企业再创新、集中创新，开发出一批具有自主知识产权的重大装备，大大提升了创新能力，实现了许多重大技术装备的跨越式发展。研制完成大批重要技术装备，质和量的快速提高超过了中国机械工业发展史上任何一个时期。

Capability of technical innovation kept improving. According to the findings of related institutions including China Academy of Machinery Science & Technology, among technologies for leading products of machinery industry, 24.5% were domestic technologies in 1980s while that rate rose to 43% in 1990s and 60% in the beginning of the 21st century. China has always highly valued the development of machine and equipment-building industry. Especially, after the State Council issued *Several Opinions on Prosper Equipment-building Industry* in Feb. 2006, the machinery industry absorbed advanced foreign technologies in combination with key engineering construction, some key equipment with proprietary intellectual property rights were developed by re-invention and centralized innovation of enterprises, innovation capability was upgraded greatly and leap-forward development was realized for many pieces of key technical equipment. Much key technical equipment was developed. The rise in both quality and quantity was the sharpest in the history of machinery in China.

1. 火力发电设备
Thermal power generating equipment

完成了超临界及超超临界1000 MW煤电机组、300 MW循环流化床锅炉、600 MW空冷机组、包括9FA重型燃气轮机在内的燃气—蒸汽联合循环机组。

1000 MW supercritical and ultra-supercritical coal-fired units, 300 MW circulating fluidized bed boiler and 600 MW air-cooling units were accomplished, including gas-steam combined cycle unit which included 9FA heavy duty gas turbine.

2002年，研发超超临界燃煤发电技术立项时，国际上仅有德国、丹麦、日本的5个电厂投产。中国首台机组于2006年12月在华能玉环电厂建成投产，2007年即生产32台，发展速度之快，中外历史未见。多台超超临界1000 MW机组的投产，使中国电力工业进入"超超临界"时代。

When the research and development project of ultra-supercritical coal-fired power generating technology was approved in 2002, only 5 power plants in Germany, Denmark and Japan were put into production in the world. China's first unit was completed and put into operation in Huaneng Yuhuan Power Plant in Dec. 2006, and 32 units were produced in 2007. The development speed was almost the fastest in the world. By operation of several 1000 MW ultra-supercritical units, China's power industry entered the "ultra-supercritical" era.

1000 MW级超超临界火电机组

1000 MW ultra-supercritical thermal power unit

600 MW空冷汽轮机

600 MW air-cooling steam turbine

9FA重型燃气轮机

9FA heavy duty gas turbine

2. 水力发电设备
Hydroelectric generating equipment

三峡（右岸）700 MW全空冷水轮发电机组、大型抽水蓄能水电机组、大型贯流式水电机组等大型水电设备都是这一时期完成的。其中自主创新的三峡（右岸）700 MW水电机组，效率和稳定性要好于引进技术的左岸机组，特别是发电机采用先进的空冷技术，处于国际领先水平。

Large-sized hydroelectric equipment was accomplished in this period, including 700 MW fully air-cooling hydraulic turbine-generator units for Three Gorges (right bank), large-sized pumped storage hydroelectric generator units and large-sized tubular-flow hydroelectric generator units. The 700 MW hydroelectric generating unit independently innovated for Three Gorges (on the right bank) was better than the unit with introduced technologies on the left bank by efficiency and stability. Especially the advanced air-cooling technology applied in generator was leading in the world.

2007年投入运行的完全由国内制造的三峡右岸电站26＃700MW水力发电机组

The 26#700MW hydroelectric generator unit for the right bank power station of Three Gorges was entirely manufactured in China and put into service in 2007

3. 输变电设备
Power transmission and distribution equipment

全面掌握了交流、直流50万伏和交流75万伏超高压输变电设备制造技术，设备国产化率2008年分别达到95%和80%以上。自主研发的百万伏级交流、±80万伏直流特高压输变电设备分别于2009年1月和12月成功投运，两条示范工程设备的国产化率分别为91%和62.9%以上。中国特高压输变电设备制造技术处于国际领先水平。

China was fully capable of manufacturing ±500 kV DC and 750 kV AC super-high voltage power transmission equipments. The import substitution rate of the equipments reached above 95% and 80% respectively in 2008. Domestically developed 1000 kV AC and ±800 kV extra-high voltage transmission and distribution equipment were successfully put into production in Jan. and Dec. 2009 respectively. The domestic content of the equipments for the two demonstration projects were 91% and 62.9% respectively. China's manufacturing technology for extra-high voltage transmission and distribution equipment was leading in the world.

ODFPS-1000000/1000单相自耦变压器

ODFPS-1000000/1000 single-phase auto-transformer

ZF-1100(L)/Y5000-50气体绝缘金属封闭开关设备(GIS)

ZF-1100(L)/Y5000-50 gas insulated metal-enclosed switchgear (GIS)

±800 kV特高压直流输电控制保护和换流阀

±800 kV extra-high DC transmission control protection and converter value

4. 大型乙烯成套设备
Complete sets of large-sized ethylene equipment

已实现了以"裂解三机"为代表的关键设备国产化。裂解气、乙烯、丙烯压缩机是百万吨乙烯的关键设备，已实现国产化；1000t加氢反应器、15万—18万t／yr裂解炉已研制成功；2006年为茂名石化制造的板翅式换热器(冷箱)，是迄今为止的世界上最大的三元制冷乙烯冷箱；大型化工空气分离装置，2004年5.2万 m^3／h空分装置投产、2005年2套6万 m^3／h空分装置出口、2008年又签订了1套8.3万 m^3／h空分装置供货合同，这些装置国外也只有德国林德公司、法国液化空气公司、美国空气产品公司等几家公司能生产。按投资计算，2009年百万吨乙烯装置的国产化率约为70%，千万吨级炼油设备为95%，百万吨级PTA装置已实现了国产化。

Domestically made equipment were used as key equipment, especially "three ethylene machines" (cracked gas compressor, propylene compressor and ethylene compressor, which were key ethylene equipment of 1 million ton). 1000 t hydrogenation reactor and 150,000—180,000 t/yr. cracking furnace were developed. Plate-fin heat exchanger (ice chest) made for Maoming Petrochemical Company in 2006 is still the largest triple-refrigeration ethylene ice chest in the world. 52,000 m^3/h air separation facility was put into operation in 2004, two sets of 60,000 m^3/h air separation facilities were exported in 2005 and supply contract was signed for another set of 83,000 m^3/h air separation facility in 2008. Only several foreign companies are capable of producing these facilities, like Linde Group, Air Liquide and Air Products and Chemicals, Inc. Import substitution rate was 70% for 1 million t ethylene plants, 95% for 10 million t oil refinery plants and 100% for 1 million t PTA plants, in terms of investment.

64万t/yr乙烯装置用裂解气
压缩机组

Cracked gas compressor unit for
640,000 t/yr ethylene plant

2006年大型乙烯项目国产化成套
乙烯冷箱

Complete set of ethylene ice chest
domestically made for large-sized
ethylene project in 2006

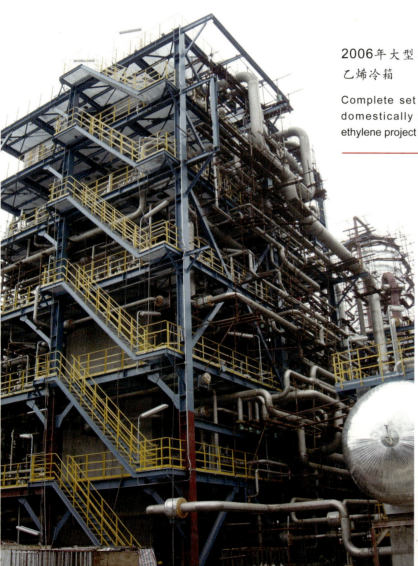

2004年研制的50000 Nm³/h(氧)空分设备

50000 Nm³/h air (oxygen) separation equipment
developed in 2004

5. 石油装备
Oil equipment

石油钻机是油田勘探开发的主要设备，2005年研制成功了9000 m深井钻机；2007年，又研制成功了12000 m特深井钻机，标志着中国在世界高端钻井设备研制上的突破。

Oil rig is a major kind of equipment for exploration and development of oil fields. 9,000 m deep drilling rig was developed in 2005, and 12,000 m extra deep drilling rig was developed in 2007, which was a breakthrough for China in development of high-end drilling equipment.

6. 大型冶金设备
Large-sized metallurgical equipment

2006—2007年，一重、二重、中重院（原西安重型机械所）等企业研制成功具有世界先进技术水平的焦化、连铸和冷、热连轧等一批大型冶金设备，并成功应用于生产。一是冷热连轧自主研制开创了新局面，除个别要求特高钢材轧机外，大型冷热连轧成套设备基本实现自主化。一重与鞍钢联合自主研制成功中国第一套1780 mm大型冷连轧成套设备、1750 mm大型热连轧成套设备。鞍钢1780 mm冷连轧机组，成品厚度0.3—3.0 mm，轧制力最大25 MN，最大轧制速度22.5 m/s，该轧机的成套集成技术已广泛应用于鞍钢2150 mm、宝钢2050 mm、京唐2250 mm等轧机上。二是大型连铸成套设备，经"十五"的关键技术攻关，2006—2007年投产的具有自主化知识产权的大型板坯连铸机达15套／20流，其中舞阳新钢2007年1月投产的300 mm×2500 mm。大型宽厚板连铸机，是在市场上与国际知名外商竞标中获得的新建项目。三是这时期国际上稀少的大型宽厚板轧机实现国产化，2005年投产的、二重为宝钢研制的5000 mm宽厚板轧机，单片牌坊重量397 t（整铸）、轧机最大速度7.3 m/s、成品厚度5—150 mm，号称"轧机之王"；其后一重又为鞍钢研制成功5500 mm大型宽厚板轧机，为中国船舶制造业提供了生产所需宽厚钢板。

China First Heavy Industries (CFHI), China National Erzhong Group Co., China National Heavy Machinery Research Institute (former Xian Heavy Machinery Research Institute) and other enterprises successfully developed a batch of large-sized metallurgical equipment at internationally top technical level for coking, continuous casting and hot and cold continuous rolling in 2006 and 2007, and such equipment was applied to production. Firstly, independent development of cold and hot continuous rolling started a new stage. Except for steel rolling mill with extra high requirements, other complete sets of large-sized cold and hot continuous rolling equipment were mostly independently developed. CFHI and Angang Steel jointly developed China's first complete sets of large-sized 1780 mm cold continuous rolling equipment and 1750 mm hot continuous rolling equipment. Finished products made by the set of 1780 mm cold continuous rolling mill of Angang Steel were 0.3—3.0 mm thick, with the maximum rolling load being 25 MN and the maximum rolling speed being 22.5 m/s. Complete integral technology of that rolling mill has been applied to 2150 mm rolling mill (Angang Steel), 2050 mm rolling mill (Baogang Steel) and 2250 mm rolling mill (Jingtang). Secondly, 15 sets (20 stands) of large-sized slab casting machines with proprietary intellectual property rights were put into production in 2006 and 2007, after key technical problems were solved in the tenth 5-year planning period. The 300 mm×2500 mm large-sized heavy plate casting machine put into production by Wuyang Iron and Steel CO.,Ltd in Jan. 2007 was a project of new construction awarded in competitive bidding against world famous foreign enterprises. Thirdly, large-sized heavy plate mill, which was rare in the world, could be produced by domestic enterprises. For the 5000 mm heavy plate mill which was developed by China National Erzhong Group Co. for Baogang Steel and put into production in 2005, each single piece of housing weighed 397 t (block cast), the maximum rolling speed was 7.3 m/s and finished products were 5—150 mm thick. This was called the "king of rolling mills". Later, CFHI developed 5500 mm large-sized heavy plate mill for Angang Steel, to provide steel plates of required width and thickness necessary for production in ship-building industry in China.

1780 mm五机架冷连轧机组

1780 mm five-stand cold continuous rolling unit

大型板坯连铸机

Large-sized slab continuous casting machine

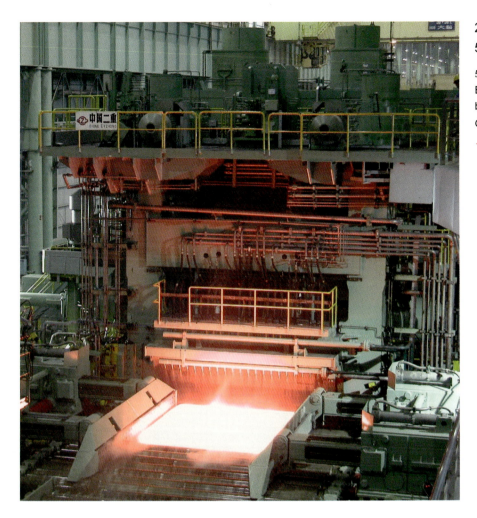

2005年二重研制的宝钢
5000 mm宽厚板轧机

5000 mm heavy plate mill of
Baogang Steel developed
by China National Erzhong
Group Co. in 2005

7. 大型煤炭井下综合采掘及大型露天矿设备
Large-sized equipment for general downhole excavation and open-pit mining of coal

2000—2007年研制了一批大型煤矿急需、长期依赖进口的大型设备，并在大型现代化煤矿中得到应用。太矿集团为井下矿研制完成了1800—2500 kW大功率厚煤层电牵引采煤机，6.5 m高端液压支架等设备，提供了年生产能力1000万t的高产高效综采综掘工作面成套设备；中信重机于2007年研制成功了具有完全知识产权、当前世界上钻凿直径最大、钻凿井筒最深的竖井钻机，最大钻凿直径13 m、最大钻进深度1000 m。太重和湘潭电机于2007年分别研制成功了具有自主知识产权的标准铲斗容量55 m³的大型矿用正铲式挖掘机，和矿用额定装载质量220t电动轮自卸车，可满足2000万t级以上大型露天矿采装作业需要，已用于中煤公司平朔分公司安家岭露天矿。

A group of large-sized equipment, which was much needed for coal mines but depended on import for a long time, was developed and applied to large-sized modern coal mines from 2000 to 2007. For underground mines, Taiyuan Mining Machinery Group Co., Ltd. developed 1800—2500 kW high-power thick-seam electric traction coal cutter and 6.5 m high-end hydraulic support and provided complete sets of equipment with the annual capacity being 10 million t for working

煤矿用3.5 m高端液
压支架

3.5 m high-end hydraulic
support for coal mines

face of high-yield high-efficiency general excavation. CITIC Heavy Industries Company Ltd. developed 1,000 m vertical shaft drill with complete intellectual property rights in 2007, which had the maximum drilling diameter of 13 m and the maximum drilling depth of 1000 m in the world at that time. Taiyuan Heavy Machinery Group Co., Ltd. and Xiangtan Electric Manufacturing Corporation Ltd. successfully developed large-sized mining face-shovel excavator with standard dipper capacity being 55 m^3 and electric-wheel dumping car for mining with rated loading weight being 220 t respectively in 2007, with proprietary intellectual property rights; the equipment were capable of large-sized open-pit mining and loading above 20 million t, and were applied to Anjialing open-pit mine of Pingshuo Branch of China National Coal Group Corp.

JkmD-5×4(III)特大型多绳摩擦式提升机

JkmD-5 × 4 (III) extra large multi-rope mining friction hoister

8. 船舶及海洋工程装备
Vessels and oceaneering equipment

近年来船舶工业对高附加值船舶的开发，实现了历史性跨越，先后完成了具有国际先进水平的14.72万m³大型液化天然气船(LNG船)、万箱级集装箱船、30万t级超大型油轮(VLCC)、30万t级海上浮式生产储油船(FPSO)、5000车位滚装船、5万hp低速大功率柴油机等高技术、高附加值船舶和船用装备；还完成了400 ft(122 m)水深自升式钻井平台及3000 m水深半潜式深海钻井平台等高技术海洋工程装备。

Development of vessels with high value added gave rise to historic leap forward in recent years. Hi-tech vessels and ship equipment with high value added at internationally advanced level were developed, including 147,200 m³ large-sized LNG vessel, 10,000 TEU container vessel, 300,000 t Very Large Crude Carrier (VLCC), 300,000 t Float Production Storage and Offloading (FPSO), 5000 car roll on/roll off ship and 50,000 hp low-speed high-power diesel engine. Hi-tech oceaneering equipment was also accomplished, including 400 ft (122 m) water-deep self-elevating drilling platform and 3000 m water-deep semi-submersible drilling platform.

9. 轨道车辆
Rolling stock

CRH2型时速300km及以上动车组于2007年12月成功下线，CRH3型时速350km动车组于2008年成功应用于京津城际铁路，为京沪高速及其他客运专线用车，2009年12月9日和谐号动车组在广武客运专线上时速达394km，创世界新纪录。世界首创的时速120km 6轴9600kW大功率货运电力机车已经于2008年完成，此前2007年，8轴9600kW电力机车已在大秦铁路进行2万t牵引运营。

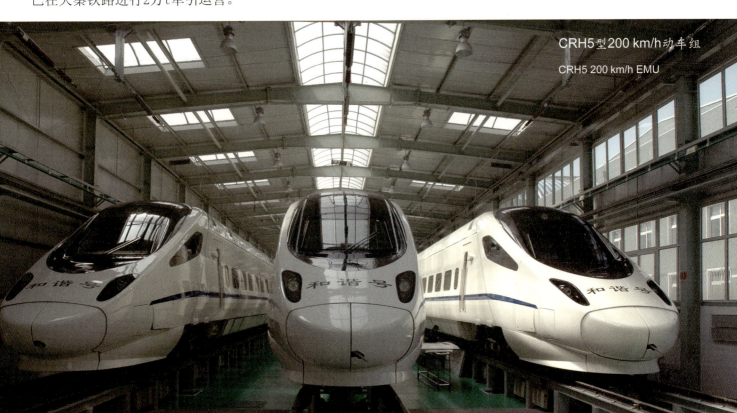

CRH5型200 km/h动车组
CRH5 200 km/h EMU

时速300 km速度级
CRH2型动车组

CRH2 EMU at 300 km/h

HXD1型大功率交流传动货运电子机车

HXD1 high-power AC drive electric freight locomotive

CRH2 Electricity Multiple Unit (EMU) at 300 km/h and above went off the line in Dec. 2007, and CRH3 350 km/h EMU was successfully applied to Beijing-Tianjin Inter-city Railway and used for Beijing-Shanghai High-Speed Railway and other passenger dedicated lines. "Harmony" EMU ran at 394 km/h on Wuhan-Guangzhou passenger dedicated line on Dec. 9, 2009, hitting a new world record. 9600 kW eight-axis electric locomotive was used for 20,000 t traction on Datong-Qinhuangdao Railway in 2007. 9600 kW high-power six-axis electric freight locomotive, which was the first of its kind in the world, was accomplished in 2008.

10. 民用飞机
Civil aircraft

2007年12月21日，自行研制生产的中国首架自主知识产权喷气支线客机ARJ21-700飞机在上海总装下线。同期，具有自主知识产权的新一代4t级多用途H425型民用直升机由哈尔滨飞机公司自主研发成功。

China's first Regional Jetliner (ARJ21-700) with proprietary intellectual property rights, which was independently developed, was assembled and went off the line in Shanghai on Dec. 21, 2007. In the same period, Harbin Aircraft Industry (Group) Co., Ltd. independently developed the new generation of 4 t H425 multirole civil helicopter with proprietary intellectual property rights.

ARJ21-700新型涡扇支线飞机
ARJ21-700 new-type turbojet regional aircraft

H425型民用直升机
H425 civil helicopter

11. 大型环保装备
Large-sized equipment for environmental protection

研制出一批重大环保装备，其中有2006年开发成功的1000 MW电力机组配套电除尘器，除尘效率达到99.7%；大型电站机组AFGD型气动脱硫装置，脱硫率极高。

A group of key equipment for environmental protection was developed, including Electrostatic Precipitator with the collection efficiency being 99.7% which was developed as auxiliary equipment for 1000 MW electric power unit in 2006. Pneumatic desulfurizer (AFGD) for large-sized power plant units was of extremely high efficiency.

AFGD气动脱硫装置

AFGD pneumatic desulfurizer

12. 大型施工机械
Large-sized construction machinery

2005年上海隧道工程公司研制出具有完全自主知识产权的ϕ6.3m土压平衡盾构机、ϕ11.9m泥水平衡盾构机；同时北方重工沈重集团也研制成功双护盾硬岩掘进机、ϕ11.38m泥水平衡盾构机等全断面掘进机，从根本上扭转了过去由外国企业垄断的局面。

Shanghai Tunnel Engineering Co., Ltd. developed ϕ6.3 m earth pressure balance shield machine and ϕ11.9 m slurry pressure balance shield machine with fully proprietary intellectual property rights in 2005. At the same time, Shenyang Heavy Machinery Group Co., Ltd. developed full-section drifting machines like double guard shield hard rock drifting machines and ϕ11.38 m slurry pressure balance shield machine. Monopoly of foreign enterprises was totally changed.

青海 ϕ 5.93 m隧道岩石全断面掘进机

ϕ 5.93 m tunnel rock full-section drifting machines in Qinghai

"先行"号国产地铁土压平衡盾构机

"Pioneer" earth pressure shield machines domestically made for subway

QAY300全地面起重机

QAY300 all terrain crane

13. 高档数控机床
High-class numerical control machine tool

大连机床集团2006年自主开发成功用于航天航空制造业的九轴五联动车铣复合中心，桂林机床公司自主开发的五轴联动龙门铣床，上海机床公司2007年开发出纳米级精度微型磨床，齐重开发出的超重型曲轴加工机床等。

Dalian Machine Tool Group Corporation independently developed CHD25 9-axis with five position turning-milling machining center for aircraft and spacecraft manufacturing in 2006. Guilin Machine Tool Co., Ltd. developed planer-type milling machine with 5 axes in an independent ways. Shanghai Machine Tool Works Ltd. developed mini grinding machine with nano-precision in 2007. Qiqihar Heavy CNC Equipment Co., Ltd. developed extra-heavy crankshaft machine.

XK2316/3-5X五轴联动
龙门铣床

XK2316/3-5X planer-type
milling machine with 5 axes

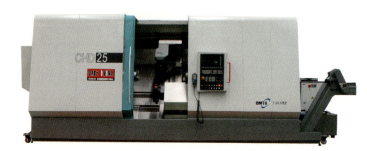

CHD25九轴五联动车
铣复合中心

CHD25 9-axis with five
position turning-milling
machining center

14. 新型纺织机械
New-type textile machinery

开发出一批对纺织行业结构调整有重大影响的成套装备。郑州纺织机械公司2006年开发的日产200t涤纶短纤维数字化成套设备，打破了过去完全进口的局面；经纬纺织机械公司的高效短流程清梳联成套设备，性能达国际先进水平；广东丰凯机械公司2007年开发了"超越"型剑杆织机，使中国织机在国际上占有了一席之地。

Complete sets of equipment, which were significant for structural adjustment of textile industry, were developed. Zhengzhou Textile Machinery Co., Ltd. developed complete sets of terylene staple fibre digital equipment with the capacity being 200 t/d in 2006, to break the structure of fully depending on import. The complete set of high-efficiency short-flow blowing-carding equipment of Jingwei Textile Machinery Co., Ltd. had internationally advanced performance. Guangdong FengKai machinery Manufacturing Co., Ltd. developed "Excellence" rapier loom in 2007, by which looms made by China found a place in the world market.

高效短流程清梳联成套设备

Complete set of high-efficiency short-flow blowing-carding equipment

日产200 t 涤纶短纤维数字化成套设备

Complete set of terylene staple fibre digital equipment with the capacity being 200 t/day

"超越"型剑杆织机

"Excellence" rapier loom

15. 新型大功率农业装备
New-style high-power agricultural equipment

一拖集团开发的288 hp大型轮式拖拉机已经批量生产，山东福田雷沃国际重工公司开发了265 hp、300 hp大型拖拉机；还有半喂入式水稻联合收割机、大型自走式玉米联合收割机等新型农业装备。

Large-sized 288 hp wheeled tractor developed by YTO Group was put into production at large scale. Foton Lovol International Heavy Industry Co., Ltd. developed 265 hp and 300 hp large-sized tractors. Other new-style agricultural equipment that was developed included half-feed rice combine and large-sized self-propelled corn combine, etc.

此外，还有上海振华港口机械公司的一次装卸两个40ft集装箱的岸边集装箱起重机等。

Furthermore, Shanghai Zhenhua Heavy Industry Co., Ltd. developed quayside container crane which could handle two 40 ft containers in one time.

东方红-1604/1804轮式拖拉机

YTO-1604/1804 wheeled tractor

福田雷沃谷神4YZ-4自走式玉米
联合收获机

Foton Lovol 4YZ-4 self-propelled corn
combine

4MZ-5型自走式采棉机

4MZ-5 self-propelled cotton picker

双40 ft集装箱岸边集装箱起重机

Quayside container crane handling two 40 ft containers

第五节 中国正由机械大国向机械强国奋进

Section 5 China Changing from a Country with Great Output of Machinery Industry to One with Advanced Mechanical Technologies

无论是从行业产销总量、技术水平，还是企业竞争力比较，21世纪以来，中国机械工业的地位和影响力迅速提升，在全球已居重要地位，逐步具备向机械强国进军的基础。

China's machinery industry keeps expanding its influence with a key role in the world in the 21st century, with respect to total production sales volume of the industry, technical level and competitive edge of enterprises. China gradually established the basis for becoming a country with advanced mechanical technologies.

(一)产销总量在全球的比重已达较高水平
Total production sales volume took a high proportion in the world

1949年，中国机械工业在世界机械工业总额中微不足道，只相当于美国的1/50左右；1989年提高到1/10左右，相当于日本的1/5、德国的1/2；2009年，从产销量看，已高于日本、美国和德国的水平，分别相当于其1.25倍、1.47倍和2.15倍。

The volume of China's machinery industry was of little influence in the global total volume in 1949, and only 1/50 of the volume of USA; It was up to 1/10 of the volume of USA, 1/5 of the volume of Japan and 1/2 of the volume of Germany in 1989. It exceeded the volumes of Japan, USA and Germany in 2009; it was equivalent to 1.25 times, 1.47 times and 2.15 times of the volume of above countries respectively.

1949—2009年中国和美国机械工业产值比较
Comparison of output value of machinery industry between China and USA from 1949 to 2009

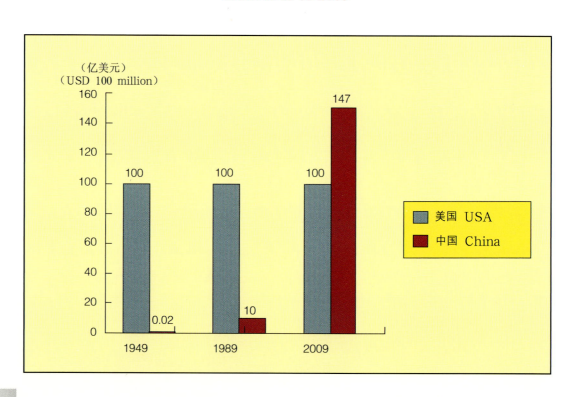

2009年中、日、美、德四国机械工业销售额
Sales volume of machinery industry of China, Japan, USA and Germany respectively in 2009

排名 Rank	国 家 Country	销售额(亿美元) Sales volume (USD 100 million)	比重(%) Proportion (%)	与中国比较(%) Comparison with China
	四国总计 Total of four countries	45140	100.00	
1	中国 China	15334	33.97	100.00
2	日本 Japan	12229	27.09	79.75
3	美国 USA	10453	23.16	68.17
4	德国 Germany	7124	15.78	46.46

注：①资料来源：根据机械工业信息中心收集的各国统计局公布数据加工。
　　②由于统计口径和汇率等原因，各项数据不尽可比，此表只能说明趋势，仅供读者参考。

Note: ① Source: based on data issued by statistics bureau of each country, collected by Machinery Industry Information Center.
② Not all the data were comparable, because of the scope of statistics and exchange rates. This tale can only show a tendency and is only for reference.

许多重要产品，从无到有，不少已居世界前列，对全球机械产品的发展作出重要贡献。以汽车、机床为例：

China has developed many important products, a lot of which are leading in the world. It made great contribution to the development of mechanical products in the world. Take automobiles and machine tools for example:

汽车。1956年中国开始生产汽车，1978年生产14.9万辆，为全球产量4230万辆的0.35%，居第18位；2008年生产930万辆，为全球产量7030万辆的13.22%，居第二位；2009年生产1370多万辆，为全球产量6300万辆的21.89%，居第一位。53年来，从无到世界第一位，走过了工业先进国家百多年的历程。

Automobile: China began to produce automobiles in 1956. It produced 149,000 automobiles in 1978, accounting for 0.35% of global production being 42.30 million automobiles, ranking the 18th. It produced 9.30 million automobiles in 2008, accounting for 13.22% of global production being 70.30 million automobiles, ranking the 2nd. It produced more than 13.70 million automobiles in 2009, accounting for 21.89% of global production being 63 million automobiles, ranking the 1st. It took only 53 years for China to go through the 100-year process of industrially developed countries, from nothing to No. 1.

世界与中国汽车产量增长情况(1978—2009年)
Growth of automobile production in China and the world (1978—2009)

（单位：万辆）

（Unit: 10,000 automobiles）

项　目 Item	1978	2000	2007	2008	2009	2009年比 1978年 2009, compared to 1978	2009年比 2000年 2009, compared to 2000
世界汽车产量 Global automobile production	4229.9	5759	7327	7030	6300		
中国汽车产量 China's automobile production	14.9	207	888	929.9	1379		
中国比重(%) China's proportion (%)	0.35	3.59	12.12	13.23	21.89		
中国汽车产量世界排名 Rank of China's automobile production in the world	18	8	3	2	1		
世界汽车比上年净增长量 Net growth of global automobile production, compared with last year		210	406	−297	−730	2070.1	541
中国汽车比上年净增长量 Net growth of China's automobile production, compared with last year		24	160	41.9	449.2	1364.2	1172
中国对世界汽车净增长量的贡献率(%) Rate of contribution by China to net growth of global automobile production (%)		11.43	39.40			65.90	216.64

世界与中国汽车产量增长情况(1978—2009年)

Growth of automobile production in China and the world (1978—2009)

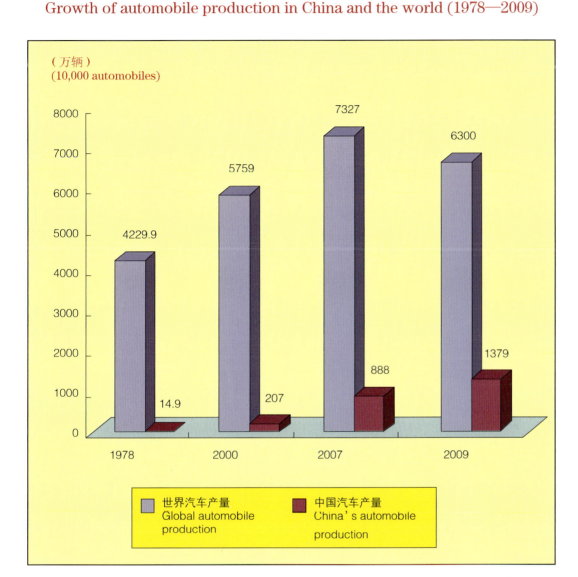

（万辆）
(10,000 automobiles)

机床(金切机床与成形机床)。1949年，中国生产了低档普通金切机床1600台，销售额很少；1987年，机床销售额4.61亿美元，为全球270.77亿美元的1.7%，居第12位；2009年生产金切机床58万台，机床销售额153亿美元，为全球554.90亿美元的27.57%，居第一位。

Machine tools (metal cutting machine tools and metal forming machine tools): China produced 1,600 low-class general metal cutting machine tools in 1949, very few of which were sold out. The sales volume of machine tool was USD 461 million in 1987, accounting for 1.7% of global volume being USD 27.077 billion, ranking the 12th. China produced 580,000 metal cutting machine tools in 2009, when the sales volume of machine tools was USD 15.3 billion, accounting for 27.57% of global volume being USD 55.49 billion, ranking the 1st.

世界与中国机床销售发展情况(1987—2009年)
Sales growth of machine tools in China and the world (1987—2009)

（亿美元）
(USD 100 million)

项目 Item	1987	1997	2007	2008	2009	1988— 2008	1988— 2009
世界机床销售额 Global sales volume of machine tools	270.77	387.00	708.58	816.00	554.9		
中国机床销售额 China's sales volume of machine tools	4.61	17.42	107.50	142.20	153.00		
中国比重(%) China's proportion (%)	1.70	4.50	15.20	17.43	27.57		
世界机床净增销售额 Net growth of global sales volume of machine tools				107.42	−261.1	284.13	545.23
中国机床净增额 Net growth of China's sales volume of machine tools				39.7	10.8	137.59	148.39
中国对世界机床净增销售额贡献率(%) Rate of contribution by China to net growth of global sales volume of machine tools (%)				32.30		25.23	52.23

1987年世界主要生产机床国家（地区）销售额
Sales volumes of major countries producing machine tools in 1987

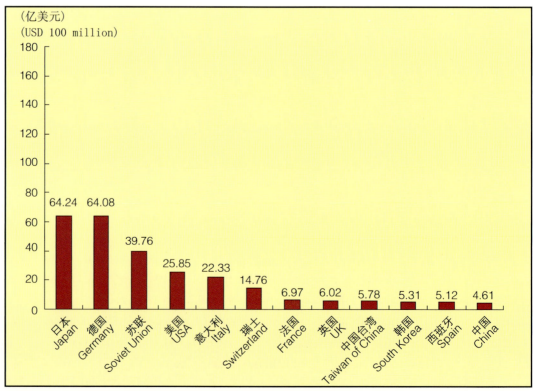

1997年世界主要生产机床国家(地区)销售额
Sales volumes of major countries (areas) producing machine tools in 1997

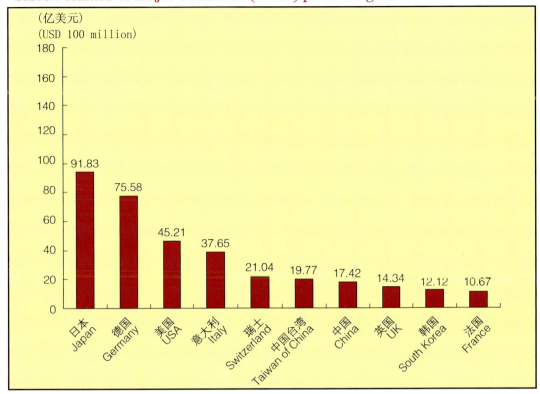

2009年世界主要生产机床国家(地区)销售额
Sales volumes of major countries (areas) producing machine tools in 2009

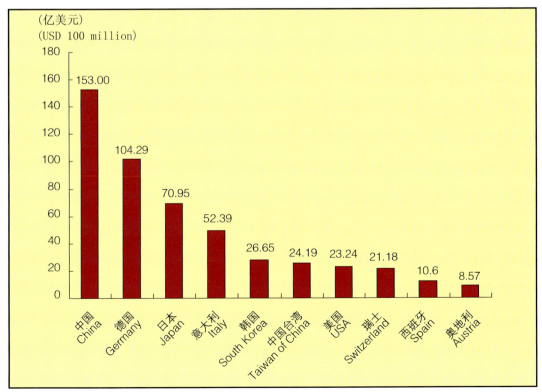

中国、日本、德国机床销售额比较
Comparison of machine tools sales volumes among China, Japan and Germany

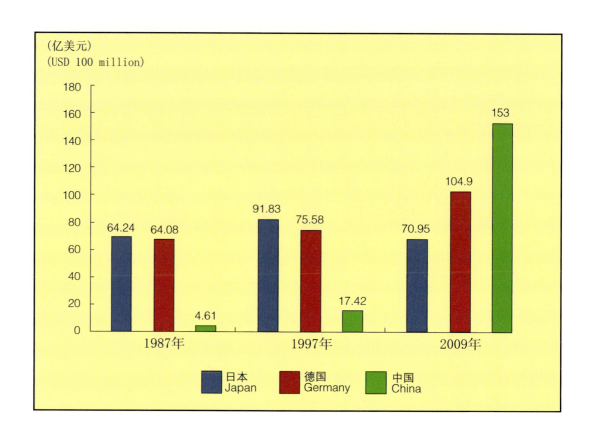

(二)中西机械工业产品技术水平差距缩小

Gap between China and western countries decreased in technologies of mechanical products

1949年，中西机械工业技术水平不在一个层次上，到20世纪60年代中期差距曾有所缩小，由于"文化大革命"的折腾，到70年代末期差距拉大到20年左右；21世纪以来，差距迅速缩小，一些重要行业、产品的差距已缩小到10年左右，中国个别的产品达到世界领先水平。

China's technologies of mechanical products were not at the same level as western countries in 1949. The gap thereof decreased in middle 1960s. However, it grew to a 20-year gap by late 1970s, due to the Cultural Revolution. It decreased swiftly in the 21st century, to a 10-year gap for some key industries and products. Some were even leading in the world.

318

21世纪初中国机械工业重大技术装备产品的技术水平
Technical level of products of key technical equipment in China's machinery industry in early 21st century

行　业 Industry	主要产品 Major products	技术水平 Technical level
重型机械 Heavy machinery	矿山设备(2200万t露天矿、1000万t井下煤矿) Mining equipment (22 million t open-pit mines and 10 million t downhole coal mines)	20世纪90年代国际水平 At the international level in the 1990s
	冶金轧制设备(冷、热连续板轧机) Rolling equipment for metallurgy (Cold continuous rolling mills and hot strip continuous rolling mills)	20世纪90年代国际水平 At the international level in the 1990s
	石化容器热壁加氢反应器 Hot wall hydrogenation reactor for petrochemical vessel	20世纪90年代国际水平 At the international level in the 1990s
	大型水、火电铸锻件 Large-sized casting and forging for thermal and hydroelectric power	20世纪90年代国际水平 At the international level in the 1990s
	工程机械(工程起重设备、混凝土泵车、盾构机) Construction machinery (Construction hoisting equipment, concrete pump, shield machine)	20世纪90年代国际水平 At the international level in the 1990s
发电设备 Power generating equipment	水电设备(三峡右岸700 MW机组) Hydroelectric equipment (700 MW unit for Three Gorges, on right bank)	国际先进水平 At the internationally advanced level
	火电设备(超超临界压力1000 MW火电机组) Thermal power equipment (1000 MW ultra-supercritical thermal power unit)	20世纪90年代国际水平 At the international level in the 1990s
	核电设备 Nuclear power equipment	20世纪90年代国际水平 At the international level in the 1990s
输变设备 Power transmission and distribution equipment	1000 kV特高压交流输变电设备 1000 kV extra-high voltage AC transmission and distribution equipment	国际先进水平 At the internationally advanced level
	±800 kV特高压直流输电设备 ±800 kV extra-high voltage DC transmission equipment	国际先进水平 At the internationally advanced level
机床 Machine tools	大型锻压机械设备 Large-sized forging and pressing machinery	20世纪90年代国际水平 At the international level in the 1990s
	数控机床 Numerical control machine tools	20世纪90年代国际水平 At the international level in the 1990s

（续表）

行　业 Industry	主要产品 Major products	技术水平 Technical level
石油及石化设备 Oil and petrochemical equipment	石油钻机(12000 m石油钻机) Oil rig (12000 m oil rig) 石化专用设备、压缩机、空分设备 Special petrochemical equipment, compressor and air separation equipment	20世纪90年代国际水平 At the international level in the 1990s 20世纪90年代国际水平 At the international level in the 1990s
机车车辆 Rolling stock	机车、客车、货车 Locomotive, passenger vehicle and freight vehicle 动车组(350 km/h) EMU (350 km/h)	20世纪90年代国际水平 At the international level in the 1990s 国际先进水平 At the internationally advanced level
船舶 Vessels	远洋船舶 Ocean vessels 海洋工程装备 Oceaneering equipment	20世纪90年代国际水平 At the international level in the 1990s 20世纪90年代国际水平 At the international level in the 1990s
航空 Aviation	"歼-10"、"歼-11"战机 J-10 and J-11 fighters 航空发动机 Aero-engine	20世纪90年代国际水平 At the international level in the 1990s 20世纪90年代国际水平 At the international level in the 1990s
兵器 Weapons	99式坦克 "99-type" tank	国际水平 At the international level

注：多数为引进消化国外先进技术。在具备自主知识产权的基础上，整合国际资源研制完成，产品技术水平未经正式评估，仅供读者参考。

Note: Most of the advanced technologies are introduced from abroad. With the intellectual property, China has further absorbed and improved these technologies by integrating international resources. Information above was not formally evaluated and only for reference.

（三）机械工业大公司开始进入"世界500强"
Large-sized machinery enterprises entered into "Global 500"

2004年，美国《财富》杂志公布的世界500强公司榜单中，中国"一汽集团"赫然在目。这是中国机械工业企业首家进入全球500强的大公司，是一个重要的进步。2005年，"上汽集团"又进入了世界500强。2009年，中国航空工业集团(中航工业)和中国南方工业集团也进入了500强。透过这个新榜单，人们可以得到一个新的信息，20世纪中国机械工业还没有一家企业上榜，方进入21世纪先后有4家进入，说明中国机械工业企业竞争力不断增强。人们期望中国机械工业更多行业的企业进入500强。

FAW (China) was listed among Global 500 issued by *Fortune* (an American magazine) in 2004. It was China's first machinery enterprise that was listed among Global 500, which was an important achievement. SAIC Group was listed among Global 500 in 2005. China Aviation Industry Corporation (AVIC) and China South Industries Group Corporation were listed among Global 500 in 2009. This new list revealed new information: the competitive edge of China's machinery enterprises grew swiftly; not one of China's machinery enterprises was among Global 500 in the 20th century, but 4 were listed at the beginning of the 21st century one after another. People wish more China's machinery enterprises can be listed.

入选《财富》世界500强中国机械工业公司名单
China's machinery companies listed among Global 500 by *Fortune*

排序 S/N	2007			2008			2009			主要业务 Principal businesses
	公司名称 Company Name	500强排名 Rank in Global 500	营业收入（亿美元）Operation revenue (USD 100 million)	公司名称 Company Name	500强排名 Rank in Global 500	营业收入（亿美元）Operation revenue (USD 100 million)	公司名称 Company Name	500强排名 Rank in Global 500	营业收入（亿美元）Operation revenue (USD 100 million)	
1	一汽集团 FAW Group	385	187.11	一汽集团 FAW Group	303	263.9	上汽集团 SAIC Group	359	248.82	汽车 Automobiles
2	上汽集团 SAIC Group	402	180.10	上汽集团 SAIC Group	373	226.07	一汽集团 FAW Group	385	236.64	汽车 Automobiles
3							中国航空工业集团 AVIC	426	217.38	航空航天 Aviation & space flight
4							中国南方工业集团 China South Industries Group Corporation	428	216.75	多样化 Diversified

第六节 存在的问题
Section Six　Problems

改革开放特别是进入21世纪以来，中国机械工业持续快速发展，总量规模已居世界前列，基本上可以满足国内经济建设发展需要。但总体上，与工业发达国家相比差距仍较大，特别是缺乏创新、自主开发能力弱。技术含量高、附加价值高的重大装备，无论是三峡700MW水轮发电机组、还是1000MW超超临界火电机组、大型石化成套设备、大型冶金轧制设备，多是直接引进专利软件，或是合作生产；精密测试仪器和关键零部件的技术水平较低；产业基础技术薄弱，基础制造设备、基础材料、基础元器件、自动化仪表、标准体系等发展滞后，制约机械工业的发展。总体来看，中国机械工业进步很快，但在国际竞争中仍然处于弱势地位，与发达国家相比仍存在着阶段性差距。

Since the reform and opening up especially since entering 21st century, the machinery industry in China continuously develops in rapid way, and with its total size ranking top in the world, it could basically meet the requirement of domestic economic development. However, on the whole, it still lags behind industrially developed countries, especially that it has poor innovation and independent developing capability. Major equipments with advanced technology and high additional value, be it 700MW hydro power generating units in The Three Gorges, 1000MW ultra supercritical thermal power generating units, large size complete sets of petrochemical equipment, or metallurgy and rolling equipment, are all made by introducing foreign patent softwares or from cooperative production; The fine measuring equipment and key components and parts technology is low-level; The industrial basic technology is poor; and the development of basic manufacturing equipment, basic materials, basic elements and components, automatic instrument and standard system lags behind, which constrains the development of machinery industry. Overall, the machinery industry in China progresses quickly, yet is still in the weak position in international competition and has phased gap with developed countries.

第一章 机床与工具
Chapter 1 Machine Tools & Tools

　　金属加工机床是机械工业的"工作母机"，是国际公认的基础装备。受到党和国家领导的特别关怀与重视。"一五"时期，第一机械工业部按中央要求在中南海举办了汇报性的机械产品展览，毛泽东主席反复看了6次，刘少奇、邓小平等也观看了这次展览；按毛泽东的指示在中南海瀛台再次举办机床展览，1960年4月4日，他又用了3个小时观看机床的操作演示。中国机床工具工业一直在党和国家领导人的关爱中不断发展壮大。

As basic equipment internationally recognized, metal working machine tools are the foundation of machinery industry and are especially valued by the Communist Party of China (CPC) and Chinese leaders. During the first 5-year Plan period, the First Ministry of Machinery industry held an exhibition of mechanical products in Zhongnanhai for reporting purpose, as required by the Central Government. Mao Zedong visited the exhibition for 6 times and Liu Shaoqi and Deng Xiaoping also paid visits. Another machine tool exhibition was held at Yingtai, Zhongnanhai, as directed by Mao Zedong who watched operation of machine tools for 3 hours on April 4, 1960. Supported by the CPC and Chinese leaders, the machine tools & tools industry of China keeps developing.

　　新中国成立初期，只有上海、沈阳、昆明等城市一些机械修配厂兼产少量皮带车床、刨床、冲床等普通机床，1952年约有30来个品种。2009年，中国机床工业以153亿美元产值居世界首位，占世界产值的27.6%。中国已成为机床工具制造大国。

In the early days of the P.R.C., only some machine repair workshops in cities like Shanghai, Kunming and Shenyang produced a few ordinary machine tools including belt-driven lathes, planers and punches, which were of 30 categories in 1952. China's machine tool industry ranked the 1st in the world in 2009, by its output value worth USD 15.3 billion accounting for 27.6% of the global output value. China became a giant manufacturing power for machine tools & tools.

　　国家一直把机床工业作为重点发展对象。1960年，为应对西方工业国家和苏联对中国发展航天航空工业设置障碍，国家计委、科委、一机部等部门成立了精密机床6人领导小组，对精密机床的发展进行统一指挥，到1965年，发展了精密机床5大类26种，有的产品达到比较先进水平，满足了国防尖端产品发展的需要；为提供第二汽车厂的冷加工成套设备，采取"聚宝"的形式，集中了机械工业的先进工艺，从1966年开始，组织了138个机床科研和生产单位共同承担这项任务，1971—1975年，共提供了较高水平的机床7664台，第二汽车厂的机床设备国产化率按台计达到98%，按金额计达到80%。数控机床是当代机械制造业的主流设备，国家从20世纪80年代开始，多次组织专项支持其发展，2006年2月颁布的《国务院关于加快振兴装备制造业的若干意见》，把"发展大型、精密、高速数控装备和数控系统及功能部件"作为对国家经济安全和国防建设有重要影响的重大技术装备和产品，加大政策支持力度。

Machine tool industry has always been considered a primary aspect of development by the state. To break the obstructs set by western industrial countries and the Soviet Union for the development of China's aircraft and spacecraft industries, a leading group for precision machine tools, which consisted of 6 members, was organized by departments including the State Planning Commission (SPC), the State Scientific and Technological Commission and the First Ministry of Machine-building Industry, to carry out united command for development of precision machine tools. Five major categories of precision machine tools, consisting of 26 kinds, had been developed by 1965, some of which reached relatively advanced level, meeting requirements for developing highly sophisticated products for national defense. To provide turnkey equipment for cold working for The Second Automobile Works, advanced workmanships in the machinery industry were gathered together to accomplish this task by organizing 138 units dealing with scientific research and production of machine tools as from 1966. Totally 7664 machine tools at high level were provided from 1971 to 1975. The import substitution rate of machine tools of The Second Automobile Works reached 98% by the number of units and 80% by value. CNC machine tools are the major type of equipment for modern machinery industry. The government organized several special programs to support the development of CNC machine tools as from 1980s. The State Council issued *Several Opinions on Prosper Equipment-building Industry* in Feb. 2006. According to the *Opinions,* "large-sized, precision and high-speed CNC equipment, systems and functional parts" were defined as significant technical equipment and products that had great influence on national economic security and defense construction, for which greater policy-based support was provided.

21世纪以来，中国机床行业年开发自主产权新产品达400多种，至2008年年底，全国更新后的金属切削机床品种，总计近3500种，其中数控机床及其他高新技术产品达1500种，基本上已无重要缺门空白，这在全球范围也是位居前列的。

In the 21st century, over 400 types of new products with proprietary intellectual property rights have been developed in China's machine tool industry every year. There were nearly 3500 categories of updated metal cutting machine tools in total by the end of 2008, among which, 1500 categories were CNC machine tools and other hi-tech products; there were generally no gap in significant products. This is among the best in the world.

锻压设备。济南第二机床厂的成系列机械压力机一直处于国际先进行列，压力吨位由20000 kN至63000 kN，居于国际前沿；上海锻压机床厂的压制12 m汽车大梁、压力吨位50000 kN的液压机，世界处于同一水平的只有德、日等国。

Forging and Pressing equipment: series of mechanical presses made by Jier Machine-tool Works are at worldwide advanced level, with the press tonnage ranging from 20000 kN to 63000 kN. In the whole world, only Germany and Japan are at the same level as that of the 12 m pressed car frames and 50000 kN hydraulic presses made by Shanghai Forging and Pressing Machine Works.

数控机床。中国在20世纪60年代即开始研制，起步并不晚，由于整个工业综合水平所限，成长较慢，1980年才逐步形成产业，但高档数控机床主要依靠进口，五轴联动等高技能产品长期被西方国家当成战略物资禁运。1999年，江苏多梭机床公司率先研制首台国产高速五轴联动数控龙门铣床，这些仍受到禁运的数控五轴联动产品技术，中国均已陆续掌控。2001年中国第七届国际机床展览会上展出5种此类产品，2009年第十一届展会上，中国已展出此类机床40种以上。21世纪以来，在国家大力支持下，高档数控机床得到迅速发展，近年来研制出一大批多坐标、复合、智能、高精、高效的新产品，用于加工神舟系列太空船、航天运载火箭的零部件，用于加工飞机发动机、汽轮机等的精密叶片，用于加工舰艇和重型远洋船推进器和曲轴……特别是2007年以来，一批世界水平的首台首套产品，如工作台宽11m的数控龙门镗铣床，加工直径16 m、20 m、22 m的超重型数控立式车床，ϕ5 m×20 m加工件重500 t的超重型卧式车床，ϕ5 m×14.5m加工250t的大型船用柴油机曲轴的旋风切削加工中心，ϕ320 mm超重型落地镗床、ϕ2.5 m×15m超重型轧辊磨床、11m超重型龙门机床的研制，新产品开发成果显著。数控机床的技术进步取得明显成效，机床复合技术进一步扩展，复合加工技术日趋成熟，"一台机床就是一个加工厂"、"一次装卡，完全加工"等理念正在被更多应用。智能化技术有了新的突破，如加工零件检测和自动补偿学习功能，高精度加工零件智能化参数选用功能等已经实用化。精密加工技术不断进展，数控金切机床的加工精度已从原来的丝级（0.01 mm)提升到2009年微米级(0.001 mm)，有些品种已达到0.05 μm左右，超精密数控机床的微细切削和磨削加工，精度可稳定到0.05 μm左右，形状精度可达0.01 μm左右；采用光、电、化学等能源的特种加工精度可达到纳米级（0.001 μm)，从而进入亚微米、纳米级超精加工时代。数控机床整体水平全面提升，数控系统和功能部件的攻关也取得进展。金切机床按产值计算的数控化率2005年47.3%，2008年48.6%，2009年52.0%；2008年按价值计算的国产数控机床市场占有率达48%。

CNC machine tools: the research of CNC machine tools began in China as early as in the 1960s. The CNC machine tool industry was not formed until 1980 due to slow growth restricted by the overall industrial level, where high-class CNC machine tools depended on import and hi-tech products like five-axis machine tools were considered as strategic goods under an embargo by western countries for a long time. Jiangsu Duosuo Machine-tool Company developed the first domestically made high-speed five-axis CNC planer-type milling machine in 1999. China was technically capable of manufacturing these 5-axis CNC products that were still under an embargo. Five types of such products were displayed by China at the 7th China International Machine Tool Show (CIMTS) in 2001, and over 40 types of such machine tools were displayed by China at the 11th CIMTS in 2009. Strongly supported by the government, high-end CNC machine tools developed swiftly in the 21st century. A lot of new products were developed in recent years, which were multi-coordinate, compound, intelligent, high-precision and highly effective. For example, parts and components for Shenzhou Spacecrafts and launch vehicles, precision blades for aeroengines and steam turbines, and propellers and crank shafts for naval vessels and heavy-duty ocean going ships, etc. Especially, a group of products at worldwide top level have been developed since 2007, such as the first CNC gantry type boring and milling machine with 11m-wide workbench, extra heavy-duty CNC vertical lathes with the machining diameter being 16 m, 20 m or 22 m, the first extra heavy-duty horizontal lathe (φ5 m×20 m) with workpiece weight being 500 t, the first thread whirling center (φ5 m×14.5 m) for machining 250 t crankshafts for large-sized marine diesels, the first extra heavy-duty floor type boring machine (φ320 mm), the first extra heavy-duty roll grinder (φ2.5 m×15 m) and the first extra heavy-duty 11m gantry machine. Great achievements were made in developing new products, remarkable technical progress was made for CNC machine tools, the technology of combined machine tools developed further and combined machining technology improved gradually. The ideas like "one machine tool means one working plant" and "complete machining with one setup" are applied more and more. New breakthroughs were made with intelligent technology, such as the functions of detecting and automatic compensating learning of machining parts, and the function of intelligent parameter selection for high-precision working parts. Precision working technology developed continuously. The machining precision of CNC metal cutting machine tools was upgraded from 0.01 mm to 0.001 mm in 2009; for some types, the precision was 0.05μm. The precision of micro cutting and grinding with ultra precision CNC machine tools can be as stable as 0.05μm, and the shape accuracy can be 0.01μm. The precision of special machining such as optical, electric and chemical energy can be nano-precision (0.001μm), which marked the start of superfinishing at submicron and nano-precision. The overall level of CNC machine tools improved, with some breakthroughs in terms of CNC systems and functional units. By output value, about 47.3% of metal cutting machine tools were CNC products in 2005; about 48.6% of metal cutting machine tools were CNC products in 2008; about 52.0% of metal cutting machine tools were CNC products in 2008. By value, about and the market share of domestically made CNC machine tools was 48% in 2008.

1950年9月，上海虬江机器厂
（上海机床厂前身）制造的
"虬13式万能工具磨床"

Qiu 13 type universal tool grinder made by Shanghai Qiujiang Machinery Plant (the former Shanghai Machine-tool Plant) in September of 1950

1986年，北京机床研究所研制的超精密轴系和JCS-027超精密车床，获国家科技进步一等奖

The ultra precision shaft type parts and JCS-027 ultra precision lathe, developed by the Beijing Machine-tool Research Institute, were awarded with the First Class National Prize for the Advancement of Sciences and Technology in 1986.

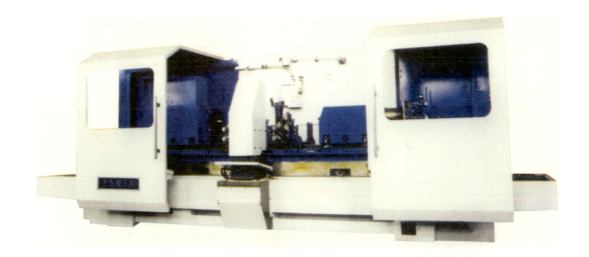

上海机床厂有限公司是制造磨床的重点骨干企业，图为20世纪80年代该公司生产的具有当代国际先进水平的H236数控曲轴主轴颈磨床

Shanghai Machine Tool Works Ltd. is a key backbone enterprise in the production of grinding machines. The photo shows model H236 CNC crankshaft journal pin grinding machine, which was designed and manufactured by this company in 1980s and reached the international advanced level.

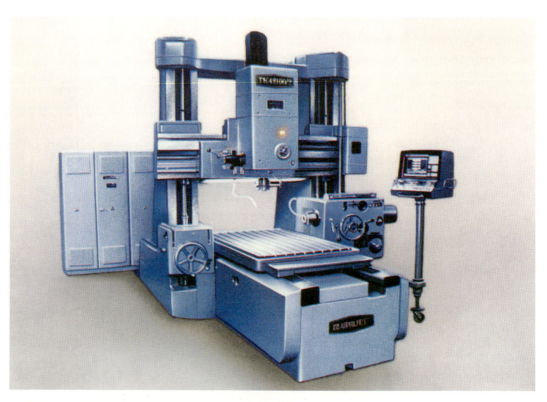

昆明机床股份有限公司（昆明机床厂）20世纪80年代研发的TK42100/2大型数控双柱坐标镗床

Model TK42100/2 large NC double-column jig boring machine developed by Kunming Machine Tool Company Limited (Kunming Machine Tool Plant) in 1980s.

北京第一机床厂为太原重型机器厂制造的5 m×20 m数控天桥铣

5 m× 20 m CNC gantry milling machine made by Beijing No. 1 Machine Tool Works for Taiyuan Heavy Machinery Works

秦川机床厂研制的可程序控制自动磨削高精度Y7032A碟形砂轮磨齿机，获国家科技进步一等奖

The photo shows model Y7032A high-precision programmable and automatic gear grinding machine with dish-shaped grinding wheel, which is made by Qinchuan Machine Tool Works and was awarded with the First Class National Prize for the Advancement of Sciences and Technology.

武汉重型机床厂是制造重型、数控机床和超重型机床的骨干企业，可为用户提供立式车床、卧式车床、龙门刨床、激光加工机床、齿轮加工机床、镗床、铣镗床、龙门镗铣床、专用机床等，图为该厂生产的CKX53I60数控单柱立式铣车床

Wuhan Heavy Machine Tool Works is a key backbone enterprise specialized in production of heavy duty, extra heavy-duty NC machine tools. It can provide customers with vertical lathes, horizontal lathes, gantry type planers, laser cutting machines, gear-cutting machines, boring machines, boring mills, gantry type boring and milling machines, special purpose machines tools, etc. The photo shows model CKX53I60 CNC single-column vertical milling and turning machine manufactured by it.

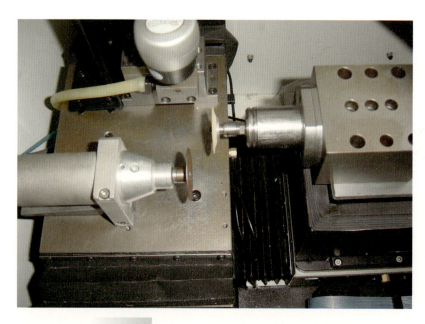

2007年上海机床公司成功开发出的纳米级精度微型磨床。砂轮主轴转速：60000 rpm，重复定位精度：X、Y轴50 nm，Z轴100 nm

The micro grinding machine at nano-precision developed by Shanghai Machine Tool Works Ltd. in 2007. Grinding wheel spindle speed: 60000 rpm; repeatability positioning accuracy: 50 nm for X and Y axes, and 100 nm for Z axis.

上海机床厂有限公司制造的PMM12106三坐标测量机

Model PMM12106 three-coordinate measuring machine made by Shanghai Machine Tool Co., Ltd.

成都工具研究所研制的CSZ500A型锥齿轮测量仪

Model CSZ500A bevel gear testing machine developed by Chengdu Tool Research Institute

昆明机床股份有限公司制造的为我国长度基准奠定基础的光电光波比长仪

Photo-electric and optical wave length comparator, made by Kunming Machine Tool Co., Ltd. has formed the basis of the length reference in China.

齐重数控装备有限公司2007年自行研制开发的数控重型曲轴旋风切削加工中心，这台机床长32.25 m、宽12.6 m、最高6.9 m，重达400 t，可加工万吨巨轮的柴油机重260 t、长14.5 m的大型曲轴

CNC heavy-duty thread whirling center for machining crankshafts independently developed by Qiqihar Heavy CNC Equipment Co., Ltd. This machine tool is 32.25 m long, 12.6 m wide, 6.9 m high at most and weighing 400 t. It can be used to machine 14.5 m-long 260 t large-sized crankshafts of diesels for 10,000-ton ships.

武汉重型机床厂自主研制的DL250多功能重型卧式镗车床，具有13个数控轴，最大工件回转直径5 m，最大加工长度20 m，是当前世界承重量最大的车床，可达500 t

DL250 multipurpose heavy-duty horizontal boring mill independently developed by Wuhan Heavy Machine Tool Works. It has 13 NC axes the maximum swing diameter of work is 5 m and the maximum machining length is 20 m. It is the machine tool with the largest loading in the world at present, which is 500 t.

2008年，上海机床厂自行研制开发的大型数控曲轴磨床，主要用于大型动力机械的曲轴主
轴颈及连杆颈加工

The large-sized CNC crankshaft grinding machine independently developed by Shanghai Machine Tool Co., Ltd. in 2008. It is mainly used to process journal pins and rod journals of crankshafts of large-sized power machines.

齐齐哈尔第二机床厂"十一五"期间自行研制开发的大型龙门式五轴混联机床

Large-sized five-axis hybrid gantry type machine tool independently developed by Qiqihar No.2 Machine Tool Works in the 11th 5-year Plan period.

北京第一机床厂2007年自主研发的XKAU2750五轴联动双龙门移动镗铣床，工作台5000 mm×22000 mm。主要用于水轮机叶片曲面的加工

XKAU2750 five-axis double gantries moving milling machine independently developed by Beijing No. 1 Machine Tool Works in 2007. The workbench is 5000 mm × 22000 mm. It is mainly used to process turbine blade surface.

北京机电院高技术公司2004年研制的立式五轴叶片加工中心

The vertical five-axis blade machining center developed by BMEI Co., Ltd. in 2004.

沈阳机床集团2001年研制的上海磁悬浮轨道梁加工生产线

Machining & production line of track beams developed by Shenyang Machine Tool (Group) Co., Ltd. in 2001, for Shanghai magnetically levitated train.

沈阳机床集团2007年推出的GMC2060u桥式龙门五轴加工中心，是航空、航天、模具等行业的关键加工设备

GMC2060u bridge type gantry five-axis machining center developed by Shenyang Machine Tool (Group) Co., Ltd. in 2007, which is a key machining equipment for aviation industry, space flight industry and die & mould industry, etc.

沈阳机床集团生产的面向船舶发动机，集车、铣、钻、镗、攻丝等功能于一身的 HTMI25600 复合车铣五轴加工中心

HTMI25600 5-axis multiturn center for turning, milling, drilling, boring and tapping, developed by Shenyang Machine Tool (Group) Co., Ltd. for marine engines.

大连机床集团"十一五"期间研制的中国首条矩形柔性加工自动线

China's first rectangular flexible transfer line developed by Dalian Machine Tool Group Corporation during the 11th 5-year Plan period.

齐齐哈尔第一机床厂"十一五"期间研制的数控DVT500X25-NC型数控双柱重型立式车床

DVT500X25-NC heavy-duty double-column vertical lathe, developed by Qiqihar No.1 Machine Tool Works in the 11th 5-year Plan period.

济南二机床集团XH2720A五轴联动定梁双龙门移动数控镗铣床

XH2720A CNC 5-axis double gantries moving milling machine with fixed crossrail, made by Jier Machine-tool Group Co., Ltd.

济南二机床集团XHSV2525X60高
架式五轴联动高速镗铣加工中心

XHSV2525X60 over-headed 5-axis high-
speed milling/machining center, made by
Jier Machine-tool Group Co., Ltd.

济南二机床集团为泰国萨密特公司提供的由1台S4-800B型、3台S4-500B型闭式四点单动
压力机组成的大型冲压生产线

The large-sized forging and pressing production line consisting of one set of model S4-800B straight-sided four-
point single action mechanical press and three sets of model S4-500B straight-sided four-point single action
mechanical presses, provided by Jier Machine-tool Group Co., Ltd. for Summit Company (Thailand).

武汉重型机床集团2007年完成的16 m数控立式铣车床

16 m CNC vertical milling machine completed by Wuhan Heavy Duty Machine Tool Group Corporation in 2007

武汉重型机床集团2007年完成的CKX5680七轴五联动车铣复合加工机床，最大加工直径8 m，高度2 m，加工件重量100 t，工作台直径ϕ7200 mm，是中国船舶工业加工远洋巨轮超重型船用螺旋桨的关键设备，打破国外技术封锁

CKX5680 7-axis with five position milling lathe completed by Wuhan Heavy Duty Machine Tool Group Corporation in 2007. The maximum machining diameter is 8 m, the height is 2 m, the workpiece weight is 100 t and the workbench diameter is ϕ7200 mm. Breaking overseas technical blockades, it is the key equipment used in China's ship-building industry to process extra heavy-duty marine propellers for large ocean vessels.

哈量集团凯狮公司生产的HSK刀柄

HSK tool holders produced by Kelch, a subsidiary of HMCT Group

第二章 机械基础零部件
Chapter 2 Basic Components for Machinery

机械基础件是机械工业关键的配套零部件。包括：轴承、模具、液压件、气动件、密封件，机械通用零部件等。

As critical ancillary components for machinery industry, basic components for machinery include bearings, molds, hydraulic and pneumatic components, sealings and universal parts for machinery, etc.

新中国成立初期只能少量生产低档标准件和球轴承。液压件、齿轮、模具等都是以后各时期逐步发展起来的。

In the early days of the P.R.C., China could only produce a few low-end standard components and ball bearings. Hydraulic components, gears and molds were developed later gradually.

轴承。至2008年，已能生产6.6万多个品种规格的轴承，覆盖了当前世界上滚动轴承的各种类型。已开发生产最小内径ϕ0.207 mm 、最轻0.017 kg的微型轴承，最大外径ϕ6.07 m 、最重16.87t的特大型轴承，套圈壁厚0.275 mm的薄壁柔性轴承，速度参数d_mn值达2.5×10^6 mm·r/min的高速轴承，以及高温（300 ℃）、超低温、防磁、耐腐蚀、防辐射、高真空和低噪音等特殊工况用轴承。为主机发展配套取得重大突破，没有受制于人，如中国航天航空和军事装备所用的轴承100%立足国内。各类飞行器的全套轴承，从发动机主轴轴承到起落架轴承、微型陀螺仪表轴承；从"99式"主战坦克开始到现在国产各种型号战车的全部配套轴承；全部国产军用舰船配套轴承；各种型号鱼雷配套的轴承；核反应堆用的原子能工业全部配套轴承；神舟系列飞船轴承；飞船导航及姿态控制系统轴承、CCD高精度照相机轴承、生命保障系统轴承、飞船返回舱、逃逸舱等有关部位用轴承及其运载火箭、发射装置和测控系统装置用的轴承等，都是中国自行研制供应。还为国民经济的发展发挥了不可替代的作用，如海上油田用的外径4.3 m、重9.503t的重大型轴承；时速140 km的提速铁路货车轴承和时速160—200 km的准高速铁路客车和机车轴承；北京世纪坛3000 t重的旋转体用组合轴承等，都是国内轴承行业经过艰苦攻关、设计、研究制造供应的。

Bearings: 66,000 types of bearings can be produced by 2008, including all the types of rolling bearings in the world at present. Some types of bearings developed and produced include micro bearings with the minimum inner diameter being $\varphi0.207$ mm and the minimum weight being 0.017 kg, oversize bearings with the maximum outer diameter being $\varphi56.07$ m and the maximum weight being 16.87 t, thin-wall flexible bearings with the ring thickness being 0.275 mm, high-speed bearings with the speed parameter (dmN) being

洛阳轴承公司为国家重点专项攻关项目（国家"863"计划）研制生产的中国首套机床主轴用高精度特大型轴承

China's first oversize high-precision bearing, developed by Luoyang Bearing Group Co., Ltd. for national key special technical programs ("863" Program)

2.5×106 mm·r/min, and bearings for special work conditions like high temperature (300 ℃), ultralow temperature, antimagnetism, anticorrosion, radiation protection, high vacuum and low noise. Great breakthroughs were made to support the development of principal machines. For example, 100% of bearings for China's aviation, spaceflight and military equipment were domestically supplied. China developed and supplied independently some types of bearings: whole sets of bearings for various aerocrafts, from engine spindle bearing to undercarriage bearing and micro gyro bearing; whole sets of ancillary bearings for "99-type" main battle tanks to various models of tanks domestically made; ancillary bearings for all the navy ships domestically made, bearings for various models of torpedos; all the ancillary bearings for nuclear reactors; bearings for Shenzhou Spacecrafts; bearings for navigation and attitude control systems for spacecrafts, for CCD high-precision cameras, for life support system, for parts of spacecrafts like re-entry module and escape module, and for launch vehicle, launcher and TT&C system. Bearings played an irreplaceable role in the development of national economy. China's bearing industry designed, developed and supplied significant bearings with the outer diameter being 4.3 m and the weight being 9.503 t for offshore oil fields, bearings for freight trains for speed-up railway at 140 km/h and bearings for freight trains and rolling stocks for sub-high speed railway; 3000 t combined bearing for rotating body of Millennium Monument in Beijing.

洛阳轴承公司生产的重量最重（16.87 t）、直径最大（φ6.07 m）的转盘轴承，填补国内空白，达到世界先进水平

The slewing bearing with the maximum weight being 16.87 t and the maximum diameter being φ6.07 m, produced by Luoyang Bearing Group Co., Ltd. This bearing is the first of its kind domestically made at worldwide top level.

瓦房店轴承公司制造的重大装备轴承

The bearings for key equipment made by Wafangdian Bearing Group Co., Ltd.

瓦房店轴承公司制造的特大精密转盘轴承

The oversize precision slewing bearing made by Wafangdian Bearing Group Co., Ltd.

哈尔滨轴承集团
的精良产品

High-quality products
made by Harbin
Bearing Group Co.

液压技术。20世纪50年代从机床行业生产仿苏的磨床、拉床、仿形车床等液压传动装置起步到20世纪60年代，液压技术的应用从机床逐渐推广到农业机械和工程机械等领域；由机床厂液压车间生产，逐步发展了一些液压件专业厂。20世纪80年代形成了一个独立的行业。改革开放以来，已成功装备了各种重点型号的军用飞机、海军舰船、主战坦克和装甲运兵车、航天领域的宇宙飞船等重大装备。中国虽已成为流体动力传动装置大国，但国内企业主要生产中低端产品，高端产品仍需大量进口，与先进国家仍有较大差距。

Hydraulic technology: in the 1950s, China began to produce hydraulic transmission devices for copying models of the Soviet Union like grinding machine, broaching machine and copying lathe. In the 1960s, application of hydraulic technology gradually expanded from machine tools to agricultural and construction machinery. The hydraulic technology developed from production in hydraulic workshops of machine tools works to some special hydraulic parts manufacturers. A separate industry was formed in the 1980s. After the start of reform and opening-up, various types of key equipment like military aircrafts, naval vessels, main battle tanks, armed personnel carriers and spacecrafts were equipped with hydraulic parts made by China itself. Though China is now a big power by manufacturing hydrodynamic power transmission devices, most of domestic enterprises produce middle and low-end products, and high-end products rely on import largely, which shows a great gap between China and the developed Countries.

北京华德液压集团研制的鞍钢1450 mm厚板液压系统

1450 mm thick plate hydraulic system developed by Beijing Huade Hydraulic Industrial Group Co., Ltd. for Angang Steel Company Limited.

北京华德液压集团研制的承钢1780热轧阀组

1780 thick hot-rolled valve group developed by Beijing Huade Hydraulic Industrial Group Co., Ltd. for Chengde Iron & Steel Group Co., Ltd.

模具。1953年第一汽车制造厂率先建立了冲模车间，1955年中国出现了第一个专业模具厂——天津电讯模具厂。模具制造发展很快，2008年生产企业已达3万多家，销售额达950亿元。产品水平从过去的只能生产简单（单工序、单型腔、单一材质、简单结构）模具发展到已能生产大型（最大模具单套重量达100t）、精密（精密度可达1μm）、复杂（多工序、多工位、多型腔、多材质、复杂结构）、长寿命（多工位级进模最长寿命可达3亿次）的模具。至2008年中国已能生产中档轿车的全部模具和高档轿车的部分模具，精度0.001mm、寿命3亿冲次以上的精密多工位级进，重达70t的大型塑料模具，60t的大型冲压模具和100t的工程轮胎橡胶模具，8注射头7800腔的精密塑封模具和精度达0.01mm、寿命100万模次以上内镶式滴灌管滴头热流道精密塑料模具及多腔精密小模数塑料齿轮模具，全钢子午线橡胶轮胎活络模等。2008年，中国模具产值已至1600亿元，约占世界模具总额的19%。除满足国内需要外，2008年出口模具已由20世纪80年代以前不足销售总额的1%，发展到15%以上。

Die & Mold: FAW established the first die workshop in China in 1953. Tianjin Telecommunication Dies Works, the first specialized die works in China, was founded in 1955. The die-making industry developed quickly. There were over 30,000 die & mold manufacturers in 2008, with the sales being RMB 95 billion. Types of products developed from simple molds (with single procedure, single cavity, single material and simple structure) to large-sized (the maximum weight of a single set of molds is 100 t), precision (to 1μm), complicated (multi-procedure, multi-position, multi-cavity, multi-material and complex structure) and long-life (the longest life of multi-position progressive die is 300 million times) molds. Products that China could produce by the year 2008 include all the dies for middle-end sedans and partial dies for high-end sedans, multi-position progressive dies with the precision being 0.001 mm and the life being above 300 million pressing times, large-sized plastic molds weighing 70 t, large-sized 60 t stamping dies, 100 t rubber dies for OTR tyres, 8-injection head and 7800-cavity precision plastic molds, internally-inlaid drip irrigation tube dropper hot-runner precision plastic molds with the precision being 0.01mm and the life being above 1 million times, multi-cavity small-modulus precision plastic gear molds and segmented molds for all-steel radial rubber tyre, etc. The output value of molds of China reached RMB 160 billion in 2008, accounting for 19% the global output value of molds. In addition to supply for domestic demands, export of molds of China accounted for more than 15% of the total sales in 2008, which was only less than 1% before 1980s.

第一汽车集团模具制造公司生产的天津威志轿车整体侧围模具

The mold of integral side body produced by the Die Manufacturing Co., Ltd. of FAW for Vizi cars (Tianjin)

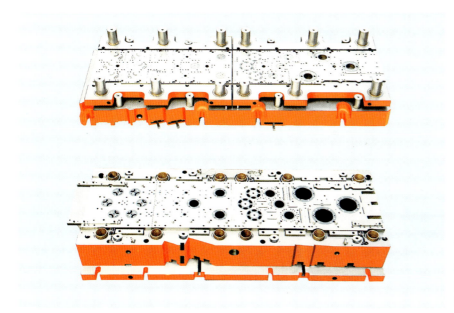

宁波鸿达电机模具公司生产的电机铁心多工位级进模具

Motor core multi-position progressive die, produced by Ningbo Hongda Motor Die Co., Ltd.

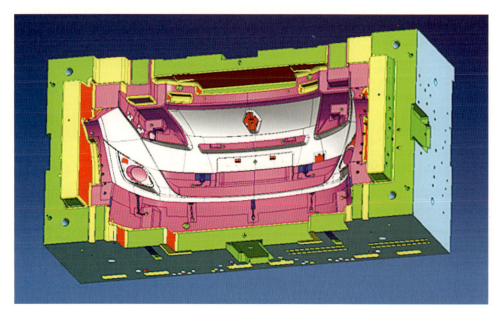

青岛海尔模具有限公司的
保险杠模具设计

Bumper mold designed by
Qingdao Haier Molds Co., Ltd.

广东巨轮模具公司生产的工
程车子午线轮胎活络模具

Segmented mould for radial tyre
for construction truck, made by
Guangdong Greatoo Molds Inc.

第三章　内燃机
Chapter 3　Internal-Combustion Engine

1908年广州均和安机器厂、1909年上海求新机器轮船厂先后制造出2.9—7.4 kW煤气机，标志着中国内燃机工业的诞生。到1949年，中国内燃机累计产量14.7万kW。1949年当年产量7300kW，均系仿制国外产品，重要零部件依赖进口。1932年以华丰机器厂仿英的15 hp柴油机为代表机型，单缸卧式，缸径/行程185/330 mm，功率/转速11.03 kW/330 rpm，平均有效压力值仅452 kPa，活塞平均速度3.6 m/s。而净重高达1950 kg，比质量为176.8 kg/kW。这就是新中国成立前中国内燃机制造业的水平。

Guangzhou Junhe'an Machine Plant and Shanghai Qiuxin Machinery Shipyard manufactured 2.9—7.4 kW gas engines respectively in 1908 and 1909, which marked the start of China's internal-combustion engine industry. The cumulative production of internal-combustion engines of China was 147,000 kW by 1949, and 7300 kW in 1949, which were all copies of overseas products. Significant components relied on import. The 15 hp diesel engine, made by Huafeng Machinery Factory by copying English product in 1932, was a representative model, which was a single-cylinder horizontal diesel engine with the cylinder bore/stroke being 185/330 mm, the power/rotary speed being 11.03 kW/330 rpm, the average effective pressure being 452 kPa, the mean piston speed being 3.6 m/s, the net weight being 1950 kg and the specific mass being 176.8 kg/kW. This was the level of China's internal-combustion industry in the early days of the P.R.C.

新中国成立之初1950—1952年恢复时期，为支援国家建设和抗美援朝，面对西方封锁，开发出几种新机型。单缸柴油机有吴淞机器厂（上海柴油机厂）的1140型，缸径/行程为140/210 mm，出力8.9 kW(12 ps)，压力446 kPa，活塞速度5.25 m/s，净重600 kg，比质量67.4 kg/kW。多缸中速柴油机有天津动力机厂的4146型，为仿美卡特彼勒公司产品，缸径/行程为146/204 mm，出力59 kW，活塞速度6.8 m/s，净重1850 kg，比质量31.5 kg/kW，从所列指标看，这些产品虽不先进，但较1949年前的水平有明显提高。柴油机的油泵油嘴也在上海柴油机厂、天津动力机厂试制成功。

In the recovery period from 1950 to 1952 after the founding of the P.R.C., several new models were developed against blockades placed by western countries, in order to support national construction and resist US aggression and aid Korea. For the Examples: model 1140 single-cylinder diesel engine made by Wusong Machine Plant (Shanghai Diesel Engine Co., Ltd.), with the cylinder bore/stroke being 140/210 mm, the output being 8.9 kW (12 ps), the pressure being 446 kPa, the piston speed being 5.25 m/s, the net weight being 600 kg and specific mass being 67.4 kg/kW; model 4146 multi-cylinder medium-speed diesel engine made by Tianjin Engine Works, which was a copy of the product of Caterpillar Inc. (American), with the cylinder bore/stroke being 146/204 mm, the output being 59 kW, the piston speed being 6.8 m/s, the net weight being 1850 kg and the specific mass being 31.5 kg/kW. According to indexes, these products were not advanced at that time, but were much better than those made before 1949. Oil pumps and oil nozzles for diesel engines were developed by Shanghai Diesel Engine Co., Ltd. and Tianjin Engine Works.

20世纪50年代，中国内燃机的生产开始走上有组织有计划的发展道路。新建和改造了一批大型企业，这些企业成为中国内燃机创业发展的骨干力量；特点是引进苏联和东欧国家技术，如第一汽车厂1956年投产的CA10型汽油机，6缸5.55L排量、最大功率70 kW/2800 rpm、升功率17.1 kW/L、比质量6.21 kg/kW，是中国批量生产车用发动机的开始；潍坊柴油机厂6160型中速柴油机，新中动力机厂的6350型柴油机及大连机车车辆厂10207型柴油机等转速较低产品，为船用或铁路内燃机车动力。这时期产品接近苏联和东欧水平，但与国际水平还有不小差距。50年代由于石油燃料供应不足，发展了不少煤气机，1952年，煤气机产量占内燃机产量的一半，直到1959年大庆油田的开发，煤气机才逐步退出市场。

The production of internal-combustion engines in China entered into a stage of well-organized and planned development in the 1950s. Some large-sized enterprises were newly founded or restructured, becoming the backbone of China's internal-combustion engine industry. Particularly, technologies were introduced from the Soviet Union and Eastern European countries. Model CA10 gasoline engine was made by FAW, with 6 cylinders, the displacement being 5.55 L, the maximum power being 70 kW/2800 rpm, the power per liter being 17.1 kW/L and the specific mass being 6.21 kg/kW. This model was put into production in 1956, marking the start of batch production of vehicle engines in China. Some low-speed products were used for ships or diesel locomotives, like model 160 medium-speed diesel engine made by Weichai Power Co., Ltd., model 6350 diesel engine made by Xinzhong Power Machine Plant as a copy of product of Czechoslovakia and model 10207 diesel engine made by Dalian Locomotive and Rolling Stock Co., Ltd. The products at this time were almost at the same technical level as these of the Soviet Union and Eastern Europe, but were still far behind the international level. Due to the lack in oil fuel in the 1950s, a lot of gas engines were developed. The production of gas engines accounted for half of that of internal-combustion engines in 1952. Gas engine was gradually abandoned after the development of Daqing Oilfield commenced in 1959.

1958年，"大跃进"虽然给中国内燃机工业带来较大的损失，但也促进了科技发展，自行设计的发动机开始问世。中国自主开发了第一个中小功率柴油机系列——上海柴油机厂135系列柴油机，在此期间得到成功发展，首先是2、4、6缸机型，每缸功率14.7 kW/1500 rpm，烧油耗238 g/kWh，比质量13.2 kg/kW，用途广泛，改进后长期生产。至1968年总计生产了68万台。沪东造船厂的6ESD243/82型低速船用柴油机，1198.5 kW/200 rpm，几经改进，到1988年总计生产了150余台，装船100余艘。

Although "the Great Leap Forward" caused giant losses to China's internal-combustion engine industry in 1958, it also stimulated scientific development, where China designed engines independently. China developed independently the first series of medium and small-power diesel engines, namely, Series-135 diesel engines developed by Shanghai Diesel Engine Co., Ltd. This series were well developed in this period, including the models of 2 cylinders, 4 cylinders and 6 cylinders, with the power of each cylinder being 14.7 kW/1500 rpm, the fuel consumption being 238 g/kWh and the specific mass being 13.2 kg/kW. These products were widely applied and still produced after improvement. In total, 680,000 sets were produced by 1968. The model 6ESD243/82 low-speed diesel engine (1198.5 kW/200 rpm) was developed for ship and improved for several times by Hudong Shipyard; over 150 sets of the model were produced totally by 1988, which were used to equip more than 100 ships.

1966年开始的十年"文化大革命"，严重干扰了内燃机的发展。河北省1970年开始，组织了200多个企业搞小柴油机会战，4年内建成16个小柴油机厂，达到了年产200万hp的生产能力，这种用政治运动完成经济任务的办法，产品质量没保证。河北省当时生产的小柴油机多数质量不高，不仅量大面广，重复生产严重。技术要求高、需要量不大的产品也是如此。如万马力大型柴油机，仅上海一地就有3个生产点；6135型160hp柴油机，全国有18个厂生产，除上海、贵阳两厂外，其他厂技术都没有过关。

"The Great Cultural Revolution", which lasted for 10 years from 1966, hindered the development of internal-combustion engines seriously. Over 200 enterprises were organized by Hebei Province to develop small diesel engines as from 1970. As a result, 16 small diesel engine plants were built in 4 years, with the production capacity reaching 2 million hp/year. To accomplish economic task by political campaigns could not guarantee product quality. Quality of most of the small diesel engines produced in Hebei Province was not good. Repetitive production was serious with large quantity and wide scope. It was the same case for products with high technical requirements and small demands. For example, there were 3 production sites in Shanghai for diesel engines at 10,000 horsepower level; there were 18 factories manufacturing model 6135 diesel engines at 160 hp in the whole country, among which, except one factory in Shanghai and another in Guiyang, the others were technically unacceptable.

根据农业发展的需要，20世纪60年代中期开发的175、195等适配小型拖拉机、小型工程机械的小型单缸柴油机，195型柴油机8.8kW/2000 rpm，油耗252 g/kWh，比质量17kg/kW，在全国各地广为生产。成为20世纪60—80年代中国内燃机生产的一大特点。

Small single-cylinder diesel engines suitable for small tractors and construction machinery were developed in the middle 1960s to meet requirements of agricultural development, including model 175 and model 195 diesel engines. Model 195 diesel engine was at 8.8 kW/2000 rpm, with the fuel consumption being 252 g/kWh and the specific mass being 17 kg/kW. These engines were produced everywhere in China, being a highlight of production of internal-combustion engines in China from the 1960s to the 1980s.

1978年改革开放以来，内燃机工业蓬勃发展，由于与信息化技术结合，已成为高新技术产品。自行研发与引进吸收并举，推进产品技术水平快速发展。引进先进技术，"六五"、"七五"期间仅整机技术即引进72项，小至0.735 kW小汽油机，大到4.2万kW的船用低速长冲程柴油机。如船舶系统1979年以来先后引进了苏尔寿（SULZER）公司、曼恩（MAN-B&W）公司等世界名牌柴油机制造技术，至1988年底引进生产的柴油机国产化率达到75%。济南柴油机厂的190系列、大连机车车辆工厂的240系列、青岛四方机车工厂的J180系列和红岩机器厂的250系列柴油机，通过与国外合作改进的方式，产品水平获得显著提高。实现了生产机型和世界当代最新技术水平同步。

The internal-combustion engine industry developed vigorously from 1978 when reform and opening-up started. Combined with information technology, internal-combustion engines developed into hi-tech products. Efforts were made through independent research and development as well as importation and absorption to promote technical development. Update technologies were introduced. About 72 items of whole-machine making technologies were introduced during the 6th and the 7th 5-year Plan periods, ranging from 0.735 kW small gasoline engines to 42,000 kW low-speed long-stroke diesel engines for ships. For example, manufacturing technologies of diesel engines with worldwide famous brands like SULZER and MAN-B&W were introduced one by one for ship system from 1979; the import substitution ratio of diesel engines was 75% by the end of 1988, for those types that were introduced for production. Series-190 diesel engines made by Jinan Diesel Engine Factory, series-240 diesel engines made by Dalian Locomotive and Rolling Stock Co., Ltd., series-J180 diesel engines made by CSR Qingdao Sifang Locomotive & Rolling Stock Co., Ltd. and series-250 diesel engines made by Hongyan Machine Plant improved a lot by cooperation with foreign parties. The models put into production were at the same level as the update technologies in the world.

内燃机企业优化资源配置，生产集中度提高。经过兼并重组，通过优化改造，使内燃机企业做大做强。如2006年，单缸机年产量超过60万台的有4家，产量占总量816万台的44%左右；通用小型汽油机销量超过100万台的5家，销量占总销量911万台的54%左右；车用汽油机销量超过20万台的10家，销量占总销量468万台的66.2%。

Resource allocation was optimized for internal-combustion engine enterprises, with a higher concentration ratio of production. Internal-combustion engine enterprises were developed and expanded by means of merger and restructuring. In 2006, there were 4 enterprises, each with the annual production of single-cylinder engines topping 600,000 sets, and the production of the four accounted for 44% of the total production (8.16 million sets); there were 5 enterprises, each with the sales volume of small universal gasoline engines topping 1 million sets, the sales volume of the five accounted for 54% of total sales volume (9.11 million sets); there were 10 enterprises, each with the sales volume of gasoline engines for vehicles topping 200,000 sets, the sales volume of the ten accounted for 66.2% of the total sales volume (4.68 million sets).

中国已经成为世界内燃机生产大国。单缸柴油机、小型汽油机、车用内燃机、大型低速柴油机产销量及内燃机总产量都名列世界前茅。

China became a big manufacturer of internal-combustion engines in the world. The volumes of production and sales of small gasoline engines, internal-combustion engines for vehicles and large low-speed diesel engines and the total production of internal-combustion engines ranked among the top in the world.

排放标准成为推动中国内燃机技术进步的主要动力。中国等效采用欧洲排放法规，2000年开始执行国 I 标准，2004年开始执行国 II 标准，2007年开始执行国 III 标准，计划2011年开始执行国 IV 标准。国 II 标准比国 I 标准CO降低30.4%，HC和NO_x降低55.8%；国 III 标准又降低了50%左右。

Emission standards became major drives for technical progresses in internal-combustion engines in China. China adopted standards equivalent to European emission laws and regulations. China I standard was executed in 2000, China II standard in 2004, China III in 2007 and China IV in 2011. CO reduced by 30.4% and HC and No_x by 55.8% from China I standard to China II standard, with another drop of 50% in China III standard.

我国正逐渐向世界内燃机强国迈进，随着电子技术及相关学科的不断发展，内燃机的产品技术和制造技术将更加完善，在21世纪再创新的辉煌。

China gradually developed into a big power of internal-combustion engines. As electronic technology and relevant disciplines develop continuously, technologies of internal-combustion engines will improve further towards another prosperity in the 21st century.

1946—1955年，无锡农具厂生产的单缸卧式柴油机

Single-cylinder horizontal type diesel engine produced by Wuxi Farm Implements Factory from 1946 to 1955.

1953年，上海柴油机厂生产的6110柴油机

6110 diesel engine produced by Shanghai Diesel Engine
Co., Ltd. in 1953

1951年，江苏江淮动力股份有限公司（原江淮农具厂）工场工作情景

The workshop of Jiangsu Jianghuai Engine Co., Ltd. (the former Jianghuai Farm Implements Factory) in 1951

1964年，上海工农动力机厂（诚孚）生产的195-1型单缸柴油机

Model 195-1 single cylinder diesel engine produced by Shanghai Industrial and Agricultural Power Machine Factory (Chengfu) in 1964

20世纪80年代初，上海内燃机厂生产的TS4100型拖拉机用柴油机

Model TS4100 diesel engine for tractor, produced by Shanghai Internal-combustion Engine Works in the early 1980s

1965年，上海沪东造船厂生产的7ESDZ75160柴油机

7ESDZ75160 diesel engine produced by Shanghai Hudong Shipyard in 1965

20世纪后期风靡我国乘用越野车
用动力——北内492汽油机

Beinei 492 Gasoline Engine—power for
off-road passenger cars that were popular
in China in the late 20th century

21世纪初诞生在常柴股份有限公司的新一
代单缸L32型柴油机

The new generation of model L32 single-cylinder
diesel engine made by Changchai Company Limited
in the early 21st century

2005年昆明云内动力公司自主开发的D19TC1型电控高压共轨轿车用柴油机

Model D19TC1 high-pressure common rail diesel engine for sedans, independently developed by Kunming
Yunnei Power Co., Ltd in 2005.

2005年潍柴动力股份
有限公司率先推出满
足"国Ⅲ排放标准"的
"蓝擎"动力

Landking China III engine,
firstly promoted by Weichai
Power Co., Ltd. in 2005

潍柴动力开发的16V200
船用柴油机

16V200 marine diesel engine
developed by Weichai Power
Co., Ltd

潍柴动力开发的226B陆
用柴油发电机组

226B land diesel generating
sets developed by Weichai
Power Co., Ltd

第四章 仪器仪表
Chapter 4 Instrumentation

1949年中华人民共和国成立以前，中国没有自己的仪器仪表工业。20世纪50年代初期，上海、天津、沈阳、大连等沿海城市有一些小型仪器仪表修理厂（点），兼产一些简易产品，如玻璃温度计、压力表、电表、低倍显微镜等；上海大华科学仪器厂、黄河理工仪器厂、天津联昌电机厂等是当时比较有影响的民营仪表制造厂。

China did not have its own instrumentation industry before the founding of PRC in 1949. There were some small instrumentation repair shops in coastal cities like Shanghai, Tianjin, Shenyang and Dalian in the early 1950s, which could produce some simple products like liquid-in-glass thermometers, pressure gauges, electricity meters and low-power microscopes. Significant private instrumentation manufacturers at that time included Shanghai Dahua Scientific Instrument Plant, Huanghe Instrument Plant and Tianjin Lianchang Electrical Machinery Plant.

"一五"计划开始，我国逐步建立仪器仪表工业，1956年建成苏联援建属于"156项"的哈尔滨电表仪器厂和太行仪表厂，生产安装式板表、电度表、汽车表、部分精密电表、仪器和航空仪表。1960年建成由民主德国设计的西安仪表厂，这是中国第一座现代化的测量温度、压力、流量和记录、调节、控制等多种系列产品的综合性热工仪表制造工厂；同期还建立了分析仪器、流量计等一批仪表仪器制造厂。1964年开始的"三线建设"，陆续建成了重庆、贵阳、湘西、甘肃、宁夏、江西等地的仪器仪表生产和科研基地，至此，中国仪器仪表制造业的布局基本完成。

The instrumentation industry was established gradually from the 1st 5-year Plan period. Harbin Electrical Measuring Instrument Factory and Taihang Instrument Factory were completed in 1956, which were among the 156 main construction projects assisted by the Soviet Union. The two factories produced mounted panel meters, kilowatt-hour meters, autometers, some precision electricity meters, instruments and aircraft instruments. Xi'an Instrument Factory, which was designed by German Democratic Republic, was completed in 1960; this was the first modern comprehensive thermal instruments manufacturer in China, making multiple series of products for measuring temperature, pressure and flow, record, regulation and control. At the same time, some instrumentation manufacturers were founded for analytic instruments and flow meters. "Third-line Construction" commenced in 1964. Instrumentation production and research bases were built one after another in Chongqing, Guiyang, Western Hunan, Gansu, Ningxia and Jiangxi, etc. Then, the structure of China's instrumentation industry was mostly completed.

通过科研开发和对外合作，形成了一定的技术基础。20世纪60年代初期重点发展了气动单元组合仪表系统和各种流程分析仪器。60年代中期，研制了电动单元组合仪表系列。70年代研制工业控制机和数据处理计算机。80年代着重开发小型、微型工业控制机、分散型控制系统、数控系统、模板系列和汉字信息系统等，并且开发出一批机电一体化产品。进入90年代实现国产化分散型自动化系统优化。至90年代末，仪器仪表工业大型工程成套率达60%，可承担30/60万kW火电机组，30万t合成氨、120 t转炉、日产30万m³城市煤气化工程、成组大型炉窑等成套任务，做到从系统设计到交钥匙。

A certain technical basis was set up by scientific research and development and cooperation with overseas partners. Pneumatic unit combination instrument system and various process stream analyzers were primarily developed in the early 1960s. Electrical unit component instrument series was developed in the middle 1960s. Industrial PC and data processing computer were developed in the 1970s. Small and micro industrial PCs, distributed control system, numerical control system, template series and Chinese character information system were primarily developed in the 1980s, together with some mechatronics products. Distributed automation system domestically made was improved in the 1990s. Ratio of complete sets of instrumentation for large projects was 60% by the end of the 1990s, where China was capable of accomplishing complete sets such as 30/600,000 kW thermal power units, 300,000 t synthetic ammonia, 120 t convertor, 300,000 m³/d urban coal gasification project and sets of large-sized kiln and furnace, etc., from system design to delivery.

21世纪以来，中国仪器仪表工业高速发展。2007年工业总产值是1978年的96.3倍；职工人数、固定资产净值分别是1978年的2.5倍、35.4倍。

China's instrumentation industry developed swiftly in the 21st century. The gross industrial value in 2007 was 96.3 times of that in 1978. The number of employees and the net value of fixed assets in 2007 were 2.5 times and 35.4 times of those in 1978.

中国为常用仪表生产大国，21世纪初年产电度表1亿只，水表2500万只，煤气表800万只，数字万用表2500万只，望远镜2000万台，显微镜500多万台，均位居世界第一；另外，变送器、执行器、测绘仪器和金属材料试验机等产品的产量也位居世界前列。

China is a big manufacturer of ordinary instruments. It produced 100 million kilowatt-hour meters, 25 million water meters, 8 million gas meters, 25 million digital AVO meters, 20 million telescopes and more than 5 million microscopes in the beginning of the 21st century, all ranking the first in the world. In addition, the volumes of products like transmission devices, actuators, instruments of surveying and mapping and metallic material testing machines ranked among the top in the world.

改革开放30年仪器仪表行业发展情况(1978—2007年)

Development of instrumentation industry in the past 30 years of reform and opening–up(1978—2007)

年 份 Year	企业数（个） Number of enterprises	职工数 （人） Number of employees	固定资产净值 （亿元） Net value of fixed assets (RMB 100 million)	工业总产值 （亿元） Gross industrial value (RMB 100 million)	人均产值（元） Output value per capita (RMB)
1978	728	302031	14.23	31.96	10581
1980	739	345840	15.49	36.84	10652
1990	983	373987	56.64	102.67	27453
2000	1681	562384	257.356	899.09	159871
2005	3391	648987	373.41	1777.00	273810
2007	3954	766603	504.39	3077.66	401467
2007/1978(倍) (times)	5.4	2.5	35.4	96.3	40

中国仪器仪表行业技术总体已达到20世纪90年代中期的国际水平，少数产品接近或达到当前国际水平。

The technical level of China's instrumentation industry reached the international level that was in the middle 1990s, with a few products approaching or reaching the current international level.

工业自动化仪表及控制系统品种系列较多，为国家重点大型工程配套能力大大提高。一般的产品掌握核心技术，产品可满足国内需要，并有出口。

There were many categories of industrial automation instruments and control systems, providing stronger support for key large national projects. For ordinary products, core technologies were in our own hands. Products could be exported, in addition to meeting domestic demands.

"十五"计划以来，自行开发研制了一批高中档产品，如中控科技集团、北京和利时、北京国电智深等公司，自主研制的DCS产品，性能水平与国外产品接近。已承接的大型工程并已投运成功的有600 MW超临界火电机组、500万t/年炼油、2万 m³/h空分装置，58 m³ PVC、 400万t/年氧化铝、265 m² 烧结装置、轨道交通信号控制项目；同时，1000 MW超超临界火电机组签约国电智深公司的国产DCS系统已于2009年完成。将改变大型工程系统长期由外商垄断的局面，在国家经济安全上有重要的战略意义。

Some high-end and middle-end products were developed independently from the 10th 5-year Plan period. For example, DCS products developed independently by SUPCON Group Co., Ltd.,

360

Beijing HollySys Co., Ltd. and Beijing GuoDian ZhiShen Control Technology Co., Ltd. were close to foreign products in performance. Large projects undertaken and put into operation successfully included 600 MW super critical thermal power generating units projects 5 million t/yr refinery projects, 20,000 m^3/h air separation facilities, 58 m^3 PVC projects, 4 million t/yr aluminum oxide projects, 265 m^2 sintering plants and urban rail traffic signal control projects. Beijing GuoDian ZhiShen Control Technology Co., Ltd. completed domestically made DCS system in 2009, which was contracted for 1000 MW ultra-supercritical thermal power generating units. The monopoly of systems for large-sized projects by foreign parties will be changed, which has significant strategic meaning for national economic security.

科学仪器具有一定的自主创新能力，色谱仪器、光谱仪器、电化学仪器、研究型光学显微镜、扫描电子显微镜等，接近或达到当前国际同类产品的先进水平。

China is capable of independent innovation of scientific instruments to some degree, including chromatograph, spectrograph, electrochemical instrument, optical microscope for study and scanning electron microscope, etc., approaching or reaching current international level of the same kinds of products.

21世纪以来，进出口贸易发展迅速。2007年仪器仪表行业进出口总额达260亿美元，其中进口172亿美元，出口88亿美元，与改革开放初期基本为进口的局面发生了根本改变。仪器仪表出口发展很快（见下表），许多出口产品在国际上已占有一定地位。年出口量较大的产品有电能表1700万只、万用表1300万只、水表1000万只、望远镜2000万台、煤气表200万只、测绘仪器3000万台、衡器8000万台。出口产品的档次逐年提升，已进入中高档产品范围，如集装箱检测系统、数字示波器、气相和液相色谱仪等都有大量出口。

Import and export trade developed swiftly in the 21st century. The total import and export volume of the instrumentation industry was USD 26 billion in 2007, among which, import was USD 17.2 billion and export was USD 8.8 billion. This was totally different from the situation that import was predominant at the beginning of reform and opening-up. The export of instrumentation grew quickly (see the table attached). Many products exported played important roles in the world. Products with great annual export volumes included 17 million energy meters, 13 million multimeters, 10 million water meters, 20 million telescopes, 2 million gas meters, 30 million instruments of surveying and mapping and 80 million weighing apparatuses. Products exported are upgraded year by year, now becoming middle-end and high-end products. Products with great export volumes also included container examination system, digital oscilloscope and gaseous phase and liquid phase chromatographs.

仪器仪表行业出口创汇情况(1981—2009年)
Foreign currency earning from export of the instrumentation industry (1981—2009)

(亿美元)
(USD 100 million)

年 份 Year	1981	1985	1990	1995	2002	2005	2007	2009
出口创汇额 Foreign currency earning	0.26	0.11	0.53	9.80	30.32	52.45	88.35	107

中国仪器仪表发展很快，但是与国家建设需要和国际同行业比较，相对比较薄弱。集中表现在产品结构不合理，成套率低。数字化、智能化、机电一体化的新型仪表品种总量不足，自动化控制系统跟不上大型成套设备配套的要求，科学测试仪器产品品种满足率仅60%左右。突出反映在外贸不平衡上，外贸逆差2007年84亿美元、2009年102亿美元，净进口率分别高达66.2%和66.14%，居机械工业各行业之首。

China's instrumentation industry developed quickly, but was not enough for national construction and lower than the global level. Major shortcomings include that product structure is irrational, ratio of complete sets is low, the total types of new instruments like digital, intelligent and mechatronics instruments are not enough, automatic control systems cannot support large complete sets of equipment and only 60% of categories of testing instruments are available. These problems are particularly reflected in the imbalance in foreign trade: the foreign trade deficits were USD 8.4 billion in 2007 and USD 10.2 billion in 2009; the net import ratios were up to 66.2% and 66.14% respectively, ranking the first among all the sub-sectors of the machinery industry.

2007年庄河电厂600 MW超临界机组采用国电智深DCS通过168 h满负荷试运行——控制室

The control room for pass-ing 168h full-loaded trial run, with DCS developed by Guo Dian ZhiShen and adopted for 600 MW supercritical power generating unit for Zhuanghe Power Plant in 2007

中国四联仪器仪表集团有限公司的自动贴片生产线

Automatic SMT production line of China Silian Instrument Group Co. Ltd.

华立集团股份有限公司仪表制造基地模块车间

Module workshop at instrument manufacturing base of Holley Group

上海自动化仪表股份有限公司生产的轨道交通主控室

Rail transit main control room, produced by Shanghai Automation Instrumentation Co., Ltd.

上海自动化仪表股
份有限公司生产的
外高桥电厂控制室

Control room, produced
by Shanghai Automation
Instrumentation Co., Ltd.
for Waigaoqiao Power
Plant

上海自动化仪表股份有限公司生产的核电主控室

Nuclear power main control room of Shanghai Automation
Instrumentation Co., Ltd.

上海自动化仪表股份有限公司生产的具有自主知识产权的分散
控制系统（SUPMAx-800）

DCS (SUPMAx-800) with proprietary intellectual property rights, produced by
Shanghai Automation Instrumentation Co., Ltd.

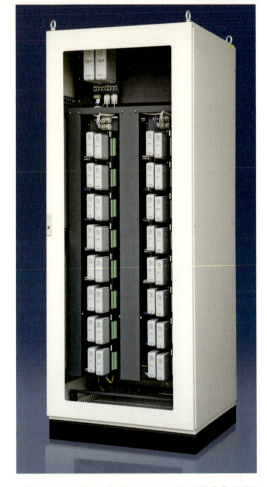

中控科技集团有限公司研发的ECS-700
大规模联合控制系统

ECS-700 large-scale combined control system,
developed by SUPCON Group Co., Ltd.

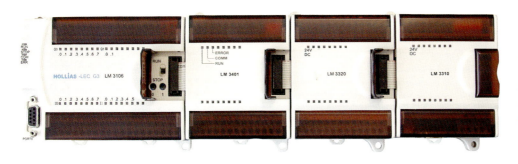

北京和利时系统工程有限公司生产的LM小型PLC产品组合

LM small PLC product combination, produced by Beijing HollySys Co., Ltd.

北京和利时系统工程有限公司生产的LK大型PLC产品

LK large PLC product, produced by Beijing HollySys Co., Ltd.

北京和利时系统工程有限公司生产的SM模块

SM module, produced by Beijing HollySys Co., Ltd.

北京北分瑞利分析仪器（集团）有限责任公司提供装备的水质自动监测站

Auto water quality monitoring system, provided by Beijing Beifen Ruili Analyzer (group) Co., Ltd.

2001年以来北京北分瑞利分析仪器（集团）有限责任公司生产的AF-610B型原子荧光光谱仪

Model AF-610B Atomic Fluorescence Spectroscopy, produced by Beijing Beifen Ruili Analyzer (group) Co., Ltd.

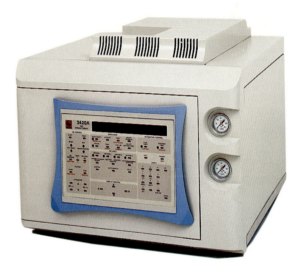

北京北分瑞利分析仪器（集团）有限责任公司生产的FHC04-8731型气相色谱仪

Model FHC04-8731 gas chromatograph, produced by Beijing Beifen Ruili Analyzer (group) Co., Ltd.

北京北分瑞利分析仪器（集团）有限责任公司生产的SP-3420A型气相色谱仪

Model SP-3420A gas chromatograph, produced by Beijing Beifen Ruili Analyzer (group) Co., Ltd.

北京北分瑞利分析仪器（集团）有限责任公司生产的AFX-110/120原子吸收分光光度仪

Model AFX-110/120 atomic absorption spectrophoto meter, produced by Beijing Beifen Ruili Analyzer (group) Co., Ltd.

北京北分瑞利分析仪器（集团）有限责任公司生产的WLD-4c型多道光电直读光谱仪

Model WLD-4c Multi-channel Opto-electronic Direct Reading Spectrometer, produced by Beijing Beifen Ruili Analyzer (group) Co., Ltd. since 2001

WAW系列微机控制全自动万能试验机

WAW microprocessor control full auto universal testing machines

北京科学仪器厂近年研制的KYKY-EM3900型扫描电子显微镜

Model KYKY-EM3900 scanning electron microscope developed by Beijing Scientific Instrument Plant in recent years

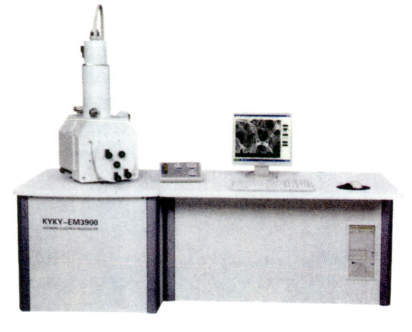

第五章　电力装备
Chapter 5　Power Equipment

　　电力工业是中国机械工业主要服务领域之一。中国电力设备制造业完全是1949年新中国成立后发展起来的，从20世纪50年代开始，陆续建立了上海、哈尔滨、四川三大动力设备制造厂和沈阳、西安两套高压电器厂，以及分布在全国各地的中小型电力装备制造厂。60年来生产了以三峡700 MW为代表的水电机组、以超超临界1000 MW为代表的火电机组、以1000 kV交流和±800 kV直流特高压输变电设备为代表的输电设备，这些装备都达到当代世界最高水平。

　　Power Sector is included in the major range of services of China's machine-building industry. China's power equipment-building industry totally developed after 1949 when the whole nation was liberated. Three major power equipment factories were built in Shanghai, Harbin with Sichuan and two HV electric appliance plants in Shenyang and Xi'an successively from the 1950s on, with some medium and small-sized power equipment plants all over China. Equipment produced in the past 60 years include hydro units represented by the 700 MW hydro power generating unit for Three Gorges Dam, thermal power generating units represented by the 1000 MW ultra-supercritical unit, and power transmission equipment represented by the 1000 kV AC and ±800 kV DC EHV transmission and transformation equipment, all reaching the highest modern level in the world.

　　从1952年中国开始制造第一台800 kW水电机组，1954年生产第一台6000 kW火电机组起，到2009年累计制造了各类发电设备约97594万kW，其中2006—2009年制造了49243万kW，占全部产量的50.44%，并连续四年产量超过1亿kW。2008年年底，中国电力发电设备装机拥有量79251万kW，其中80%以上为国产机组。近年来每年出口机组都是1500万kW以上。

　　China manufactured its first 800 kW hydro power generating unit in 1952 and the first 6000 kW thermal power generating unit in 1954. All the power generating equipment produced from 1952 to 2009 totaled 975.94 million kW, among which, 492.43 million kW were produced from 2006 to 2009, accounting for 50.44% of the total production. The production exceeded 100 million kW in every of four years from 2006 to 2009. The installed capacity of power generating equipment in China reached 792.51 million kW by the end of 2008, of which above 80% were domestically made. Generating units totaling more than 15 million kW were exported every year recently.

第一节 火力发电设备
Section 1 Thermal Power Generating Equipment

燃煤火力发电设备。50多年来，单机容量从2.5 MW、6 MW、25 MW发展到1000 MW；参数从低压、中压、高压、超高压、亚临界压力到超临界和超超临界压力；能耗从每千瓦时500多g标准煤降至不到300 g。

Coal-fired power generating equipment: in the past 50 years, the single-machine capacity grew from small capacity as 2.5 MW, 6 MW and 25 MW to 1000 MW, the parameter developed from low pressure to medium pressure, high pressure, extra-high pressure, subcritical pressure, supercritical pressure and to ultra supercritical pressure, and the energy consumption decreased from more than 500 g/kWh to less than 300 g/kWh.

1952年从捷克斯洛伐克引进6 MW和12 MW火电机组制造技术，1953年从苏联引进6—50 MW机组的制造技术。1956年在上海生产了第一台6 MW火电机组。国产125 MW、200 MW和300 MW机组分别于1966年和1969年完成设计，于1969年、1972年和1974年相继投入运行。由于当时中国尚未掌握火电设备核心技术，这些机型基本上是按简单放大的思路发展的，性能质量满足不了国民经济发展的需求。1977年开始酝酿引进国外制造技术，1980年与美国西屋公司（WH）和燃烧工程公司（CE）签订了引进亚临界压力300 MW、600 MW火电机组成套制造技术，除三大主机和电站工程设计技术之外，还包括按火电机组工艺流程的10大系统240项配套设备和有关自动控制系统等168种产品，涉及的主辅机制造工厂、科研院所和电力设计院等约200家。在消化引进技术过程中，共派出近千名技术人员分别到美国等8个国家38家厂商进行培训提高；共转化了4万张图纸、上千个计算程序；还同步对发电设备制造业主机、辅机、自动化等企业进行了相应的技术改造，仅"六五"期间国家即投资近1亿美元和30亿元人民币进行工厂改造。亚临界压力300 MW、600 MW火电设备制造技术是中国机械工业最大的一项成套设备技术引进项目。经过300多家主辅机承制企业七八年的努力，引进型第一套300 MW、600 MW考核机组分别于1985年12月20日和1987年12月17日完成，并于1987年6月30日和1988年11月4日投入运行。其后在"七五"、"八五"期间还进行了优化攻关，提高了国产化率，降低了煤耗。300/600 MW火电设备技术引进消化吸收和再创新的扎实工作，为尔后中国研制超临界和超超临界火电设备打下了基础，创造了条件。

The manufacturing technology for 6 MW and 12 MW thermal power generating units was introduced from Czechoslovakia in 1952, and the manufacturing technology for 6—50 MW units was introduced from the Soviet Union in 1953. China's first 6 MW thermal power generating unit was produced in Shanghai in 1956. China-made 125 MW, 200 MW and 300 MW units were designed in 1966 and 1969 respectively, and were put into operation in 1969, 1972 and 1974 successively. Because China was not capable of core technology for thermal power generating equipment, these models were mostly developed in the principle of simple magnification, the performance and quality of which failed to support national economic development. Preparation for introduction of foreign manufacturing technologies began in 1977. Agreements were signed with Westinghouse (WH) and CE in 1980s, to introduce manufacturing technologies for complete 300 MW and 600 MW subcritical thermal power generating units. In addition to the design technologies for the three major machines and power station projects, the introduction covered 168 products including 10 systems, 240 auxiliary facilities and relevant automatic control systems involved in the process flow of thermal power generating units. About 200 organizations were engaged, including manufacturers of main units and auxiliary machines, research institutes and electric power design institutes. In the process of learning from the technology introduced, about 1,000 technicians were assigned to 38 manufacturers in 8 countries including USA, to improve through training; 40,000 pieces of drawings and over 1,000 calculation programs were transformed; relevant technical transformation was carried out in enterprises dealing with main units, auxiliary machines and automation in the power generator-building industry. China invested nearly USD 100 million and RMB 3 billion in transformation of plants during the 6th Five-year Plan period. Introduction of the manufacturing technology for 300 MW and 600 MW subcritical thermal power generating equipment is the largest introduction project of technology for complete equipment in China's machine-building industry. The first 300 MW unit and the first 600 MW unit for appraisal of foreign manufacturing technologies introduced were completed on Dec. 20, 1985 and Dec. 17, 1987 respectively, and put into operation on June 30, 1987 and Nov. 4, 1988 respectively, by common efforts of more than 300 enterprises manufacturing main units and auxiliary machines. After that, more technical problems were solved to improve performance and quality in the 7th Five-year Plan period and the 8th Five-year Plan period, where the ratio of China-made equipment increased and coal consumption decreased. The steady and effective introduction, absorption and innovation of technologies for 300/600 MW thermal power generating equipment laid a foundation for China's development of supercritical and ultra supercritical thermal power generating equipment later.

超临界和超超临界火电机组。具有明显的高效节能和低排放优势，是世界各国竞相发展的成熟的发电新技术。中国从2002年开始，在已能批量生产亚临界300/600 MW火电机组的基础上决定发展超临界和超超临界机组。沁北电厂为中国首台生产600 MW超临界火电机组的依托工程，机组参数为24.2MPa/566℃，于2004年11月23日投产发电。

Supercritical and ultra supercritical thermal power generating units have remarkable advantages including high efficiency, energy saving and low emission. The technologies of such units are new and mature power generating technologies desired by all the countries in the world.

China decided to develop supercritical and ultra supercritical units in 2002, when it was capable of mass production of 300/600 MW subcritical thermal power generating units. By the project of Qinbei Power Plant, China produced its first 600 MW supercritical thermal power generating unit with the parameter being 24.2 MPa/566 ℃, which was put into operation on Nov. 23, 2004.

2002年中国开始超超临界机组研发应用立项时，国际上仅有德国、丹麦、日本的5座电厂投产。2003年下半年中国开始了超超临界机组的建设，起步为1000 MW级，参数为26.25MPa/600℃,以华能玉环电厂为依托工程，于2006年11月18日正式投运。宣告了中国首台国产大型节能环保型燃煤机组的诞生，从而使中国火电装备技术水平步入国际先进水平。上海电气（与西门子合作生产）、哈尔滨电气（锅炉与三井巴柏葛、汽轮机及电机与三菱合作生产）和东方电气（与日立合作生产）三大集团依靠国外公司的性能和质量保证等合作方式制造了1000 MW超超临界机组。到2008年年底累计共制造了19台，已有11台国产1000 MW超超临界机组成功投入运行，同期全球只投入运行70台，中国占15.71%，中国电力工业开始进入"超超临界"时代。（注：至2010年年底在运机组已达33台，还有11台在建。）

When China approved its project of research and application of ultra supercritical units in 2002, totally only 5 power plants with such units were put into service in Germany, Denmark and Japan. China started the building of ultra supercritical units with a 1000 MW unit by constructing Huaneng Yuhuan Power Plant in the second half of 2003, and the unit was put into operation formally with the parameter being 26.25 MPa/600 ℃ on Nov. 18, 2006. This marked the completion of the first large-sized, energy-efficient and environment-friendly coal-fired unit made by China, by which China's technology for thermal power generating equipment reached international top level. Shanghai Electric Corporation (producing in cooperation with Siemens), Harbin Electric Corporation (producing boilers in cooperation with Mitsui Babcock Energy Limited and producing steam turbines and generators in cooperation with Mitsubishi) and Dongfang Electric Corporation(producing in cooperation with Hitachi) manufactured 1000 MW ultra supercritical units with performance and quality guaranty made by foreign companies. In total, there were 19 1000 MW ultra supercritical units made in China and 11 China-made 1000 MW ultra supercritical units were put into operation successfully by the end of 2008, accounting for 15.71% of 70 units which were the global number of the same kind put into operation in the same period. China's Power Sector entered into the "ultra supercritical" era.(Note: Until the end of 2010, 33 units had been put into operation and 11 units were being built.)

中国电力工业火电设备的主力机组，20世纪50—70年代为50—100 MW，70—80年代为125—200 MW，80年代以后长期为125—300 MW机组，2005年以后600—1000 MW超临界和超超临界机组产量占整个火电设备的45%以上，已经开始进入电力工业主力机组范围。

Major models of thermal power generating units in China's Power Sector were 50—100 MW units from the 1950s to the 1970s, 125—200 MW units from the 1970s to the 1980s and 125—300 MW units after the 1980s. The production of 600—1000 MW supercritical and ultra supercritical units accounts for more than 45% of the production of all the thermal power generating equipment after 2005, and such equipment is now a major model of thermal power generating unit.

经对玉环电厂投运机组考核，机组每度电能耗为282.6g标准煤，比2006年全国火电平均煤耗低80多g；发电热效率45.4%。

According to assessment of units operating at Yuhuan Power Plant, energy consumption per kWh by the units is 282.6g standard coal, being 80g lower than the national average coal consumption for thermal power generation in 2006, and the thermal efficiency of power generation is 45.4%.

大型空冷机组。燃煤电厂是耗水大户，一个百万千瓦电厂年耗水约2000万t左右，富煤缺水的三北地区急需大型空冷机组。20世纪80年代，中国从匈牙利引进了混合式凝气器的间接空气冷却系统后，自主开发了200 MW间接空冷汽轮机，在山西大同电厂成功投运。2007年中国掌握了亚临界参数300/600 MW和超临界600 MW直接空冷机组，首台600 MW超临界间接空冷机组在山西阳城电厂投运，1000 MW直接空冷机组于2010年在宁夏灵武电厂投运，为世界上最大的直接空冷机组。到2007年，中国累计有1600万kW空冷机组在运行，是世界上拥有空冷机组最多的国家，各项指标达到世界先进水平。

Large-sized air-cooling units: coal-fired power plants consume lots of water. A 1000 MW power plant consumes about 20 million t water in a year. Large-sized air-cooling units are desired in Northwestern China, Northern China and Northeastern China where coal resources are rich but water is insufficient. China developed independently 200 MW indirect air-cooling steam turbine in the 1980s, which was put into operation at Datong Power Plant, after introducing indirect air-cooling system for direct contact condenser from Hungary. China developed independently 300/600 MW subcritical and 600 MW supercritical direct air-cooling units in 2007, when the first 600 MW supercritical indirect air-cooling unit was put into operation at Yangcheng Power Plant, Shanxi Province and 1000 MW direct air-cooling unit was put into operation at Lingwu Power Plant, Ning Xia Hui Autonomous Region, which was the largest air-cooling unit in the world. Air-cooling units operating in China totaled to 16 million kW in 2007, making China the country with the most air-cooling units in the world and with various indices reaching top level in the world.

循环流化床锅炉（CFB）。循环流化技术是国际公认的经济有效的低污染燃煤技术，20世纪七八十年代得到迅速发展，90年代向大型化发展。中国从1995年首台国产50 MW级CFB锅炉投运以来，开发了100/200 MW和300 MW级CFB锅炉，2006年又启动自主研制和建设600 MW级超临界CFB锅炉示范电站的计划。中国现有35—1100 t/h循环流化床锅炉2000台，是世界上拥有CFB锅炉最多的国家。

Circulating fluidized bed (CFB): Circulating fluidization technique is an economic and effective coal-fired technique recognized in the globe. It was developed vigorously in the 1970s and the 1980s and developed to mass scale in the 1990s. China's first home-made 50 MW CFB was put into operation in 1995. From then on, China developed 100/200 MW and 300 MW CFB, and later, initialized a plan of independent development and building of a model power station with 600 MW supercritical CFB in 2006. China possesses 2,000 sets of 35—1100 t/h CFB at present, which was the largest number of CFB among all the countries in the globe.

重型燃气轮机。随着"西气东输"工程建设的进行，E级、F级燃气轮机及联合循环机组的需求不断增长。从2002年开始，国家发改委组织了三次以市场换技术的"打捆招标"，国内4家企业（哈、沪、川、宁）分别从GE、三菱、西门子3家公司引进了E级、F级燃气轮机制造技术，并为制造燃气轮机的高温热部件相继成立了合资厂，已经制造了一批燃气轮机，国产化率30%—60%。F级燃气蒸汽联合循环的效率可达57%，发供电标准煤耗约215 g/kWh、220 g/kWh，以天然气为燃料的燃机电厂，SO_X的排放约45 mg/m^3，NO_X的排放控制在51 mg/m^3。

Heavy-duty gas turbine: the demand for Grade E and Grade F gas turbines and combined cycle units is growing, as the West-to-East Gas Transmission Project is being constructed. From 2002 on, the State Development and Reform Commission organized three times of lump-sum bidding with the "Market for Technology" strategy. Four domestic enterprises (in Harbin, Shanghai, Sichuan and Xining) introduced the manufacturing technologies for Grade E and Grade F gas turbines from GE, Mitsubishi, Siemens, established joint-venture plants of high-temperature components for gas turbines, and produced some gas turbines which made the rate of China-made equipment 30%—60%. The efficiency of Grade F gas and steam combined cycle can reach 57% and the standard coal consumption for power generation is about 215 g/kWh or 220 g/kWh. For a gas turbine power plant fueled with natural gas, the SO_X emission is about 45 mg/m^3 and the NO_X emission is controlled at 51 mg/m^3.

1954年，上海电机厂制造的国产第一台6000 kW汽轮发电机组用于淮南电厂

China's first 6000 kW steam turbine generator set, manufactured by Shanghai Electric Machine Factory, was used at Huainan Power Plant in 1954.

1958年4月，哈尔滨汽轮机厂
生产的首台2.5万kW汽轮机组

The first 25,000 kW turbine unit
produced by Harbin Steam Turbine
Works in April 1958

1959年，哈尔滨汽轮机厂制造
的5万kW单轴式汽轮机组

50,000 kW single-shaft turbine unit
produced by Harbin Steam Turbine
Works in 1959

上海电机厂制造的世界第一台双水内冷1.2万
kW汽轮发电机组，获国家科技进步一等奖

The first 12,000 kW turbo-generator with double internal
water-cooling system in the world, manufactured by
Shanghai Electric Machine Factory, was awarded with
the First Class National Prize for the Advancement of
Sciences and Technology.

1960年4月，哈尔滨汽轮机厂生产的首台10万kW汽轮机组

The first 100,000 kW turbine unit produced by Harbin Steam Turbine Works in April 1960

1960年8月，哈尔滨汽轮机厂生产的首台20万kW汽轮机组

The first 200,000 kW turbine unit produced by Harbin Steam Turbine Works in Aug. 1960

东方汽轮机厂制造的东方-日立型60万kW汽轮机在山东邹县电厂运行

Dongfang-Hitachi 600 MW steam turbine made by Dongfang Steam Turbine Works was operating at Zhouxian County Power Plant, Shandong Province.

东方汽轮机厂制造的我国最大电站出口项目——伊朗4台32.5万kW空冷型汽轮机总装现场

General assembly field for 4 × 325 MW air cooling type steam turbine in Iran, China's largest power station export project undertaken by Dongfang Steam Turbine Works

哈尔滨电机有限责任公司引进美国西屋公司技术并与之合作制造的60万kW汽轮发电机组，1988年11月在安徽平圩电厂运行

600 MW generator, made by Harbin Electric Machinery Co., Ltd. in cooperation with Westinghouse of USA with technology introduced from Westinghouse, was working at Anhui Pingwei Power Plant in Nov. 1988.

哈尔滨汽轮机厂正在装配首台60万kW汽轮机组

The first 600 MW steam turbine generating set was being assembled at Harbin Steam Turbine Works.

上海电气电站集团制造的浙江玉环电厂1000 MW超超临界火电机组

1000 MW ultra-supercritical thermal power generating unit produced by Shanghai Electric Power Generation Group for Yuhuan Power Plant in Zhejiang Province

2006年，哈尔滨锅炉厂为
华能浙江玉环电厂生产了国
内首台1000 MW超超临界
锅炉机组

China's first 1000 MW ultra-
supercritical boiler unit was
produced by Harbin Boiler
Plant for Yuhuan Power Plant in
Zhejiang Province in 2006.

哈电集团制造的泰州电厂1000 MW超超临界汽轮发电机组

1000 MW ultra-supercritical steam turbine generator set manufactured by Harbin Electric
Corporation for Taizhou Power Plant

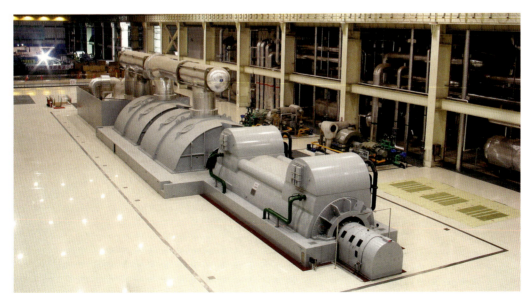

东方电气为山东邹
县制造的1000 MW
超超临界发电机组

1000 MW ultra-
supercritical steam
turbine generator
set manufactured by
Dongfang Electric
Corporation for Zou
County,Shandong

东方电气大型火电设备汽轮机转子吊运

The hoisting of the steam turbine rotor for large-sized thermal power equipment, produced by Dongfang Electric Corporation

上海电气电站集团工人正在吊装百万千瓦火电机组汽轮机转子

A worker of Shanghai Electric Power Generation Group was hoisting the steam turbine rotor for 1000 MW thermal power generating unit.

哈尔滨电气集团的两缸结构
600 MW超超临界汽轮机

600 MW ultra-supercritical steam turbine with two cylinders, made by Harbin Electric Corporation

哈尔滨电气集团制造的
600 MW直接空冷汽轮机组
用于大同发电厂

600 MW direct air-cooling turbine unit, made by Harbin Electric Corporation, was used at Datong Power Plant.

2006年哈尔滨锅炉厂
的首台国产300 MW
循环流化床锅炉——
开远电厂锅炉机组

China's first 300 MW
circulating fluidized bed
boiler was made by Harbin
Boiler Plant for Kaiyuan
Power Plant in 2006.

上海电气电站集团制造的镇江电厂600 MW超临界火电机组

600 MW supercritical thermal power generating unit, produced by Shanghai Electric Power Generation Group
for Zhenjiang Power Plant

2005年6月哈尔滨电气集团制造的首台国产半山1号9FA燃气轮机

China`s first "BS-1" 9FA Gas Turbine was produced by Harbin Electric Corporation in June 2005.

东方电气首台
M701F级重型燃机
转子吊入汽缸现场

The first M701F heavy-duty gas turbine rotor, produced by Dongfang Electric Corporation, was being hoisted into the cylinder field.

第二节 水力发电设备
Section 2 Hydroelectric Power Generating Equipment

新中国成立初期曾生产了0.8 MW的小型水电机组，1955年制造首台官厅10 MW混流式机组，以后陆续发展了新安江72.5 MW机组、刘家峡225 MW机组。1978年改革开放以来，先后发展了一些水平较高的大型机组。1979年研制成功转轮直径达11.3 m葛洲坝170 MW机组，至今仍是世界上转轮直径最大的轴流式机组。1984年制造了转轮直径6m的龙羊峡320 MW混流式机组，1991年制造了转轮直径8 m的岩滩302.5 MW混流式机组。1996年以来与国外阿尔斯通、伏依特、西门子、东芝、通用电气等公司合作制造了达到世界先进水平的三峡左岸700 MW混流式机组，其转轮直径9.8 m，推力轴承负荷5500 t。随后在消化国外先进技术的基础上创新提高，2004年实现三峡右岸700 MW水电机组的完全国产化，其水平高于左岸进口机组。此前，中国只设计制造了300 MW级混流式水电机组，而国外制造三峡机组等级的特大型水电机组已有30年历史，三峡工程大型机组，从介入到完成只用7年时间，一步跨越30年，是成功消化吸收引进国外先进技术的典范。国内外对此都给予高度评价。

Small-sized 0.8 MW hydro units were produced in the early days of the P.R.C. China's first 10 MW mixed-flow turbine unit (for Guanting) was produced in 1955, after which, 72.5 MW unit (for Xin'anjiang) and 225 MW unit (for Liujiaxia) were developed successively. Since 1978 when the reform and opening-up began, high-level large-sized units have been developed. The 170 MW axial-flow turbine unit for Gezhouba were developed in 1979, with the rotor diameter being 11.3 m which is still the largest one in the world now. The 320 MW mixed-flow turbine unit (for Longyang Gorge) was manufactured in 1984, with the rotor diameter being 6 m. The 302.5 MW mixed-flow turbine unit (for Yantan) was made in 1991, with the rotor diameter being 8 m. The 700 MW mixed-flow turbine unit (for the left bank of the Three Gorges) was produced to global top level after 1996, by cooperation with foreign companies like Alstom, Voith, Siemens, Toshiba and GE, with the rotor diameter being 9.8 m and the thrust bearing load being 5500 t. Later, innovation and improvement were made based on absorption of foreign advanced technology. The 700 MW hydro unit on the right bank of the Three Gorges was totally composed of equipment made by China in 2004, at a level superior to the imported unit at the left bank. Before that, China's experience was only the design and manufacturing of 300 MW mixed-flow turbine hydro unit while other countries had manufactured oversize hydro units like those used at the Three Gorges for 30 years. China took only 7 years from the initialization to completion of the large-sized unit for the Three Gorges. This is a great leap over the 30-year development in foreign countries and a success in introduction and absorption of foreign advanced technology, which is highly praised at home and abroad.

葛洲坝水力发电站鸟瞰图

A bird' s-eye view of Gezhouba Hydropower Station

东方电机厂为葛洲坝水电站制造的170 MW轴流式水
轮机转轮正在组装

The rotor of 170 MW Axial-flow hydro-turbine, made by Dongfang
Electrical Machinery Works for Gezhouba Hydropower Station,
was being assembled.

哈尔滨电机厂制造的125 MW轴流式水轮机正在
葛洲坝水力发电站安装

The 125 MW kaplane hydro-turbine made by Harbin
Electrical Machinery Works was being installed at Gezhouba
Hydropower Station.

20世纪80年代，东方电机厂制造的龙羊峡320 MW水轮发电机的直径11.8 m、重878 t的发电机轮子正在吊装

The generator rotor (diameter being 11.8 m and weight being 878 t) for 320 MW Hydro-turbine Generating Set, manufactured by Dongfang Electrical Machinery Co., Ltd. for Longyang Gorge Hydropower Station, was being lifted in the 1980s.

三峡大坝泄洪

Flood discharge at Three Gorges Dam

哈尔滨电机厂自主研制的三峡右岸电站700 MW水轮机转轮（外径10.44 m，净重440 t）

700 MW turbine rotor at the right bank of Three Gorges Dam, which was developed independently by Harbin Electrical Machinery Works. The outer diameter of the rotor was 10.44 m and the net weight of the rotor was 440 t.

东方电气自主研制的三峡右岸电站700 MW水轮机转轮（外径9.88 m，净重473.3 t）发运出厂

700 MW turbine rotor, developed independently by Dongfang Electric Corporation for the power plant at the right bank of the Three Gorges Dam, was delivered from the factory. The outer diameter of the rotor was 9.88 m and the net weight of the rotor was 473.3 t.

拥有自主知识产权的国产首台特大型水电机组——三峡右岸26号机组吊装

No. 26 unit at the right bank of Three Gorges Dam was being hoisted, which was the first oversize hydro unit made by China with proprietary intellectual property rights.

首台三峡机组定子机座制造成功

The first stator frame for the unit at Three Gorges Dam was manufactured.

第三节 核电设备
Section 3 Nuclear Power Generating Equipment

　　核电与火电、水电一起，是世界三大电力支柱，作为一种清洁、经济的一次性能源，受到国家重视。1980年12月国务院决定自主研制第一座核电站——秦山一期300 MW等级的压水堆核电机组，国内首台300 MW核电机组于1987年制造完成，国产设备占价值总量的70%，1991年12月15日投入商运，结束了中国无核电的历史。随后中国为巴基斯坦建设一座300MW核电站恰希玛一号电站，主设备于1997年交付，其中第一重型机器厂制造的反应堆压力容器和大连起重机厂制造的安全壳内环形吊车两项设备于1996年9月获得国家"八五"科技攻关重大科技成果奖。继秦山一期之后又进行了二期核电工程，分批建设4台650 MW核电机组，1993年初二期工程开工，我国首台650 MW压水堆核电机组于2002年4月15日投入运行，第二台由于上海锅炉厂制造时严重质量事故，拖到2004年5月才商用发电，国产化率55%。引进法国设备建设的大亚湾2×900 MW核电机组分别在1993年8月和1994年2月投运。截至2009年，我国已运行核电机组11个，总装机910万kW；正在建设核电机组11个，装机1100万kW；已核准拟建设核电机组22个，装机2400万kW。截至2010年年底，我国已运行核电机组13个，总装机1080万kW，是当今全世界在建和已定建设核电机组最多的国家。

　　Nuclear power, thermal power and hydropower are three pillars of the world's power sector. As a clean, economically efficient and non-regenerable energy, nuclear power is highly valued by China. The State Council decided to develop independently the 300 MW PWR nuclear unit for Phase I of Qinshan Power Station, which was China's first nuclear power station, in Dec. 1980s. The first 300 MW nuclear unit made by China was completed in 1987. China-made equipment accounted for 70% of total value. The nuclear unit was put into commercial operation on Dec. 15, 1991, which started China's nuclear power history. Later, China constructed Charshima No. 1 300 MW Nuclear Power Station in Pakistan, which was delivered in July 1996. In the project, the pressure vessel for nuclear reactor was made by First Heavy Machinery Works and the polar crane in containment was manufactured by Dalian Crane Factory. These two equipments were awarded the National Prize for Significant Scientific and Technological Achievement for the 8th Fiveyear Plan period in Sept. of the same year. Phase II of Qinshan Power Station commenced at the beginning of 1993, for which 4 sets of 650 MW nuclear units were built successively; the first 650 MW PWR nuclear unit made by China was put into operation on April 15, 2002. The second one began to generate power commercially in May 2004, delayed by a serious quality accident in the process of manufacturing by Shanghai Boiler Works; the ratio of China-made equipment was 55%. The 2×900 MW nuclear units for Daya Bay Nuclear Power Station, which were built by introducing equipment from France, were put into operation respectively in Aug. 1993 and in Feb. 1994. In total, 11 nuclear units have been put into operation in China with the installed capacity being 9.1 million kW, 11 nuclear units are being built with the installed capacity being 11 million kW, and 22 nuclear units are approved to be built with the installed capacity being 24 million kW by the year 2009. By the end of 2010, 13 nuclear units have been put ino operation in China with the installed capacity being 10.8 million kW. China is the country with the most nuclear units being and to be built in the world.

　　国内装备制造企业基本掌握了二代改进型核电站设备设计制造技术，引进型AP1000三代核电站关键设备正在消化引进技术或合作制造，逐步掌握其设计制造技术。现已基本形成了东北、上海、四川三套核电设备主辅机制造基地。

Domestic equipment-building enterprises are technically capable of designing and producing equipment for the second-generation improved nuclear station. As for equipment introduced for AP1000 third-generation nuclear station, absorption of the technology introduced or cooperative manufacturing is in process to gradually master the design and manufacturing technology thereof. At present, the three production base for nuclear main units and auxiliary machines are established mostly in Northeastern China, Shanghai and Sichuan.

国产首座秦山核电站一期外景
Phase I of Qinshan Nuclear Power Station, the first nuclear power station built by China

东方电气1000 MW
核电部套装配

The assembly of
1000 MW nuclear
components made
by Dongfang Electric
Corporation

东方电气1000 MW
核电蒸发器

1000 MW nuclear
evaporator made by
Dongfang Electric
Corporation

上海电气电站集团制
造安装于浙江秦山
核电站的国内首台
310 MW核电机组

China's first 310 MW
Nuclear Power
Generating Unit was
made by Shanghai
Electric Power
Generation Group,
which was installed
at Qinshan Nuclear
Power Station, Zhejiang
Province.

百万级核电高压
给水加热器

High pressure feed
water heater for
1000 MW nuclear unit

上海电气电站集团吊装完成后的
万吨级海水淡化蒸发器筒体——
为火力发电设备提供冷却水

The barrel of the 10,000 t sea water
desalting evaporator providing cooling
water for thermal power generating
equipment, after being hoisted by
Shanghai Electric Power Generation
Group.

组装完的万吨级海水淡化蒸发器——为火力发电设备提供冷却水

10,000 t sea water desalting evaporator was providing cooling water for thermal power generating equipment, after assembly

第四节 风力发电设备
Section 4 Wind Power Generating Equipment

长期以来，中国的风力发电设备停留在内蒙古、新疆为解决农牧民用电的离网小型机。21世纪以来，节能减排已成共识，风电是重要的新能源，2005年，国家《可再生能源法》明确了国家支持风电等能源发展的政策，中国风力发电设备得到始料不及的迅猛发展。通过引进259 W、1 MW、1.5 MW、2 MW、3 MW和5 MW级机组制造技术，中国很快与世界先进技术接轨，中国的风电设备制造业迎来了大发展。2006年国家尚没有关于风电设备产量的统计，2007年即生产了230多万kW，2009年生产了7551台/107.6万kW。2008年以后，1.5 MW机组为主力机组，在2009年生产了5530台/829.5万kW，2 MW机组和3 MW机组已批量生产，湘潭电机厂等正在研制5 MW直驱式海上风电机组。主机制造企业约80家，年产能超千万千瓦。

For quite a long time, the wind power generating equipment in China were only off-grid small machines used in Inner Mongolia and Xinjiang to supply power for farmers and herders. The idea of energy saving and emission reduction is popular in China in the 21st century, when people realize that wind power is an important new energy. *Regerable Energy Law of the People's Republic of China* defined the national policy of supporting development of energies including wind power in 2005. From then on, wind power generating equipment develops vigorously in China and China's manufacturing industry of wind power generating equipment soars. China integrated its technologies with top technologies in the world soon by introducing the manufacturing technologies for 259W, 1 MW, 1.5 MW, 2 MW, 3 MW and 5 MW units. There was no national statistics of the production of wind power generating equipment in China in 2006. More than 2.3 million kW were produced in 2007 and 7551 sets/107.6 million kW in 2009. After the year 2008, 1.5 MW units are considered as the major model, the production of which is 5530 sets/8.295 million kW in 2009. Mass production of 2 MW units and 3 MW units already began. Some enterprises, like Xiangtan Electric Manufacturing Corporation Ltd., are developing 5 MW direct driven offshore wind power generating units. There are about 80 main unit manufacturers, with the annual capacity exceeding 10 million kW.

2009年由湘电集团生产的国内第一套5 MW海上风力发电机组

China's first set of 5 MW offshore wind power generating unit was produced by Xiangtan Electric Manufacturing Corporation Ltd (XEMC) in 2009.

大连重工·起重集团公司生产的风电机组

The wind power generating unit manufactured by DHI·DCW Group Co., Ltd.

第五节 输变电设备

Section 5 Power Transmission and Transformation Equipment

1949年新中国成立前中国只能少量生产部分10 kV以下输变电产品。20世纪50年代，中国已掌握了110 kV、60年代220 kV、70年代330 kV高压输变电成套设备的制造技术。改革开放后，80年代自行研制了锦辽线500 kV交流输变电成套设备和舟山±100 kV直流输电设备，但技术水平与国外仍有一定差距。

China could only produced a few power transmission and transformation products below 10 kV before the founding of PRC in 1949. The development was swift after the founding. China was technically capable of manufacturing complete sets of 110 kV HV power transmission and transformation equipment in the 1950s, 220 kV in the 1960s and 330 kV in the 1970s. After the reform and opening-up began, China developed independently the complete set of 500 kV AC power transmission and transformation equipment for Jinliao Transmission Line and the ±100 kV DC power transmission equipment for Zhoushan in the 1980s. However, a certain technical gap still exists between China and foreign countries.

"十五"计划期间，自行研制成功西宁至兰州的750 kV超高压交流输变电设备，创造了世界上海拔最高（3000 m）、运行电压最高的输变电技术。其后，与国外合作生产三峡的输变电线路装备，先后全面掌握了500 kV超高压交直流输变电技术装备的制造。

During the 10th Five-year Plan period, China developed independently the 750 kV EHV AC power transmission and transformation equipment for Xining-Lanzhou line, developed the technology of power transmission and transformation with the highest operating voltage and the highest elevation (3000 m) in the world. Later, China cooperated with foreign partners to produce power transmission and transformation equipment for the Three Gorges Dam and mastered the entire manufacturing technology for 500 kV EHV AC/DC power transmission and transformation equipment.

"十一五"规划期间攻关1000 kV交流和±800 kV直流特高压设备。国外特高压交流输变电技术的研究始于20世纪60年代前后，苏联、日本、意大利均建设了特高压试验站、线段，但都没有进行商业运作。巴西依泰普±600 kV直流输电工程是世界上电压等级最高的直流工程。建设特高压电网是优化我国能源资源配置方式的途径，而且已掌握了500 kV和750 kV超高压交流输变电工程和±500 kV直流输电工程的装备制造，为特高压技术装备研制打下基础。世界首个1000 kV交流特高压示范工程，晋东南—南阳—荆门线已于2009年1月6日正式运行，国产化率达到90%。2009年12月世界首个±800 kV直流输电特高压示范工程在云南—广东线开始单极运行，2010年6月18日全面建成双极运行，国产化率62.9%以上。这两个特高压交直流输变电设备的研制成功，把中国输变电产品技术提高到世界最高水平。

During the 11th Five-year Plan period, technology was developed for 1000 kV AC and ±800 kV DC EHV equipment. The study of EHV AC power transmission and transformation began in foreign countries in the 1960s. The Soviet Union, Japan and Italy built EHV testing stations and lines which were not put into commercial operation. The Itaipu ±600 kV DC power transmission project in Brazil has the highest voltage class in the world. To build EHV power grid is a way to improve allocation of energy resources in China. China is technically capable of producing equipment for 500 kV and 750 kV EHV AC power transmission and transformation projects and ±500 kV DC power transmission projects, which lays the foundation for developing EHV equipment. Southeastern Shanxi-Nanyang-Jinmen Line was put into formal operation on Jan. 6, 2009, as the first 1000 kV AC EHV trial project in the world, with domestic content reaching 90%. The world's first trial EHV project of ±800 kV DC power transmission was put into operation under monopolar mode in Yunnan-Guangdong Line in Dec. 2009 and was accomplished on Jun. 18, 2010 running under bipolar mode, with the domestic content topping 62.9%. By the successful development of the aforesaid EHV AC/DC power transmission and transformation equipment, China's technology of power transmission and transformation products is upgraded to the top level in the world.

西安高压电器研究所合成试验回路大厅

The synthetic test circuit laboratory of Xi' an High Voltage Apparatus Research Institute Co., Ltd.

锦辽线董家变电站出线——20世纪80年代我国自行研制的500 kV输变电线路

The out-going line of Dongjia Substation on Jinliao Transmission Line, which was the 500 kV power transmission and transformation line developed independently by China in the 1980s

舟山100 kV高压直流输电工程——20世纪80年代我国自行研制±100 kV直流输电工程

100 kV High Voltage DC Power Transmission Project at Zhoushan, ±100 kV DC Transmission Project developed independently by China in 1980s

2009年12月甘肃实施电网升级，跨入750 kV主电网时代。这是永登750 kV变电站设备区

Electrical grid was upgraded in Gansu Province in Dec. 2009, by which the times of 750 kV mains began. This picture shows the equipment area of Yongdeng 750 kV Substation.

1100 kV气体绝缘金属封闭开关设备（DS、ES、母线、出线套管试验场景），西安电器开关有限公司生产

1100 kV gas insulated metal-enclosed switchgear (test scene for DS, ES, busbar and outgoing line bushing), produced by Xi'an XD Switchgear Electric Co., Ltd.

在武汉特高压试验基地运行的1100 kV变压器套管，西安电器开关有限公司生产

1100 kV transformer bushing, which was produced by Xi'an XD Switchgear Electric Co., Ltd. and operating at Wuhan Extra-high Voltage Test Base.

中国首台自主研发的±500 kV直流换流变压器，用于贵广二回直流输电工程，特变电工生产

The first ±500 kV DC converter transformer independently developed by China, produced by Tebian Electric Apparatus Stock Co., Ltd. for the second circuit of Guizhou-Guangdong DC Transmission Project.

为我国首条1000 kV交流特高压试验线路研制的400 MVA、1000 kV变压器，特变电工生产

400 MVA & 1000 kV transformer produced by Tebian Electric Apparatus Stock Co., Ltd. for China`s first 1000 kV AC Extra-high Voltage Test Line

为南方电网公司云南至广东世界首条±800 kV特高压直流输电工程研制的±800 kV干式平波电抗器，西安变压器有限公司生产

±800 kV Dry-type smoothing reactor, developed and manufactured by Xi`an XD Transformer Co., Ltd., for Yunnan-Guangdong ±800 kV Extra-high Voltage DC Transmission Project which was the first of its kind in the world and was affiliated to China Southern Power Grid Co., Ltd.

为南方电网公司云南至广东世界首条±800 kV特高压直流输电工程研制的±800 kV干式平波电抗器，特变电工生产

±800 kV Dry-type smoothing reactor, developed and manufactured by Tebian Electric Apparatus Stock Co., Ltd., for Yunnan-Guangdong ±800 kV Extra-high Voltage DC Transmission Project which was the first of its kind in the world and was affiliated to China Southern Power Grid Co., Ltd.

2008年2月西电集团自主研制成功
的世界首台1000 kV、200 Mvar并
联电抗器，是世界上电压等级最
高、容量最大的并联电抗器

The first 1000 kV & 200Mvar Shunt
reactor with the highest voltage level and
maximal capacity in the world. It was
successfully developed by Xi' an XD
Transformer Co., Ltd in Feb. 2008.

西安变压器有限公司换流变压器
直流极性翻转试验同时局部放电

DC Polarity Reversal Test with partial
discharge, for converter transformer
produced by Xi' an XD Transformer
Co., Ltd.

贵广Ⅱ回工程换流阀运行现场

Operation of the converter valve
produced for the second circuit of
Guizhou-Guangdong DC Transmission
Project

新沈高1100 kV GIS用隔离开关开合小电流试验

The low switching current test for 1100 kV GIS disconnector made by New Northeast Electric (Shenyang) High Voltage Switchgear Co., Ltd.

新沈高1100 kV GIS在特高压南阳开关站现场安装

1100 kV GIS, made by New Northeast Electric (Shenyang) High Voltage Switchgear Co., Ltd., was being installed at Nanyang EHV Switching Station.

国家电网公司荆门变电站的世界第一组投入商业运行的特高压1000 MVA，1000 kV变压器，特变电工生产

1000 MVA & 1000 kV transformer produced by Tebian Electric Apparatus Stock Co., Ltd. to serve Jingmen Substation affiliated to State Grid Corporation of China. This transformer is the first of its kind put into commercial operation in the world.

云广工程用±800 kV换流
变压器，特变电工生产

±800 kV converter transformer
produced by Tebian Electric
Apparatus Stock Co., Ltd. for
Yunnan-Guangdong Project

中国西安集团自主研发的
800 kV气体绝缘金属封闭
开关设备（GIS）

800 kV gas insulated metal-
enclosed switchgear (GIS),
developed independently by
China XD Group

西安西电电力整流器有限
责任公司制造的±500 kV
直流换流器

±500 kV DC converter
produced by Xi' an XD Rectifier
Co., Ltd.

第六章　农业机械
Chapter 6　Agricultural Machinery

新中国成立以来，党和国家十分重视农业机械的发展。1959年4月毛泽东作出"农业的根本出路在于机械化"的论断；1991年中共十三届八中全会提出"大力发展农用工业，推进农业机械化"；2004年颁布《农业机械化促进法》；中央财政投入购置农机具补贴，从2004年0.7亿元开始，3亿元、6亿元、20亿元、40亿元到2009年的130亿元，一年比一年大幅提高。

The Chinese Communist Party and the state have attached great importance to the development of agricultural machinery ever since the founding of new China. Mao Zedong has asserted in April 1959 that "the fundamental way out for agriculture lies in mechanization"; and it was put forward in the 8th plenary session of the 13th CPC Central Committee in 1991 that "to vigorously develop agro-industry and push ahead the agricultural mechanization". In 2004, "Law of People's Republic of China on the Promotion of Agricultural Machinery" was enacted, after which the central government has subsidized the purchase of farm machinery, from RMB 70 million in 2004, followed by 300 million, 600 million, 2 billion, 4 billion to RMB 13 billion in 2009, a substantial increase year after year.

1949年，中国的农业机械工业基本上是空白。1951年，国家召开农具工作会议，提出了迅速增补旧式农具和制造推广新式农具的工作方针。为了配合国营农场和拖拉机站的迅速发展，从1953年开始研制机械化农具，到1957年已能生产犁、耙、播及谷物联合收割机等机械化农机具。20世纪60年代到70年代，农机工业有了较快发展，开发了大批新产品，如东方红系列履带式拖拉机、铁牛系列轮式拖拉机、3—12 hp（2.6—8.8 kW）手扶拖拉机、东风牌自走式联合收割机等，到1978年已拥有农机产品2100多种。1959年第一拖拉机厂建成投产，各地还建设了一批大中型农机具制造企业。到1978年底，全国共拥有大中型拖拉机厂65个，小型拖拉机厂143个。

In 1949, the agricultural machinery industry in China was basically blank. Change did not happen until the national work conference on farm implements in 1951 when the principle for producing and promoting new farm implements while rapidly improving old ones was brought out. To match up with the rapid development of state-run farms and tractor stations, China started developing mechanized farm implements in 1953 and was able to produce plows, harrows, sowers and grain combines in 1957. The period of 1960s to 1970s witnessed the fast development of agricultural machinery industry, with the launch of a large number of new products, including the YTO series of crawler tractors, Iron Ox series of wheeled tractors, 3—12 hp (2.6—8.8 kW) walking tractors, Dongfeng self-propelled harvesters. By 1978, there have been over 2,100 kinds of farm implements. The first tractor plant was put into production in 1959, followed by the establishment of manufacturing enterprises of medium and large farm implements, resulting 65 medium and large tractor plants, and 143 smaller tractor works in China by the end of 1978.

1978年改革开放以前，中国农机产品主要是满足拖拉机站、国营农场（农垦）集体耕作的需要，产品以大型化为主。改革开放以后，农村经济改革，土地经营规模变小，多种经营有所发展，原有的农机产品适应不了"三农"发展的需要。根据农村新的需求，相应调整农业机械的产品结构，之后发展了农用运输车、小型农业机械、多种谷物联合收割机及农村多种经营所需农机产品。

Before the reform and opening up in 1978, China's agricultural machinery products, featuring large size, mainly met the demand of collective cultivation in tractor stations and state-run farms (reclamation). However, as the reform and opening up went on, rural economy changed which resulted in small-scale land operation and the development of diversified operation, the existing farm implements could not meet the need of "agriculture-rural areas-farmers". To cope with the new demand of rural development, the product mix of agricultural machinery was adjusted, followed by the development of the farm transport, small agricultural machinery, a variety of grain combines, as well as various farm implements required for the rural multi-operation.

进入21世纪，随着工业化、城市化进程加快，孕育了土地规模化经营方式的发展，中国农机行业的规模经济水平显著提高，逐步培育出一拖、时风、福田雷沃重工等多家大型农机制造企业集团，形成了具有产业集群效应凸显的山东、河南、江苏、浙江和河北等农机生产大省。通过技术引进、自主开发，开发了一大批高科技含量的农机具，21世纪初还依靠进口的120—180 hp大功率轮式拖拉机，现已批量生产并出口；在具备自主知识产权整机技术的基础上，通过整合国际资源开发研制出一拖东方红2884（288 hp）和福田雷沃2854（285 hp）、3004（300 hp）等大功率拖拉机，已成为新一轮带动中国农机工业经济增长的引擎；大型自走式玉米联合收割机技术获得突破，延吉春苗插秧机走向成熟等，为加速中国农业现代化的进程发挥重要作用。

As the curtains of 21st century opened, the speed-up industrialization and urbanization has nurtured the large-scale operation of land, and the scale and economic level of China's agricultural sector witnessed significant increase. A number of large agricultural machinery manufacturing enterprises and groups such as YTO Group, Shifeng Group, Foton Lovol International Heavy Industry Co.,Ltd were gradually fostered, while such large agricultural machinery manufacturing provinces as Shandong, Henan, Jiangsu, Zhejiang and Hebei with prominent industrial cluster effect took shape. Thanks to the introduction of technology and independent research, a large number of high-tech farm machinery was developed. 120—180 hp high-power wheeled tractors which relied on import in the early 21st century have been put into mass production and exported; With the intellectual property, China has developed high power tractors as YTO2884(288hp) and Foton 2854(285hp) and Foton 3004(300hp) by integrating international resources, which has driven the new round of growth of China's agricultural machinery industry; the technology breakthrough of large self-propelled corn combine harvester and much maturely developed Yanji spring seedling transplanter have played a significant role in expediting the agricultural modernization in China.

60年来，中国农业机械工业为农村提供了1.2万亿元以上的农业机械，使我国农业机械保有量快速增长。

China's agricultural machinery industry has contributed to the rapid growth of agricultural machinery in China with the provision of agricultural machinery worth more than RMB 1.2 trillion to rural areas for the past 60 years.

中国主要农业机械1952—2008年末拥有量增长情况
Growth of China's major agricultural machinery by the end of 1952—2008

年份 Year	农业机械 总动力 (万kW) Total Power of Agricultural Machinery (10,000 kW)	大中型 拖拉机 (万台) Medium and Large Tractor (10,000 sets)	小型 拖拉机 (万台) Small Tractor (10,000 sets)	联合 收割机 (万台) Combine Harvester (10,000 sets)
1952	18	0.13		0.03
1957	121	1.47		0.18
1978	11750	55.74	137.3	1.90
2000	55172	97.45	1264.4	
2007	76590	206.27	1619.1	
2008	82190	299.52	1722.4	

随着农业机械保有量的增加，农业机械化水平不断提高。全国耕种收综合机械化水平2004年底为35.7%，2008年为45%，其中全国机耕面积占全国耕地面积的比重，1977年为38.7%，2007年为57.0%；机播面积占播种面积的比重，1977年为7.30%，2007年增为33.00%；机收面积占收获面积的比重，1977年为1.8%，2007年为27%（注：2008年小麦机收面积占82%、水稻54%、玉米12%）。

With the growth of agricultural machinery, agricultural mechanization also stepped to a higher level with the level of farming mechanization in the country rising to 45% in 2008 from 35.7% at the end of 2004. The area plowed and sown by machine accounted for 57.0% and 33.00% of the total respectively in 2007 rather than the original 38.7% and 7.30% in 1977. The proportion of land harvested with the help of machine in the total area climbed to 27% in 2007 from 1.8% in 1977. (Note: the area of wheat, rice and maize harvested by machine took up 82%, 54% and 12% of the total respectively in 2008.)

全国农业机械作业水平(1977—2008年)
National level of agricultural machinery operation (1977—2008)

年份 Year	机 耕 Mechanical Farming		机 播 Mechanical Sowing		机 收 Mechanical Harvest	
	面积 (100 km²) Area (10,000 hectares)	水平 (%) Level (%)	面积 (100 km²) Area (10,000 hectares)	水平 (%) Level (%)	面积 (100 km²) Area (10,000 hectares)	水平 (%) Level (%)
1977	3841	38.70	1087	7.30	267	1.80
1978	4067	40.90	1333	8.9	313	2.10
1986	3931	40.85	1316	9.12	492	3.41
1996	5518	57.81	3259	21.38	1835	12.05
2007	6933	57.00	5200	33.00	4067	27.00
2008		61.80		35.30		32.00

　　中国已经成为世界农业机械制造大国，主要农机产品产量远远超越其他国家。2009年中国大中型拖拉机产量37.1万台，高于德国、日本，约占全球总产量的30%以上；小型拖拉机年产量200万台，是日本的10倍；中国联合收割机产量居世界首位，2007年生产10万台，是欧美的4倍，日本的3倍多。除特殊产品外，农业生产主要所需机械基本自给，为中国农业生产的现代化、机械化的发展提供了坚实的物质基础。

China has developed into a large manufacturer of agricultural machinery in the world with the output of major agricultural machinery products far more than that of other countries. In 2009, China manufactured 371,000 large and medium tractors, higher than Germany and Japan, accounting for over 30% of the global production, and 2 million small tractors which is 10 times that of Japan. China also tops the first in the production of combine harvesters, with an output of 100,000 sets, which is 4 times that of the U.S. and Europe and more than triple that of Japan. Except certain special products, the basic self-sufficiency of the main agricultural machines needed for farming is realized, laying solid material foundation for the modernization and mechanization of agricultural production.

20世纪80年代，一拖集团生产的东方红1202型履带
拖拉机带五铧犁在田间作业

The YTO 1202 crawler tractor with five-share plough made by
YTO Group in 1980s, was working in the farm.

20世纪80年代，一拖集团生产的东方红1202型履带
拖拉机带联合播种机在田间作业

The YTO 1202 crawler tractor with the combined drill produced
by YTO Group in 1980s was working in the farm.

20世纪80年代，一拖集团生产的东方红1202型轮式拖拉机牵引犁带合墒器作业

The YTO 1202 wheeled tractor produced by YTO Group in 1980s was drawing plough with a device keeping moisture in the soil.

新联（集团）公司研制的摘棉机，填补了国内空白

The newly developed cotton-harvester developed by Xinjiang Combined Machinery (Group) Co.ltd. filled the domestic gaps.

20世纪90年代中期以来发展的 "新疆-2" 自走式联合收割机在田间作业

The Xinjiang-2 self-propelled harvester developed in the middle 1990s is operating on the farm.

20世纪90年代中期以来逐步形成的跨地区的收割机队（整装待发的 "新疆-2" 收割机队）

Cross-region harvester teams have gradually come into being since the middle 1990s (The Xinjiang-2 harvester team is ready to departure).

20世纪90年代中期以来
发展的手扶拖拉机稻田
机耕作业

The walking tractor
developed in the middle
1990s was plowing the
paddy field.

20世纪80年代中期以来
发展的小型拖拉机翻耕
水田

The small size tractor
developed in the middle
1980s was plowing the
paddy field.

20世纪90年代以来发展的水稻收割机收稻作业

Rice harvester developed in the 1990s was working in the farm.

牧草收割机作业

Hay crop harvester was working in the grasslands.

牧草搂草作业

Hay crop raker was working in the grasslands.

第一拖拉机厂2008年研制的国内最大功率拖拉机之一的东方红-2884大功率轮式拖拉机

The YTO-2884 high-power wheeled tractor, one of the highest-power tractors in national wide developed and produced by YTO Group in 2008

20世纪80年代以来发展的钢架玻璃温室内景

The internal scene of a steel frame glass greenhouse developed in the 1980s

20世纪80年代以来发展的三层全阶梯蛋鸡笼养设备

The 3-layer staircase laying house developed in the 1980s

21世纪初中国一拖大功率轮
式拖拉机总装配线

General assembly line of high-
power wheeled tractor of YTO
Group at the beginning of the 21st
century

21世纪初的福田欧豹拖
拉机生产线

Production line of Europe
Leopard tractor of Futian
Automobile Co. at the
beginning of the 21st century

一拖集团生产的4LZ-2.5YA
玉米籽粒收获机

4LZ-2.5YA maize harvester
produced by YTO Group

410

20世纪末以来中国农业机械化科学研究院组织研发的部分农机具

Part of the Agricultural Machinery Researched and Developed by Chinese Academy of Agricultural Mechanization Sciences since the end of 20th century

20世纪末以来开发的部分农机具：4Mz-5型自走式采棉机演示

Part of the agricultural machinery developed since the end of 20th century: demonstration of 4Mz-5 self-propelled cotton harvester

8120甘蔗种植机

8120 sugarcane planter

半喂入水稻联合收割机

Half-feed rice combine harvester

1240A四行马铃薯种植机（牵引）

1240A four-row potato planter (traction)

6119免耕播种机

6119 no-tillage seeder

9265A自走式饲料收获机

9265A self-propelled forage harvester

1710马铃薯联合收获机

1710 potato harvester

山东时风（集团）有限责任公司生产的低速货车、三轮车和拖拉机

Low-speed Vehicles, Tricycles and Tractors Produced by Shifeng Group, Shandong

第七章 矿山采掘及起重、运输机械
Chapter 7 Mining, Lifting and Transport Machinery

20世纪50年代中国只能生产少量小型矿山设备。1978年改革开放前装备年产500万 t 露天矿的设备主要是冲击式钻孔机和4 m³电铲、80 t 矿用电机车，以此装备了攀枝花钢铁公司矿山；井下矿沿用打眼放炮、凿岩台车等设备。

In 1950s, China was only able to produce a small amount of small mining equipment. Before the reform and opening up in 1978, major equipment for open pit with an annual output of 5 million tons were impact drills and 4 m shovels, 80 t mining electric locomotives, which have been installed the mines of Panzhihua Iron and Steel Company, while drill and blast, and drill jumbo were applied in underground mines.

改革开放后我国开始研制现代化大型露天矿装备。"七五"、"八五"计划期间提供了首钢水厂铁矿1000万 t 级露天矿成套设备，采用单斗电铲加汽车运输工艺，主要装备为10 m³矿用挖掘机、108 t 电动轮矿用自卸车等；井下矿开始采用综采装备，液压支架和割煤机等先进装备。"九五"计划期间，已能提供总体水平相当国际20世纪80年代水平的平朔煤矿2000万 t 级露天矿成套设备，主要装备为16 m³和23 m³单斗挖掘机、154 t 电动轮矿用自卸车等；还开发了3600 m³/h采矿型斗轮挖掘机和5000 m³/h排土机的连续开采露天矿成套设备。20世纪90年代为矿山采掘提供的装备能力，大体是2000万 t/yr 露天煤矿、300万 t/yr井下煤矿，年处理能力300万—400万 t 选煤厂和2000 t/d熟料干法工艺水泥厂成套装备。

Following the reform and opening up, the research and development of modern large-scale open pit equipment kicked off. During the period of "Seventh and Eighth Five-Year Plan", Shuichang Iron Mine of the Capital Iron & Steel Works was equipped a complete set of equipment for 10-million-tons's class large open-pit mine, including 10 m³ electric shovels and 108 t motorized wheel dumping trucks, which adopted the technique of mono-bucket electric shovel and vehicle transport. Underground mining began to use some advanced equipment such as combined mining equipment, hydraulic support and coal cutter. During the "Ninth Five-Year" period, a complete set of equipment was equipped for Pingshuo 20-million-tons class open-pit mine, which was generally up to the international level in the 1980s. Apart from the main equipment such as 16 m³ and 23 m³ mono-bucket excavators, and 154 t electric wheel dump trucks, a complete set of 3600 m³/h bucket-wheel excavators and 5000 m³/h soil displacer was also developed and equipped for continuous operation. In 1990s, complete sets of equipment were able to be equipped for 20-million-tons/yr. open-pit mine, 3-million-tons/yr. underground mine, coal dressing plant with an annual handling capacity of 3 to 4 million tons/yr., and 20 million tons/d cement works adopting clinker dry process.

进入21世纪，我国开发了很多高档装备，如太重集团的35 m³、55 m³巨型矿用挖掘机、1800—2500 kW采煤机、7.5 m高井下液压支架、湘电集团的220 t电动轮矿用自卸车和中信重工的ϕ13 m竖井钻机等。综合起来看，21世纪初，中国机械工业有能力提供较高水平的矿用采掘设备。主要有装备水平较高的2000万 t/yr露天金属矿和煤矿、60万—70万 t/yr井下金属矿、1000万 t/yr井下煤矿（单井工作面）、300万—400万 t/yr选煤厂、单系列300万 t/yr选矿厂、1万 t/d熟料干法工艺水泥厂成套设备等。中国是世界上

20世纪80年代，第一重型机器厂和湘潭电机厂引进美国P&H公司技术合作制造的2800XP型斗容23 m³挖掘机

The Model 2800XP Excavator with bucket volume of 23 m³ co-produced in 1980s by No.1 Heavy Machinery Works and Xiangtan Electrical Machinery Works with the imported technology from P&H Corp. of USA

少数能成套提供各类矿山设备的国家之一。

Since the 21st century, a number of high-end equipment was developed, such as the giant 35 m³ and 55 m³ excavators, 1800—2500 kW coal cutters, and 7.5 m high underground hydraulic support of Taiyuan Heavy Machinery Group, 220 tons electric wheel dump trucks of Xiangtan Electric Manufacturing Corporation Ltd, as well as φ13 m shaft drills of CITIC Heavy Industries Co., Ltd. Generally speaking, the Chinese machinery industry was capable of providing mining equipment of a high level in the early 21st century. Complete sets of higher-level equipment were installed in 20-million-tons/yr. open-pit metal mines and coal mines, 0.6—0.7-million-tons/yr. underground metal mines, 10-million-tons/yr. underground coal mines (single well face), 3—4-million-tons/yr. coal dressing works, single series 3-million-tons/yr. ore dressing plants, 10000-tons/d cement works adopting clinker dry process and so on. China is one of the few countries that are able to provide complete sets of mining equipment for various mines.

20世纪80年代，太原重型机器厂与湘潭电机厂引进美国P&H公司技术合作制造的2300XP型挖掘机，斗容16 m³（2000万吨级露天矿成套设备）

The Model 2300XP Excavator with bucket volume of 16 m³ (open-pit mine complete plant with production capacity of 20 million tons/yr.) co-produced in 1980s by Taiyuan Heavy Machinery Works and Xiangtan Electrical Machinery Works with the imported technology from P&H Corp. of USA

20世纪80年代，湘潭电机厂研制的SF3103型108 t耐寒型电动轮自卸车在霍林河煤矿使用（千万吨级露天矿成套设备）

The Model SF3103 (108 t) Cold-resistant Motorized Wheel Truck (open-pit mine complete plant with production capacity of over 10 million tons) developed in 1980s by Xiangtan Electrical Machinery Works is in operation at Huolinhe Coal Mine.

20世纪90年代，上海彭浦机器厂引进日本小松公司技术制造的用于年产2000万t露天矿的410 hp履带推土机

The 410 hp Caterpillar Bulldozer used at 20 million tons/yr. open-pit mine was manufactured in 1990s by Shanghai Pengpu Machinery Plant with the imported technology from Komastu Company of Japan.

20世纪80年代，中信重型机械公司制造的KY-380型牙轮钻机

The Model KY-380 Rotary Drill made in 1980s by Zhongxin Heavy-duty Machinery Co.

20世纪80年代，柳州工程机械厂研制的ZL100型斗容5 m³轮式装载机

The Model ZL100 Wheel Loader with bucket volume of 5 m³ developed and manufactured in 1980s by Liuzhou Construction Machinery Factory

20世纪80年代，湘潭电机厂与美国德莱赛公司合作生产的154 t电动轮自卸车在平朔露天煤矿使用

The 154 t Motorized Wheel Dump Trucks co-produced in 1980s by Xiangtan Electrical Machinery Works with US Dresser Corp. are working at Pingshuo Open-pit Coal Mine.

20世纪80年代，抚顺挖掘机厂研制的WD-1200型挖掘机，斗容12 m^3

The Model WD-1200 Excavator with bucket volume of 12 m^3, developed in 1980s by Fushun Excavator Plant

20世纪80年代，湘潭电机集团有限公司制造的150 t工矿电机车

The 150 t Mining Electric Locomotive manufactured in 1980s by Xiangtan Electrical Machinery Group Co.Ltd

20世纪80年代，天津工程机械研究所、杭州重型机器厂、沈阳矿山机器厂、大连重型机器厂等研制的每小时1500—2000 m^{3}斗轮连续开采成套设备在云南小龙潭煤矿使用

The 1500—2000 m^3/h complete plant-bucket wheel continuous mining equipment developed in 1980s by Tianjin Construction Machinery Research Institute, Hangzhou Heavy Machinery Plant, Shenyang Mining Machinery Plant and Dalian Heaving Machinery Plant etc. is operating at Xiaolongtan Coal Mine, Yunnan Province.

20世纪90年代，沈阳重型机械集团有限责任公司与德国MAN/TAKRAF公司合作为元宝山露天煤矿制造的每小时3600 m³矿用大型斗轮挖掘机

The 3600 m³/h Mining Large Bucket Wheel Excavator was manufactured in 1990s for Yuanbaoshan Open-pit Coal Mine by Shenyang Heavy Machinery Group Co.Ltd in cooperation with MAN/TAKERAF Company of Germany.

20世纪90年代，大重集团公司与德国MAN/TAKRAF公司合作为元宝山露天煤矿制造的每小时5000 m³矿用大型排土机

The 5000 m³/h Large Mining Soil Displacer was manufactured in 1990s for Yuanbaoshan Open-pit Coal Mine by Dazhong Group Co. in cooperation with MAN/TAKRAF Company of Germany.

20世纪90年代，沈阳矿山机械集团公司与德国MAN/TAKRAF合作制造的元宝山矿带式输送机驱动站

The Driving Station for Belt Type Conveyer，manufactured in 1990s for Yuanbaoshan Open-pit Coal Mine by Shenyang Mining Machinery Group Co. in cooperation with MAN/TAKERAF Company of Germany

20世纪90年代，沈阳矿山机械集团公司与德国MAN/TAKRAF公司合作为元宝山露天煤矿制造的重型卸料车

The Heavy-duty Unloader，manufactured in 1990s for Yuanbaoshan Open-pit Coal Mine by Shenyang Mining Machinery Group Co. in cooperation with MAN/TAKERAF Company of Germany

20世纪80年代，中信重型机械公司制造的AS9/500型钻孔φ9 m竖井钻机

Model AS9/500 φ 9 m Shaft Drill Rig manufactured in 1980s by Zhongxin Heavy Machinery Co.

20世纪80年代，中信重型机械公司制造的矿用竖井JKMD-6×4型多绳摩擦式提升机

The Model JKMD-6×4 Multi-rope Friction Type Lift for mine shaft, made in 1980s by Zhongxin Heavy Machinery Co.

20世纪80年代，中信重型机械公司制造的年处理200万t洗煤成套设备装备的洗煤厂

The coal washing plant equipped with the complete set of coal washing equipment that was made in 1980s by Zhongxin Heavy Machinery Co. with annual disposing capacity of 2 million tons.

1986年，太原矿山机器集团有限公司制造的AM500型采煤机已用于阳泉、枣庄等20多个煤矿，年创百万吨水平

The AM500 coal cutter was produced by the Taiyuan Mining Machinery Group in 1986, which has been used in Yangquan, Zaozhuang and other 20 coal mines. The annual capacity reaches 1 million tons.

20世纪80年代，在首钢水厂铁矿进行工业试验的"一铲四车"（一台10 m³电铲和四台108 t电动轮自卸车）千万吨级大型露天矿成套设备

"One Shovel with Four Trucks" (a 10 m³ electric shovel and four 108 t motorized wheel trucks)—the complete set of equipment for 10-million-tons's class large open-pit mine in 1980s was in industrial operation test at Shuichang Iron Ore Mine of the Capital Iron & Steel Works.

20世纪80年代，太原重型
机器厂研制的WK-10A型挖
掘机，斗容10—14 m³（获
1988年国家质量金牌奖）

The Model WK-10A Excavator
with bucket volume of 10—14 m³,
developed in 1980s by Taiyuan
Heavy Machinery Works (awarded
the National Quality Gold Medal)

20世纪80年代，宣化采掘机械厂
制造的露天潜孔钻机在鞍钢弓长岭
铁矿作业

Open Air Down-the-hole Drill
manufactured by Xuanhua Excavating
Machinery Works in 1980s is working at
Gongzhangling Iron Mine, Anshan Iron &
Steel Co.

2007年，中信重工生产的竖井钻机，钻孔ϕ13m，创世界纪录

The shaft drill rig drilling ϕ13 m, produced by Zhongxin Heavy Machinery Works in 2007, broke the world record.

大连重工·起重集团制造的出口澳大利亚的12500 t/h斗轮取料机

12500 t/h bucket wheel reclaimer was produced by DHI·DCW Group Co.,Ltd. and exported to Australia.

大连重工·起重集团被国家发改委确定为第三代核环吊研制基地

DHI·DCW Group Co.,Ltd is identified as the development base of third-generation ring overhead crane for nuclear power plant by the State Development and Reform Commission.

2007年太重集团制造的900 t 架桥机

900 t bridge girder erection machine produced by DHI·DCW Group Co.,Ltd in 2007

大连重工·起重集团制造的国内第一台直径8 m敞开式岩石隧道掘进机

The first open-style rock tunnel boring machine with a diameter of 8 m in China, produced by DHI·DCW Group Co.,Ltd

2003年太原重工集团制造的三峡1200 t桥式起重机

1200 t Three-Gorges bridge crane produced by Taiyuan Heavy Machinery Group in 2003

2008年1月26日，国内首台、世界最大的矿用55 m³挖掘机在山西太原重型机械集团下线，这是2000万吨级以上大型露天矿成套设备中的关键设备，具有完全自主知识产权

55 m³ Mining Excavator, the first in China and the biggest in the world, rolled off the production line in Taiyuan Heavy Machinery Group in Shanxi on January 26th, 2008. It is a key part with full independent intellectual property right among the complete set of equipment for large open-pit mines with annual production capacity of over 20 million tons.

WK-55挖掘机正在平朔安家岭施工中

WK-55 Excavator is operating in Anjialing open-pit mine in Pingshuo.

2008年，湘电集团研制生产拥有完全自主知识产权的SF33900型220 t电动轮自卸车，这是我国2000万吨级大型露天矿成套设备的关键设备

In 2008, Xiangtan Electric Manufacturing Group developed SF33900 Model 220 t Electric Wheel Dump Truck with full intellectual property right. It is a key part with full independent intellectual property right among the complete set of equipment for large open-pit mines with annual production capacity of 20 million tons.

上海振华港机集团制造的一次性可翻三节火车车皮的三翻式旋转车钩翻车机

Three-turn rotary dumper with rotary coupler produced by Shanghai Zhenhua Port Machinery Co.,Ltd could turn three train wagons at a time.

2007年，上海建设路桥机械设备公司制造的5.5—6.0 m大型掩护式液压支架

5.5—6.0 m large hydraulic shield support produced by Shanghai Jianshe Luqiao Machinery Co., Ltd in 2007

2006年，上海振华港机集团制造的安装在法国勒哈佛码头的全自动化双小车岸桥

Fully automatic Quayside Container Gantry Crane produced by Shanghai Zhenhua Port Machinery Co.,Ltd in 2006 was installed in the Port of Le Havre, France.

2006年，上海振华港机集团制造的ZPMC可吊三个40 ft集装箱的岸桥

ZPMC Quayside Container Gantry Crane produced by Shanghai Zhenhua Port Machinery Co.,Ltd in 2006 is able to lift 40-ft three containers.

2007年，北方重工集团有限公司生产的φ11 m双护盾硬岩掘进机

φ11 m double shield hard rock tunnel boring machine produced by Northern Heavy Industries Group in 2007

2007年，沈重集团研制成功φ11m全断面隧道掘进机（盾构机）

Full-face tunnel boring machine of φ11 m (Shield tunneling Machine) successfully developed by Northern Heavy Industries Group (Shengyang) in 2007

2009年9月，太原矿山机器集团制造的世界最大的2500 kW电牵引采煤机成功下线，该机以25 m/min的速度前进，每小时采煤3500 t，该机为当前世界上最大的年产千万吨综采成套设备，现在山西西山煤电集团斜沟煤矿运行

2500 kW electrically driven coal cutter produced by Taiyuan Mining Machlnery Group Co.,Ltd   rolled off the production line successfully in September, 2009. It moves at a speed of 25 m/min and can excavate 3500 tons of coal per hour. It is the world's biggest complete set of mining equipment up to now and is in operation in the Xiegou Coal Mine of Xishan Coal Electricity Group in Shanxi Province.

中信重工"十一五"规划时期提供
的10000 t/d水泥生产线

10000 t/d cement production line provided
by Zhongxin Heavy Machinery Group during
the "Eleventh Five-Year Plan" period

安徽海螺集团日产万
吨新型干法水泥生
产线

The new dry cement
production in Anhui
Conch Cement Company
Limited with a daily
production capacity of
10000 tons

第八章 石油和石油化工设备
Chapter 8 Oil Equipment and Petrochemical Equipment

第一节 石油工业装备
Section 1 Oil Equipment

从1957年太原重型机器厂制造了中国第一台钻深1200m轻型石油钻机起步，20世纪70年代，兰州石油机器厂和兰州通用机器厂等，已能批量生产适应中浅陆上油田的钻深1500m、 3000m钻机为代表的钻、采、集设备，大庆油田基本依靠国产设备装备。为适应油气开发向海洋大陆架、沙漠油田和深层油田开发的需要，20世纪80年代中期以来，我国先后研制了4500m丛式钻机和6000m电驱动钻机。2005年宝鸡石油机械公司成功研制了9000m交流变频顶部驱动特深井钻机，2007年又研制了12000m特深井钻机，标志着我国在世界高端钻井装备上的突破。目前国内87%的大中型钻机、90%的修井机、100%的抽油机都是国内制造；国产9000 m等钻机已实现了对俄罗斯、美国、中东等地的批量出口。

Taiyuan Heavy Machinery Works manufactured China's first 1200 m light oil rig in 1957. As a start, Lanzhou Petroleum Machinery Works and Lanzhou General Machinery Plant were capable of mass production of drilling, extracting and collecting equipment in the 1970s, represented by 1500 m and 3000 m rigs for medium and shallow onshore oilfields. Equipment at Daqing Oilfield was mostly domestically made. For exploration of oilfields in continental shelf and deserts and of deep oilfields, 4500 m cluster-well drilling rig and 6000 m electric drive drilling rig were developed successively as from the mid 1980s. Baoji Oilfield Machinery Co., Ltd. developed 9000 m AC VF top-drive extra-deep drilling rig in 2005 and 12000 m extra-deep rig in 2007, marking a breakthrough for China in terms of high-end drilling equipment. At present, 87% of large and medium-sized drilling rigs, 90% of workover rigs and 100% of pumping units in China are domestically made; China-made rigs like 9000 m rig are exported in batches to Russia, USA and the Middle East.

海上油气钻采集运装备在20世纪80年代即开始研制，21世纪以来获得重大进展。30万t大型油轮、14万㎥大型液化气船、深海钻井平台都已出口，中国已成为世界上少数几个石油装备制造强国之一（另详见海洋工程介绍）。

Research and development of offshore oil & gas drilling, extracting, collecting and transporting equipment started in the 1980s and saw significant progress in the 21st century. Deep-water drilling platforms, 300,000 t large-sized oil tankers and 140,000 m³ large liquefied gas carriers are exported. China is now one of a few big manufacturers of oil equipment in the world (Introduction of oceaneering on a separate sheet).

2007年，宝鸡石油机械公司成功研制了12000 m特超深井钻机，此前只有美国、德国和挪威等少数国家具备生产此类钻机的能力

Baoji Oilfield Machinery Co., Ltd. developed 12,000 m ultra deep well drilling rig in 2007. Only a few countries like USA, Germany and Norway could produce this kind of drilling rigs before that.

四川宏华石油设备公司研制成功ZJ90DBS型9000 m超深井钻机

Model ZJ90DBS 9000 m ultra deep well drilling rig developed by Sichuan Honghua Petroleum Equipment Co., Ltd.

2006年，南阳二机石油装备
集团研制的ZJ700B/7000 m
型撬装钻机

Model ZJ700B/7000 m skid-
mounted drilling rig developed by
RG Petro-machinery (Group) Co.,
Ltd. in 2006

四川宏华石油设备有限公司的高寒
钻机在北极圈附近作业

Drilling rig developed by Sichuan Honghua
Petroleum Equipment Co., Ltd. is working
near the Arctic Circle.

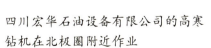

1998年，南阳二机石油装备集团研制的3000 m
车装钻机

3000 m truck-mounted drilling rig developed by RG
Petro-machinery (Group) Co., Ltd. in 1998

江汉油田第四机械厂
生产的车载钻机

Truck-mounted drilling
rig produced by No.4
Machinery Plant under
Jianghan Petroleum
Administration (JHPA)

2005年，南阳二机石油装备集团研制成功的适应-45℃高寒环境的低温钻机

Cryogenic rig for -45℃ temperature developed by RG Petro-machinery (Group) Co., Ltd. in 2005

华油一机厂抽油机测试

Pumping unit made by the First
Machinery Works of Oil Field of North
China is being tested.

荣盛机械公司生产的泥浆泵

Slurry pump produced by Rongsheng
Machinery Manufacture Ltd.

四川宏华公司生产的泥浆泵

Slurry pump produced by Sichuan Honghua
Petroleum Equipment Co., Ltd.

第二节　石油化工设备
Section 2　Petrochemical Equipment

　　中国在炼油、石化以及煤化等重大设备国产化方面也取得了可喜的成绩。

China made remarkable achievements in domestic production of significant equipment for oil refinery, petrochemistry and coal chemistry, etc.

20世纪80年代，由国内成套供应装备的四川化工总厂年产20万t的合成氨装置

The 200,000 t Synthetic Ammonia Plant at Sichuan Chemical Complex for which complete plant domestically made was supplied in the 1980s

20世纪70年代末，我国自行研制成套装备的上海吴泾化工厂30万t氨装置鸟瞰图

The Bird's-eye view of 300,000 t Synthetic Ammonia Plant at Shanghai Wujing Chemical Works, independently developed by China as a complete plant in the late 1970s

20世纪80年代，我国自行研制的镇海石油化工总厂第一套年产52万t二氧化碳汽提法尿素装置，设备国产化率达77%，随后第二套、第三套相继建成投产

The first set of 520,000 t CO_2 Stripping Urea Plant independently developed by China for Zhenhai Petrochemical Complex in the 1980s, with domestic content reaching 77%. The second and third sets were also completed and put into operation successively.

沈阳鼓风机集团为四川华天股份有限公司30万t合成氨装置研制的氨冷冻压缩机

The Ammonia Refrigeration Compressor developed and manufactured by Shenyang Blower Works for 300,000 t Synthetic Ammonia Plant of Sichuan Huatian Co., Ltd.

沈阳鼓风机集团为四川华天股份有限公司30万t合成氨装置研制的天然气压缩机

The Natural Gas Compressor developed and manufactured by Shenyang Blower Works for 300,000 t Synthetic Ammonia Plant of Sichuan Huatian Co., Ltd.

陕西鼓风机集团研发的高效节能TRT成套装置

High efficient energy-saving complete TRT unit developed by Shaanxi Blower (Group) Co., Ltd.

按项目的装备投资计算：千万吨级炼油设备的95%，百万吨级乙烯装置的78%（天津乙烯）以及百万吨级PTA装置的主要装备已实现国产化。针对国内乙烯、合成氨、尿素、常减压、催化裂化和催化重整、重油加氢脱硫等装置，以及丙烯腈、聚丙烯等配套装置的需要，解决了所需装置设备的研制。

By investment in equipment for projects: 95% of 10 million t refining equipment, 78% of 1 million t ethylene plants (Tianjin ethylene) and major equipment of 1 million t PTA plants were domestically made. Equipment were researched and developed for ethylene plants, Synthetic ammonia plants, urea plants, atmospheric-vacuum distillation plants, catalytic cracking plants, catalytic reforming plants and heavy oil hydrodesulfurization plants, as well as accessories like acrylonitrile plants and polypropylene plants.

高压热壁加氢反应器。1991年，上海重型机器厂和上海锅炉厂成功研制出镇海80万t/yr加氢裂化装置中的560t和400t热壁加氢反应器；20世纪90年代末，第一重型机械集团研制了千吨级加氢反应器；2007年，第一重型机械集团又为神华百万吨级煤直接制油装置，成功制造了世界上最大、单台重量2103 t、高64m的煤液化反应器。

High-pressure hot wall hydrogenation reactor: Shanghai Heavy Machinery Factory and Shanghai Boiler Works developed 560 t and 400 t hot wall hydrogenation reactors for 800,000 t/yr. hydro cracking plant for Zhenhai Petrochemical Complex in 1991. CFH MW developed 1000 t hydrogenation reactor by the late 1990s and 1 million t coal direct liquefaction plant for Shenhua project in 2007, successfully manufacturing the largest coal-liquefying reactor in the world with the single unit weight being 2103 t and the height being 64 m.

1991年，上海锅炉厂、上海重型机器厂为镇海石化总厂制造的560 t锻焊结构加氢裂化反应器

The 560 t forge-weld structured hydro generation cracking reactor was manufactured by Shanghai Boiler Works and Shanghai Heavy Machinery Factory for Zhenhai Petrochemical Complex in 1991.

1998年，第一重型机械集团公司为齐鲁石化公司制造的首台千吨级热壁加氢反应器

The first thousand ton class Hot Wall Hydrogenated Reactor manufactured by China First Heavy Industries(CFHI) for Qilu Petrochemical Corporation in 1998.

2000年，第一重型机械集团制造世界第一台两千吨级煤液化反应器，安装于神华煤制油工程

The first 2000 t-grade coal-liquefying reactor in the world, manufactured by CFHI and installed for the coal liquefaction project of Shenhua Group in 2000

第一重型机械集团于21世纪初制造的我国第一台1400 t 加氢裂化反应器

China's first 1400 t hydro generation cracking reactor manufactured by CFHI at the beginning of the 21st century

　　裂解装置。这是乙烯成套设备中的关键装置，1985年开始，我国先后研制了CBL型2万、3万、4万、5万、6万t/yr的裂解炉，应用于辽化、抚顺、扬子、齐鲁乙烯的改造工程，国产化率90%以上。21世纪初与国外合作制造了年产10万t、12万t大型裂解炉，已投产运行；年产15万—18万t和20万t的裂解炉已验收或正在开发，可满足百万吨级乙烯裂解装置的需要。

Crackers: crackers are key elements of complete ethylene plants. China developed Model CBL 20,000, 30,000, 40,000, 50,000 and 60,000 t/yr. cracking furnaces successively as from 1985, which were applied to reconstruction projects of Liaoyang Chemical Plant, Fushun Petrochemical Machinery Factory, Yangzi Chemical Plant and Qilu Chemical Plant, where more than 90% of equipment was domestically made. By cooperation with foreign parties, 100,000 t/yr. and 120,000 t/yr. large-sized cracking furnaces were manufactured at the beginning of the 21st century, which were put into operation already. More cracking furnaces at 150,000 t/yr., 180,000 t/yr. and 200,000 t/yr. were accepted or are under development, which can support 1 million t ethylene cracking plant.

　　乙烯三机。裂解气压缩机、乙烯压缩机、丙烯压缩机是乙烯装置的核心动力设备，世界上只有少数国家具备设计制造能力，曾经是乙烯装备国产化的禁区。"九五"以来，乙烯装置设备国产化取得了突破，沈阳鼓风机集团于1998年成功为大庆48万t/yr乙烯改造项目提供了裂解气压缩机和丙烯压缩机之后，为中国石化行业第二轮大中型乙烯改造奠定了基础，陆续为金山、扬子、茂名等石化60万—80万t/yr乙烯改造工程提供了乙烯装置用离心压缩机；2006年，该厂承制的茂名80万t/yr乙烯改造工程用乙烯裂解气压缩机一次开车成功，实现了国产裂解气压缩机大型化的工程应用。2007年，沈阳鼓风机集团承接了镇海、天津、抚顺3个百万吨级乙烯工程的裂解气压缩机、乙烯压缩机、丙烯压缩机各1台，已经陆续完成，实现了百万吨级乙烯裂解三机的国产化。

Three typies of ethylene machines: cracked gas compressors, ethylene compressors and propylene compressors are key power equipment for ethylene plants. Only a few countries in the world are capable of designing and manufacturing such equipment. This used to be a key problem prohibiting domestic production of ethylene plants. As from the"9th five-year Plan"period, breakthroughs were made in domestic production of ethylene plants. Shenyang Blower Works Group Co., Ltd. supplied cracked gas compressors and propylene compressors for Daqing 480,000 t/yr. ethylene reconstruction project in 1998, establishing a foundation for the second large and medium-sized ethylene reconstruction in China's petrochemical industry. After that, it supplied centrifugal compressors for ethylene plants for 600,000 — 800,000 t/yr. ethylene reconstruction projects of Jinshan, Yangzi and Maoming successively. The initial start-up of cracked gas compressor succeeded in 2006, which was manufactured by Shenyang Blower Works for ethylene plant for Maoming 800,000 t/yr. ethylene reconstruction project, which was the first large-sized project application of China-made cracked gas compressor. Shenyang Blower Works was entrusted with the manufacturing of one cracked gas compressor, one ethylene compressor and one propylene compressor respectively for the three 1 million t ethylene projects in Zhenhai, Tianjin and Fushun in 2007, which were completed successively realizing China's capability of producing the three ethylene machines at 1 million t level.

1988年，兰州化工机械研究院等单位研制辽阳石油化纤公司使用的CBL型2万t乙烯裂解试验炉，采用2-1炉管、二次注入蒸汽、二级急冷等技术

The Model CBL 20,000 t Experimental Ethylene Cracking Furnace developed by Lanzhou Chemical Machinery Research Institute and others for Liaoyang Petrochemical Fiber Company in 1988, by using technology such as 2-1 type furnace coils, secondary steam injection and two-stage deep freezing techniques, etc.

1993年，兰州石油化工机器总厂等单位为大庆石化总厂研制的 CF-62 钢制 1500 m³ 大型乙烯球罐

The 1500 m³ Model CF-62 Large Size Ethylene Spherical Steel Tank developed and manufactured by Lanzhou Petrochemical Machinery Works, etc., for Daqing Petrochemical Complex in 1993

2007年，沈阳鼓风机集团为上海金山石化70万t乙烯装置生产的 DMCL804+2MCL804+2MCL706 裂解气体压缩机

DMCL804+2MCL804+2MCL706 cracked gas compressor produced by Shenyang Blower Works for 700,000 t ethylene plant of SINOPEC Shanghai Petrochemical Co., Ltd. in 2007

沈阳鼓风机集团生产的大型炼油装置富气压缩机

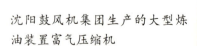

Unstripped gas compressor produced by Shenyang Blower Works for large-sized refinery unit

锦西化工机械厂研制的
聚乙烯90 m³聚合反应釜

The 90 m³ Polyethylene
Polymer Reactor developed
and made by Jinxi Chemical
Machinery Works

杭州制氧机集团自行设计制造的
乙烯冷箱用于齐鲁石化72万t/yr
改扩建工程

Ethylene ice chest developed and
manufactured independently by
Hangyang Group for 720,000 t/yr.
reconstruction & expansion project of
Qilu Petrochemical Corporation

沈阳鼓风机集团的4M80往复式压缩机

4M80 reciprocating compressor made by Shenyang Blower Works

沈阳鼓风机集团的800万 t 炼油装置用裂解气压缩机

Cracked gas compressor developed by Shenyang Blower Works for 8,000,000 t refinery unit

沈阳鼓风机集团的空分装置用压缩机

Compressor developed by Shenyang Blower Works for air separation plant

沈阳鼓风机集团的乙烯装置用裂解气和丙烯压缩机

Cracked gas compressor and propy compressor developed by Shenyang Blower Works for ethylene plant

上海压缩机厂为镇海石化总厂制造的循环氢压缩机

Hydrogen recycling compressor produced by Shanghai Compressor Factory for Zhenhai Petrochemical Complex

陕西鼓风机集团大型冶金装置高炉鼓风机

Blast furnace blower for large-sized metallurgical plant, made by Shaanxi Blower (Group) Co., Ltd.

大型化工用空气分离装置。大型空分装置是石化、煤化及冶金工业装置的重要设备。2002年，杭州制氧机集团设计制造的首台3万m³/h大型空分设备在上海宝钢开车成功，结束了中国长期以来3万m³/h以上大型空分设备依赖进口的历史。2004年，5.2万m³/h空分装置成功应用于中原大化项目，2005年，有2套6万m³/h空分装置出口国外，显示了我国的技术水平。2007年，开封空分集团研制的5.3万m³/h特大型双泵内压缩空分装置成功后，又中标煤制烯烃项目4组6万m³/h特大型空分装置；2008年，签订了1套8.3万m³/h的大型空分装置。这类大型空分装置国外也只有德国林德公司，法国液化空气有限公司和美国空气产品公司能生产。

Large-sized air separation plants for chemical industry: large-sized air separation plants are key equipment for petrochemistry, coal chemistry and metallurgy. The start-up of the first 30,000 m³/h air separation plant designed and manufactured by Hangyang Group succeeded at Shanghai Baoshan ISC in 2002, which ended the long period in which large-sized air separation plants above 30,000 m³/h relied on import. In 2004, a set of 52,000 m³/h air separation plant was applied to Zhongyuan Dahua project, and in 2005 two sets of 60,000 m³/h air separation plants were exported, showing China's technical level. Kaifeng Air Separation Group Company Limited (KFAS) developed 53,000 m³/h oversize dual-pump internal-compression air separation plant in 2007, after which, it was awarded the contract for 4 sets of 60,000 m³/h oversize air separation plants for Coal-to-Olefin (CTO) project. KFAS signed the contract for 1 set of 83,000 m³/h large air separation plant in 2008; only three foreign companies could manufacture such equipment, including Linde Group (Germany), Air Liquide (French) and Air Products and Chemicals, Inc. (America).

杭州制氧机集团自行设计制造的4.8 Nm³/h空分设备

4.8 Nm³/h air separation plant developed and manufactured by Hangyang Group

2006年杭州制氧机集团研制的60000 m³/h "宝钢6万" 空分设备

60000 m³/h "Baogang 60,000" air separation plant developed by Hangyang Group in 2006

2005年开封空分集团研发
制造的、安装在永城龙宇
煤化工的53000 m³/h大型
空分设备

53000 m³/h large-sized air
separation plant developed by
Kaifeng Air Separation Group
Company Limited (KFAS) and
installed at Henan Longyu Coal
Chemical Co., Ltd. in 2005

杭州制氧机集团板式钎接炉

Plate-fin brazing furnace made by Hangyang Group

第九章 冶金设备
Chapter 9 Metallurgical Equipment

20世纪50年代末"大跃进"时期，为"大炼钢铁"提供了大量小高炉及低档轧机。现代化大型冶金设备是20世纪70年代以来为"备战"而开始的。曾研制完成"九大设备"和攀枝花钢铁公司一期年产150万 t 的钢铁联合企业成套设备，主要有1200 m^3高炉、130 m^2烧结机等，自动化水平低，大体相当于工业发达国家20世纪50年代水平。还研制了本溪钢铁公司1700 mm热连轧板机，轧速6—8 m/s、厚度公差0.2 mm，手动控制，只相当于20世纪60年代初期水平，因设计、质量等原因，该机当时未能正常投产。

A lot of small blast furnaces and low-class rolling mills were supplied for "large-scale steelmaking" during the "Great Leap Forward" in the late 1950s. The development of large-sized modern metallurgical equipment started in the 1970s, to prepare for possible wars. "Nine major sets of equipment" were developed, together with 1.5 million t/yr. complete plant for iron and steel complex for Phase I of Pangang Group Company Ltd., mainly including 1200 m^3 blast furnace and 130 m^2 sintering machine, etc. The automation level was as low as that of industrially developed countries in the 1950s. What's more, 1700 mm hot strip continuous rolling mill was developed for Benxi Iron & Steel Co., with the rolling speed being 6—8 m/s, the thickness tolerance being 0.2 mm and manual control; this machine was only at the level of industrially developed countries in the early 1960s, which was not put into operation normally due to reasons like design and quality at that time.

1984年以来，通过宝钢三期工程装备的联合设计、合作生产，冶金设备的水平和国产化率迅速提高。宝钢一期工程（1979—1985年）国产化率12%，二期（1984—1991年，高炉、焦炉、烧结机、1900 mm板坯连铸机、2050 mm热连轧板机、2030 mm冷连轧板机、制氧机等工程）为61%，三期工程(1991—1999年，包括4350 m^3高炉、250 t 转炉、150 t 超高功率电炉，450 m^2烧结机，1450 mm板坯连铸机，及轧速分别为25.4 m/s和40 m/s的1580 mm热连轧板机和1400 mm及1550 mm冷连轧板机等）为80%，其中轧钢设备国产化率70%，冶炼设备国产化率达95%。通过宝钢二、三期现代化冶炼轧制设备的合作制造，为尔后自主研制年产300万—600万t钢的高水平成套设备打下基础，当时制造的宝钢第三期工程成套设备，要求其技术水平在21世纪初仍能保持世界一流水平。

The level and ratio of domestically made metallurgical equipment soared due to joint design and cooperative production of equipment for the three Phases of Baoshan ISC as from 1984. The ratio of China-made equipment was 12% in Phase Ⅰ (1979—1985) of Baoshan ISC, 61% in Phase Ⅱ (1984—1991, involving blast furnace, coke oven, sintering machine, 1900 mm continuous slab caster, 2050 mm hot strip continuous rolling mill, 2030 mm cold continuous rolling mill and oxygenerator, etc.) and 80% in Phase Ⅲ (1991—1999, involving 4350 m^3 blast furnace, 250 t convertor, 150 t UHP electrical furnace, 450 m^2 sintering machine, 1450 mm continuous slab caster, 1580 mm hot strip continuous rolling mills and 1400 mm & 1550 mm cold continuous rolling mills with the rolling speeds being 25.4 m/s and 40 m/s respectively), among which, the ratio of domestic content was 70% for rolling equipment and 95% for smelting equipment. Joint manufacturing of modern smelting and rolling equipment for Phase Ⅱ and Phase Ⅲ laid a foundation for independent development of high-level complete plant with the capacity being 3—6 million t steel/year. For the complete plant manufactured by China in cooperation with foreign parties for Phase Ⅲ, it was required that the technique thereof would still be of first class in the world at the beginning of the 21st century.

21世纪以来，通过鞍钢1780 mm和1700 mm冷、热连轧板机等高水平设备的自主研发，特别是鞍钢500万t现代化板材精品基地从冶炼到连续冷、热连轧板机的锻炼，国内设计、制造技术已臻成熟。此后鞍钢建设所需2150 mm、2130 mm热、冷连轧机和5.5 m宽厚板轧机等大型成套设备，均由国内制造。首钢搬迁建设的曹妃甸钢厂是新一代钢厂，具有很高的技术含量，按设备重量计，国产化率达93%以上。

After independent development of high-level equipment in the 21st century, like 1780 mm and 1700 mm cold continuous rolling mill and hot strip continuous rolling mill for Angang, especially from smelting equipment to cold continuous rolling mill and hot strip continuous rolling mill for Angang 5 million t modern high-class plate base, China's design and manufacturing technologies are well developed to a mature level. After that, all the large-sized complete plants necessary for construction of Angang were domestically made, including 2,150 mm and 2,130 mm cold continuous rolling mill and hot strip continuous rolling mill and 5.5 m heavy plate mill. Caofeidian Steel Works, built by Shougang Group for relocation, is of a new generation, with quite high technical level, where the ratio of China-made equipment tops 93% by the weight of equipment.

综合起来看，到21世纪初期，中国机械工业有能力提供年产600万t级以上钢铁联合企业所用常规流程的成套设备。包括4350 m^3高炉，7.63 m焦炉， 450 m^2烧结机，方坯、圆坯和板坯连铸机，大型冷、热连轧板机，无缝钢管热连轧机，高速线材轧机，大型中厚板轧机及大型螺旋焊管机组等成套设备。

In general, China's machinery industry is capable of supplying complete plants for normal workflows of iron and steel complex with the annual capacity above 6 million t. at the beginning of the 21st century, including 4350 m³ blast furnaces, 7.63 m coke ovens, 450 m² sintering machines, square billet and round billet and slab continuous casters, large-sized cold continuous rolling mills and hot strip continuous rolling mills, seamless-tube hot continuous rolling mills, high-speed wire rolling mills, large-sized medium-thick plate mills and large-sized spiral coil tube welding machine sets.

1967年，沈阳重型机器厂为西南铝加工厂研制的12500 t有色金属卧式挤压水压机（九大设备之一）

The 12500 t Non-ferrous metal horizontal extrusion hydraulic press (one of the nine major sets of equipment), developed by Shenyang Heavy Machinery Works for Southwest Aluminum Processing Factory in 1967

1970年，第一重型机器厂、太原重型机器厂为西南铝加工厂联合研制的2800 mm铝板轧机（九大设备之一）

The 2800 mm aluminum plate rolling mill (one of the nine major sets of equipment), jointly developed by China First Heavy Industries (CFHI) and Taiyuan Heavy Industries (TYHI) for Southwest Aluminum Processing Factory in 1970

1967—1970年，第一重型机器厂、机械科学研究院为西南铝加工厂联合研制的30000 t模锻水压机(九大设备之一)

The 30000 t die forging hydraulic press (one of the nine major sets of equipment), jointly developed by CFHI and Academy of Machinery Science & Technology for Southwest Aluminum Processing Factory from 1967 to 1970

一重集团为宝山钢铁公司三期(1991—1999年)制造的1450 mm板坯连铸机（1998年投产）

The 1450 mm slab continuous caster (put into operation in 1998) manufactured by CFHI for Phase III (1991 — 1999) of Baosteel Group Co.

455

二重集团1996年为宝山钢铁公司三期
工程制造的1580 mm热连轧机

The 1580 mm hot strip continuous rolling mill
made by China National Erzhong Group for
Phase III of Shanghai Baoshan Iron & Steel
Co. in 1996

第二重机器厂、太原重型机器厂、洛阳矿山机器厂1974年为舞阳钢铁公司联合承制的4200 mm特厚板轧机

The 4200 mm exceptionally thick plate rolling mill, jointly made by China No. 2 Heavy Machinery Works, Taiyuan Heavy Machinery
Works and Luoyang Mining Machinery Works for Wuyang Iron & Steel Co. in 1974

第一重型机械集团公司建厂初期（20世纪50年代末期）为包头钢铁公司制造的高炉

The blast furnaces made by CFHI at its early period (end of the 1950s) for Baotou Iron & Steel Co.

第一重型机械集团公司于建厂初期（20世纪50年代末期）为包头钢铁公司制造的第一代1150 mm方坯初轧机

The first generation of 1150 mm square billet blooming mill made by CFHI at its early period (end of the 1950s) for Baotou Iron & Steel Co.

1986年上海重型机器厂与德国、美国、日本等外国公司联合设计、合作制造安装在宝山钢铁公司二期工程
（1984—1991年）的2030 mm冷轧板机

The 2030 mm cold plate rolling mill, which installed at Phase II (1984—1991) of Shanghai Baoshan ISC and was jointly designed and manufactured by Shanghai Heavy Machinery Works and foreign companies from Germany, USA and Japan, etc. in 1986

西安重型机械研究所、天津重型机器厂联合为太原钢铁公司研制的国产第一台160 mm×1280 mm立式回转出坯型不锈钢板连铸机，1985年投产

The first China-made vertical rotary billet out type 160 mm×1280 mm stainless steel plate continuous caster, jointly developed and manufactured by Xi'an Heavy Machinery Works and Tianjin Heavy Machinery Works for Taiyuan Iron & Steel (Group) Co., Ltd.; it was put into operation in 1985.

第一重型机械集团公司为本溪钢铁公司制造的
1150 mm万能初轧机

The 1150 mm universal blooming mill made by CFHI for Benxi
Iron & Steel Co.

以太原矿山机器厂为主要单位，为沙市钢管厂制造
的第一套1020 mm螺旋焊管机组

The first 1020 mm spiral coil tube welding machine set
manufactured mainly by Taiyuan Mining Machinery Works for
Shashi Steel Pipe Works

年产400万t的板坯连铸机，两机四流，1988年第一重型机械
集团、太原重型机械集团、西安重型机器研究所和上海东风
机器厂与日本日立造船公司合作制造，供宝钢二期工程

The two twin-strand continuous slab casters with the annual capacity being
4,000,000 tons, jointly manufactured by CFHI, DHMG·DCW Group Co.,
Ltd., Xi'an Heavy Machinery Research Institute, Shanghai Dongfeng
Machinery Works and Hitachi Zosen Co. of Japan in 1988, for Phase II of
Baoshan ISC

沈阳重型机器厂与日立造船公司合作制造，于1991年投产的
宝钢二期工程450 m²烧结机在工作

The 450 m² sintering machine is working, which was produced by
Shenyang Heavy Machinery Plant and Hitachi Zosen Co. of Japan for
Phase II of Baoshan ISC and was put into operation in 1991.

大连重型机器厂为宝钢二期工程研制的6 m焦炉推焦机（1991年投产）

The pusher for 6 m coke oven, developed by Dalian Heavy Machinery Works for Phase II of Baoshan ISC (put into operation in 1991)

2006年一重集团自行设计制造的我国第一台15000 t自由锻造水压机试车成功

Test run of China's first 15000 t free-forging hydraulic press succeeded in 2006, which was independently developed and manufactured by CFHI.

二重集团2007年自行研制的
160 MN水压机

The 160 MN hydraulic press
independently developed by China
Erzhong Group in 2007

上海重型机器厂有限公司2008年
制造的165 MN自由锻造油压机

The 165 MN free-forging oil press
manufactured by Shanghai Heavy
Machine Works Co., Ltd. in 2008

2007年大连重工·起重集团生产的7.63 m焦炉机械

The 7.63 m coke oven machinery manufactured by DHM·DCW Group Co., Ltd. in 2007

上重集团生产的万吨铝挤压机（获2003年工业博览会金奖）

The 10,000 t aluminum extruder produced by Shanghai Electric Heavy Machine Group (wining the golden prize at 2003 Industry Exposition)

2003年，一重集团与鞍钢联合研制、具有自主知识产权、荣获国家科技进步一等奖的鞍钢1780 mm冷连轧机

The 1780 mm cold continuous rolling mill jointly developed by CFHI and Angang Steel Company Limited in 2003, with proprietary intellectual property rights and being awarded with the First Class National Prize for the Advancement of Sciences and Technology

一重集团制造的我国第一套2300 mm宽厚板坯连铸机

China`s first 2300 mm heavy slab continuous caster manufactured by CFHI

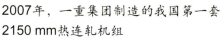

2007年，一重集团制造的我国第一套2150 mm热连轧机组

China's first 2150 mm hot strip continuous rolling mill manufactured by CFHI in 2007

一重集团制造的我国第一台2000 t多连杆压力机

China's first 2000 t multi-tie rod press manufactured by CFHI

一重集团制造的我国第一套1780 mm热连轧机

China's first 1780 mm hot strip continuous rolling mill manufactured by CFHI

4300锻造支承辊，一重产品

4300 forged steel back up roll of CFHI

1000 MW超超临界低压转子，
一重产品

1000 MW Supercritical Low Pressure
Rotor of CFHI

600 MW核反应堆压力容
器，一重产品

600 MW pressure vessel for
nuclear reactor of CFHI

二重集团2006年为波兰制造的2250 mm热轧机

The 2250 mm hot strip rolling mill manufactured by China Erzhong Group for Poland in 2006

二重集团为武钢制造的
2250 mm热连轧机

The 2250 mm hot strip
continuous rolling mill
manufactured by China
Erzhong Group for Wuhan
Iron and Steel (Group) Corp

二重集团为攀钢制造的
1350 mm连铸机

The 1350 mm continuous
caster manufactured by China
Erzhong Group for Pangang
Group Company Ltd

二重集团的150 t LRF钢
包精炼炉

The 150 t LRF ladle furnace
of China Erzhong Group

上重集团为鞍钢制造的1700 mm中薄板连铸连轧工程——精轧机组

Finishing mill train for 1700 mm medium-thin slab continuous casting and rolling works, manufactured by Shanghai Electric Heavy Machine Group for Angang Steel Company Limited

上重集团生产的船用
曲轴

Ship crankshaft produced
by Shanghai Heavy Ma-
chine Group

2009年中信重工为18500 t自由锻造油压机制造，成功组织829.5 t钢水合浇了世界最大的550 t铸钢件

CITIC Heavy Industries Co., Ltd. casted the largest 550 t steel casting in the world with 829.5 t melten steel in 2009, for manufacturing 18,500 t free-forging oil press.

2007年二重集团为宝钢生产制造的5000 mm宽厚板轧机

The 5000 mm heavy slab rolling mill manufactured by China Erzhong Group for Baoshan ISC in 2007

2008年中国一重研制的5500 mm 厚板轧机

5500 mm heavy plate rolling mill, developed by CFHI in 2008

第十章　工程机械
Chapter 10　Construction Machinery

1949—1952年国民经济恢复时期，中国开始制造一些经济建设急需的低端工程机械产品，如凿岩机、混凝土搅拌机、压路机、柴油机打桩锤等。经过"一五"、"二五"计划的建设，中国工程机械制造业逐步成型；经过"三五"、"四五"计划期间国家的建设改造，整个行业已初具规模。挖掘机、装载机、推土机、压路机、工程起重机等都已能系列生产。但直到20世纪七八十年代，工程机械的发展仍满足不了军民建设的急需，推土机等产品依靠大量进口，是当年机械工业能力薄弱的典型表现。

China began to produce some low-end construction machinery necessary for economic construction during the recovery period from 1949 to 1952, such as rock drills, concrete mixers, rollers and diesel pile hammers, etc. China's construction machinery industry developed gradually after construction in the first and the second five-year Plan periods, and took shape primarily after construction in the third and the fourth five-year Plan period. Series of excavators, loaders, bulldozers, rollers and construction cranes could be produced. However, the development of construction machinery failed to satisfy military and civil construction in the 1970s and the 1980s. The large import volume of products like bulldozers was a typical problem showing the poor machinery industry at that time.

1978年改革开放以来，工程机械行业是机械工业各行业中经济活动最活跃的行业之一。特别是进入21世纪，工程机械行业异军突起，发展势头强劲。这期间，三峡建设，西部开发，南水北调，西气东输，西电东送，高速公路网建设，铁路提速，海空港口建设和城镇化建设等，为工程机械开辟了越来越宽广的国内市场，促进了行业的快速发展。到2007年，已由机械工业中的一个小行业，发展成为仅次于汽车、电工、石化和机床的行业，居第五位。

The construction machinery industry has seen the most living in economic activities among all the sectors of machinery industry since the start of reform and opening-up in 1978. Especially in the 21st century, the construction machinery industry is soaring with a vigorous momentum. In this period, more and more opportunities are available to construction machinery industry in domestic market, which result in swift growth of the industry, due to projects like Three Gorges Project, Western Development, south-north water diversion, west-east natural gas transmission, west-east electricity transmission, expressway network construction, railway speed-up, construction of harbors and airports and urbanization. The construction machinery industry used to be a small sector in the machinery industry, but ranked the 5th in 2007, following automobile industry, power industry, petrochemical industry and machine tool industry.

中国工程机械行业发展主要指标(1978—2007年)
Major indices for development of China's construction machinery industry(1978—2007)

	单 位 Unit	1978	1997	2007
企业数 Number of enterprises	个 Nr.	380	1008	1488
固定资产原值 Original value of fixed assets	亿元 RMB 100 million	35.0	210	360
固定资产净值 Net value of fixed assets	亿元 RMB 100 million	17.5	140	270
工业总产值 Gross industrial output	亿元 RMB 100 million	18.8	350	2223
利润总额 Total profits	亿元 RMB 100 million	4.6	14	180

实施改革开放政策，走国际化发展道路。"八五"时期以来，工程机械行业逐步进入国际化发展轨道。国际上卡特匹勒公司、小松公司等知名跨国公司，看准了中国市场和中国工程机械工业的薄弱，蜂拥般进入中国，除兴办独资企业外，还兼并了一批中方企业，曾一度成为中国机械行业的主要力量。工程机械工业内资企业也逐步振兴发展，跨地区、跨行业、境内外兼并重组活跃。中联重科于2004年与国有企业湖南浦沅工程机械集团联合后，规模和技术水平都跃上新台阶，2008年收购了黄河工程等企业发展推土机和挖掘机等产品，同时在海外收购了英国保路捷公司、世界排名第三的意大利GFA混凝土机械制造商，大力推进混凝土机械国际业务。三一重工集团在国内重组兼并多家企业的同时，高速进军海外。徐工集团、柳工集团兼并许多企业，在国外设立子公司。

The reform and opening-up policy was implemented to take an international way of development. The construction machinery industry took an international way of development gradually after the 8th five-year Plan period. Noted international companies like Caterpillar

Co.Ltd and Komatsu Ltd. rushed into the Chinese market to take advantage of the weakness of China's construction machinery industry in domestic market. They founded wholly foreign-funded enterprises, merged some Chinese enterprises and used to be the largest players in China's construction machinery industry. Domestically-funded enterprises also thrived, with plenty of mergers and restructuring involving enterprises in different regions, industries and countries. Changsha Zoomlion Heavy Industry Science & Technology Development Co., Ltd. upgraded its scale and technical level by the integration with Hunan Puyuan (Holdings) Co., Ltd. in 2004, purchased enterprises like Shaanxi Xin Huanggong Machinery CO., Ltd. to develop products such as bulldozers and excavators in 2008 and purchased foreign companies including Powermole International (British) and GFA (an Italian concrete machinery manufacturer ranking the 3rd in the world), to expand its international business of concrete machinery vigorously. Sany Heavy Industry Group Co., Ltd. ("Sany" for short) merged and restructured several enterprises in China on the one hand and operated business in overseas market vigorously on the other hand. Xugong Group and LiuGong Machinery Corp. merged a lot of enterprises in domestic market and established branches in other countries.

自主创新能力增强，开发了许多高水平新产品。工程机械的重点骨干企业，都非常重视自主创新发展，每年投入的研发经费达到销售额的2%—4%，有的企业甚至达到5%以上。近年来开发了500 t全路面起重机、900 t履带起重机、68 m登高平台消防车，130 t汽车起重机、6.4 m³装载机、臂架长度72 m的混凝土泵车，创造了以492 m单泵垂直泵运送混凝土的业绩等等。

Capability of independent innovation improved, with a lot of new products developed at high level. Key enterprises dealing with construction machinery valued independent innovation highly, with the input by each in R&D accounting for 2%—4% and even above 5% of the sales amount every year. Products developed in recent years include 500 t all terrain crane, 900 t crawler crane, 68 m elevating platform fire truck, 130 t truck crane, 6.4 m³ loader and 72 m-boom concrete pump. Other achievements include vertical delivery of concrete by 492 m single pump.

对外贸易大发展，我国已成为工程机械产业大国。2007年，进入世界工程机械50强企业中的中国内资企业有8家。2006年，工程机械进出口贸易由长期逆差转变为顺差；2007年，出口额达87亿美元， 是进口额的1.76倍，产品销售台数仅次于美国，居世界第二位；出口拉动已经成为中国工程机械发展的主要动力之一。

Foreign trade increased remarkably. China is now a big power of construction machinery in the world. In 2007, 8 domestically-funded enterprises were listed among Global 50 of Construction machinery. Deficit of import and export trade existing for a long time in the past was changed into surplus in 2006. The export amount reached USD 8.7 billion being 1.76 times of the import amount in 2007, when the number of products sold by set ranked the 2nd following USA in the world. Export has become a major drive for the development of China's construction machinery industry.

中国工程机械产品进出口情况(2000—2007年)
Import and export of construction machinery (2000—2007)

		2000	2001	2002	2003	2004	2005	2006	2007
金额 （亿美元） Amount (USD 100 million)	进口 Import	13.1	15.5	20.5	35.6	36.4	30.26	39.1	49
	出口 Export	5.09	6.86	7.47	10.5	18.5	29.4	50.12	87
增长率 （%） Growth rate (%)	进口 Import	−10.27	18.32	32.26	73.66	2.25	−16.87	29.21	25.31
	出口 Export	21.24	34.77	8.89	40.56	76.19	58.92	70.48	73.58

1953年，我国第一台机械式挖掘机在抚顺挖掘机厂试制成功。到1985年，该产品的国内市场占有率达90%

Trial production of China's first mechanical excavator succeeded in Fushun Excavator Works in 1953. The domestic market share of this product reached 90% in 1985.

473

三一重工集团自主研发的66 m长臂架混凝土输送泵车，2008年1月24日在美国拉斯维加斯西曼哈顿商住群楼宇工地泵送混凝土

The 66 m Truck-mounted Concrete Pump developed independently by Sany Group Co., Ltd. This photo shows the product pumping concrete on the construction site of a commercial/residential compound in Las Vegas, USA on Jan. 24, 2008.

2007年，三一重工集团生产的泵送设备在上海环球金融中心施工

The pumping equipment produced by Sany was operating at the construction site of Shanghai World Financial Center in 2007.

2008年，三一重工集团研制成功世界最长72 m臂架SY5650THB72混凝土泵车

Sany developed SY5650THB72 72 m Truck-mounted Concrete Pump with the longest boom in the world in 2008.

上海环球金融中心492 m混凝土泵
送现场

The 492 m concrete pump at the
construction site of Shanghai World
Financial Center

现代化的长沙中联重科泵车生产线

This photo shows the modern concrete
pump production line of Changsha
Zoomlion Heavy Industry Science &
Technology Development Co., Ltd.

2008年，徐工集团开发成功国内最大吨位的QAY500型全地面起重机

Xugong Group (XCMG) developed the QAY500 model all terrain crane with the largest tonnage in China in 2008.

多家企业的工程机械在"5.12"汶川地震的抗震救灾现场

Construction machinery provided by several enterprises were working at the area hit by Wenchuan Earthquake on May 12, 2008.

2008年，三一重工集团研制的SCC9000型900 t履带起重机，被誉为"亚洲第一吊"

The SCC9000 model 900 t crawler crane developed by Sany in 2008 was called "the No. 1 crane in Asia".

三一重工集团有限公司自主研发的大吨位SR360旋挖钻机，填补了国内大功率大口径旋挖钻机的空白

The large-tonnage SR360 rotary drilling rig developed independently by Sany is the first large-power large-diameter rotary drilling rig domestically made.

中国最大轮式装载机CLG899III型斗容6.4 m³，2009年在柳工集团诞生

The CLG899III model wheel loader with the bucket capacity being 6.4 m³, which was the largest of its kind made by China, was developed by LiuGong Machinery Corp. in 2009.

天水风动机械公司的凿岩钻车

This photo shows the rock drills produced by Tianshui Pneumatic Machinery Co. Ltd.

第十一章 汽 车
Chapter 11 Automobiles

生产汽车在新中国成立初期还是可望不可即的事，毛主席曾在论述"论十大关系"时感叹："什么时候我们能坐上自己生产的小汽车就好了。"国家非常重视汽车工业的建设，第一汽车制造厂是国家"一五"计划的156项重点建设项目之一。1953年，毛主席签发《中共中央关于力争三年建设长春汽车厂的指示》。第一汽车厂的建设，1953年7月15日奠基，在全国的支援下，1956年7月13日第一辆解放牌汽车下线，标志着一汽三年建厂目标的如期实现，结束了中国自己不能制造汽车的历史。

The People's Public of China was not able to produce its own vehicles in its early days. When Chairman mao was giving the report "On ten Relationships", he said, "If only we could go for meetings in cars developed by our people…" The government valued the building of the auto industry highly. The First Automobile Works was one of the 156 key construction projects planned by the government for the first five-year Plan period. Chairman Mao signed *The Central Government's Instruction on Building Changchun Automobile Factory in Three Years* in 1953. The foundation for construction of FAW was laid on July 15, 1953. The first "Jiefang" brand vehicle was released off the assembly line on July 13, 1956, supported by the whole country, which indicated the goal of building FAW in 3 years was accomplished. From then on, China can produce vehicles independently.

汽车发明于1796年，批量生产于1886年，到2009年分别为213年和123年。中国1956年生产出第一辆汽车，1958年生产出第一辆轿车；2009年中国年产汽车1379.10万辆，其中轿车747.12万辆，都位居全球第一位，超过了世界上几个汽车生产大国历史最高年产量（美国2000年1278万辆，日本1990年1325万辆，德国2007年621万辆）。汽车产量从开始生产出第一辆到总量居世界第一，历经53年时间，超越了西方工业国家200多年历史。

China produced its first vehicle in 1956 and the first sedan in 1958. China produced 13,791,000 vehicles in 2009, including 7,471,200 sedans, ranking the first in the world by either vehicle or sedan. This annual production in 2009 exceeded the max. annual production of each of several big auto manufacturing countries (USA produced 12.78 million in 2000, Japan produced 13.25 million in 1990 and Germany produced 6.21 million in 2007). It took China 53 years from the manufacturing of its first vehicle to the total production ranking the first in the world. This is much faster than the development of auto industry in western industrial countries which took more than 200 years (It was 213 years from 1796 when the first vehicle was invented to 2009, and 123 years from 1886 when batch production began to 2009).

中国汽车在全球汽车产量中的比重逐年上升，1970年0.31%、1978年0.35%、2000年3.59%、2008年13.28%，2009年跃升至21.89%。

The proportion taken by China's auto production in global auto production rose year by year, from 0.31% in 1970 to 0.35% in 1978, to 3.59% to 2000, to 13.28% in 2008 and then to 21.89% in 2009.

中国汽车生产对全球汽车产量的增长作出重要贡献。1978年全世界共生产汽车4230万辆，其中中国14.9万辆，居世界第18位；2000年分别为5759万辆和207万辆；2008年分别为7030万辆和934.6万辆，居世界第二位。2008年比1978年和2000年，全世界增加汽车产量2800万辆和1271万辆，其中中国净增915万辆和723万辆，中国对世界汽车新增产量的贡献率1978—2008年为32.6%，2000—2008年为56.9%。至2009年则更高一些。

China's auto production was a major drive to the rise in global auto production. In 1978, 42.3 million vehicles were produced in the world, among which, 149,000 were made by China ranking the 18th. Global auto production was 57.59 million and China's auto production was 2.07 million in 2000, and 70.3 million and 9.346 million respectively in 2008 (China's production ranked the 2nd in the world). Global auto production rose by 28 million and 12.71 million from 1978 and 2000 respectively, among which, the rise of China was 9.15 million and 7.23 million respectively. The ratio of contribution by China to the world's new auto production was 32.6% from 1978 to 2008, 56.9% from 2000 to 2008 and even higher in 2009.

中国在世界汽车产量中的比重(1970—2009年)
Proportion of China's auto production in global auto production (1970—2009)

（单位：万辆）
(Unit: 10,000)

年份 Year	全球 总计 Global production	中 国 China		美国 U.S.A.	德国 Germany	日本 Japan
		产量 Production	在全球比重 （%） Proportion (%)			
1970	2940	9	0.31	827	384	529
1975	3300	14	0.42	899	319	694
1978	4230	15	0.35			
1980	2857	22	0.77	801	388	1104
1985	3229	44	1.36	1165	445	1227
1990	3611	51	1.41	881	503	1325
1995	5015	145	2.89	1199	467	1020
2000	5759	207	3.59	1278	553	1014
2001	5577	233	4.18	1143	561	978
2002	5878	325	5.53	1227	547	1026
2003	6058	444	7.33	1211	551	1029
2004	6396	507	7.93	1199	557	1051
2005	6655	572	8.60	1195	353	1080
2006	6921	728	10.52	1129	582	1148
2007	7327	888	12.12	1078	621	1160
2008	7030	930	13.23	868	604	1156
2009	6300	1379	21.89	570	521	793

注：数据来源：1990年以前来自《世界汽车工业参考》，以后年份据《中国汽车工业年鉴》。

Source: data dated before 1990 are from *Reference for World Automotive Industry*, and data dated after 1990 are from *China Automotive Industry Yearbook*.

中国制造汽车是从载货汽车开始的。1956年7月13日第一辆解放牌CA10型4t载货汽车在第一汽车厂下线；1958年5月一汽试制成功东风牌71型轿车，送到北京中南海向中共八大二次会议献礼，毛主席等党中央和国务院领导同志观看试坐，毛主席高兴地赞许："坐上我们自己制造的小轿车了"；6月21日，北京第一汽车附件厂试制成功井冈山牌轿车；7月，一汽试制成功第一辆红旗牌CA72型高级轿车，1959年9月，35辆"红旗"牌高级轿车发送北京，其中6辆参加国庆10周年游行，2辆"红旗"牌敞篷轿车提供国家领导人阅兵乘用，成为载入中国汽车工业史册的一个重要篇章。同时还有上海试制的凤凰牌中级轿车。但长期以来，能商品供应的轿车只有上海牌轿车，而且数量很少。

China's auto manufacturing began with freight trucks. The first "Jiefang" brand CA10 4t freight truck was released off the assembly line of FAW on July 13, 1956. The first "Dongfeng" Model 71 sedan was manufactured by FAW in May 1958, and was sent to Zhongnanhai for the Second Plenary Session of the Eighth National Congress of the CPC. Chairman Mao and other leaders of the Central Committee and the State Council visited and rode the sedan. Mao said with pleasure, "I've had a ride on the car made by ourselves". Beijing No. 1 Auto Parts Works manufactured the first "Jinggangshan" brand sedan on June 21 and FAW manufactured the first "Red Flag" brand CA72 limousine in July in the same year. In Sept. 1959, 35 "Red Flag" limousines were delivered to Beijing, 6 out of which were used for the ceremony celebrating the 10th anniversary of the founding of PRC and 2 open-topped limousines were used by state leaders to review the armed forces. This was a key milestone for China's auto industry. "Fenghuang" brand middle-class sedans were made in Shanghai at that time. However, only a small quantity of sedans made by Shanghai was supplied as commodities for quite a long time.

中国汽车工业发展，得益于改革开放，得益于轿车进入家庭。1987年，国务院北戴河会议确定了通过加快发展轿车工业来振兴中国汽车工业的发展战略；同时确定一汽、二汽、上汽作为我国轿车生产的三大基地。此后中国汽车工业的发展逐步加快。特别是2001年11月11日加入WTO后，进入高速发展期。从2002年开始，基本上每年新增汽车100万辆，而2009年一年就增加了450万辆。

Development of China's auto industry benefits from reform and opening-up and from application of sedans by households. At the conference of the State Council at Beidaihe in 1987, the strategy was determined to develop China's auto industry by promoting the development of sedan, and FAW, The Second Automobile Works and SAIC Group were made three major sedan production bases of China. From then on, China's auto industry soared. Especially, it has grown swiftly since China's admission to the WTO on Nov. 11, 2001. Generally, the auto production increased by 1 million every year from 2002 on, and 4.5 million in 2009.

改革开放初期，中国生产的汽车主要是中型载货汽车，外人形容中国汽车制造的产品结构为"缺重、少轻、轿车近乎无"，20世纪80年代末这一状态逐步改观，轿车、客车、货车三类汽车的产品结构比例，1990年为8.33%:25.04%:66.63%；至1995年已调整为26.69%:19.52%:53.79%；21世纪以来，特别是"轿车进入家庭"以来，三类车型构成比例迅速改善，2007年已调整为71.83%（包括MPV、SUV，如仅为轿车则为52.10%）：3.87%：24.34%。过去载货车的结构是缺重少轻，现在也发生很大变化，2007年重型、中型、轻型三类货车之比为6.12%：8.52%：85.34%。中国汽车产品结构已经与世界比例相衔接，基本适应汽车市场需求。

In the early days of reform and opening-up, the major category of automobiles produced by China was medium freight truck. It was described that, the product structure of automobiles made by China "lacked of heavy and light trucks and had almost no sedans". This situation changed gradually in the late 1980s. The ratio of sedans, passenger cars and trucks in the auto product structure was 8.33%：25.04%：66.63% in 1990, which was adjusted to 26.69%：19.52%：53.79% in 1995. In the 21st century, especially after "common households began to use sedans", the ratio was improved quickly to 71.83% (including MPV and SUV; and it would be 52.10% if only sedan was included)：3.87%：24.34% in 2007. In the past, both heavy and light trucks were lacked in the structure of freight trucks. This situation changed. The ratio of heavy truck, medium truck and light truck was 6.12%：8.52%：85.34% in 2007. The structure of auto products made by China has been adjusted to the global ratio to mostly satisfy the auto market.

产品品种和技术水平。轿车，从A级、B级到C级，低、中、高档品种俱全。从排量0.6 L的微型轿车到5.6 L的红旗高级轿车应有尽有；近几年每年都会有几十个、一百多个车型品种上市。载货汽车，从总质量1.8 t及以下微型车至总质量≤40 t的重型车；重型载货汽车技术含量提高，达到了国际同类产品水平；发展了各种要求的特种车，在2009年国庆节大阅兵中表现突出。客车从车长3.5 m以下的微型客车至车长10 m以上的大型客车；中高客车水平不断提升，城市客车宽敞、舒适、低地板、超长双铰接产品，尤其是BRT（快速公交）车型投入运营，成为城市一道亮丽风景线。改革开放前，中国汽车工业与发达国家在技术上整体有30年左右的巨大差距，通过技术引进和自主开发相结合，至21世纪前5年，在商用车领域已经与国际先进水平接近，轿车已基本完成了全面自主化开发的准备，新能源汽车研制基本与国外同步。

Categories and technical level of products: all the categories of sedans are available, from Grade A to Grade B, Grade C and Grade D, from low class to middle class and to high class, and from 0.6 L mini-car to 5.6 L "Red Flag" brand limousine. Dozens and even over hundred of car models were issued every recent year. Categories of trucks range from mini-truck weighing 1.8 t or below in total to heavy truck at≤40 t. The level of technology in heavy trucks was upgraded to the international level. Various special vehicles were developed, which gave people a remarkable impression in the big parade on the National Day in 2009. Categories of passenger cars range from minibus at 3.5 m long or below to large buses at 10 m long or above. The level of middle and top passenger cars keeps improving. City buses are broad and comfortable with low floor and overlong twin-twisted products. Especially, BRT models were put into service, becoming a nice view in cities. Before reform and opening-up, China's auto industry was 30 years behind developed countries technically. By the combination of technology introduction with independent development, in the last 5 years of the 20th century, commercial vehicles made by China approached international advanced level, preparation was mostly completed for fully independent development of sedans and R&D of new-energy vehicles went in line with international level generally.

1984年1月15日，中美合资经营的北京吉普汽车有限公司开业，10月10日中德双方签署上海大众汽车有限公司合营合同，以此为契机，排名在世界汽车工业前列的国际轿车生产商和最大汽车零部件企业绝大部分进入中国投资设厂。

Beijing Jeep Corporation Ltd., a Sino-American joint venture, began business operation on Jan. 15, 1984. The Chinese party and the German party signed the contract for the joint venture named Shanghai Volkswagen Automotive Co., Ltd. on Oct. 10. By this, most of the international sedan producers ranking among the top in global auto industry and the largest auto parts enterprises began to invest or set up factories in China.

2007年前10名跨国汽车公司在中国生产情况
Production of top 10 international auto companies in China in 2007

单位：万辆
Unit: 10,000

	企业名称 Company	全球产量 Total production in the world	在华企业产量 Production in China
1	丰田 Toyota	949.8	45.5
2	通用 GM	881.8	98.9
3	福特 Ford	636.5	18.0
4	大众 Volkswagen	621.3	95.6
5	现代起亚 Hyundai Kia	398.7	33.8
6	本田 Honda	391.2	46.4
7	日产 Nissan	343.1	28.8
8	菲亚特 Fiat	323.3	16.7
9	PSA集团 PSA Group	281.4	21.3
10	铃木 Suzuki	259.6	20.5

中国汽车工业已有上汽集团、一汽集团和南方工业集团（长安汽车）入选美国《财富》世界500强，2009年营业收入分别为248.82亿美元、236.64亿美元和216.75亿美元的业绩，排名分别为359、385和428位。在入选世界500强企业中的汽车板块21家企业中，上汽、一汽和南方分别居17、19和20位。虽然中国汽车企业已有三家入选500强，规模空前，但仍需增强竞争力。

Among all the Chinese automobile enterprises, SAIC Group, FAW and China South Industries Group Corporation (CSIGC) were listed among Global 500 by *Fortune* (an American magazine), the operating income of which was USD 24.882 billion, USD 23.664 billion and USD 21.675 billion in 2009 respectively, ranking the 359th, the 385th and the 428th. Among all the 21 auto enterprises listed among Global 500, SAIC Group, FAW and CSIGC ranked the 17th, the 19th and the 20th respectively. Although three Chinese auto enterprises have been listed among Global 500, which hits a record high, China's competitiveness still needs improvement.

入选《财富》500强的中国汽车企业
Chinese auto enterprises listed among Global 500 of *Fortune*

	2008			2009		
	营业收入（亿美元）Operating income (USD 100 million)	排名 Rank 在500强中 Among Global 500	排名 Rank 在汽车板块中 Among all the auto enterprises in Global 500	营业收入（亿美元）Operating income (USD 100 million)	排名 Rank 在500强中 Among Global 500	排名 Rank 在汽车板块中 Among all the auto enterprises in Global 500
上汽 SAIC Group	226.07	373	20	248.82	359	17
一汽 FAW	263.91	303	17	236.64	385	19
南方工业集团 CSIGC	–	–	–	216.75	428	20

我国第一辆国产"东风"牌
轿车

The first "Dongfeng" sedan made
by China

1956年7月13日，我国
第一汽车制造厂建成并
试制出第一批国产"解
放"牌载重汽车

The First Automobile Works
(FAW) was completed and
produced the first batch of
"Jiefang" brand heavy-
duty truck on July 13, 1956.

1958年9月28日，第一辆凤凰牌轿
车诞生，开创了"上海"牌轿车制
造的历史

The first "Fenghuang" (phoenix) sedan
was produced on Sept. 28, 1958, starting
the manufacturing history of sedans
"made by Shanghai".

1983年4月11日，第一辆上海桑塔纳
轿车组装成功，开创了上海汽车工业
面向世界、开门造车的新纪元

The first "Santana" brand sedan was
assembled on April 11, 1983, opening a new
era for Shanghai's auto industry to make
products for the whole world.

道路模拟试验

Road Simulation Test

上海大众和一汽大众汽车有限公司是中德合资企业，2009年分别生产轿车70.8万辆和67.1万辆，图为上海大众桑塔纳轿车在20世纪90年代初期，总装后调试厂房一角

FAW-VW Automobile Co., Ltd. and Shanghai Volkswagen Automotive Co., Ltd. are Sino-German joint venture enterprises, which produced 708,000 sedans and 671,000 sedans respectively in 2009. The photo shows "Santana" brand sedans at a corner of the commissioning plant after final assembly in the early 1990s.

东风汽车公司襄樊试车场

Xiangfan Testing Ground of Dongfeng Motor Corporation

一汽大众捷达轿车生产线

Production line for Jetta Passenger Cars

1992年，东风合资轿车公司刚下线的富康轿车

Fukang (Citroen) Sedans just released off the production line of Shenlong Automobile Co., Ltd. in 1992

1992年8月27日，二汽第一辆合资轿车"富康"在神龙襄樊装试厂顺利通过工艺调试，它拉开了东风汽车公司轿车发展的序幕

The first "Fukang" (Citroen) brand sedan made by Shenlong Automobile Co., Ltd. (a joint venture of Dongfeng Motor Corporation and PSA Peugeot-Citroen) passed process commissioning in Xiangfan Works on Aug. 27, 1992. This is the start of sedan development of Dongfeng Motor Corporation.

488

改革开放30年中国汽车成就展上展示的红旗检阅车

This photo shows "Red Flag" brand limousine displayed at "Exhibition of China's Achievements in Auto Industry due to Reform and Opening-up in the Past 30 Years".

红旗检阅车

"Red Flag" Brand Limousine

　　一汽从10周年国庆时便开始为国家元首制造检阅车。2008年产红旗检阅车：重量4.5 t，车长6 m，前高后低的船型车身看上去低调而气势非凡，前脸的水箱面罩是扇形格栅，继承了老式红旗的基因。轮辋造型也设计成太阳花状，旋转起来轮盘光芒四射。红旗检阅车搭载一汽自主研发的V12发动机，采用"双电脑动力控制系统"，每6个汽缸用一套电控单元控制，以保证正常行驶。红旗检阅车达到了"重度防弹级别"，国内目前的常规军用、警用制式武器都不能奈何得了它。它的防弹轮胎，即使中弹，仍可以50 km/h的速度行驶50 km；油箱采用防爆炸技术，几乎没有被点燃的可能。它还有达到军事标准的抗电磁干扰能力。

FAW has manufactured limousines for state leaders since the 10th anniversary of the founding of PRC. The "Red Flag" brand limousine for the National Day of 2008: weight is 4.5 t, length is 6 m; the body in the ship form which is high in the front and low at the rear looks extraordinary. The radiator grill in the front is fan-shaped, which is a classical element of "Red Flag" brand. Each rim is designed in the shape of sunflower, which makes it splendid by rotating. V12 engine which is developed independently by FAW is applied to the "Red Flag" brand limousine, and "double-computer power control system" is applied which overrides all the domestic conventional standard arms for army and police. The bullet proof tyres can still run 50 km at 50 km/h even if they are shot. The fuel tank is protected against explosion and can hardly be fired, which has resistance against electromagnetic interference up to military standard.

北京吉普汽车有限公司生产的第50万辆汽车下线仪式

The photo shows the ceremony for the 500,000th off-line vehicle produced by Beijing Jeep Co., Ltd. (BJC).

2006年10月12日，中国第一个中高级自主品牌——"上汽荣威"出世，图为上汽荣威550轿车

"Roewe" brand was developed by Shanghai Automotive Industry Corporation (Group) on October 12, 2006, as China's first middle-class and high-class original brand. This photo shows Roewe 550.

21世纪战地越野车"勇士"

"Yong Shi"（Warrior）military off-road vehicle developed in the 21st century

东风猛士

"Meng Shi" made by Dongfeng Motor Corporation

长城MPV嘉誉

菱智

长安奔奔

金刚

天津一汽夏利N3

奇瑞A5

一汽奔腾

长丰猎豹CS6

2008年群车像

Car Products in 2008

出口的吉利轿车

"Geely" brand sedans exported

2002年6月14日，一汽集团与天汽集团公司在北京签署重组协议

FAW Group and Tianqi Group signed the restructuring agreement in Beijing on June 14, 2002.

2006年12月26日，上汽和南汽在北京人民大会堂正式签署全面合作协议，这是中国汽车工业的里程碑

SAIC Group and Nanjing Automobile (Group) Corporation signed the formal cooperation agreement in the Great Hall of the People in Beijing on Dec. 26, 2006. This cooperation became a milestone for China's auto industry.

2007年12月17日，中国重汽集团2007年第10万辆重卡下线。中国重汽集团位居国内行业之首，产量规模进入全球前五大重卡制造商行列

The 100,000th heavy truck made by CNHTC in the year 2007 was released off the assembly line on Dec. 17, by which CNHTC ranked the first in the domestic industry. CNHTC ranked among global top 5 heavy truck manufacturers by production scale.

2008年7月11日，"奥运节能与新能源汽车示范运行交车仪式"在北京奥运公交车场站举行

"Ceremony for Demonstration and Delivery of Energy-efficient Vehicles and New-energy Vehicles for Olympic Games" was held at Olympic Bus Station in Beijing on July 11, 2008.

纯电动客车

Pure Electric Bus

奇瑞混合动力轿车

Hybrid Power vehicle made by Chery
Automobile Co., Ltd.

2009年10月20日10时45分，
中国年产1000万辆汽车在长春
一汽诞生（中国是继美、日之
后第三个年产量突破千万辆的
国家）

The 10,000,000th vehicle made by
China in 2009 was completed by FAW
Group in Changchun at 10:45 on Oct.
20 (China is the third country with the
annual vehicle production above 10
million, following USA and Japan).

第十二章　航空工业
Chapter 12　Aviation Industry

1951年4月17日，中央军委和政务院颁发《关于航空工业建设的决定》，从而正式宣告中国航空工业的创建。近60年来，逐步形成了专业门类齐全、科研、试验、生产相配套，具备研制生产当代航空装备能力的高科技工业体系。发展了多类型、多用途的飞机、发动机、导弹，已跻身于能够研制先进的歼击机、歼击轰炸机、直升机、运输机、教练机、特种飞机和航空发动机等多种航空装备的少数国家之列。2009年7月8日，中国航空工业集团公司成功入选美国《财富》世界500强，以营业收入217.38亿美元、利润5.68亿美元的业绩排名第426位，成为首家跻身世界500强的中国军工企业，并在航空航天与防务板块位居全球第11位。历经58年努力，中国航空工业终于站在了与欧洲宇航防务集团(EADS)、波音公司等世界级航空企业同台竞技的新起点上。

The Military Commission of the CPC Central Committee and the Government Administration Council issued *Decision on Construction of Aircraft Industry* on April 17, 1951, formally declaring the initialization of China's aircraft industry. A hi-tech industrial system has been developed over 50 years, which is capable of researching, developing, testing and manufacturing modern aviation equipment in all the specialized fields. Various kinds of multi-purpose aircrafts, engines and missiles were developed. China is now one of a few countries that are capable of developing many kinds of advanced aviation equipment like fighter, fighter-bomber, helicopter, transport aircraft, trainer aircraft, special-purpose aircraft and aeroengine. Aviation Industry Corporation of China was listed among Fortune Global 500 on July 8, 2009, ranking the 426th by the operating income being USD 21.738 billion and the profit being USD 568 million. It is the first Chinese military enterprise listed among Global 500, which ranks the 11th in the field of aviation, spaceflight and defense in the world. China's aviation industry is capable of competing with the world's top aviation enterprises like EADS and Boeing after 58 years of efforts.

1954年7月25日，中国生产的第一架飞机"初教-5"（仿苏雅克-18型）试制成功；1956年9月8日，中国又成功生产了第一架喷气式歼击机"歼-5"飞机（仿苏米格-17F型）。此后，中国第一架直升机——"直5"、超音速喷气式飞机——"歼-6"相继试制成功。20世纪60—70年代，虽然受到"文化大革命"的严重干扰和破坏，但中国航空工业继续发展，由"歼-5"、"歼-6"发展至"歼-7"、"歼-8"，1968年中国第一架自行设计制造的高空高速歼击机——"歼-8"飞机首飞成功，飞机性能和速度不断提高，由亚音速到超音速再到2倍音速。60年代，中国的"霹雳"1号空对空导弹、"红旗"1号、2号地对空导弹、"上游"1号舰对舰导弹相继试制成功、批量生产，结束了中国不能制造战术导弹的历史。

China manufactured its first aircraft named "CJ-5" (a copy of Yak-18 aircraft developed by the Soviet Union) on July 25, 1954, and its first jet fighter named "J-5" (a copy of Mig-17F aircraft developed by the Soviet Union) on Sept. 8, 1956. After that, China developed its first helicopter name "Z-5" and its first supersonic jet named "J-6" successively. China's aviation industry kept developing in the 1960s and the 1970s, even with serious interference and damage caused by the Cultural Revolution. "J-5" and "J-6" were developed into "J-7" and "J-8" aircrafts. "J-8" aircraft, which was the first high-altitude and high-velocity fighter developed and manufactured by China, finished its maiden flight successfully in 1968. The performance and speed of aircrafts were improved continuously, from subsonic velocity to supersonic speed and then to twice sound velocity. China developed and started mass production of "PL-1" air-to-air missile, "HQ-1" and "HQ-2" surface-to-air missiles and "SY-1" ship-to-ship missile one after another in the 1960s, with which China began to produce tactical missiles.

进入21世纪，中国航空工业迎来了发展的重大机遇，突破了一大批具有自主知识产权的航空工业核心技术，以"歼-10"飞机为代表，实现了中国军机从第二代向第三代的跨越；以"太行"发动机为代表，实现了中国航空发动机从第二代向第三代，从涡喷向涡扇，从中推力向大堆力的跨越；空空、空地导弹实现了从第三代向第四代的跨越；重大特种飞机实现了从无到有，直升机专项研制取得重大成果的一系列历史性跨越，一批赶超世界先进水平的国产第三代战斗机"FC-1"（枭龙）、"歼-10"（猛龙、轻型战斗机）、"歼-11"（重型战斗机）的问世，标志着中国歼击机研制取得突破性进展。民机产业发展翻开了崭新的一页，继2000年2月，中国第一个品牌民用客机"新舟-60"涡桨支线客机首飞成功后， 2008年11月，中国首架具有自主知识产权的92座支线飞机ARJ21成功首飞。国家重大专项150座干线大飞机项目于2007年2月获国家批准立项，现已进入预发展阶段，预计2014年实现首飞。

China's aviation industry found great opportunities of development in the 21st century, with breakthroughs in many core aviation technologies with proprietary intellectual property rights. Many historic milestones were achieved. For example, military aircrafts were developed from the 2nd generation to the 3rd generation, represented by "J-10" aircraft; aeroengines were developed from the 2nd generation to the 3rd generation (from turbojet to turbofan, from medium thrust to heavy thrust), represented by "TH" aeroengine; air-to-air and air-to-surface missiles were developed from the 3rd generation to the 4th generation; major special aircrafts were developed for the first time; significant achievements were made in research and development of special helicopter projects. A group of third-generation fighters were designed and made domestically at or above international level, including "FC-1"(Thunder), "J-10"(Vigorous Dragon, light fighter) and "J-11"(heavy fighter), marking China's breakthroughs in the R&D of fighters. Development of civil airplanes stepped into a new stage. China's first civil airplane, i.e., "XZ-60" turbo-prop regional airplane, finished its maiden flight successively in Feb. 2000. ARJ21 finished its maiden flight successively in Nov. 2008, which was China's first regional airplane with 92 seats and proprietary intellectual property rights. The special project of arterial airplanes each with 150 seats was approved by the state as a significant project in Feb. 2007. This project is now under preliminary development now and the maiden flight is planned to be accomplished in 2014.

航空工业主要成就（1954—2007年）
Major achievements in aviation industry （1954—2007）

年份 Year	成　就 Achievement
1954	我国生产的第一架飞机——"初教-5"试制成功 China manufactured its first aircraft named "CJ-5".
1956	第一架喷气歼击机——"歼-5"飞机试制成功 "J-5" jet fighter was developed, which was China's first jet fighter.
1958	多用途运输机——"运-5"飞机和我国第一架直升机——"直-5"试制成功 "Y-5" transport aircraft (multi-purpose) and "Z-5" helicopter (China's first helicopter) were developed.
1959	超音速喷气式飞机——"歼-6"试制成功 "J-6" aircraft (supersonic jet) was developed.
1965	自行设计的强击机——"强-5"实现设计定型，投入成批生产 The design of "Q-5" attack aircraft was finalized, for which mass production began.
1966	2倍音速的歼击机——"歼-7"试制成功 "J-7" fighter (at twice sound velocity) was developed.
1968	第一架自行设计制造的高空高速歼击机——"歼-8"飞机首飞成功 "J-8" fighter (with high altitude and high velocity) finished its maiden flight successfully, which was the first of its kind designed and manufactured by China independently.
1998	第一架自主设计的第三代战斗机——"歼-10"（猛龙、轻型战斗机）首飞成功 引进研发、改进的第三代战斗机——"歼-11"（重型战斗机）试制成功 "J-10" light fighter (Vigorous Dragon) finished its maiden flight successfully, which was the first third-generation fighter designed independently by China. "J-11" heavy fighter was manufactured successively, which was a third-generation fighter improved based on introduction.
2000	第一个世界品牌民用客机"新舟-60"首飞成功 "XZ-60" finished its maiden flight, which was China's first brand of civil aircrafts.

年份 Year	成 就 Achievement
2003	面向国内外两个市场的新一代轻型战斗机——"枭龙FC-1"首飞成功 "FC-1" (Thunder) finished its maiden flight, which was a light fighter of a new generation designed for domestic market and overseas market.
2005	"太行"大推力发动机、涡扇发动机试制成功 "TH" heavy-thrust aeroengine and turbofan engine were manufactured.
2007	首架自主研制的90座支线客机——ARJ21-700下线 国务院批准150座干线客机项目立项 ARJ21-700 was released off the assembly line, which was the first regional airplane with 90 seats developed by China independently. The State Council approved the project of arterial airplanes each with 150 seats.

新中国制造的第一种飞机——"初教-5"，1954年7月首飞成功。"初教-5"的试制成功，标志着中国航空工业从修理阶段跨入制造阶段。1954年8月1日，毛泽东为"初教-5"的试制成功签署嘉勉信，称赞"这在建立我国的飞机制造业和增强国防力量上都是一个良好的开端"。

"CJ-5" trainer finished its maiden flight in July 1954, which was the first aircraft made by PRC. By the success of "CJ-5", China's aviation industry developed from repair business to manufacturing business. Chairman Mao signed the congratulation letter for "CJ-5" on Aug. 1, 1954, saying that "this is a good beginning for establishing China's own aircraft-manufacturing industry and consolidating national defense".

新中国自主研制的第一种飞机——"歼教-1"，1958年7月首飞成功。它是为了满足喷气式飞机的训练要求而设计、制造的。该机从图纸发完到首飞上天不超过100天，在新中国航空史上占有重要的地位。

"JJ-1" trainer finished its first maiden flight in July 1958, which was the first kind of aircraft developed and manufactured independently by PRC. It was designed and manufactured to support training of jet planes. It was no more than 100 days from completion of drawings to maiden flight. This aircraft played an important role in the aviation history of China.

新中国生产的第一种喷气式战斗机——"歼-5"，1956年7月首飞成功。1956年10月1日，4架"歼-5"战斗机参加庆祝中华人民共和国成立七周年庆典，从天安门上空飞过。1959年下半年停产，共生产767架。

"J-5" jet fighter finished its maiden flight in July 1956, which was the first jet fighter manufactured by PRC. Four "J-5" fighters flew over Tian'anmen on Oct. 1, 1956, to serve the ceremony celebrating the 7th anniversary of the founding of PRC. The production of "J-5" was shut down in the second half of 1959, when 767 "J-5" jet fighters were produced in total.

新中国制造的第一种战术轰炸机——"轰-5"，1966年9月首飞成功，是一种亚音速轻型战术轰炸机，在当时是相当先进的一种前线轰炸机。1967年4月，该机正式投入批量生产，并开始装备空军部队。"轰-5"的众多改进型号在空军和海军航空兵中担负了重要角色。

"H-5" finished its maiden flight in Sept. 1966, which was the first kind of tactical bomber produced by PRC. It was a light bomber at subsonic velocity and a very advanced front-line bomber at that time. Mass production began in April 1967, and from then on, China's air force was equipped with this product. Many improved models of "H-5" played an important role in air force and naval air force.

新中国第一种大型水上巡逻反潜轰炸机——"水轰-5"，1976年4月首飞成功，具有超低空、大航程、全天候、大载弹量、短距起降和抗波浪性好等特性，主要用于中近海域海上侦察、巡逻警戒、搜索反潜等任务，也可监视和攻击水面舰艇。

"SH-5" anti-submarine bomber finished its maiden flight in April 1976, which was the first large-sized anti-submarine bomber developed by China. Its characteristics include super low altitude, long range, all-weather capacity, heavy bombload, short take off and landing, and anti-wave capacity. It mainly serves for reconnaissance, patrol surveillance and antisubmarine search on sea areas in middle and short ranges, as well as for monitoring and attacking surface ships.

新中国研制生产的第一代中型/中程运输机——"运-8"，1974年12月首飞成功。"运-8"是我国批量生产的最大的飞机，主要用于装备部队，也有一定数量的飞机进入民用市场和国际市场。该机是我国当前唯一能进西藏的国产飞机，用途广泛，具有空投、空降、空运、救生及海上作业等多种功能，一次可装载货物20 t，可同时装载两辆解放牌卡车，可运载直升机。

"Y-8" finished its maiden flight in Dec. 1974, which was the first generation of medium-sized/medium-range transport aircraft developed and manufactured by PRC. This was the largest aircraft for mass production in China, mainly for military use with a certain quantity for civil use or for international market. This is the only aircraft domestically made which can fly to Tibet at present. It can serve for multiple purposes with functions including air drop, air-borne use, air transportation, life saving and offshore operation. Its loading capacity is 20 t. Two "Jiefang" brand trucks can be loaded at the same time. It can also be used to convey helicopters.

新中国第一种取得通往世界市场"绿卡"的飞机——"运-12"，1982年7月首飞成功，对中国民机走向世界飞机市场、提升我国飞机的制造和管理水平具有开拓性意义。该机可载客17人，也可用于运输、跳伞、海上巡逻和农业飞行。

"Y-12" finished its maiden flight in July 1982, which was the first aircraft domestically made that is accepted by international market. This was the start for civil aircrafts made by China to compete in international aircraft market and to upgrade China's level of aircraft manufacturing and management. Each "Y-12" can carry 17 passengers, and can also serve for transportation, parachute jump, offshore patrol and agriculture.

中型多用途直升机——"直-9"，1982年2月首飞成功，主要用于人员运输、近海支援、海上救护、空中摄影、海上巡逻、鱼群观测、护林防火等，并可作为舰载机使用。军事用途包括侦察、火力支援、反坦克、搜索救护、反潜、通信等。1997年，12架"直-9"随驻港部队进驻中国香港特别行政区。"直-9"还多次参加极地科学考察，并在2008年汶川抗震救灾、海军索马里护航行动中发挥了重要作用。

"Z-9" medium-sized multi-purpose helicopter finished its maiden flight in Feb. 1982. It mainly serves for personnel transportation, offshore support, maritime rescue, aerial photography, offshore patrol, fish observation and fire protection. It can be used as carrier-based aircraft. It can serve for military uses like reconnaissance, fire support, anti-tank use, searching & rescue, anti-submarine use and communications. In Dec. 1997, "Z-9" helicopters were assigned to Hong Kong, China along with Peoples Liberation Army garrison in Hong Kong.

"Z-9" helicopters were used for polar scientific exploration for many times and played an important role in Wenchuan Earthquake relief in 2008 and naval convoy in Somalia.

新中国第一个世界品牌民用客机——"新舟-60"，2000年2月首飞成功，是我国已在航线上运营的性能最好的涡桨支线客机，该机在安全性、经济性、舒适性、维护性等方面达到或接近世界同类飞机的水平。截至2009年8月，"新舟-60"飞机已累计获得国内外订单160余架，已经交付津巴布韦、刚果（布）、赞比亚、老挝、印尼、玻利维亚等国。

"XZ-60" aircraft finished its maiden flight in Feb. 2000, which was the first brand of civil aircraft of PRC. It is the best turbo-prop regional airplane of China serving air routes. It approaches or equals to the international level of its kind in terms of safety, economy, comfort and maintenance. Over 160 "XZ-60" aircrafts in total have been ordered by clients at home and abroad by Aug. 2009, which were already delivered to countries like Zimbabwe, the Republic of the Congo, Zambia, Laos, Indonesia and Bolivia.

2007年，我国首架具有自主知识产权的新支线飞机ARJ21成功下线，2008年11月28日成功实现首飞。

ARJ21 was release off the assembly line in 2007, which was China's first regional aircraft with proprietary intellectual property rights. Its maiden flight was finished on Nov. 28, 2008.

"空警-2000"预警机，是一种大型全天候、多传感器、高性能、多用途的空中预警与指挥控制飞机，是空军未来战争中夺取空中优势、实施战略、战术及战役打击的重点武器装备。由载机和任务电子系统两部分组成。

"KJ-2000" AWACS has an all-weather airborne warning and control system with multiple sensors, high performance and multiple uses. It is a key weapon for air force to take air superiority and to realize strategic, tactical and campaign attacks. It is composed of two parts, i.e., aerial carrier and mission electronic system.

空警-200预警机，采用"运-8"作为基础平台，安装平衡木式相控阵雷达，是我国自行研制的另外一种轻型、全天候、多传感器空中预警飞机，是我军预警探测系统、指挥控制系统的重要组成部分。

"KJ-200" AWACS adopts "Y-8" as the basic platform, where balance-beam phased array radar is mounted. It is another kind of light and all-weather AWACS with multiple sensors, which is developed by China independently. It is a core element of the early warning detection system and the command and control system of the People's Liberation Army.

我国目前最先进的高级教练机——L-15"猎鹰"，2006年3月首飞成功。"猎鹰"飞机集成了许多当代最尖端的技术，整体技术水平在国际上处于一流。该机能完全模拟三代战斗机的飞行性能，是中国教练机发展史上的一个重要里程碑。

China's most update advanced trainer named L-15 "Falcon" finished its maiden flight in March 2006. L-15 "Falcon" integrates many most sophisticated technologies at present, so the overall technical level is among the best in the world. This product can totally simulate the flight performance of the third-generations of fighters and is a key milestone for the development of China's trainers.

新中国第一种面向国内国际两个市场的新一代轻型战斗机——"枭龙"FC-1，2003年8月首飞成功，具有突出的机动能力、较大的航程、留空时间和作战半径，以及较好的截击和对地攻击能力。"枭龙"战机的研制充分利用了国内国外两个市场、两种资源，使得军工高技术出口成为我国外贸经济中一道亮丽的风景线。

FC-1 "Thunder" finished its maiden flight in Aug. 2003, which was China's first kind of light fighter of new generation for domestic and overseas markets. It features excellent mobility, long range, long hovering time and long fight radius, as well as good performance of interception and ground attack. Domestic market and international market, as well as two kinds of resources, were fully leveraged to develop and manufacture "Thunder", by which, the export of high technology for military industry became a nice view in China's foreign trade economy.

新中国第一种自主设计的第三代战斗机——"歼-10"，1998年3月首飞成功。"歼-10"具有高可靠性、高生存力和高机动性能，作战半径大，起降距离短，攻击能力强，综合作战效能达到国际同类战斗机的先进水平。"歼-10"的研制成功，标志着我国成为少数几个能独立研制先进战斗机的国家之一。

"J-10" finished its maiden flight in March 1998, which was the first kind of the third-generation fighters developed independently by PRC. "J-10" is highly reliable, survivable and mobile, with long fight radius, short takeoff/landing distance and strong offensive capacity. Its comprehensive fighting efficiency reaches the advanced international level of the same kind. The successful development of "J-10" indicates that China became one of a few countries that could develop and manufacture advanced fighters independently.

"歼-11"飞机，是我国于20世纪90年代以来，引进、研发、改进的第三代战机，是人民空军的新型主战飞机。

"J-11" aircraft was the third-generation fighter introduced, researched and improved by China in the 1990s, as a main battle aircraft for the People's Liberation Army Air Force.

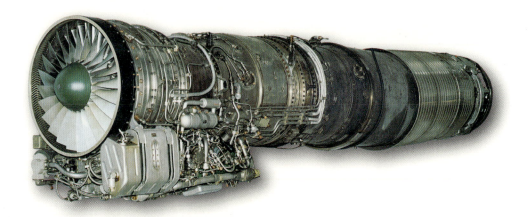

昆仑发动机是我国第一台走完自行设计、试制、试验、试飞全过程的航空发动机，是国内目前最先进的中等推力级的军用涡喷发动机。该发动机经过几百项严格的地面考核试验和空中考核试飞后，于2002年7月被国家军工产品定型委员会正式批准设计定型。它的研制成功使我国成为继美、俄、英、法之后世界上第五个能够独立研制航空发动机的国家。

KL aeroengine is China's first aeroengine that went through the whole process from independent design, manufacturing, testing and test flight. It is the most advanced turbojected engine with medium thrust that is domestically made for military use at present. After it passed hundreds of strict ground tests and test flight, its final design was approved formally by National Military Product Approval Committee in July 2002. Due to the success of KL aeroengine, China became the fifth country in the world, following USA, Russia, UK and France, that could develop and manufacture aeroengines independently.

太行发动机是20世纪80年代初期面对中国航空界的严峻局面，发展的新一代大推力涡扇发动机。太行发动机研制成功，标志着中国在自主研制航空发动机的道路上实现了重大跨越，对今后加速中国航空发动机事业跨越式发展打下了基础。

TH aeroengine was a heavy-thrust turbofan engine of new generation, developed against the tough situation of China's aviation industry in the early 1980s. The success of TH aeroengine marked a great leap forward of China on the road of independent research and manufacturing of aeroengines, and laid a foundation for promoting leap-forward development of China's aeroengine industry in the future.

第十三章 船 舶
Chapter 13　Ships

　　中国船舶工业是典型的外向型产业，中国作为世界上最重要的船舶出口国之一，每年建造的船舶70%以上用于出口。2008年，我国造船完工量、新接订单和手持订单三大造船指标已经超过日本，排在韩国之后，成为居世界第二位的造船大国。

China's shipbuilding industry is typically export-oriented. 70% of the ships built every year in China are exported, making China one of the world's most important exporter. In 2008, China exceeded Japan in terms of three main shipbuilding indicators, namely, shipbuilding capacity, newly received and hand-held shipbuilding orders, and became the world's second largest shipbuilding country following Korea.

　　中国船舶工业，从1865年江南制造局发轫，至新中国成立初期虽已有80多年历史，相对机械工业其他行业基础较好，但旧中国钢质船累计产量只有50万t。

Starting from 1865 in Jiangnan Manufacturing Bureau, China's shipbuilding industry has a relatively sound base as compared other machinery industries given its 80 years of development till the early days of the founding of People's Republic of China. However, the accumulative output of steel ships in old China only totals 500,000 tons.

　　旧中国一直是"有海无防"，因此新中国成立后，为海军研制技术装备，成为当时中国船舶工业的首要任务。在改革开放前，中国已成为世界上第五个制造核潜艇和第三个拥有远洋靶场船队的国家。

There was nearly no maritime defense in Old China; therefore the development of technical equipment for the navy becomes top priority for China's shipbuilding industry once the new China was founded. Before the reform and opening up, China was the fifth country to build nuclear submarines and the third to have ocean-going target fleet.

　　核潜艇的研制。1958年7月，中共中央批准正式研制核潜艇，1959年6月苏联中止对华援助，当时，毛泽东说："核潜艇，一万年也要搞出来"；1975年8月，第一艘鱼雷攻击型核动力潜艇"长征"1号定型；1983年8月20日，中国第一艘导弹核潜艇建成，1988年9月，导弹核潜艇水下发射运载火箭成功，从1958年上马至核潜艇水下发射试验成功，历时30年（20世纪60年代初期曾一度下马停建）。

The research and development of nuclear submarines was officially approved by the CPC Central Committee in July 1958. When the Soviet Union suspended aid to China in June 1959, Mao Zedong said: "Submarines shall be built, even if it would take 10 thousand years." The first nuclear-powered torpedo-attack submarine, named "Long March 1" was modeled in August 1975 and China's first nuclear-powered missile submarine was manufactured on August 20, 1983. After 30 years of development since the kickoff of research in 1958 (including a temporary break in early 1960s) the underwater launch of carrier rocket by means of nuclear submarine was recorded as a success in September 1988.

远洋靶场船队舰船的研制。1965年8月，中央专委决定建立远洋靶场测量船队（即远洋测量船队），1968年6月，毛泽东、周恩来正式批准研制工程计划，1977年12月到1979年远洋测量船队各船陆续建成，此后还在不断扩建。2007年以来，中国自主设计研制的新一代航天远洋测量船"远望"5号、"远望"6号交付中国卫星海上测控部使用，这是两艘具有国际先进水平的大型航天远洋测量船。

On ocean-going target fleet, the decision to establish ocean-going target surveying fleet (i.e., ocean-going surveying ships) was made in August 1965 by Special Commission of the Central Committee of CPC and Mao Zedong and Zhou Enlai formally approved the development project in June 1968. Vessles of ocean-going fleet were built successively during the period December 1977 to 1979 and the fleet was further expanded later. Since 2007 "Yuanwang 5" and "Yuanwang 6" (gaze afar), a new generation of space surveying ships independently designed and developed by China, have been delivered to China Satellite Maritime Tracking and Control Department for use. These two large-scale ships have reached the internationally advanced level.

1977年12月6日对于中国船舶工业来说，是一个具有历史转折意义的日子，邓小平在接见三机部、五机部、六机部主要负责同志时指出：国防工业应"军民结合，以军为主，发展民用，以民养军"；1978年6月28日，邓小平在听取六机部、海军汇报造船工业情况时指出："我们造船工业应该打进国际市场。我们的船比日本便宜，我们的劳动力便宜，一定可以竞争过，要多造船，出口船，赚外汇，主要多搞小型船，以民养军。"邓小平积极支持船舶工业选择我国香港作为突破口，并亲自作香港船东包玉刚家族的工作，2.7万t散货船"长城"号就是包氏家族订购的首船，是新中国成立以来的首条出口船，也是新中国首次按照国外船级社规范和标准建造的船舶；1982年1月4日"长城"号散货轮交船，英国劳氏船级社主席表示，"长城"号的建造标志着中国船舶工业跨入了一个新纪元。

December 6, 1977 is of historic significance for China's shipbuilding industry when Deng Xiaoping met with the leading comrades from the third, fifth and sixth ministries (in charge of aviation, weapon and shipping industry respectively) and pointed out that: the defense industry should be military-civil integration, with military industry in a leading position. Civil industry should be developed to support military industry. When Deng Xiaoping listened to reports from the sixth ministry and the navy on June 28 the next year, he also said: "We should enter into the world shipbuilding market. Our ships are cheaper than that of Japan, so is our labor. It would be sure that we are competitive and we shall build and export more ships to earn foreign exchange. We shall focus on small ships and development of civil industry to support military industry." Deng Xiaoping also actively supported Hong Kong as a breakthrough of shipbuilding industry and convinced the ship-owner Bao Yugang family in person who then ordered their first ship "Great Wall", a bulk cargo carrier with tonnage of 27,000 tones which was delivered on January 4, 1982. It is for the first time that China exported ships and built ships as per the regulations and standards of international classification societies. "The manufacturing of "Great Wall", said the Chairman of Lloyds Register of UK Shipping, "marks a new era of shipping industry of China."

20世纪80年代初，改革开放伊始，中国造船产业敏捷地完成了"军转民"，产品主体从舰艇改为商船，开创了船舶工业新局面；进入21世纪，抓住机遇，向世界造船大国、强国挺进。从20世纪90年代中期开始，中国船舶工业生产能力已跃居世界前列，到1994年，中国已成为继日本、韩国后的世界第三船舶生产国，2008年仅次于韩国，居世界第二位，2009年已居全球第一位。

Shortly after the reform and opening up began in the early 1980s, China shipbuilding industry enjoyed the smart transition from military use to civil use, and the shift of main product from naval vessels to merchant ships, creating a new situation of shipbuilding industry. Stepping into the new century, China seizes opportunities and advances to be a big and strong shipbuilding country in the world. China's shipbuilding capacity has leaped to the front ranks in middle 1980s and toped the third, following Japan and Korea in 1994, and was only second to Korea in 2008 and ranked the first in 2009.

中国已经能够自主设计和建造几乎所有类型的船舶，14.7万m^3液化天然气（LNG）船、10000TEU集装箱船、11300 t滚装船、钻井生产储油船（EDPSO）、半潜式深海钻井平台等高附加价值（高技术）*船舶和海洋工程陆续建造完成。出口船舶中90%以上为自主品牌船型。

China has been able to independently design and manufacture ships of almost all types. A range of high value-added (hi-tech)* ships and ocean projects, including 147000 m^3 liquefied natural gas (LNG) ships, 10000 TEU container ships, 11300 t Ro-Ro ships, drilling production storage and offloading vessel (EDPSO), and semi-submersible deep-sea drilling platform, are successively made and completed. More than 90% of exported ships are of independent brand.

中国造船产量(1980—2009年)
China's shipbuilding output (1980—2009)

年份 Year	总产量 （万t） Output (10,000 t)	占世界总产量 份额(%) Share in the World Output (%)	中国 排序 Ranking of China	船舶产量超过 中国的国家(地区) Country（Area）with more output than China
1980	20.0	0.6	17	
1990	40.4	2.5	8	日、韩、德、 中国台湾、南斯拉夫、 苏联、丹麦 Japan, Korea, Germany, China Taiwan, Yugoslavia, the Soviet Union, Denmark
1993	72.1	3.5	5	日、韩、德、丹麦 Japan, Korea, Germany, Denmark
1994	103.9	5.0	3	日、韩 Japan, Korea
2000	346.3	6.4	3	日、韩 Japan, Korea
2005	1000	18	3	日、韩 Japan, Korea
2006	1453	19	3	日、韩 Japan, Korea
2007	2164	25.0	3	韩、日 Korea, Japan
2008	2882	29.5	2	韩 Korea
2009	4243	40	1	—

注：*高附加值船舶是一个相对概念，泛指依靠先进技术、技能、工艺、复杂劳动、创造性等要素设计和建造的，比同吨位船舶具有更高价位的船舶。主要包括LNG船（液化天然气船）、超大型集装箱船、化学品船、豪华游船、汽车运输船、滚装船、挖泥船、冷藏船；特种船舶和海洋平台，比如破冰船、科考船和海洋工程装备，通常也属于高附加值船舶。高附加值船舶价位高。如，一艘15万m³容积的LNG船价格高达2.2亿美元，一艘超大型集装箱船价格1.5亿美元，一艘豪华游轮价格高达5亿美元以上，而普通油船或散货船价格仅为3000—8000万美元。

中国船舶工业成就概览(1958—2007年)
Overview of shipbuilding industry achievement（1958—2007）

年份 Year	成 就 Achievement
1958	5000 t 级沿海散货船"和平"25号与"和平"28号建成，建造速度创当时纪录 5000 t–class coastal bulk carrier "Heping" 25 and "Heping" 28 were completed at a record speed.
1960	第一艘自行设计建造的万t级货轮"东风"号下水 The first self–designed and built 10 000 t–class cargo ship "Dongfeng" was launched.
1979	建成首批远洋航天测量船"远望"1号和"远望"2号，成为世界上第3个（美、俄、中）拥有此类船舰的国家；首艘万t级远洋科学考察船"向阳红"10号建成 The first ocean–going space surveying ship "Yuanwang" 1 and "Yuangwang" 2 was built and China became the third (following United States and Russia) country to have such ships; the first 10,000 t–class ocean–going scientific–exploration ship "Xiangyanghong" 10 was completed.
1982	首艘按国际船舶通行规范建造的出口船"长城"号建成 "Great Wall", the first exported ship made according to prevailing international specification was built.
2002	首艘自行建造的30万t 级超大型油轮（VLCC）"远大湖"号首航 The first self–built 300 000 t class VLCC "Yuandahu" (Great Lake) made the maiden voyage.
2007	第一艘自主设计建造的8530TEU超大型集装箱船下水。我国自主建造的第一座有海洋工程中"航空母舰"之称的3000 m深水半潜式钻井平台 The first 8530TEU large container ship independently designed and built was launched. The first 3000 m semi–submersible deep–sea drilling platform was independently built by China and known as the "aircraft carrier" marine projects.

Note: * High value-added ship is a relative concept. It refers to ships that are designed and built by relying on advanced technology, skills, technique, complex work, creativity, and etc, and have higher price than those of the same tonnage. It mainly includes liquefied natural gas (LNG) ships, ultra large container ships, chemical tankers, luxury cruise ships, car carriers, Ro-Ro Ships, dredgers, refrigerated ships; special ships and offshore platforms, such as icebreakers, surveying ships and ocean engineering equipment, also fall within this category. These high value-added ships usually are of higher price . For instance, a LNG ship with a volume of 150,000 m^3 prices as high as 220 million U.S. dollars, an ultra large container ship 150 million U.S. dollars, a luxury cruise ship 500 million U.S. dollars, while the price of ordinary oil tanker or bulk carrier is only 30 — 80 million U.S dollars.

21世纪初，中船重工研制的战略导弹核潜艇

Strategic nuclear missile submarine developed by China Shipbuilding Industry Corporation at the beginning of 21st century

中船重工研制的新型导弹驱逐舰（海军成立60周年阅兵式阅兵舰）

New guided missile destroyer developed by China Shipbuilding Industry Corporation (reviewed at the 60th anniversary parade of PLA navy)

大连造船厂制造的"长城"号27000 t大湖型散装货船是1982年我国船舶行业第一艘出口船舶，也是第一次按照国际规范和标准建造的船舶

The 27000 tons-class Great Lakes bulk carrier "Great Wall" was built by Dalian Shipyard and exported in 1982. It is for the first time that China exported ships and built ships as per the specification and standards of international classification societies.

自行开发研制的水下智能机器人 (ARV)

Self-developed Autonomous and Remote-operated Vehicle (ARV)

第一节 航天测量船和科考船
Section 1 Space Surveying Ship and Research Ship

2009年，"远望"6号航天测量船航行在黄浦江上（可见主桅和第一个测控天线之间预留了一个天线的位置，这个部位以后可以根据需要加装一个大型测控天线）

Space surveying ship "Yuanwang" 6 sailing on the Huangpu River in 2009 (Room for another antenna is left between mainmast and the first monitoring antenna, which would enable to install a large-scale monitoring and control antenna if needed.)

2009年在南极冰海中的"雪龙"号科考船

Research ship "Snow Dragon" in the Antarctic ice in 2009

第二节　工作船
Section 2　Work Boat

中国交通建设集团研发的世界最大浮吊——7500 t "蓝鲸"号浮吊

The world's largest floating cranes developed by China Communications Construction Company Ltd: 7500 tons-class floating crane "Blue Whale".

10000TEU超巴拿马型集装箱船建造图　2007年12月24日，南通中远川崎公司为中远集装箱运输公司建造的集装箱船下水。该船长349 m，型宽45.6 m，造价10亿人民币，可装载10062个20 ft标准集装箱，最大服务航速25.8节，入级美国ABS船级社。是4艘同型船中的第一艘，是中远川崎公司继2001年成功交付两艘5400TEU集装箱船之后再次建造出中国最大箱位的集装箱船。它的建造刷新了中国造船业承接高箱位船的纪录，是亚洲首艘、世界第三艘超1万个标准箱的集装箱船。

As-built Plan of 10000TEU Post-Panamax container ship: The container ship built by Nantong COSCO KHI Ship Engineering Co., Ltd. (NACKS) for COSCO Container Line Co., Ltd. was launched on December 24, 2007. The ship is 349 m long and 45.6 m wide, and costs 1 billion yuan. Being able to carry 10,062 20-foot standard containers and move at the maximum service speed of 25.8 knots, being classified in American Bureau of Shipping. It is the first among all 4 ships of the same type and boasts the largest container ship slot in China, overshadowing two 5400TEU container ships successful delivered by NACKS in 2001. It broke the record of China's shipbuilding industry to undertake the construction of high-slot ships, but also tops the first in Asia and the third in the world that is able to carry over 10,000 TEU container ships.

中国造亚洲最大集装箱船公海试航　由南通中远川崎船舶工程有限公司建造的10000TEU(标准箱)集装箱船
"中远川崎"48号于2008年3月16日开始的试航，从长江南通水道航行至东海，为期5天。

Trial trip of Asia's largest container ship made in China in high seas：10000TEU container ship built by Nantong COSCO KHI Ship
Engineering Co., Ltd named "NACKS" 48 began its trial trip on March 16, 2008, navigating from the Nantong canal of Yangtze River to
the East China Sea for a period of 5 days.

16888 m³自航耙吸挖泥船"新海凤"号　由中国船舶工业集团公司第708研究所设计、广
州文冲船厂有限责任公司建造的16888 m³自航耙吸挖泥船"新海凤"号，于2008年11月28
日交付中港疏浚股份有限公司使用。该船载泥量23750 t，总载重量25000 t，泥舱舱容约
16888 m³，吸泥管内径为1.2 m，满载航速16节。

16888 m³ trailing suction hopper dredger "Xinhaifeng"：16888 m³ trailing suction hopper dredger
"Xinhaifeng", designed by No. 708 Institute (Marine Design and Research Institute) of China State
Shipbuilding Corporation and built by Guangzhou Wenchong Shipyard Co., Ltd, was delivered to CHEC
Dredging Co., Ltd on November 28, 2008. With a total tonnage of 25000 t and full speed of 16 knots, the vessel
is capable of carrying 23750 t mud. The volume of hopper tank and the internal diameter of suction tube are
about 16888 m³ and 1.2 m respectively.

11300 t滚装船　　2008年1月18日，南京金陵船厂为瑞典船东建造的一艘万吨级滚装船顺利下水。该船总长187 m，载重11300 t，主要用于装运卷纸及拖车等。

11,300 t Ro-Ro ship：10000 tons-class Ro-Ro ship made by CSC Jinling (Nanjing) Shipyard for Swedish ship-owner was launched on January 18, 2008. The ship is 187 m long with a tonnage of 11300 tons and mainly used for transporting rolls of paper and trailers.

■ 第三节　油气运输船
Section 3　Oil and Gas Transport Ship

中国第一艘LNG船顺利交付船东　　2008年4月3日，中国第一艘液化天然气船(LNG)在上海顺利交付船东。该船由中船集团公司所属沪东中华造船公司建造，历经三年多。它的建成，标志着我国基本掌握了世界造船尖端技术。该船是为广东大型LNG运输项目建造的第一艘147000 m³LNG船，船长292 m，船宽43.35 m，型深26.25 m，航速19.5节。贷舱类型为GTNO．96E-2薄膜型，是当前世界上最大的薄膜型LNG船。

China`s first LNG ship was smoothly delivered to the owner in 2008:
China`s first liquefied natural gas (LNG) ship, which took 3 years for Hudong-Zhonghua Shipbuilding (Group) Co., Ltd. under the leadership of China Shipbuilding Group Corporation to build, was successfully delivered in Shanghai on April 3. It marks that China basically grasps the world cutting-edge shipbuilding technology. The vessel is 292 m long, 43.35 m wide and 26.25 m high and moves at a speed of 19.5 knots, and is first 147000 m³ LNG ship of the large-scale Guangdong LNG transport project. With the adoption of GTNO. 96E-2 thin film in the cabin, the vessel now is the world`s largest film-type LNG vessel.

30.8万t原油船(VLCC)"新埔洋"号出坞 2009年6月19日，由中船龙穴造船有限公司、中国船舶及海洋工程设计研究院联合研发设计的"新埔洋"号30.8万t原油船出坞。该船长333 m、宽60 m、型深29.8 m，采用国际船级社协会双壳油船结构统一规范设计，用于装载闪点低于60℃的原油，甲板设有直升机平台，航速15.7节。该船是中国拥有自主知识产权的最大型原油船。

308,000 tons very large crude oil carrier (VLCC)"Xinpuyang"undocked：The very large crude oil carrier "Xinpuyang", with a tonnage of 308000 tons, jointly developed and designed by Longxue Shipbuilding Co., Ltd and Marine Design and Research Institute of China, was undocked on June 19, 2009. It is 333 m long, 60 m wide, 29.8 m deep and moves at a speed of 15.7 knots. The ship with a helicopter pad on the deck was built as per the unified standard of double-hull oil tanker of International Association of Classification Societies and used to carry crude oil with flash point below 60℃. It is the largest crude oil tanker in China with independent intellectual property right.

"海洋石油"116号海上浮式生产储油船　2007年，大连船舶重工为中海石油基地建造的文昌油田群海上浮式生产储油船(FPSO-5)。该船长234 m，型宽46 m，型深24.6 m。采用了分段建造、后在船坞对接合拢的建造方式，船体和上部模块前期异地建造，后期同地进行联调，上部模块首次采用浮吊在FPSO上进行模块安装。

Floating production storage and offloading vessel "Offshore Oil" 116: In 2007, the Dalian Shipbuilding Industry Co., Ltd built floating production storage and offloading vessel (FPSO-5) for Wen-chang Oilfields Group of China National Offshore Oil Corporation. The vessel is 234 m long, 46 m wide and 24.6 m high. The parts of vessel were built first and then interconnected and closed in the dock. The hull and superstructure were made in different places in the earlier stage, and then transported to the same place for uniting and adjustment later. Floating crane was introduced for the first time in the installation of superstructure blocks in FPSO.

首艘30万t级矿砂运输船(VLOC)"合恒"号　船长327 m，型宽35 m，型深29 m，服务航速17节。该船由南通中远川崎船舶工程有限公司自主设计、建造，为当前中国至巴西和澳大利亚航线的主流船型，2008年12月17日交付中远香港航运公司，并投入使用，为中国进口铁矿石运输船队主力。

The first 300,000 tons-class ore carriers (VLOC) "Heheng": "Heheng" is China's first 300,000 tons-class ore carriers (VLOC). It is 327 m long, 35 m wide and 29 m high, with a service speed of 17 knots. The vessel, now the main ship in the route from China to Brazil and Australia, was independently designed and built by the Nantong COSCO KHI Ship Engineering Co., Ltd, and delivered to COSCO Hong Kong shipping company and put into use on December 17, 2008. The ship is the main force of China's imported iron ore transport fleet.

中国第一艘完全自主设计建造的全球最大的30万吨级FPSO "海洋石油117" 号，2009年由中船集团外高桥造船公司建造。

The world`s largest 300,000 tons-class FPSO "Offshore Oil 117", the first one independently designed and built by China, was built by Waigaoqiao Shipping Company of China Shipbuilding Group Corporation in 2009.

第四节　海洋工程
Section 4　Ocean Projects

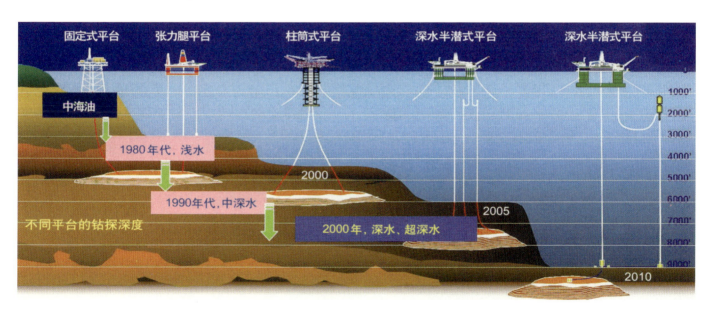

中国不同平台的海洋油田的钻探深度示意图

Diagram of drilling depth of different platforms for offshore oilfield in China

半潜式深海钻井平台　　2009年1月5日，大连船舶重工海洋工程有限公司为美国NOBLE公司建造的、也是中国船企第一次完整建造的半潜式深海钻井平台交付。该平台总长111.6 m，宽66.4 m。作业水域最大水深3048 m，钻井最大深度为10668 m。此前国内建造半潜式深海钻井平台大都是造其主体部分及部分上体，而此次交付的半潜式深海钻井平台则全部在国内完成。该平台作业水深在3000 m左右，工作时必须保证在固定的位置才能进行钻井工作。在深海无法通过锚链或者桩腿固定，因此采用动力定位技术，通过本身8个360°回旋推进器，保证该平台在固定的位置。该产品属于第六代深水半潜式钻井平台，代表当今世界海洋石油钻井的最高水平。标志着中国钻井平台已进入超深水领域。

Semi-submersible deep-sea drilling platform：The semi-submersible deep-sea drilling platform, built by Ocean Engineering Company of Dalian Shipbuilding Industry Co., Ltd for US Nobel Corporation, was delivered on January 5, 2009. It is also the first one that is completely made by China. The platform is 111.6 m long and 66.4 m wide. The maximum depth of operating waters and drilling are 3048 m and 10668 m respectively. Unlike the past practice that China made the main part and some of upper body, this semi-submersible deep-sea drilling platform delivered was completely built at home. The platform operates at a depth of about 3,000 m and must be in a fixed location to conduct drilling. In deep sea where the platform can be fixed through anchor chain or spud leg, dynamic positioning technology is adopted to ensure the platform in a fixed position through its eight 360° swing thrusters. It is the six generation semi-submersible deep-sea drilling platform, representing the highest level of today's offshore oil drilling in the world. It marks that the drilling platform of China has entered the super deep water field.

中国首座出口400 ft自升式钻井平台 由大连船舶重工为美国诺贝尔钻井公司设计建造的400 ft(122 m)自升式钻井平台，整个平台设备安装与调试均达到世界先进水平。这是中国首次为国外专业钻井公司自主设计建造的深水自升式钻井平台。

该座钻井平台全部实现自动控制。其悬臂梁可以外伸23 m，钻台可以左右移动5 m。平台一次定位能钻40多口井，可在全球范围内122 m水深以内进行作业。能抵御百年一遇风暴和在零下20 ℃环境正常作业。钻井深度可达9144 m。通过此项工程，掌握了变频系统、自动化控制钻井设备技术等核心技术，完全具有自主知识产权。

China's first export of 400 ft jack-up platform：The 400 feet (122 m) jack-up platform was designed and built by the Dalian Shipbuilding Industry Corporation for the United States Nobel Corporation. The equipment installation and commissioning of the platform reached the world advanced level. It is for the first time that China independently designed and built deep-water jack-up platform for international professional drilling company.

Completely automatic control is realized in this platform, whose cantilever beam can be extended 23 upto meters and drilling tower can move around for 5 meters. The platform can drill 40 wells in one fixed position and operate in waters at the depth of 122 m around the world. It can also withstand a-hundred-year storms and work normally when temperature falls to minus 20 centidegrees. The drilling depth is up to 9144 meters. Through this project, China has mastered such core technology as frequency conversion system and automatic control on drilling equipment, with independent intellectual property rights.

圆筒形海洋钻探平台　2009年6月28日，世界首座圆筒形超深水海洋钻探储油平台在位于南通的江苏启东中远海洋工程基地建成并正式命名。标志着我国海洋工程装备设计与建造能力已跻身世界先进水平。

该平台属于当今世界海洋石油钻探平台中技术水平最高、作业能力最强的高端领先产品。平台总造价近6亿美元，工作水深可达3000 m以上，钻井深度约12000 m，配置了全球最先进的DP-3动态定位系统和系泊系统，是世界首座兼具钻探和储油功能的平台，拥有15万桶原油的存储能力。独特的圆筒形外观使其对恶劣海域环境的适应能力更强，可以适应零下2℃的低温条件。其甲板可变载荷达15000 t，生活楼可容纳150人居住，居住舱室达到45 dB超静音标准，生活设施可比五星级酒店，而平台的设计和主体建造仅用24个月，比国际同类产品的建造周期缩短近半年。

Cylindrical offshore drilling platform was built：On June 28, 2009, the world's first ultra-deepwater cylindrical offshore oil drilling and storage platform was built and formally named as Qidong COSCO Ocean Engineering Base in Nantong, Jiangsu province. It marks the design and construction capacity of ocean engineering equipment has been up to the international advanced level.

The high-end leading product of world's offshore oil drilling platforms boasts the highest technical level and strongest work capacity. It costs about 600 million U.S. dollars, and can work in waters 3000 m deep, with a drilling depth of 12,000 m. Equipped with the most advanced DP-3 dynamic positioning system and mooring system, it is the world's first platform capable of both drilling and oil storage, to be more specific, with a capacity of 15 million barrels of crude oil. The unique cylindrical appearance contributes to strong adaptability to harsh marine environment, even when the temperature falls as low as minus 2 ℃. The deck has a variable loading capacity of 15,000 t; the life floor can accommodate 150 people; the living cabin is up to ultra-silent standard of 45 dB, with facilities comparable to those in five-star hotel. However, it only took 24 months to design the platform and build the main part, almost 6 months shorter than construction period of similar international products.

中国建造的全球首座圆筒形海上石油钻井平台

China built the world's first cylindrical offshore oil drilling platform

第十四章 铁路车辆
Chapter 14 Railway Vehicles

　　铁道运输设备，1949年新中国成立前绝大部分依赖国外进口，新中国成立后逐步建立起自己的机车车辆工业，但满足不了铁道运输发展的需要。1986年，铁道部贯彻中央指示，痛下"宁可少修一条线，也要加快机车车辆工业发展"的决心，使机车车辆工业得到较好发展。60年来，铁路运输，由蒸汽机车时代发展到内燃和电力机车时代，又发展到现在的高速动车组时代，从而支持路网质量发生了巨大的变化，由时速60 km以下的低速铁路，发展到120 km的常速铁路，又提速到140—160 km，2008年8月又建成200—350 km的高速铁路。

　　Rail transport equipment mostly relied on imports from abroad until the founding of People's Republic of China in 1949, after which China gradually established its own rolling stock industry. However, it was still hard to meet the needs of rail transport development. In 1986, the Ministry of Railways was determined to "speed up the development of rolling stock industry first, instead of railroad construction" in accordance with the directive from the central government, which achieved good results. Over the past 60 years, rail transport successively experienced the era of steam locomotive, internal-combustion and electric locomotive, and now steps into the times of high-speed EMU. Meanwhile, the network quality has undergone tremendous changes and the speed jumped from a low speed of less than 60 km/h, to a constant speed of 120 km/h, and later 140—160 km/h, which further rose to 200—350 km/h in the high-speed railway in August 2008.

　　机车制造。1952年制造出新中国第一台蒸汽机车，1958年开始自制内燃机车，1960年开始自制电力机车，牵引动力从蒸汽到内燃、电力，机车功率和单轴功率不断提高，形成了比较完整的机车车辆系列；1988年停止生产蒸汽机车，标志着中国铁路全面进入了内燃、电力牵引的时代。20世纪90年代以来，大连机车厂研制的东风4B型内燃机车，株洲电机车厂的韶山4型大功率（640 kW）货运机车水平不俗，韶山8型电机车和东风11型内燃机车成为牵引时速160 km准高速客车的主型机车。

　　Locomotive manufacturing. China produced the first steam locomotive in 1952 and started developing internal-combustion and electric locomotive in 1958 and 1960 respectively. With increasing traction powcr from stcam, to internal combustion, and electric engine, as well as locomotive power and unishaft power, a relatively complete locomotive vehicle series took shape. The production of steam locomotive stopped in 1988, marking the full entry to internal-combustion and electric era. Since 1990s, Dongfeng 4B diesel locomotives of Dalian Locomotive Works, and Shaoshan 4 model high-power (640 kW) freight locomotives developed by Zhuzhou Electric Locomotive Works are quite impressive, while Shaoshan 8 model electric locomotives and Dongfeng 11 model diesel locomotives have become the main part of quasi-high speed passenger train with a speed of 160 km per hour.

客车制造。1994年开发了准高速双层及25型新型客车，实现了时速160 km行车，实现了客车增容、提速、上水平的跨越。

Passenger coach manufacturing. The successful development of quasi-high speed double-deck passenger coaches and 25 model passenger coaches in 1994, with a speed of 160 km/h, achieved a leap in capacity, speed and standard.

货车制造。1949—1957年为仿制国外产品阶段，1967年以后为自行开发阶段。实行了三次大的升级换代：1956—1957年，实现了载重由30吨级向50吨级升级换代；1976—1978年，实现了由50吨级向60吨级的第二次升级换代；2005—2006年，实现了载重由60吨级向70吨、时速由70—80 km向120 km第三次大的升级换代。提速、重载并举创世界新纪录，还研制开发了载重80吨级C80型铝合金运煤敞车及C80B型不锈钢运煤敞车等高端产品，满足大秦线开行2万吨级重载单元列车的运输要求，使中国铁路重载运输技术进入世界先进行列。

Freight wagon manufacturing. The production relied on the imitation of foreign products from 1949 to 1957, and China has not independently developed freight wagons until 1967. Three major upgrades have occurred so far: firstly, the load capacity increased from 30 t in 1956 to 50 t in 1957; and secondly, from 50 t to 60 t during the period from 1976 to 1978; and thirdly from 60 t to 70 t during the period from 2005 to 2006 with the speed rising to 120 km/h from the original 70—80 km/h, making a record of upgrading in both speed and load capacity. Moreover, high-end products such as 80 t-class C80 model aluminum alloy coal gondola and C80B model stainless steel coal gondola have been developed and meet the transport requirements for the open of 20,000 t-class heavy unit train in Datong-Qinhuangdao line. The Chinese heavy-haul rail transport technology has reached the international advanced level.

2000年，中国铁路机车车辆工业总公司与铁道部"脱钩"，改组为中国南方机车车辆工业集团公司和中国北方机车车辆工业集团公司。管理体制发生了历史性的变革，形成国内铁路机车车辆市场的竞争性格局。

21世纪以来，中国机车车辆制造业，按照"引进先进技术、联合设计生产、打造中国品牌"的要求，坚持"先进、成熟、经济、适用、可靠"的基本方针，低成本引进了法、日、加、德公司的时速200 km及300 km以上动车组技术以及法、德、美公司的大功率电力、内燃机车技术，成功地实现了国产化。客运动车组和货运重载方面都取得了长足进步。

In 2000, China Railway Rolling Stock Industry Corporation was decoupled from the Ministry of Railway and restructured to be China South Locomotive & Rolling Stock Corporation Ltd (CSR) and China North Locomotive & Rolling Stock Corporation Ltd (CNR). Management system has undergone historic changes, and the competition structure of domestic railway rolling stock market took shape. As of the 21st century, in accordance with the requirement of "introduction of advanced technology, joint design and production, building Chinese brand", the Chinese rolling stock manufacturing industry, has introduced the technology of EMU with a speed of over 200 km and 300 km per hour from Japan, France, Canada and Germany at a low cost, as well as high-power electric and diesel technology from French, German and U.S. enterprises on the principle that the introduction should be "advanced, mature, economical, applicable and reliable", but also successfully put them into domestic production. Both passenger EMU and heavy-haul freight wagons have witnessed great progress.

动车组列车。通过再创新，设计制造具有自主知识产权的时速250 km的长编组座车和卧铺动车组、时速300—350 km及以上动车组，形成高速动车组系列产品。2007年4月10日上午8时40分，京广铁路许昌至安阳段首次试用了国产时速200 km及以上"CRH"动车组，这是中国第一列动车组（"CRH"为"China Railway High-speed"的缩写，意为"中国高速铁路"）。CRH2型时速300—350 km级动车组于2007年11月在南车集团四方公司成功下线；CRH3型时速350 km动车组（最高试验速度达394.3 km/h，处于世界领先地位），是引进德国技术由北车集团唐山机车车辆厂制造，于2008年4月11日下线，8月1日开始在京津城际高速铁路运行，是全球商业运行的最高速。具有自主知识产权的时速380 km/hCRH动车组于2010年4月在北车集团下线，刷新了世界高速动车组的纪录。

EMUs. Through re-innovation, China has designed and manufactured with independent intellectual property rights long-marshalling carriage and sleeper EMUs of 250 km per hour and EMUs with a speed of 300—350 km and above, forming high-speed EMU series. At 8:40 on April 10, 2007, the home-made "CRH" EMU, also the first EMU of China, with a speed of over 200 km/h, made its first trial operation in the section of Xuchang-Anyang in Beijing-Guangzhou railway ("CRH", the acronym of "China Railway High-speed"). The 300—350 km/h-class CRH2 EMUs got off the CSR production line successfully in Sifang in November 2007; 350 km/h-class CRH3 EMUs (a world leader with a maximum test speed of 394.3 km/h), developed by CNR Tangshan Locomotive & Rolling Stock Works with the introduction of German technology, got off the assembly line on April 11, 2008 and are used in Beijing-Tianjin high-speed inter-city railway as of August 1. CRH3 boasts the highest speed among commercially operating trains in the world. The 380 km/h-class CRH EMUs with independent intellectual property rights that got off the CNR assembly line in April 2010, set a world record of high-speed EMUs.

通过京津城际铁路建设与运营实践，初步形成了中国时速350 km高速铁路技术标准体系，是全球商业运行的最高速，并将用于京沪高速铁路。2009年以来已成功开通了武（昌）广（州）和郑（州）西（安）两条高速铁路。

With the construction and operation practices of Beijing-Tianjin inter-city railway, the technical standard system of 350 km/h-class high-speed railway which is the world's highest speed of trains commercially operated initially forms in China. It will also be used in Beijing-Shanghai high speed railway. Since 2009, China has successfully launched Wuchang-Guangdong and Zhengzhou-Xi'an high-speed railway lines.

大功率交流电机车。南车株机公司于2006年11月与国外公司联合设计生产出具有世界先进技术水平的HXDI型9600 kW八轴大功率交流电机车批量下线，在大秦线进行2万t牵引。通过八轴机车技术引进消化吸收再创新，2009年1月，拥有自主知识产权的大功率六轴9600 kW电力机车又在株洲下线，该车型是世界上最先进的大功率机车。

High-power AC locomotives. HXDI model 9600 kW 8-axis high-power AC locomotives, jointly designed and produced by CSR Zhuzhou Electric Locomotive Co.,Ltd (ZELC) and foreign enterprises, have reached the world advanced technology level. They got off the assembly line in November 2006 and were put into 20000 t traction operation in Datong-Qinhuangdao railway line. By means of introduction and absorption eight-axle locomotive technology, as well as innovation based on it, high-power six-axis 9600 kW electric locomotive with independent intellectual property rights got off the ZELC assembly line in January 2009. This model is the world's most advanced high-power locomotive.

南车集团四方公司2007年11月研制成功的CRH2型时速300—350 km动车组

CRH2 EMU with a speed of 300—350 km/h successfully developed by CSR Sifang Locomotive and Rolling Stock Corporation in November 2007

南车集团株洲机车厂HXD1B型9600 kW 6轴大功率交流传动电力机车，运行时速120 km

HXD1B model 9600 kW 6-axis high-power AC electric locomotive developed by CSR Zhuzhou Locomotive Co.,Ltd runs 120 km per hour.

南车集团株洲电力机车厂制造的9600 kW 8轴大功率交流传动货运电力机车，运行时速120 km，已于2007年在大秦线投入运行

9600 kW 8-axis high-power AC electric freight locomotive model developed by CSR Zhuzhou Locomotive Co.,Ltd runs 120 km per hour and was put into operation at the Datong-Qinhuangdao line in 2007.

北车集团大连机车厂HXD3B庞巴迪9600 kW 6轴大功率交流传动货运电力机车，运行时速120 km

HXD3B Bombardier 9600 kW 6-axis high-power AC electric freight locomotive developed by CNR Dalian Locomotive Works runs 120 km per hour.

北车集团长客公司CRH5型200—250 km/h动车组，首批动车组于2007年4月18日在全国铁路第六次大提速中正式投入运营

The first batch of CRH5 trains with a speed of 200—250 km/h, developed by CNR Chuangchun Railway Vehicles Co.,Ltd, was put into operation on April 18, 2007, the date of the sixth national railway speed-up.

时速200 km以上的动车组

EMU with a speed of over 200 km per hour

株洲机车厂制造的出口伊朗的电力机车

The electric locomotive manufactured by Zhuzhou Electric Locomotive Co.,Ltd is exported to Iran.

大连机车厂制造的出口马来西亚的内燃机车

Internal combustion manufactured by Dalian Locomotive Works is exported to Malaysia.

浦镇厂制造的南京地铁车辆

Nanjing metro subway vehicles produced by Puzhen Vehicle Factory

大连机车厂制造的城市轨道交通车辆

Urban transit vehicles produced by Dalian Locomotive Works

第十五章　航天工业
Chapter 15　Aerospace Industry

1956年1月，中共中央发出"向科学技术进军"的伟大号召。同年10月，中国第一个导弹研究机构——国防部第五研究院诞生，拉开了中国航天科技工业创业和发展的序幕。50多年来，经过努力奋斗，已经具备一定规模，成为具有战略意义的高科技产业，跨入世界航天先进行列。

In January 1956, the CPC Central Committee issued the great call of "marching forward to science and technology". In October the same year, the fifth Academy of Ministry of National Defense, China's first missile research institution, was established and China's aerospace science and technology entrepreneurship and development pulled the curtain. After more than 50 years of arduous efforts, it has become a strategic high-tech industry with a certain scale and advanced to be in the leading position in the world aerospace industry.

航天工业成就概览表（1960—2009年）
Overview of achievements in aerospace industry（1960—2009）

年份 Year	成　就 Achievement
1960年11月5日 November 5, 1960	中国第一枚仿制近程导弹"东风"1号发射成功 China's first imitative short-range missile "Dongfeng" 1 was launched successfully.
1966年10月27日 October 27, 1966	导弹核武器试验成功，中国有了自己的导弹核武器 China has its own missile nuclear weapon after the test succeeded.
1970年4月24日 April 24, 1970	"长征"1号火箭成功发射中国第一颗"东方红"1号卫星，中国成为世界上第五个独立研制和发射卫星的国家，宣告中国进入航天时代 LM-1 rocket successfully launched China's first satellite "Dongfanghong" 1, making China the fifth country in the world that can independently develop and launch satellites and declaring China has entered to the space age.

年份 Year	成　就 Achievement
1980年5月18日 May 18, 1980	"东风"5号洲际导弹飞行试验成功，中国成为世界上第三个进行洲际导弹全程飞行试验的国家 "Dongfeng" 5 intercontinental missile flight test succeeded and China became the third country in the world to have full flight test of intercontinental missiles.
1984年4月8日 April 8, 1984	第一颗地球静止轨道通信卫星由"长征"3号火箭成功发射并准确定点，中国成为世界上第三个掌握液氢液氧发动机技术，第二个掌握低温发动机高空二次点火技术和第五个能独立研制发射静止轨道通信卫星的国家 The first geostationary communication satellite was successfully launched by rocket LM-3 and placed accurately. China has become the third country to master liquid hydrogen-liquid oxygen engine technology, the second to master high-altitude secondary ignition technology of low-temperature engine and the fifth to independently develop and launch geostationary telecommunication satellites in the world.
1988年9月7日 September 7, 1988	"长征"4号甲火箭发射"风云"1号气象卫星成功，中国成为世界上第三个独立研制发射太阳同步轨道卫星的国家 LM-4 rocket successfully launched FY-1 weather satellite. China became the third in the world that can independently develop and launch sun-synchronous orbit satellites.
1999年11月20日 November 20, 1999	"神舟"1号试验飞船成功，发射成功回收，随后在2001—2002年又成功发射和回收三艘"神舟"无人飞船 "Shenzhou" 1 experimental spacecraft was successfully launched and recovered, followed by successful launch and recovery of 3 "Shenzhou" unmanned spacecrafts from 2001 to 2002.
2003年10月15日 October 15, 2003	中国第一艘载人飞船"神舟"5号，载着航天员杨利伟进入太空成功，中国成为世界上第三个能独立开展载人航天活动的国家 China's first manned spaceship "Shenzhou" 5, carrying astronaut Yang Liwei was successfully launched. China became the third country in the world to be capable of independent manned space activities.
2008年9月25—28日 September 25 to 28,2008	"神舟"7号载人航天飞行任务成功，并首次成功实验空间出舱活动和科学实验，成为世界上第三个掌握独立出舱技术的国家 "Shenzhou" 7 manned space mission was a success, so was the first test of space extravehicular activities and scientific experiments. China became the third country in the world to master independent extravehicular techniques.
2007年10月24日—2009年3月1日 October 24, 2007 to March 1, 2009	"嫦娥"1号卫星发射成功，2009年3月1日完成预定探测工程，中国首次月球探测成功。标志着中国已经进入具有深空探测能力的国家行列 "Chang'e" 1 satellite was successfully launched, and has completed scheduled exploration project by March 1, 2009. China's first lunar exploration was a success, indicating that China has developed to be a country capable of deep space exploration.

第一节　导弹武器装备
Section 1　Missile Weapons and Equipment

　　中国航天科技工业从研制导弹武器装备起步。1960年11月5日，中国第一枚仿制的近程地地导弹"东风"1号（仿苏P2导弹）试射成功，这是中国军事装备史上一个重要转折点。中国自行设计的"东风"2号导弹，1962年3月21日发射失败，直到1964年6月29日才发射成功，从此中国导弹走上独立研制之路，逐步形成工业生产能力。1966年10月27日导弹核武器试验成功，中国拥有了自己的导弹核武器。从1966年到1971年"东风"2号甲中近程导弹、"东风"3号中程导弹和"东风"4号中远程导弹相继研制成功，航天科技工业体系基本形成。1980年5月18日，"东风"5号洲际导弹飞行试验成功，中国成为世界上第三个进行洲际导弹全程飞行试验的国家。进入21世纪，新型远程地地导弹得到重大改进。经过50多年的建设和发展，中国的战略战术导弹，品种比较齐全，功能比较完备，已成为巩固国防、保卫祖国安全的重要保障。

China's aerospace science and technology industry starts from the development of missile weapons and equipment. In November 5, 1960, China's first imitative short-range "Dongfeng" 1 ground-to-ground missile (imitation of Soviet missile P2) was successfully tested, which is an important turning point in the history of military equipment. The launch of "Dongfeng" 2 missile independently designed by China in March 21, 1962 turned out to be a failure and did not succeed until June 29, 1964. Since then, China has started independent missile development and gradually formed industrial production capacity. The successful test of missile nuclear weapon in October 27, 1966 marked that China had its own nuclear missiles. With successful development of "Dongfeng" 2 short-range missile, "Dongfeng" 3 medium-range missile and Dongfeng 4 long-range missile successively from 1966 to 1971, an aerospace science and technology industrial system generally took shape. The successful flight test of "Dongfeng" 5 intercontinental missile in May 18, 1980 enabled China to be the third country in the world to have full flight test of intercontinental missiles. The new long-range ground-to-ground missiles are significantly improved in the 20th century. After more than 50 years of construction and development, China's strategic and tactical missiles boast relatively various types and fairly comprehensive functions, and have been a vital guarantee for national defense consolidation and homeland security safeguard.

1966年10月27日，导弹原子弹结合飞行试验获得圆满成功

The test flight of missile combined with atomic bomb in October 27, 1966 was a complete success.

国庆35周年阅兵式上的导弹方队

Missile square team in the 35th anniversary National Day military parade

国庆50周年阅兵式上的导弹方队

Missile square team in the 50th anniversary National Day military parade

国庆60周年阅兵式上的导弹方队

Missile square team in the 60th anniversary National Day military parade

第二节 运载火箭和人造卫星
Section 2 Carrier Rockets and Man-Made Satellites

1965年，中国开始实施第一颗人造地球卫星工程。1970年4月24日，"长征"1号火箭在酒泉卫星发射中心成功发射"东方红"1号卫星，中国成为世界上第五个能独立研制和发射卫星的国家①，宣告中国进入航天时代。1975年11月20日，"长征"2号火箭发射返回式卫星获得成功，三天后卫星成功收回，中国成为世界上第三个掌握卫星回收技术的国家。1975年4月，国家批准卫星通信工程，至1984年4月8日，第一颗地球静止轨道通信卫星在西昌卫星发射中心由"长征"3号火箭成功发射并准确定点，中国成为世界上第三个掌握液氢液氧发动机技术，第二个掌握低温发动机高空二次点火技术和第五个能独立研制发射静止轨道通信卫星的国家。1977年11月，国家批准"风云"1号气象卫星工程，1988年9月，"长征"4号甲火箭在太原卫星发射中心成功发射，中国成为世界上第三个独立研制发射太阳同步轨道卫星的国家。20世纪90年代，中国除发射新一代通信广播卫星、气象卫星和地球资源卫星，研制成功第一枚大型捆绑式火箭外，还开始实施了载人航天工程，用7枚"长征"2号F火箭，先后完成了4艘无人试验飞船和3艘载人飞船的成功发射和成功回收，载人航天技术取得突破。进入21世纪，中国空间技术又有很大发展，初步具备了满足深空探测要求的测控能力。

China began the first man-made earth satellite project in 1965. The successful launch of "Dongfanghong" 1 satellite by LM-1 rocket in Jiuquan Satellite Launch Center on April 24, 1970 made China the fifth country in the world that is able to independently develop and launch satellite① and declared China has entered into the space age. The recoverable satellite was successfully launched by LM-2 rocket in November 20, 1975 and recovered three days later, indicating China has become the world's third to master satellite recovery technology. Satellite communication project was approved by the State in April 1975. The first geostationary communication satellite was successfully launched by LM-3 carrier rocket in Xichang Satellite Launch Center and accurately placed on April 8, 1984. China has become the third country to master liquid hydrogen-liquid oxygen engine technology, the second to master high-altitude

---

①中国是第五个能独立研制和发射卫星的国家。按时间顺序为：苏联（1957年10月4日）、美国（1958年）、法国（1965年）、日本（1970年）、中国（1970年4月24日）、英国（1975年）、印度（1980年）、以色列（1988年）、俄罗斯（1992年）、乌克兰（1992年）、伊朗（2009年）。

① China is the fifth country that can independently develop and launch satellites. Countries with this capability in chronological order are: Soviet Union (October 4, 1957), United States (1958), France (1965), Japan (1970), China (April 24, 1970), United Kingdom (1975), India (1980), Israel (1988), Russia (1992), Ukraine (1992), Iran (2009)

secondary ignition technology of low-temperature engine and the fifth to independently develop and launch geostationary telecommunication satellites in the world. FY meteorological satellite project was approved by the State in November 1977. In September 1988, LM-4 rocket successfully launched FY-1 weather satellite. China became the third in the world that can independently develop and launch sun-synchronous orbit satellites. In 1990s, in addition to successful launch of a new generation of communication and broadcast satellites, meteorological satellites and earth resources satellites, and development of the first large-scale strap-on rocket, China also started manned space program and achieved breakthroughs, in which 4 unmanned experimental spacecrafts and 3 manned spacecrafts were successively and successfully launched and recovered by 7 LM-2 F rockets. In the 21st century, China's space technology witnesses great development and China generally possesses monitoring and control capabilities that meet the requirements of deep space exploration.

中国研制的长征系列运载火箭，具备了发射近地轨道、太阳同步轨道和地球静止轨道空间飞行器能力，成为中国为数不多的具有自主知识产权和较强国际竞争力的高科技品牌。截至2009年4月，中国自己研制的14种长征系列运载火箭，分别从酒泉、西昌和太原3个卫星发射中心进行了117次发射，成功110次，成功率94%以上，成功地发射了122颗国内外卫星和7艘飞船。自1996年10月以来，长征系列运载火箭连续75次发射成功，在国际上赢得了很高的信誉。

LM series of carrier rockets developed by China, are capable of launching low-earth orbit, sun-synchronous orbit and geostationary orbit spacecrafts, and become one of the few high-tech brands with both independent intellectual property rights and strong international competitiveness. By the end of April 2009, 14 LM carrier rockets, independently developed by China, have undertook 117 launches from Jiuquan, Xichang and Taiyuan Satellite Launch Center respectively, 110 of which were successful, with a success rate as high as 94%. In total they successfully launched 122 satellites and 7 spacecrafts at home and abroad. Moreover, LM series of carrier rockets have succeeded in 75 continuous launches since October 1996, winning a high international reputation.

1970年4月24日，"长征"1号运载火箭成功发射我国第一颗人造地球卫星"东方红"1号

LM-1 carrier rocket successfully launched China's first man-made earth satellite Dongfanghong 1 on April 24, 1970.

1980年5月18日，我国向太平洋预定海域发射的第一枚运载火箭获得圆满成功

The launch of the first carrier rocket of China to predetermined waters of the Pacific Ocean in May 18, 1980 was a complete success.

第三节 载人航天工程和月球探测工程
Section 3 Manned Space Program and Lunar Exploration Program

载人航天是衡量一个国家综合国力的重要标志。1992年，中国载人航天工程正式列入国家计划。1999年11月，"神舟"1号试验飞船成功发射和回收，中国载人航天技术取得重大突破。2001—2002年，中国又成功发射和回收了3艘"神舟"号无人飞船，为实现载人飞行奠定了基础。2003年10月15日，中国第一艘载人飞船"神舟"5号载着中国第一名航天员杨利伟进入太空成功，中国成为世界上第三个能够独立开展载人航天活动的国家。2005年10月、2008年9月，"神舟"6号、"神舟"7号实现两名、三名航天员飞行成功，"神舟"7号首次成功实施空间出舱活动和科学实验，成为世界上第三个独立掌握出舱关键技术的国家。

Manned space flight is an important symbol of comprehensive national strength. China's manned space program was formally included in the national plan in 1992. The successful launch and recovery of "Shenzhou" 1 experimental spacecraft in November 1999 marked a major breakthrough in manned space technology. 3 more Shenzhou unmanned spacecrafts were successfully launched and recovered from 2001 to 2002, laying foundation for manned flight. In October 15, 2003, China's first manned spaceship "Shenzhou" 5 carried China's first astronaut Yang Liwei into space. China became the third country in the world to be capable of independent manned space activities. "Shenzhou" 6 and "Shenzhou" 7 carrier rockets successfully sent 2 and 3 astronauts into space in October 2005 and September 2008 respectively. Space extravehicular activities and scientific experiments were realized for the first time in "Shenzhou" 7, making China the third country in the world to master independent extravehicular techniques.

月球探测工程。2004年1月国务院批准立项，2007年10月24日嫦娥一号卫星在西昌发射中心成功发射，2009年3月1日圆满完成多项预定探测工程。中国首次月球探测成功，是继"两弹一星"工程、载人航天工程取得成功后，中国航天事业发展的又一重要里程碑。标志着中国已经进入世界上具有深空探测能力的国家行列。

Lunar exploration program was approved by the State Council in January 2004; Chang'e 1 satellite was successfully launched at the Xichang Launch Center in October 24, 2007 and has successfully completed a number of scheduled exploration projects by March 1, 2009. The success of China's first lunar exploration is another important milestone in the aerospace industry development, following the "two bombs and one satellite" (nuclear bomb, hydrogen bomb and artificial satellite) program and manned space program. It indicates that China has entered the rank of countries with deep space exploration capability.

2003年10月15—16日，我国首次载人航天飞行任务取得圆满成功，图为"长征"2号F运载火箭发射"神舟"5号飞船和航天员杨利伟

China`s first manned space mission from October 15 to 16, 2003 was a complete success. LM-2 F carrier rocket is launching the "Shenzhou" 5 spacecraft and astronaut Yang Liwei in the photos.

2005年10月12—17日，"神舟"6号载人航天飞行任务取得圆满成功，图为"长征"2号F运载火箭发射"神舟"6号飞船和航天员费俊龙、聂海胜

The Shenzhou 6 manned space mission from October 12 to 17, 2005, was a complete success. LM-2 F carrier rocket is launching the "Shenzhou" 5 spacecraft and astronauts Fei Junlong and Nie Haisheng in the photos.

2008年9月25—28日，"神舟"7号载人航天飞行任务取得圆满成功，图为"长征"2号F运载火箭发射"神舟"7号飞船和航天员翟志刚、刘伯明、景海鹏及航天员出舱

The "Shenzhou" 7 manned space mission from September 25 to 28, 2008 was a complete success. The photos show the LM-2 F carrier rocket launching the "Shenzhou" 7 spacecraft and astronauts Zhai Zhigang, Liu Boming, Jing Haipeng, as well as the extravehicular activity respectively.

我国首次月球探测工程取得圆满成功。图为2007年10月24日"嫦娥"1号卫星在西昌卫星发射中心成功发射及我国首次月球探测工程第一幅月面图像

China's first lunar exploration program was a success. The photos show the successful launch of "Chang'e" 1 satellite at the Xichang Launch Center in October 24, 2007 and the first image of moon's surface during China's first lunar exploration respectively.

中国文化办公设备制造行业起步于20世纪50年代，但主要是1978年改革开放后逐步发展起来的。现已发展成为以三资企业为主导的多种经济类型并存的、以加工贸易为主的外向型高新技术产业。中国已成为世界照相机、数码照相机、数字复印机、数字多功能复合机、碎纸机等产品的生产和出口大国。

China office equipment manufacturing industry kicked off in 1950s, but generally enjoyed gradual development since the reform and opening up in 1978. It has now developed into an export-oriented high-tech industry featuring processing and trade, where various economic types coexist with foreign-invested enterprises (Sino-foreign joint ventures, enterprises with Sino-foreign cooperation, and wholly foreign-owned enterprises) as main player. China has become a major producer and exporter of cameras, digital cameras, digital copiers, multi-functional digital complex machine, shredder and other products.

文化办公行业根据中央"以市场换技术"的方针，走出一条引进技术、开放市场、合作生产、合资办厂的发展之路，全面提升了行业的技术水平和生产能力，缩短了与国外的差距。照相机行业虽曾在"文化大革命"时期大发展，但技术上没有过关。照相机和复印机都是20世纪80年代初期开始引进国外先进制造技术，经过消化吸收，到80年代后期初步形成具有一定规模的产业。由于自主开发能力不足，跟不上国外产品更新的速度，为摆脱困境，不少企业选择了与外商合资、贴牌生产、进料加工和来料装配等方式发展生产，使中国文化办公设备制造行业发展为新兴产业。2007年与1978年相比，企业从65个增加到439个，职工人数从3.53万人增加到23.45万人，分别增加5.75倍和5.64倍。工业总产值从2.09亿元提高到1450.86亿元；利润总额从0.37亿元提高到55.76亿元；分别增长693倍和150倍。

In line with the policy of the central government "market for technology", the office equipment industry has explored a development road of "imported technology, open markets, co-production, joint venture", which reduces the gap with foreign countries while comprehensively enhancing the technological level and production capacity. In spite of great development in the Cultural Revolution, the camera industry did not meet the standards technically. The production of cameras and copiers were based on imported advanced technology in the early 1980s, and formed an industry with certain scale in the late 1980s through digestion and absorption of imported technology. Due to inability to keep up the pace of foreign product updates as result of self-development capacity deficiency, many companies resort to such means as joint ventures, OEM production, processing of supplied materials, and assembling of supplied components to navigating out of the dilemma. China office equipment production is developing as an emerging industry. In 2007 as compared with 1978, the number of companies increased from 65 to 439, employees from 35,300 to 234,500, up by 5.75 times and 5.64 times respectively. The industrial output value jumped from RMB 209 million to 145.086 billion with total profit rising to RMB 5.576 billion from 37 million, up by 693 times and 150 times respectively.

产品产量快速增长。2007年与1978年相比，照相机从17.91万台增加到8630.46万台，其中数码相机从2000年的410万台增加到7493.47万台，复印机从470台增加到452.36万台，均居世界前列。已形成数码相机8000万台、复印机500万台、光导鼓3800万台、墨粉1.6万t的年生产能力。国产文化办公设备生产已融入世界市场，全球数码相机年产量的60%、复印设备的55%、喷墨盒的30%、光导鼓的12%、墨粉盒的12%均在中国制造。

The product output grows rapidly. The output of camera climbed to 86,304,600 in 2007 from 179,100 in 1978, while the output of digital cameras increased to 74,934,700 in 2007 from 4.1 million in 2000. The output of copiers increased from 470 in 1978 to 4,523,600 in 2007. The output of all these three products tops in the world and now China has an annual production capacity of 80 million digital cameras, 5 million copiers, 38 million photosensitive drums, and 16,000 t toner. Domestic office equipment has been integrated into the world market. The amount of digital cameras, copying equipment, inkjet cartridges, photosensitive drums, toner cartridges made in China account for 60%, 55%, 30%, 12%, and 12% of the global output respectively.

全行业主要产品实现了从模拟技术向数字技术的全面转变。传统的胶片照相机、静电复印机、胶片电影放映设备等产品已被相关的数码产品取代，数码产品已占行业的主导地位。

A full transition from analog technology to digital technology for major products in the industry has been realized. Traditional film cameras, electrostatic copiers, film projecting equipment, and related products have been replaced by digital products which take a dominant position in the industry.

文化办公设备生产技术已国际化，产品的发展与世界同步。如数码相机实现了高像素、超薄、水印、防抖、脸部识别、场景识别、阴影自动识别、双十字自动对焦、超声波除尘、多媒体功能等技术，开发出从35万像素、500万像素、800万像素到1200万像素的数码相机和1000万像素、1160万像素和1600万像素三代数码机。复印机的发展主要体现在功能的不断扩大、自动化和智能水平不断提高，彩色化、复合化、多功能化已成为产品发展的主要趋势，这些方面保持与国际同步发展。

The internationalized office equipment technology enables in-phase product development with international counterparts. For instances, with such technologies as high-pixel, ultra-thin, watermark, image stabilization, face recognition, scene identification, automatic identification shadow, Double Cross AF, ultrasonic dust removal, multimedia, digital camera backs of 10 million, 11.6 million and 16 million pixels, as well as digital cameras with pixels from 350,000, 5 million, 8 million to 12 million, have been developed. The development of copier is mainly reflected in the expanded functions and rising levels of automation and intelligence, with more colorful, composite and multi-functional product as the main trend of development. China has kept in line with international development in this regard.

文办设备行业是外向型行业，据2004年全国经济普查数据，行业出口率高达84.51%。进出口贸易发展很快，2007年与1978年相比，进出口贸易总额从0.19亿美元增加到303.4亿美元，增长1596倍，其中出口额从0.01亿美元增加到217.9亿美元，增长21789倍。出口产品结构不断改善，2007年数码照相机出口77.65亿美元，占照相机出口额的98.9%；数字复印机和多功能一体机出口41.86亿美元，占复印机出口额的98.8%。

Office equipment industry as an export-oriented industry, its export rate recorded as high as 84.51% according to the national economic census of 2004. Import and export trade has developed rapidly. In 2007 as compared with 1978, the total volume of import and export trade rocketed from 19 million U.S. dollars to 30.34 billion U.S. dollars, an increase of 1596 times, of which export value jumped from 1 million U.S. dollars to 21.79 billion U.S. dollars, up by 21,789 times. Meanwhile, export product mix continued to improve. In 2007, the export value of digital cameras reached 7.765 billion U.S. dollars, or 98.9% of that of all cameras, while the export figure of digital copiers and multifunction machines, numbering 4.186 billion U.S. dollars, accounts for 98.8% of that of all exports copiers.

中国文化办公设备进出口额情况表（1978—2007年）
Total volume of import and export of office equipment（1978—2007）

（亿美元）

(USD 100 million)

项目/年份 Item/Year	1978	1980	1985	1990	1995	2000	2002	2005	2007
进出口总额 Total volume of import and export	0.19	0.28	3.93	1.73	19.47	45.81	53.61	149.24	303.38
进口额 Value of import	0.18	0.26	3.91	0.93	7.13	16.75	16.20	33.73	85.46
出口额 Value of export	0.01	0.02	0.02	0.80	12.34	29.06	37.41	115.5	217.92

20世纪70年代，我国生产的座式35 mm电影放映机

China-made block-type 35 mm film projector in 1970s

1964年上海生产的"海鸥4A"型120双反相机

"Seagull 4A" 120 twin-lens reflex (TLR) camera produced in Shanghai in 1964

1969年上海照相机厂生产的"东风"120单反相机

"Dongfeng" 120 single-lens reflex (SLR) camera produced by Shanghai Camera Plant in 1969

1971年上海照相机二厂制造的"红旗20"型135单反相机及与之配套3只专用镜头是当年照相机极品

"Red Flag 20" 135 SLR camera and its 3 dedicated camera lens, made by No. 2 Shanghai Camera Plant in 1971, were superb among products of same kind.

2008年华旗资讯开发的全球首款GPS卫星导航数码相机P-1

The world's first GPS satellite navigation digital camera P-1 developed by Huaqi Information Digital Technology Co., Ltd. in 2008

天津佳能公司制造的佳能多
功能数码复印机

Canon multi-function digital copier
manufactured by Tianjin Canon
Co. Ltd

2008年上海富士施乐公司制
造的Workcentre7132彩色
多功能复印机

Workcentre7132 multi-function
color device manufactured by
Fuji Xerox Industry Development
(Shanghai) in 2008

参考文献
References

[1] 卢嘉锡, 席泽宗.彩色插图中国科学技术史.北京:中国科学技术出版社,祥云（美国）出版公司，1997.

[2] 卢嘉锡, 王兆春.中国科学技术史·军事技术卷.北京:科学出版社，1998.

[3] 卢嘉锡, 席飞龙.中国科学技术史·交通卷.北京:科学出版社，2004.

[4] 卢嘉锡, 陆敬严, 华觉明.中国科学技术史机械卷.北京:科学出版社，2000.

[5] 卢嘉锡, 陈美东.中国科学技术史·天文学卷.北京:科学出版社，2003.

[6] 卢嘉锡, 杜石然.中国科学技术史·通史卷.北京:科学出版社，2003.

[7] 卢嘉锡, 赵承泽.中国科学技术史·纺织卷.北京:科学出版社，2002.

[8] 卢嘉锡, 丘光明.中国科学技术史·度量衡卷.北京:科学出版社，2001

[9] 卢嘉锡, 潘吉星.中国科学技术史·造纸与印刷卷.北京:科学出版社，1998

[10] 中国科学技术馆.中国古今科技图文集.北京:中国科学技术出版社，2005.

[11] 中国机械工业年鉴编辑委员会.中国机械工业60年图鉴.北京:机械工业出版社，2010.

[12] 中国机械工业联合会, 中国机械工业企业管理协会. 中国机械工业改革开放30年辉煌成就.北京:机械工业联合会，2008.

[13] 姜鸣.龙旗飘扬的舰队:中国近代海军兴衰史.北京:三联书店，2002.

[14] 李滔, 陆洪洲.中国兵工企业史.北京:兵器工业出版社，2003.

[15] 纪江红.中华上下五千年.北京:北京出版社，2003.

[16] 周瀚光.中国科技史.上海:华东师范大学出版社，2001.

[17] 冯国超.中国通史.北京:光明日报出版社，2003.

[18] 齐豫生.中国通史彩图版.长春:吉林摄影出版社，2000.

[19] 周继烈, 姚建华.机械制造工程实训.北京:科学出版社，2005.

[20] 机电产品相关贸易壁垒报告.商务部机电产品进出口公司，2003.

[21] 陈效曾. 中国汽车工业专业史.北京:人民交通出版社，1996.

[22] 宋晓超.辉煌的三十年.北京:中国统计出版社，2008.

[23] 朱维盛.新中国五十年.北京:中国统计出版社，1999.

[24] 郑斯林.共和国辉煌五十年.北京:中国经济出版社，1999.

[25] (日)中山秀太郎.世界机械发展史.石玉良, 译.北京:机械工业出版社，1986.

[26] 刘仙洲.中国机械工程发明史　第一篇.北京:科学出版社，1962.

[27] 周伟.中国兵器史稿.天津:百花文艺出版社，2006.

[28] 王振德.兵器百科全书.桂林:广西师范大学出版社，2006.

[29] 吴熙敬.中国近现代技术史.北京:科学出版社，2000.

[30] 张彦宁.中国企业史.北京:企业管理出版社，2002.

[31] 李庄.共和国的记忆.北京:人民出版社，1994.

[32] 周日新.神鹰凌空——中国航空史话.北京:北京航空航天大学出版社，2003.

[33] 汪海波.新中国工业经济史:1979—2000.北京:经济管理出版社，2000.

[34] 汪海波.新中国工业经济史.北京：经济管理出版社，1986.

[35] (美)费正清，(美)麦克法夸尔.剑桥中华人民共和国史：1949—1965.王建朗等译.上海:上海人民出版社，1990.

[36] (美)麦克法夸尔，(美)费正清.剑桥中华人民共和国史——革命的中国的兴起：1949-1965.谢亮生等译.北京:中国社会科学出版社，1990.

[37] (美)麦克法夸尔，(美)费正清.剑桥中华人民共和国史：1966—1982.金光耀等译.上海:上海人民出版社，1992.

[38] (美)麦克法夸尔，(美)费正清.剑桥中华人民共和国史——中国革命内部的革命:1966-1982.俞金戈等译.北京:中国社会科学出版社，1992.

[39] (美)麦克法夸尔，(美)费正清.剑桥中华人民共和国史——革命的中国的兴起:1949-1965.谢亮生等译.北京:中国社会科学出版社，1990.

[40] 薄一波.若干重大决策与事件的回顾(上卷).北京：中共中央党校出版社，1991.

[41] 薄一波.若干重大决策与事件的回顾(下卷).北京：中共中央党校出版社，1993.

[42] 人民出版社.光辉的成就——中华人民共和国建国35年.北京:人民出版社，1984.

[43] 周恩来.伟大的十年.北京:人民出版社，1959.

[44] 清庆瑞.抗战时期的经济.北京:北京出版社，1995.

[45] 强重华.抗日战争时期重要资料统计集.北京:北京出版社，1997.

[46] 郭祖玉.军事科技发展史.北京:军事谊文出版社，1998.

[47] 中国电工技术学会中国电器工业发展史专业委员会.中国电器工业发展史.北京:机械工业出版社，1995.

[48] 图说中国历史编委会.图说中国历史.北京:中央编译出版社，2007.

[49] 白寿彝.中国通史.上海:上海人民出版社，2007.

[50] 中国内燃机工业协会组.中国内燃机工业诞辰一百周年纪念文集.2008.

[51] 景晓村.当代中国的机械工业.北京:中国社会科学出版社，1990.

[52] 中国历史大辞典编委会.中国历史大辞典.上海:上海辞书出版社，2000.

[53] 邱梅贞.中国农业机械技术发展史.北京:机械工业出版社，1993.

[54] 张小平.中华人民共和国1995年第三次全国工业普查资料汇编.北京:中国统计出版社，1997.

[55] 陈坚.最新彩图袖珍兵器百科.南宁:接力出版社，2005.

[56] 郑祺耀.机械工业六十年史.台北:台湾区机械工业同业协会，2005.

[57] 董光壁.中国近现代科学技术史论纲.长沙:湖南教育出版社.1992.

[58] 吴连赏.台湾地区工业发展的过程及其环境结构的变化.台北:台湾文史哲出版社，1991.

[59] 何东君.中华人民共和国改革开放30年年鉴.北京:新华出版社，2008.

[60] 姚开建.改变中国(中国的十个"五年计划").北京:中国经济出版社，2003.

[61] 房维中.中华人民共和国经济大事记.北京:中国社会科学出版社，1984.

[62] 王佳宁.中国经济改革30年.重庆:重庆大学出版社，2008.

[63] 汪敬虞.中国近代工业史资料.北京:科学出版社，1957.

[64] 孙毓棠.中国近代工业史资料.北京:中华书局,1957.

[65] 陈真,姚洛,逄先知.中国近代史资料.北京:三联书店,1961.

[66] 北京师范大学,中国人民大学政治经济系.中国近代经济史.北京:人民出版社,1976.

[67] 中国社会科学院近代史研究所《中国近代史稿》编写组.中国近代史稿.北京:人民出版社,1981.

[68] 庄前鼎,刘仙洲.三十年来之中国机械工程.中国工程师学会,1946.

[69] 王世铨.三十年来中国之造船工程.中国工程师学会,1946.

[70] 钱昌祚.三十年来中国之航空工程.中国工程师学会,1946.

[71] 恽震.三十年来中国之电机制造工业.中国工程师学会,1946.

[72] 顾毓瑔.三十年来中国之机械工业.中国工程师学会,1946.

[73] 杨占昌.中国兵器工业发展历史梗概.兵工学会兵工史编辑部编印,1984.

[74] 孙云龙.延安兵工厂的始末.兵器工业部编印《军工战歌》,1984.

[75] 吴东才.黄崖洞兵工厂.兵器工业部编印《军工战歌》,1984.

[76] 上海工商行政管理局,第一机电工业机器工业史料组.上海民族机器工业.北京:中华书局,1966.

[77] 上海经济研究所.江南造船厂厂史.南京:江苏人民出版社,1983.

[78] 张果为.台湾经济发展.台北:正中书局,1970.

[79] 周任,等.台湾经济.北京:中国财经经济出版社,1980.

[80] 张柏春.中国近代机械简史.北京:北京理工大学出版社,1992.

[81] 黄开亮.中国机械工业技术发展史.北京:机械工业出版社,2001.

[82] 李冶,屈贤明.2006—2007年中国装备制造业发展报告.北京:中国计划出版社,2008.

[83] 徐从才.汽车与装备制造业发展研究.北京:中国物资出版社,2006.

[84] 中国经济年鉴编辑委员会.中国经济年鉴(1981—2009).北京:中国经济年鉴社.

[85] 程栋,霍用灵,刘树勇.20世纪中国史(1980—1989).广州:广东旅游出版社,1999.

[86] 蔡桂林.炎黄天梦——中国航天发展50年纪实.桂林:漓江出版社,2003.

[87] 孟赤兵,李周书.神鹰临空——中国航空史话.北京:北京航空航天大学出版社,2003.

[88] 舰船知识杂志.2003—2009.

[89] 航空知识杂志.2003—2009.

[90] 现代军事杂志.2003—2009.

[91] 军事历史杂志.2003—2009.

[92] 世界制造技术与装备市场.2003—2009.

[93] 国家地理杂志.2003—2009.

[94] 经济日报.2003—2009.

[95] 人民日报.2003—2009.